Regulated Exchanges

Regulated Exchanges

Dynamic Agents of Economic Growth

Edited by

Larry Harris

The World Federation of Exchanges
Centre for European Policy Studies

UNIVERSITY PRESS

2010

Oxford University Press, Inc., publishes works that further
Oxford University's objective of excellence
in research, scholarship, and education.

Oxford   New York
Auckland   Cape Town   Dar es Salaam   Hong Kong   Karachi
Kuala Lumpur   Madrid   Melbourne   Mexico City   Nairobi
New Delhi   Shanghai   Taipei   Toronto

With offices in
Argentina   Austria   Brazil   Chile   Czech Republic   France   Greece
Guatemala   Hungary   Italy   Japan   Poland   Portugal   Singapore
South Korea   Switzerland   Thailand   Turkey   Ukraine   Vietnam

Published by Oxford University Press, Inc.
198 Madison Avenue, New York, New York 10016

www.oup.com

Oxford is a registered trademark of Oxford University Press

Library of Congress Cataloging-in-Publication Data
Regulated exchanges : dynamic agents of economic growth/
edited by Larry Harris.
p. cm. — (The World Federation of Exchanges Centre for European Policy Studies)
Includes bibliographical references and index.
ISBN 978-0-19-977272-8
1. Stock exchanges. 2. Economic development. I. Harris, Larry, 1956–
HG4551.R38 2010
332.64'2—dc22   2010036971

9 8 7 6 5 4 3 2 1
Printed in the United States of America
on acid-free recycled paper

CONTENTS

The World Federation of Exchanges (WFE) promotes knowledge and best practice in the exchange space. It helps exchanges—and the governmental agencies that regulate them—to better understand the financial markets in which they and their customers operate. The WFE fulfills its mission through a variety of programs, not least of which is the sponsorship of research and publications.

In keeping with this mission, this book—commissioned by the WFE Board of Directors to commemorate the 50th Anniversary of the WFE—presents various perspectives on how exchanges have changed through time, how they are presently changing, and how they will likely change in the future.

The eleven sets of authors who present these perspectives are all authorities in their fields. In many cases, they shaped the events that they discuss. They include leading exchange officials, accomplished academics, and long-time observers of the exchange industry. WFE Secretary General Thomas Krantz and I asked the authors to share their views freely and honestly with the hope that they could help readers better understand the forces that have formed—and continue to form—exchanges and the traders that operate in them.

Given this mandate, the opinions that appear in their essays are obviously those of the authors and not necessarily mine or those of the WFE. Growth in knowledge comes from the exposure of different viewpoints. The WFE, as a promoter of knowledge and best practice, is merit worthy for its willingness to expose controversial ideas for further discussion. Indeed, much of the value created over the years by this organization has come from honest debate over important issues. If the answers were obvious, there would have been no need for the WFE.

As editor, I let the authors speak in their own voices. In particular, I did not mandate a common style for their prose. To do otherwise would have made the book less informative: How people express themselves often helps us better understand what they say. I did suggest many changes where I thought that readers would benefit from further development of ideas, or where I was aware of counterarguments or evidence that would balance the presentation.

Where necessary, I suggested revisions to help the authors better express themselves for readers less informed than they are. I also provided assistance to several of our authors who are not native English speakers. Composing in a second language is difficult even for the most accomplished of linguists.

All chapters in this book are completely self-contained. They thus can be read in any order. The essays in the Part I present three essential perspectives about exchanges. Professor Ranald Michie first provides a history of exchanges during the last 50 years. I wrote the next essay, which discusses the economics of trading and of regulated exchanges. The third essay, by Karel Lannoo and Piero Cinquegrana, surveys regulatory issues that involve exchanges. Like all essays in this volume, each of these essays includes many forward-looking discussions of public policy issues.

The essays in Part II discuss five innovations that shaped today's exchange markets. These five essays constitute the core of this book. They describe in detail how exchange markets dealt with the most important drivers of change over the last 50 years. Understanding these forces is essential for appreciating why today's exchanges are structured as they are. Since these forces remain important, they also will shape exchanges in the future.

The first essay in this part, by former Securities and Exchange Commission (SEC) Commissioner Roberta Karmel, addresses the deregulation of fixed commissions. Former Stockholmbörsen CEO Bengt Rydén then explains why exchanges demutualized to provide better services to their customers in the face of competition. Next, Hal Weitzman of the *Financial Times* discusses the introduction of financial futures in the 1970s. The fourth essay, by Professor Michael Gorham, traces the development of screen-based trading. Finally, the last essay of this section, by former Warsaw Stock Exchange Chairman Wieslaw Rozlucki, explains how Eastern European and Asian countries with communist histories founded new exchanges and how those exchanges have contributed to their economic welfare.

The final part of the book provides three complementary visions for the future. The first, by Edemir Pinto, CEO of BM&FBOVESPA, highlights the role that regulated exchanges have played in promoting social corporate responsibility. This movement has grown in the last few years, and the authors argue that it will become more important in the future. The second essay, by Tokyo Stock Exchange Group President and CEO Atsushi Saito, addresses ethical issues in the capital markets. The final essay, by Stephan Malherbe of Genesis Analytics, and Nicky Newton-King and Siobhan Cleary from the Johannesburg Stock Exchange, provides an informative and thought-provoking survey of the issues that will shape exchanges in the future.

Biographies for all authors and contributors to this volume appear at the front of the book. In keeping with its identity as a commemorative fiftieth anniversary volume, this book also includes a preface by Mr. Pedro Rodríguez Ponga, the last surviving attendee of the October 12–13, 1961, original organizing meeting of the Conference of European Stock Exchanges, the earliest name for the WFE. That name was soon changed to *La Fédération Internationale des Bourses de Valeurs*, and later in 2001 to the World Federation of Exchanges. Mr. Ponga—then Vice President of the *Bolsa de Madrid*—is a Past President of that exchange and a Past Chairman of the WFE.

Finally, this book also includes an annex with reproductions of important documents and images from the first 50 years of the WFE. Although unrelated to the essays, these memorabilia are interesting in their own right.

Acknowledgements

The authors all worked very hard on their essays, and I greatly appreciate their efforts. The result is an interesting and highly informative book of which we all should be proud.

I have been delighted to work closely with Thomas Krantz, Secretary General of the WFE. His commitment to, and care for, the WFE and its mission is always apparent. Thomas was instrumental in identifying most of the authors. He also read and commented upon every essay. I am particularly grateful to Thomas for the freedom he gave me to structure this book, and for the constructive comments that he gave me on my essay.

I also appreciate the diligent efforts of WFE Research & Projects Manager Romain Devai, who read and commented on every essay.

I am very indebted to our managing editor, Piero Cinquegrana, of the Centre for European Policy Studies (CEPS). Piero was the most conscientious of assistants—I could not have asked for anything more. His work went well beyond assistance to include much valuable editorial advice. His service as a sounding board was unexpectedly special to me. Piero presently is working toward his Ph.D. in Political Science at the University of California, Los Angeles. I wish him and his new wife all success and joy in the world.

Karel Lannoo, CEO of the CEPS, hired me, managed the contract with WFE, assigned Piero Cinquegrana to this project, and, of course, co-wrote the essay on regulation with Piero Cinquegrana. I greatly appreciate his confidence in me and the care that he exercised over this project from beginning to end.

We all appreciate the effort that Oxford University Press Executive Editor Terry Vaughn undertook to promote this book within OUP. Terry and I have worked together before as he also serves as the managing editor of my book *Trading and Exchanges: Market Microstructure for Practitioners*. It was a pleasure to work with him again. I was delighted that he shared our vision for this book and that he was willing to stake OUP's extraordinary reputation for publishing valuable contributions to human knowledge on this volume.

Lisa Stallings, Jais K. Alphonse and Vasu Pillai helped project manage and copyedit this book, and in doing so, made this volume much easier to read. The authors and I greatly appreciate their meticulous efforts.

Finally, I want to thank WFE Chairman Bill Brodsky and his colleagues on the WFE board for their vision for this book. I can think of no more fitting way to honor the jubilee of an organization committed to advancing learning and best practice than to commission a volume that promotes that mission.

This project has excited me from the start through the end. It has been a great pleasure for me to associate with the WFE, an organization that I have long respected.

Larry Harris
Los Angeles
May, 2010

Why this book?

Commemorative books celebrating the achievements of an institution on the occasion of a major anniversary are customary. Such books recall what has been accomplished, and usually include pictures of the people who led and did the work.

Although the traditional approach is not without merit, our directors envisioned a different path from the start of this project. In first considering the idea of a fiftieth jubilee book, our thoughts went beyond our own institutions and the Federation itself to the economic role of exchanges in the global marketplace. Our goal was to assess the role of organized, regulated exchanges in the financial system and their contribution to economic growth, and to communicate that perspective in the form of this book.

Rather than a list of what member exchanges and the World Federation of Exchanges (WFE) have achieved over the past five decades, the board of directors determined that a more lasting contribution would be made in attempting to answer a more outward looking question: what have the world's regulated exchanges contributed to the development of the global capital markets these past five decades? This time span covers most of the post-Second World War period, and essentially all of what we refer to as the establishment of today's global financial system. At our founding, people did not know their colleagues on a worldwide basis. Airplane travel was not common in 1961, international phone calls were rare and made by appointment, and the Internet was unimaginable. In most cases, with only one exchange per jurisdiction, the need to share expertise across national borders was logical; usually no local partners were available for consultation. In these past five decades, the mix of persons and ideas and business has gone well beyond that original conception of what WFE might do for its member exchanges.

With this overarching goal in mind, the Board of Directors commissioned essays addressing the major issues faced by exchanges today, and shorter chapters on key milestones that mark the challenges that were overcome during this past half-century in the course of building today's global exchange industry. The jubilee book ends with thought pieces that consider where exchanges may go in the years ahead.

The Essays

Why and how regulated markets work are complex questions that cannot be answered in simple sound bites too often seen in the popular media. This book provides deeper analyses. Each essay casts a different light on the role of exchanges and their associated pre- and post-trade services within the broader financial services industry. Taken together, these essays provide the reader with a better sense of the role of exchanges in today's global financial system and, more importantly, the role that regulated exchanges will play in shaping a better and stronger global marketplace for tomorrow.

In the book's preface, Mr. Pedro Rodriguez Ponga shares his recollections of the first WFE meeting in 1961, and his perspective on what the WFE has accomplished since. Mr. Ponga was President of the Madrid Stock Exchange and, later, Chairman of this Federation.

The opening section of the book covers three essential matters at greater length than the rest, all highlighting the distinctiveness of exchanges:

- Professor Ranald Michie on "Exchanges in Historical and Global Context."

- Professor Larry Harris on "The Economics of Trading and Regulated Exchanges."
- Messrs. Karel Lannoo and Piero Cinquegrana on "Capital Markets Regulation Revisied."

The next section of the book covers a selection of significant milestones, including the resolution of management challenges and policy issues, which ultimately lead to moments of significant transformation:

- Professor Roberta Karmel on "A Retrospective on the Unfixing of Rates and Related Deregulation".
- Mr. Hal Weitzman on "Chicago's Decade of Innovation: 1972–82"
- Professor Michael Gorham on "The Long, Promising Evolution of Screen-based Trading"
- Dr. Bengt Rydén on "Demutualization and self-listing"
- Dr. Wieslaw Rozlucki on "The Creation of Exchanges in Countries with Communist Histories"

The final section presents three essays that contemplate the future:

- Mr. Edemir Pinto on "The World's Exchanges as Social Agents"
- Mr. Atsushi Saito, President & CEO of Tokyo Stock Exchange Group on "Regulated Exchanges and the Ethos of Public Capital Markets"
- Ms. Nicky Newton-King, Mr. Stephan Malherbe and Ms. Siobhan Cleary share the view from Johannesburg on "A Free Option on the Future: Regulated Securities Exchanges Beyond 2010"

On behalf of the WFE, I hope that this book sheds new light on the importance of regulated exchanges in the world's economy.

William J. Brodsky
Chairman, WFE
Chairman and Chief Executive Officer,
Chicago Board Options Exchange

ACKNOWLEDGEMENTS

Before expressing my thanks to the many professionals who became involved in this jubilee book project, a brief presentation of the World Federation of Exchanges is in order.

WFE is the global association for the exchange industry; its members broadly represent the world's regulated market segments. WFE appropriately represents this industry because its membership is comprehensive. Here, briefly, is how WFE came to have this authoritative voice:

The founding moment is captured in the Preamble to the Statutes:

> *"Whereas it was considered beneficial to have a more formal organization of organized stock exchanges, the Amsterdam Stock Exchange, the Brussels Stock Exchange, the London Stock Exchange, the Luxembourg Stock Exchange, the Madrid Stock Exchange, the Milan Stock Exchange, the Paris Stock Exchange, the Vienna Stock Exchange, the Association of German Stock Exchanges and the Association of Swiss Stock Exchanges have decided to create an International Federation of Stock Exchanges. The official creation date was October 12–13, 1961."*

Article 2 of the Statutes gives the direction: *"The purpose of the Federation is to contribute to the development, support and promotion of*

*organized and regulated securities and derivatives markets, in order to meet
the needs of the world's capital markets in the best interest of their users."*

The Federation's membership quickly moved beyond the European founders, themselves propelled to act together in the aftermath of the Treaty of Rome in 1957, which first established the Common Market. The idea of an organized and regulated market for raising capital, providing facilities for fair and transparent price discovery and hedging or taking on risk is well established—with one proviso: all these markets must be grounded in laws and regulations which are publicly known and enforceable. The success of the exchange idea as sketched in this book is demonstrated by having WFE members present on all continents.

How to achieve the purpose of the Federation was left open to what might prove workable. In practice, gathering together industry leaders—senior executives as well as business-line managers—from all regions of the world has been most productive. Over time, member exchanges defined common aims, leading to useful studies and statistics. The ability to share business issues engendered new perspectives on common problems. Member exchanges have since developed best practices in the form of: (1) admission criteria requiring that new member candidates demonstrate the quality of their market operations and (2) regulatory infrastructure visible during the Federation's inspection.

Organized exchange trading often preceded the establishment of governmental securities commissions; the WFE itself came into being before the founding of many global financial policy bodies. As those bodies were formed in recent decades, WFE actively supported their work to foster global coordination. WFE member exchanges publicly endorsed the development of the International Organization of Securities Commissions' *Principles of Regulation*, the Organization of Economic Cooperation and Development's *Principles of Corporate Governance*, and the ongoing development of International Financial Reporting Standards and International Audit Standards—all in the belief that sound global standards must underpin the growth in cross-border transactions. As I write this page of acknowledgments, this Federation is sharing market policy ideas among members for use in their local jurisdictions, while at the same time also addressing major issues of concern to global financial policy-makers.

Together with our members, I first wish to thank the WFE Board of Directors. We greatly appreciate the substantial meeting time that the directors devoted to the structure and content of this jubilee work, even in the midst of a severe financial crisis.

I particularly want to thank the numerous exchange officials who made detailed suggestions as to book content and structure. We regret that not all those good ideas could be included in this book in the manner in which they were proposed due to space constraints, but I believe that the majority of ideas were incorporated in the course of writing the chapters.

The Centre for European Policy Studies (CEPS) in Brussels was instrumental in coordinating this work, and we thank especially Messrs. Karel Lannoo, its Chief Executive, and Piero Cinquegrana, who served as managing editor. Pulling together in coherent fashion a serious set of essays on this complex industry from various corners of the globe was never obvious or easy. We commend and thank them both for their masterful work.

Likewise, I also wish to express our thanks to the general editor, Professor Larry Harris of the University of Southern California, Marshall School of Business, for maintaining a high level of thought and expression across these essays, and assuring that our contributing authors kept focused on the agreed themes. Without his orchestration, the variety of submissions deemed necessary by the subject matter could not have achieved a cohesive whole.

The publisher, Oxford University Press, has offered all manner of practical experience and suggestions and demonstrated remarkable patience as the essays have been gathered from around the world.

My colleague Romain Devai, who heads research here at WFE, has been my unfailing partner and planner and co-thinker on this book. I owe him the most sincere thanks of all.

At the WFE secretariat, we find the work of exchanges uniquely compelling. We are honored to work with exchange leaders who are dedicated, not only to improving their home markets, but to improving a global marketplace for all. We hope that the WFE fiftieth anniversary jubilee book channels our enthusiasm for this work outward from Paris to readers everywhere.

Thomas Krantz
Secretary General
Paris, May 2010

PREFACE

PEDRO RODRÍGUEZ PONGA

We as exchanges have learned to survive in fast-changing, challenging, and on occasion, even hostile environments without forgetting for a single day the role that our function plays in the development of nations.

Since my very first days at *Bolsa de Madrid*, back in the 1940s, I have always tried to be conscious of this responsibility, that as exchanges we undertake before society and that commits us to societal advancement.

Achievement of such an honorable aim laid at the heart of an initiative that a few exchanges undertook in the early 1960s when they mutually committed to co-operate closely, to join efforts, and to share their knowledge, views, and expertise gathered from very different experiences. By these means and with their foresight, those exchanges would eventually improve the value of their contributions to capital markets—and, hence, to the financial system. They started from a European perspective that quite soon began to encompass a much wider scope. The result was *La Fédération Internationale des Bourses de Valeurs*—FIBV.

For some of us, the foundation of the Federation was the first step in the quest for a dream: to build an institution of reference in the global securities markets industry. This entity would establish international standards for the correct functioning of markets while respecting the idiosyncrasies of each exchange, and the guidelines of the Organization for Economic Cooperation and Development and other international organizations. It would make the securities industry highly visible by promoting knowledge and understanding to the public. It also would establish and maintain close links of cooperation with the highest representatives of finance, academia, and civil administration.

Fifty years of work later, after that first morning meeting in 1961 in London without fog—which today seems to me to have taken place just yesterday—I can now express my modest satisfaction that all of us have made that dream come true.

I remember with emotion when, at the time of the General Assembly of 2001 in Madrid—which I had the honor to inaugurate—FIBV changed its name to the current World Federation of Exchanges (WFE). This seemingly small change was natural for an organization that gathers over fifty regulated markets throughout the five continents. It represented the victory—as enormous as it was discreet—of the men and women working at securities exchanges that I had the privilege to know. They committed themselves, half a century ago, to friendship and institutional cooperation in the increasingly globalized environment that, hardly discernable at the time, would eventually become the world in which we are now living.

Exchanges always should keep in mind their essential role—to facilitate the channeling of savings towards productive investment—which, as repeatedly has been demonstrated, is of the utmost relevance for economic development, and thus for the welfare of humankind.

The hopes of millions of families, and the business projects of thousands of companies, have passed throughout the engines of our institutions: from the overseas trading companies in the seventeenth century to the construction of the railways in the nineteenth, to the design and deployment of modern telecommunications networks that connect the world in this still fresh millennium.

The passing of time has revealed how the WFE, previously known as the FIBV, has promoted our market model within a framework for coordination and cooperation that has proven essential when facing difficulties arising in global finance.

Throughout the last fifty years, we have witnessed massive changes in the financial industry in general, and in the securities markets in particular. The transformation has affected every aspect of exchanges and their business contexts. Among many others, these changes include the deregulation of securities markets, the demutualization of exchanges, exchange self-listing, and the move from open outcry pits and floors to screen trading. These changes allowed exchanges to adopt robust, state-of-the-art technologies that now enable investors to access our prices and services from anywhere in the world.

My intention is not to evaluate either the correctness or the opportunities represented by these changes. They have resulted from the very realities to which exchanges have duly adapted. They arose not only as exchanges pursued the fulfillment of their users' needs in efficient and safe ways, but also as part of their endeavors to survive.

When principles such as transparency, neutrality and investor protection are left aside for factors that are not essential for the functioning of markets, innocent bystanders have paid a high price. We shall not forget that at the end of the day, it is investors—especially retail investors—who bear the consequences of sacrificing those principles for mechanisms that are faster, more lax, or that provide lesser guarantees.

As an example, I would mention the introduction in the last decade of new, highly complex financial instruments. In the vast majority of cases, such instruments have been bilaterally traded with little transparency, and their valuation has been extremely difficult to calculate, if not impossible. If we wish to prevent such mistakes, abuses and bad practices committed in the past from happening again in the future, a detailed and honest analysis of such derivative and structured products—including their nature, their risks, their transparency, as well as the way they are traded and settled—is of essence. At this time of writing, it would not be necessary to remind anybody of the magnitude of the repercussions of every kind that this philosophy of unsupervised markets—so different from the principles governing regulated markets—has brought to the world economy since September 2008, as well as to the very existence of the financial system.

The ongoing financial crisis has demonstrated that the smooth running of the financial markets needs—as a *conditio sine qua non*—a bedrock that provides market players with a framework of legal certainty, without risks other than those intrinsic to any investment. Moves towards further sophistication of the financial system that do not duly account for the need for a safe, level playing field as described could eventually have dramatic consequences for public confidence, the cornerstone upon which finance rests and which for now still shows the serious fractures incurred in recent years.

These events invite us to reflect on the features that characterize securities markets that are sound and safe. They bring to our minds, once again, the principles mentioned earlier on which we, exchanges, regardless of our geographical and temporal contexts, must base our activity. Markets must be transparent, markets must be neutral, markets must be multilateral, and market activity must be supervised with the ultimate goal of guaranteeing the protection of bona fide investors.

The recent transformations in the financial system, and the adaptation of exchanges to them, clearly demonstrate the great difficulties that our industry faces in respecting those principles while remaining competitive in the marketplace. Exchanges must prosper to provide regulated marketplaces. In this tough task, exchanges have been left alone in recent times.

Although in recent months, regulators and supervisors again seem to be taking into account the worthiness of regulated markets, no one should think that social, financial or regulatory tensions will end here. If History teaches us anything, it is that the world will take less time to forget the abuses and the mistakes that have ignited the latest crisis than the time it will take to recover from its effects.

Hence, I am convinced there are still a number of dangers out there. I believe that new temptations will arise for reducing the vigorous application of our market model and principles for the sake of uncertain and implausible objectives.

Those of us who have lived long have the privilege of hindsight. We know that new trends and theories will come along in the future calling for dramatic changes in the securities industry, sometimes confusing the real values contributed by regulated markets.

We also know that, despite the many mistakes and obvious imperfections our institutions must acknowledge, building what we have today is a result of many years of difficult toil and effort. We should be generous in valuing it. There is still a hard, long way forward to achieve sound, efficient and fully transparent securities markets that enjoy the benefit of investors' full confidence and that prove resilient under highly stressful conditions. Nevertheless, we only will meet that goal by respecting and preserving those essential exchanges principles. This is the fundamental argument for our future.

WFE has always supported the view that fair markets result from the responsible exercise of the freedom of action granted to market players, on the one hand, combined, on the other, with a sound supervisory system that guarantees the protection of well-meaning investors.

For all these reasons, I feel truly honored to be writing the foreword to this WFE Jubilee Commemorative Book, as well as for having the opportunity to share this extraordinary space with such a remarkable cast of prominent academics and market practitioners who have contributed to it.

I would like to offer a few words of appreciation and gratitude to all the people and institutions who have actively contributed, in some way or another, to the success of the Federation since its first steps. I am most confident that with the determination of all of you, the future will provide us with many such brilliant results and moments as those that we already have had the fortune to see.

Happy Birthday, World Federation of Exchanges! Happy Fiftieth Anniversary! I wish you, at the very least, another half a century of success in supporting regulated markets. God bless our exchanges.

Ranald Michie, Professor of History, Durham University. Author of Chapter 1, "Exchanges in Historical and Global Context."

Ranald Michie is one of the United Kingdom's leading financial historians, with an internationally recognized specialty in the history of stock exchanges. Beginning with research on the Scottish stock exchanges, his interests have become international over the last 25 years. Among his books on the subject are *The London and New York Stock Exchange, 1850–1914* (1987); *The London Stock Exchange: A History* (1999); and *The Global Securities Market: A History* (2006). His interest in stock exchanges is not a narrow institutional one but extends to the role they played both as markets and their connections to other aspects of the financial system, especially banks. This research on stock exchanges and securities market has also led him to study financial centers, especially London and New York. Through that, he has investigated the relationship between markets, regulators and governments resulting in an edited volume, R. C. Michie and P. A. Williamson (eds.), *The British Government and the City of London in the Twentieth Century* (2004). He is currently working on a detailed study documenting the transformation of exchanges from 1970 to the present day.

Larry Harris, Fred V. Keenan Chair in Finance, Marshall School of Business, University of Southern California. Editor-in-chief and author of Chapter 2, "The Economics of Trading and of Regulated Exchanges."

Larry Harris holds the Fred V. Keenan Chair in Finance at the USC Marshall School of Business. His research, teaching, and consulting address regulatory and practitioner issues in trading and in investment management. He has written extensively about trading rules, transaction costs, index markets, and market regulation. His introduction to the economics of trading, *Trading and Exchanges: Market Microstructure for Practitioners* (Oxford University Press: 2003), is widely regarded as a "must read" for entrants into the securities industry.

Chairman Harvey Pitt appointed Dr. Harris to serve as Chief Economist of the US Securities and Exchange Commission in July 2002 where he continued to serve under Chairman William Donaldson through June 2004. As Chief Economist, Harris was the primary advisor to the Commission on all economic issues. He contributed extensively to the development of regulations implementing Sarbanes-Oxley, the resolution of the mutual fund timing crisis, the specification of Regulation National Market System (NMS), the promotion of bond price transparency, and numerous legal cases. Harris also directed the SEC Office of Economic Analysis in which 35 economists, analysts, and support staff engage in regulatory analysis, litigation support, and basic economic research.

Professor Harris currently serves on the boards of Interactive Brokers, Inc. (IBKR), the Clipper Fund, Inc. (CFIMX), and CFALA, the Los Angeles Society of Financial Analysts. He is the director of the USC Marshall School Center for Investment Studies and the research coordinator of the Institute for Quantitative Research in Finance (the Q-Group). In the past, he has served as an associate editor of the *Journal of Finance*, the *Review of Financial Studies*, and the *Journal of Financial and Quantitative Analysis*. Other professional service has included year-long assignments to the US Securities and Exchange Commission and to the New York Stock Exchange immediately following the Stock Market Crash of 1987. Dr. Harris has also worked at UNX, Inc., an electronic pure agency institutional equity broker, and at Madison Tyler, LLC, a broker–dealer engaged in electronic proprietary trading in various markets.

Dr. Harris received his Ph.D. in Economics from the University of Chicago in 1982.

Karel Lannoo, Chief Executive Officer, Centre for European Policy Studies. Co-author of Chapter 3, "Capital Markets Regulation Revisited."

Karel Lannoo (born 1961) has been Chief Executive of the Centre for European Policy Studies (CEPS) since 2000 and senior research fellow since 1997. CEPS is one of the leading independent European think tanks, with a strong reputation in economic and foreign policy research.

Before joining CEPS, Karel Lannoo was employed in the cultural sector, worked for the Italian conglomerate Ferruzzi and for a professional federation. He was also active as a freelance journalist for specialized financial sector publications.

He has published some books and numerous articles in specialized magazines and journals on the European Union (EU), financial regulation and corporate governance matters. He has given speeches at several European Parliament, Commission and related institutions hearings and participated in studies for national and international bodies (EU institutions, OECD, ADB, and the World Bank). He is a regular speaker at international conferences and in executive training programs.

Karel Lannoo holds a baccalaureate in philosophy and an M.A. in history from the University of Leuven, Belgium (1985) and obtained a postgraduate in European studies (CEE) from the University of Nancy, France (1986).

Karel Lannoo is an independent director of BME (Bolsas Y Mercados Espanoles), the company that runs the Madrid Stock Exchange.

Piero Cinquegrana, Associate Research Fellow, Centre for European Policy Studies; Ph.D. Candidate in Political Science, University of California, Los Angeles. Co-author of Chapter 3, "Capital Markets Regulation Revisited."

Piero Cinquegrana joined CEPS in July 2008 and has published articles on commodity markets, credit rating agencies, MiFID, short selling, and capital markets regulation in general. His research interests are in international political economy, politics and economics of regulation, monetary and exchange rate policy, and institutional reform. Prior to joining CEPS, Piero Cinquegrana worked at a think tank at Columbia University, where he dealt with issues of conflict resolution. He resides in Los Angeles, where he is a Ph.D. candidate in Political Science at the University of California, Los Angeles, specializing in quantitative methods, formal models, and international relations. Piero obtained a B.A. and M.A. in International Relations from the University of Bologna, Italy.

Roberta Karmel, Centennial Professor of Law, Brooklyn Law School. Author of Chapter 4, "A Retrospective of the Unfixing of Rates and Related Deregulation."

Professor Karmel's area of expertise is international and domestic securities regulation. She is widely called upon to teach and lecture all over the world on this subject. She is a former Commissioner of the Securities and Exchange Commission, a Public Director of the New York Stock Exchange, and was in private practice for 30 years. She was also a Fulbright Scholar studying the harmonization of the securities laws in the European Union. Professor Karmel is the author of *Regulation by Prosecution: The Securities and Exchange Commission Versus Corporate America*, and has widely published articles on securities regulation and international securities law in dozens of law reviews and journals. She also authors a monthly column, "Securities Regulation," that appears in the *New York Law Journal*.

Professor Karmel's professional activities and affiliations are numerous. She is a trustee of the Practising Law Institute, a member of the American Law Institute, and a Fellow of the American Bar Foundation. She also serves on the American Bar Association's (ABA) Presidential Task Force on Financial Markets Regulatory Reform. She previously served as a director of the New York Chapter of the National Association of Corporate Directors and was the Vice Chair of the International Coordinating Committee of the American Bar Association Business Law Section.

A member of the faculty since 1985, Professor Karmel has played an instrumental role in leading the activities of The Dennis J. Block Center for the Study of International Business Law, where she serves as its codirector. In 2009, she was the Harry Cross Visiting Professor at the University of Washington School of Law. Other recent honors include Phi Beta Kappa Alpha Iota of Massachusetts at Harvard College (Hon.) and the American Bar Association Women Lawyers of Achievement Award. She received her B.A. from Radcliffe College and LL.B. from New York University School of Law.

Hal Weitzman, Chicago and Midwest Correspondent, *Financial Times*. Author of Chapter 5, "Chicago's Decade of Innovation, 1972–82."

Hal Weitzman's beat includes coverage of the US futures and options exchanges. He grew up in Cardiff, Wales, and was educated at Leeds University, Oriel College, Oxford, and the Kennedy School of Government at Harvard. Weitzman joined the *FT* in 2000 as a subeditor on the Comment and Analysis section. In 2002, he was appointed the

FT's Americas News Editor based in London, in which role he coordinated the newspaper's coverage of the 2004 US presidential election. In 2004, he transferred to Lima, Peru, where he took up the post of Andes correspondent. During his three years in the region, he reported from Peru, Bolivia, Ecuador, Venezuela, and Chile. He is currently writing a book about the spread of leftwing nationalism in South America, based on his coverage of the rise of leaders such as Evo Morales in Bolivia and Rafael Correa in Ecuador, who are closely associated with Hugo Chávez, the Venezuelan president. In October 2007, he moved to Chicago, where he lives with his wife, Lorna, and their daughter, Orlie.

Michael Gorham, Industry Professor of Finance, Stuart School of Business, Illinois Institute of Technology. Author of Chapter 6, "The Long, Promising Evolution of Screen-based Trading."

Michael Gorham is Industry Professor and Director of the IIT Stuart Center for Financial Markets at the Illinois Institute of Technology. He is also Adjunct Distinguished International Professor of Finance at Escuela de Graduados en Administracion y Direccion de Empresas (EGADE), the graduate business school of Monterrey Tec, at the Santa Fe Campus in Mexico City. In addition, he currently serves on the board of directors for the Chicago Board Options Exchange (CBOE) Futures Exchange in Chicago and, until July 2008, served on the board of the National Commodity and Derivatives Exchange in Mumbai, India. He serves on the business conduct committee of the Chicago Mercantile Exchange, the editorial boards of the Global Association of Risk Professionals (GARP) Risk Review and of Futures Industry magazine. He is regional director of the Global Association of Risk Professionals for Chicago.

He is co-author of two books; *India's Financial Markets: An Insider's Guide* (July 2008) and *Electronic Exchanges: The Global Transformation from Pits to Bits* (May 2009), both published by Elsevier.

From 2002 to 2004, Mr. Gorham served as the first director of the Commodity Futures Trading Commission's new Division of Market Oversight, a division of 100 economists, lawyers, futures trading specialists, and others dedicated to the oversight of the nation's 12 futures exchanges. Earlier, Mr. Gorham was an economist at the Federal Reserve Bank of San Francisco and Vice President of international market development at the Chicago Mercantile Exchange.

He has been involved in consulting projects to create a stock index futures market in India, establish a commodities market in the United Arab Emirates, evaluate the feasibility of Parmesan cheese futures in

Italy, and to modernize financial markets in Egypt. He also served as Managing Editor of the *Journal of Global Financial Markets*.

He has written for newspapers, journals and magazines in Argentina, China, Japan, Mexico, and the US and has given talks on derivatives in 14 countries. After university, he was a Peace Corps volunteer working on an agricultural modernization project in Malawi, Africa. He holds a B.A. in English literature from the University of Notre Dame, an M.S. in food and resource economics from the University of Florida and a Ph.D. in agricultural economics from the University of Wisconsin.

Bengt Rydén, Former CEO, Stockholm Stock Exchange. Author of Chapter 7, "Demutualization and Self-listing."

Dr. Bengt Rydén graduated from Stockholm School of Economics in 1960, where he received a Ph.D. in 1972. His research was carried out at The Industrial Institute for Social and Economic Research, where he finished his dissertation on corporate mergers and acquisitions. He has during several periods been doing research in finance and industrial organization at Stanford University and University of Virginia. Having early shown an interest and talent in writing, Dr. Ryden was editor-in-chief of a leading Swedish business magazine in 1971–73.

During 1974–84, Dr. Ryden was CEO of Centre for Business and Policy Studies in Stockholm. He was also President and Chairman of Stockholm Stock Exchange from 1985 to 2000. During these years, he played an active role in FIBV/WFE, where he was Chairman of the Working Committee and of the Board of Directors. He was an early advocate for structural change and new directions for stock exchanges and for developed corporate governance practices in public companies.

Bengt Rydén has held and is still holding leading positions in boards of private and public companies, organizations, and foundations and has been a member of several government committees and commissions. He has also been serving as advisor to company boards and leaders. He was active in creating a Swedish code of corporate governance. He was a member of The Committee of Wise Men for the Regulation of European Securities Markets, set up by the Council of Ministers of the European Union. He has authored, co-authored, and edited books on economic, social, and political issues and published a large number of articles and columns in newspapers and magazines. Privately, his main interest has for many years been the tasting of fine wines. He recently co-authored a book on wine and wine makers in Languedoc, France.

Wiesław Rozłucki, Chairman of the Supervisory Board, Bank BPH; Former Chairman, Warsaw Stock Exchange. Author of Chapter 8, "The Creation of Exchanges in Countries with Communist Histories."

Dr. Wiesław Rozłucki graduated from the Foreign Trade Faculty of the Warsaw School of Economics in 1970. He has a Ph.D. in economic geography. Between 1973 and 1989, he worked as a researcher at the Polish Academy of Sciences. Between 1990 and 1994, he was an adviser to the Minister of Finance, a director of the Capital Markets Department in the Ministry of Privatization and a member of the Polish Securities and Exchange Commission. Between 1991 and 2006, Dr. Rozłucki was the President and CEO of the Warsaw Stock Exchange. He was also the Chairman of the Supervisory Board of the National Depository for Securities and a member of the working committees of the World Federation of Exchanges and the Federation of European Securities Exchanges. Dr. Rozłucki has been actively engaged in the corporate governance movement in Poland. He is the Chairman of the Programming Council of the Polish Institute of Directors. He is also a member of supervisory boards of large public companies: Telekomunikacja Polska, TVN, Polimex-Mostostal. He runs a strategic and financial consultancy.

Edemir Pinto, Chief Executive Officer, BM&FBOVESPA. Author of Chapter 9, "The World's Exchanges as Social Agents."

Mr. Edemir Pinto serves as Chief Executive Officer and Member of the Executive Board of BM&FBOVESPA SA. Mr. Pinto joined BM&F in January 1986. In July 1987, he was promoted to the position of Derivatives Clearinghouse Officer and was responsible for risk management, settlement, participant registration, collateral, custody, and controllership. He graduated in Economics from Faculdade de Ciencias Economicas e Administracao de Empresas de Sao Jose do Rio Preto.

Atsushi Saito, Board Member, President and CEO, Tokyo Stock Exchange Group, Inc.; President and CEO, Tokyo Stock Exchange, Inc. Author of Chapter 10, "Regulated Exchanges and the Ethos of Public Capital Markets."

Born in October 1939 in Kumamoto prefecture, Mr. Saito graduated from Keio University in 1963 then went on to work at Nomura Securities Co., Ltd. for 35 years. During that time, he was stationed twice in New York for a total of ten years, and in 1986, he was appointed a member of the board. At Nomura, Mr. Saito worked in Treasury and Fixed Income

Dealing and several other divisions, overseeing operations in a broad range of areas from treasury to legal affairs. During his tenure there, he served as Deputy President and in many other executive roles.

While in New York in the latter half of the 1980s, Mr. Saito was actively involved in the securitization of nonperforming loans, real estate and commodities, as well as the development and sale of index funds and other products.

He also has committed his efforts to the liberalization of financial services in Japan, participating in the planning of the Japanese financial "Big Bang" policy promoted by the Hashimoto cabinet by acting as a member of several governmental deliberation councils.

After retiring from Nomura, Mr. Saito served successively as President, then Chairman of Sumitomo Life Investment Co., Ltd., where he participated in company administration and the management of ten trillion yen in pension capital.

In April of 2003, Mr. Saito became president of the Industrial Revitalization Corporation of Japan—a part of the government's financial revitalization project—where he engaged in many revitalization support programs. While at this corporation, he played a significant role in the resolution of the country's nonperforming loan problem, and blazed a trail for corporate restructuring in the future.

Mr. Saito was appointed President and CEO of Tokyo Stock Exchange, Inc., in June of 2007, and in August of the same year, he became the first president and CEO of Tokyo Stock Exchange Group, Inc., the holding company for the market operation company and the self-regulation corporation. Many have high expectations for his expertise towards strengthening the international competitiveness of Japan's financial markets.

Stephan Malherbe, Chairman and Founder, Genesis Analytics. Co-author of Chapter 11, "A Free Option on the Future: Regulated Exchanges beyond 2010."

Stephan is the founder and Chairman of Genesis Analytics, the largest economics consultancy in Africa. He is also the Chairman of sister Genesis companies in India and Dubai providing advice in the areas of regulatory and competition economics and financial services policy and strategy, respectively. He was educated in law at the University of Stellenbosch in South Africa, and in economics and policy at the Kennedy School of Government, Harvard University.

Stephan's work on capital markets combines macro, market development and competition perspectives. He was a principal co-author of the benchmark report of the International Organization of Securities Commission on the emerging markets financial crisis of 1997–98. The report focused on the role sound capital market institutions can play to reduce the incidence of financial crises precipitated by private cross-border capital flows. He also authored capital markets development strategies for the South African government and has advised on nascent capital markets in low-income countries. This work links sound design of capital markets to ensuring sound allocation of capital and risk management in virtually all types of economies. Corporate governance work for, amongst others, the Development Centre of the OECD has focused on the potential role for long-term institutional investors and exchanges in improving the quality of decision-making in large, publicly traded businesses. As a competition economist practicing in a number of jurisdictions, he has worked on both merger and conduct cases dealing with equity and bond markets, derivatives markets, and central securities depositories.

Stephan has provided economic policy advice to a number of African countries at a presidential level, including Mozambique, Rwanda and Liberia. He played an influential role in the drafting of South Africa's democratic Constitution with respect to the economic aspects of the Bill of Rights and the constitutionally guaranteed independence of the country's central bank. He was also a member of the team that designed the country's competition policy.

Currently, Stephan splits his time between practicing in India and South Africa.

Nicky Newton-King, Deputy CEO and Member of the Executive Committee and Board of Directors, Johannesburg Stock Exchange. Co-author of Chapter 11, "A Free Option on the Future: Regulated Exchanges beyond 2010."

At the JSE, Miss Newton-King leads the JSE's legal, strategy and investor relations teams. Over the years, she has been part of various teams which were responsible for drafting key legislation affecting the South African financial markets, including the Insider Trading Act, 1998, the Securities Services Act, 2004 and the new Companies Act. She is also a member of the Financial Markets Advisory Board, the Standing Advisory Committee on Company Law and the Presidential

Remuneration Commission which determines the remuneration of all South African Public Office Bearers.

Nicky led the development of the JSE's Socially Responsible Investment Index, the first such index in the world sponsored by an exchange and has led most of the JSE's group-level transactions, including the acquisition by the JSE of the South African Futures Exchange and the Bond Exchange of South Africa.

Nicky was one of the South African Global Leaders of Tomorrow appointed by the World Economic Forum in 2003 and is a WEF Young Global Leader. She was South Africa's 2003 Businesswoman of the year and in 2006, spent five months at Yale University as a Yale World Fellow.

Nicky is married with two young sons and prefers to spend her private time with her family.

Siobhan Cleary, Senior Manager, Johannesburg Stock Exchange. Co-author of Chapter 11, "A Free Option on the Future: Regulated Exchanges beyond 2010."

Siobhan Cleary heads up the JSE's strategy team and forms part of the Strategy, Investor Relations and Legal Counsel Division headed by Nicky Newton-King, Deputy CEO.

Prior to joining the JSE at the start of 2006, Siobhan worked as a Business Law lecturer at the University of Cape Town and was a Manager (Strategy) with global management consulting firm, Accenture. Her Accenture clients included several major South African financial services firms as well as one of the world's largest NGOs. As part of the consulting engagement for this last client, she spent six months in Bangladesh. She has also published in the field of development economics.

Since joining the JSE, Siobhan has worked on (amongst other projects) the JSE's listing, the JSE's acquisition of the Bond Exchange, the strategic review of the Socially Responsible Investment (SRI) Index and the establishment of the JSE's All Africa Indices. Siobhan's interests are varied but she is particularly fascinated by the interplay between the private and the public and not-for-profit sectors.

PART I

ESSENTIAL PERSPECTIVES

Exchanges in Historical and Global Context

RANALD MICHIE

1. Abstract

Exchanges have transformed dramatically over the last 50 years with the evolution of telecommunications and computing technologies. Electronic trading, demutualization, and new regulations increased competition and substantially lowered transactions costs. During this period, the role that exchanges play in our economy also changed substantially. This chapter traces the recent development of exchanges, identifies the forces that shaped today's exchange structures, and discusses the effects that exchanges had on economic development. Failure to appreciate these changes too often has led to unproductive criticisms of exchanges.

2.1 Criticism of Exchanges

Those who believe in the importance of unrestrained market behavior see the rules and regulations imposed by exchanges as a limit to competition. Conversely, those who favor government control over economic activity are critical of exchanges as obvious symbols of unrestrained market capitalism. Even those who accept the need for both competitive markets and government intervention remain critical of exchanges because of the behavior they appear to have encouraged.

Writing in the 1930s at the time of the Great Depression, no less an economist than J. M. Keynes equated stock exchanges with casinos and suggested that their operations be subjected to a high degree of government control. "When the capital development of a country becomes the by-product of the activities of a casino, the job is likely to be ill-done. It is usually agreed that casinos should, in the public interest, be inaccessible and expensive. And perhaps the same is true of Stock Exchanges."[1]

Exchanges were believed to encourage gambling on the rise and fall of prices, whether of stocks and bonds, wheat and oil, or exchange and interest rates.[2] Such behavior encouraged price volatility and so created economic instability. Under these circumstances, the behavior of producers was driven by short-term considerations, because prices were constantly fluctuating. Consumers faced rapid fluctuations in prices that could either encourage unwarranted expenditure or dramatic cutbacks in purchases. Investors experienced either irrational exuberance or profound despair which led to rapid swings between over-optimism and deep pessimism. Overall, the consequences were believed to discourage long-term investment, undermine confidence, and foster an economic system characterized by booms and slumps.

If these were the consequences that exchanges had, it is not surprising that they have been condemned, outlawed and marginalized by those seeking to influence economic behavior generally and financial systems specifically.

At the root of the criticism made of exchanges lies a failure to understand fully the role played by exchanges in economies. Businesses are essential components of dynamic economies whether they are family-run enterprises or multinational corporations. Each business played its role by organizing and providing the goods and services required by consumers of all kinds and at all levels. It is also easy to appreciate the importance of markets in the allocation of resources and the pricing and distribution of products.

The value of markets becomes clear when they collapse due to natural disaster, war, political upheaval, or financial crisis because of the damage inflicted on populations dependent upon the ability to buy and sell. Even the imperfect functioning of particular markets can have important consequences for comparative economic performance. Jorion and Goetzman have shown this for global stock markets in the twentieth century.[3]

Governments also occupy a central role in modern economies. The contribution made by governments ranges from the basic underpinning of society through the imposition of law and order to the ability to mobilize and organize people and resources on a scale beyond that possessed by either individuals or business. Emergencies and wars reveal what governments are capable of. Governments also play an important role in framing the environment within which business operates as with the laws which dictate the behavior of companies. A degree of government involvement is also necessary if markets are to function efficiently.

Those using a market must have confidence that it will operate without favoring either buyers or sellers, and that agreements to buy and sell will be honored. At the most basic level, governments provide that confidence through the maintenance of legal systems that enforce contracts. Governments are also on hand to intervene when particular groups abuse their power within the market, whatever form it may take. Governments can also intervene to prevent market activity that endangers the whole economy.

2.2 Role of Exchanges

In contrast to businesses, markets and governments, the contribution made by exchanges was both hidden and indirect, once they ceased to be places where merchants went to buy and sell. Exchanges serve the needs of business and occupy the middle ground between the free operation of markets and the regulatory role of governments.

At the most basic level, exchanges provide a fundamental service in a market economy by matching buyers and sellers over space and time. This role has gradually become more indirect, because so much economic activity is undertaken by governments and large businesses, and so internalized within such organizations. Nevertheless, it remains a core activity of exchanges.

By creating permanent and visible marketplaces, exchanges provide buyers and sellers with a high degree of certainty. Exchanges provide certainty that sales and purchases can take place both now and in the future. Exchanges provide the certainty that the price achieved fully reflects the balance of supply and demand. Without certainty, there would be a reluctance to rely on the market with major consequences for production, consumption, saving, and investment.

By responding to the constant fluctuations in supply and demand, exchanges generate prices that provide key signals within a market economy. These signals determine investment behavior by providing reference points for purposes of comparison. Fluctuations in exchange rates are the market's verdict on a nation's international economic standing and point to the need for correction. Movements in interest rates reflect the actions of savers and borrowers and influence their behavior. Volatility of stock prices is driven by investor confidence in future performance and can lead to a change of management, mergers, or acquisitions. Rising and falling commodity prices are driven by expectations and stimulate changes in supply and demand.

Though the public may see in these price movements the random behavior of the market or the hand of the speculator, they are simply the means by which a dynamic global economy constantly adjusts to ever-changing circumstances. Without such price movements, neither producers and consumers nor savers and borrowers would alter their behavior so as to avoid future economic problems. Rising prices, whether of money, stocks, commodities, or products encourage both an increase in supply to meet growing demand and a reduction in demand to balance available supply. Falling prices act to restrain supply and stimulate demand. As the source of so many of these prices, exchanges are thus central to the operation of a market economy.

2.3 Changes in Exchanges

To perform these basic functions, exchanges have changed many times over their history, though this has been little understood. In a 2008 special issue of the Banker, it was observed that, "Until the 1980s, exchanges would, in their essentials, have been recognizable to a merchant who was trading in the fourteenth century—the time of their inception."4 To many, change only came in the late twentieth century with the disappearance of the physical trading floor, the end to national monopoly, and loss of control by members. In reality, exchanges have long had to accommodate the changing nature of business organization, especially the growth of the company, and the globalization of economic activity driven by revolutions in technology, transport, communications, production, and distribution. The actions of governments have also impacted on exchanges to a greater or lesser degree in different countries at different times. In this process of change, exchanges have moved far from a position where buyers and sellers met and public auctions were held to dispose of products, commodities, or property.

The role played by exchanges has become much more indirect as the supply lines involved in production and consumption or saving and investment have become ever more extended and complex. As a result, the prices generated in exchanges are no longer the end result of the buying and selling process but key reference points which are integral to all economic activity through their dissemination and use.

The role of exchanges has also become much more hidden as the nature of the products traded have ceased to be the everyday items that are familiar to people. From their foundation, exchanges encouraged the use of complex financial instruments, involving promises to pay. Exchanges are permanent, nontransitory institutions compared to the fairs and markets of earlier periods.

One consequence of permanency was that payment could take the form of bills of exchange rather than gold and silver, because buyers and sellers remained in place and could be called upon to fulfill the promises made. The effect of this was to liberate trade from artificial monetary constraints as the movements of commodities and products was financed by credit not cash. The use of credit gave purchasers time to recoup their expenditure from consumers, giving producers the means to continue their operations while awaiting payment. Governments and business could also raise finance by promising to pay interest and dividends, because a market existed for the financial instruments created. This did involve risk as promises were not always met, creating problems for those who relied on the expected payments. History abounds with financial and commercial crises when this occurred, with government defaults having the most serious consequences.[5]

2.4 Continuity in Exchanges

Though change has been a constant feature of exchanges, certain of their fundamental features have been present (throughout) from their beginnings in medieval Italy.[6] The central role played by an exchange is to provide a means through which products and assets can be priced. Prices transmit signals to both producers and consumers that determine levels of both production and consumption and saving and investment. These signals have far reaching consequences for short- and long-term economic activity. A process of constant adjustment between supply and demand becomes possible both in the present and the future. By providing accurate prices and disseminating them widely, exchanges provide a key service for the operation of a market economy.

Much of what an exchange does is related to achieving accuracy and ensuring dissemination. By bringing buyers and sellers together exchanges ensure that prices reflect current market conditions as well as expectations about the future. To achieve accurate prices, and disseminate them widely, exchanges must attract as many buyers and sellers as possible.

Exchanges also exist to police market behavior. Though governments make and enforce laws governing buying and selling, most transactions take place on a basis of trust, with each transaction following on from the previous and leading to the next. When that trust breaks down, buyers and sellers are reluctant to trade and the market shrinks or even ceases to operate, with very serious consequences for economic activity. The rules and regulations governing market activity in an exchange are there to ensure that buyers and sellers honor the bargains they have made or face exposure and punishment.

As exchanges became more and more markets for promises, it became essential for them to create an environment where trust prevailed both between those directly participating in the trading process and the buyers and sellers for whom they acted. The ultimate sanction exchanges had available to them was expulsion, and so preventing future participation in the market.

Exchanges thus face a dilemma between trying to create an open market, so as to deliver and disseminate as accurate prices as possible, and the need to enforce a market discipline that makes all participants aware of the consequences that would arise from any failure to deliver, pay, or otherwise abuse the facilities provided. This dilemma existed even before the formation of exchanges: the creation of exchanges was a means of resolving this dilemma.

Exchanges provided a closed environment to which all buyers and sellers could go to conduct business in the knowledge that those who failed to deliver on their promises would be identified and refused entry in the future. The problem was that maintaining this environment and enforcing these regulations involved a cost that had to be met if an exchange was going to operate successfully. The most obvious people to meet these costs were those who used the exchange, because they obtained entry to the market in which they could do business. Here again was another dilemma: those who paid to enter an exchange had to be guaranteed that they would receive something in return that was denied to those unwilling to pay.

Exchanges thus faced a difficult balancing act between providing a market as open as possible, and thus capturing virtually all transactions, and one that restricted entry only to those least likely to default, most likely to obey the rules, and best able to pay the charges. Achieving this balance was not a once-and-for-all act but the product of constant adjustment as circumstances changed. There were always demands from those excluded for governments to intervene to force open the market. Conversely, there were also demands from those who paid for entry for greater privileges in return for the charges made. A government inquiry in the mid-nineteenth century into the operation of the London Stock Exchange correctly identified the maintenance of this balance as critical. In keeping with the spirit of the times, it concluded that an exchange was best positioned to determine this balance, though it did recommend some changes.

> We shall have to suggest details in which we think their rules may
> be advantageously modified and varied, and in parts of the
> existing system we shall have some serious changes to propose,
> but speaking generally of the institution itself as a whole, and of
> the rules by which its operations are regulated, we recognize a
> great public advantage in the fact that those who buy and sell for
> the public in a market of such enormous magnitude in point of
> value, should be bound in their dealings by rules for the
> enforcement of fair dealing and the repression of fraud, capable of
> affording relief and exercising restraint far more prompt and often
> more satisfactory than any within the reach of the courts of law.[7]

In contrast, a different conclusion was reached in the mid-twentieth century in the wake of the Wall Street Crash. Given the magnitude of that speculative bubble and its collapse, exchanges could no longer be trusted to balance the interests of the members who paid for entry and the public who were excluded from direct participation. As early as 1934, a report by the influential Twentieth Century Fund concluded that ". . . public policy requires that speculative activities be brought under such control that they will add to and not detract from the value of the functions which security exchanges are designed to perform; and so that such activities will no longer create credit disturbances and other maladjustments throughout our economic structure."[8]

Throughout their history exchanges have had to balance their private function of serving the needs of those who paid to use them and their public function of providing a market that was accessible and delivered accurate prices that were widely disseminated. Simple as that seems to be, it was no easy matter to achieve. What made the task increasingly difficult were the changes that took place especially over the last 150 years. These changes affected what was traded in exchanges, the scale of those who participated, the relationship with governments, and the technology of communications. All these were to have a profound impact on exchanges, forcing them to transform themselves many times and in such ways that they were recognizable only in name compared with the institutions they had once been.

▓▓▓▓ 3. The Nature, Role, and Use of Securities

The modern development of exchanges has been closely related to the market they provide for securities, especially stocks and bonds. Stocks and bonds were highly flexible instruments that freed finance from all spatial and temporal constraints.

3.1 Stocks

Ownership of stocks could be easily changed both over time and between investors without affecting the continuity of business, which was the problem for enterprises controlled by individuals or partnerships. Bonds could be bought, held or sold even by those with modest savings, so providing both governments and business with an almost inexhaustible source of funding to meet all types of needs.

Though securities had long been in use, it was in the nineteenth century that they became central components of financial systems within advanced economies. To achieve that position, it was essential that securities possessed a market where they could be bought and sold at prices that commanded the trust of investors.

Stock exchanges provided that market. In doing so, exchanges became the bridge that connected the market for money with the market for capital.

To understand why requires an explanation of the contribution made by securities to modern finance. Companies sold stocks, otherwise known as shares or equities, to investors in order to provide themselves with the capital necessary to finance their operations. Through the sale of stocks, companies were able to engage in a far larger scale of operations than was possible for individuals operating alone. It was companies that were responsible for building much of the world's railway system in the nineteenth century. By owning stocks, investors bought the right to share in any profits generated as well as control over the management of a company. Stocks thus opened up a riskier form of investment to investors of more limited means, because their stake could be easily tailored to the savings they had available, unlike land or property.

3.2 Bonds

In contrast to stocks, bonds offered no direct participation in the fortunes of a business, promising investors instead a guaranteed rate of interest. As long as that interest was paid, those investors holding bonds had no control over the direction of the company. Only if the company failed to pay interest on its bonds could those investors owning them exercise their legal rights and take control.

Bonds were also extensively used by governments to raise finance, especially for capital extensive projects with interest paid out of future earnings. Governments also resorted to bond issues to finance wars with the burden placed on later generations of tax payers to meet the costs of interest and eventual redemptions. Default on these war debts was only too likely, and it was difficult for investors to force governments to honor their promises until they needed to borrow again.

3.3 Divisibility and Transferability of Stocks and Bonds

Despite these differences between stocks and bonds, they shared very important common characteristics. By issuing a stock or bond, the vendor obtained money for immediate use. By buying a stock or bond, a purchaser received a promise of future gain.

Compared with a direct investment or loan, the two advantages that securities possessed were *divisibility* and *transferability*. Both these characteristics had far-reaching consequences. Divisibility expanded the absolute amount that could be raised at any one time, through the ability to access the pool of passive investors. This made it possible for companies to finance large and expensive long-term projects. Divisibility also mobilized funds for high-risk ventures through the ability to spread the investment among numerous individuals.

Transferability changed the time horizon associated with an investment as regular interest payments or a share in annual profits replaced repayment. This encouraged long-term investment in such areas as infrastructure. Transferability also permitted a better matching between investor and investment as investors could exit or enter according to preferences and changing circumstances. This lowered the cost of capital. Transferability also meant that control of a business was divorced from the way it was financed. This permitted the employment of professional management and eased the creation of new business units whether through mergers or subdivisions.

3.4 Price Changes

The combination of divisibility and transferability also meant that securities generated constantly changing prices, as investors bought and sold according to their circumstances and perceptions. This price information transmitted signals which informed decision-making in business, whether regarding investment or control.

Pricing signals were also of value to the wider financial community. Knowledge of accurate and reliable prices allowed securities to be used for collateral. Banks, in particular, possessed deposits from savers that could not be invested for the long term as they could be withdrawn on demand. Lending to those providing securities as collateral provided an easy and remunerative means of employing these deposits. If the deposits were withdrawn, the loans could be recalled and the investors could repay, because the securities could be sold.

There existed a complex chain that connected the stocks and bonds issued by companies and governments to the deposits placed in banks by savers. Underpinning that chain were exchanges, because they provided both the means through which securities could be bought and sold and the prices that guaranteed the value of the loan.

From time to time, this mechanism broke down as speculators sought to manipulate individual stocks or bonds for personal gain, or a collective euphoria arose that created a belief that prices would continue to rise inexorably. When this happened, the signals emanating from exchanges encouraged investors to drive prices higher and higher and banks to lend them more and more based on these inflated values. When the manipulation or euphoria ended, prices collapsed, leaving investors with large losses and banks with irrecoverable loans. Recovery then took time as investors were left poorer and banks adopted more cautious lending policies while some had ceased to do business. However, such were the attractions possessed by stocks and bonds to both issuers and investors that their use quickly recovered once confidence in future economic prospects returned.

4. The Value of Exchanges: Markets and Regulation

4.1 Confidence in Future Economic Prospects

Critical for this confidence was the ability of exchanges to deliver a forum where securities could be easily, quickly, and cheaply traded, and delivered prices that could be generally relied on. Without such a market, the advantages that securities possessed in terms of divisibility and transferability would be largely lost.

Securities and the market were mutually reliant, with the use of the former being dependent upon the development of the latter. Though mercantile exchanges did provide securities with a means through which they could be bought, this proved to be increasingly inadequate as securities developed in importance and generated a specialist set of intermediaries in the process.

What these intermediaries required, whether they were brokers or dealers, was a market in which transactions could be completed quickly with those who could be relied upon. To achieve that required a set of regulations governing the conduct of business. Based on these regulations, all who bought and sold could do so in the relative certainty that any transaction would be honored.

Enforcing these rules and regulations was achieved through the power to deny entry to those whose actions might create unacceptable risks and punish those who broke the rules. This led to the creation of an exclusive organization whose membership contained all those whose livelihood depended on buying and selling securities. In doing so, securities exchanges differentiated themselves from both the mercantile exchanges and the informal securities markets out of which they had grown.

Once these securities exchanges had achieved an independent existence, they continually refined their rules and regulations to deal with abuses and improve the matching of buy and sell orders. The effect of this was to make stock exchanges, as they were generally known, increasingly better markets for the trading of securities.

A process of mutual dependency and common advantage took place in which the growing sophistication of the market provided by stock exchanges popularized the use of stocks and bonds by issuers and investors. In turn, the popularity of securities encouraged the formation of more stock exchanges and advanced the quality of the markets they provided. And so the process continued.

4.2 Formation of Specialized Exchanges

What took place with stock exchanges was also replicated in other markets. As the trading process moved away from a simple matching of current supply and demand, many of those involved sought ways to improve the market and reduce risk simultaneously. The result was the formation of other specialized exchanges devoted to trading specific products under mutually agreed rules and where admission was restricted. By creating closed markets, specialized exchanges were able to introduce a greater degree of trust among the members compared with a situation in which all could participate.

With regulation and supervision, there was greater trust in the prices being collected for dissemination. Enforcement of either open outcry, where buyers and sellers had to shout out prices, or the use of a dealer as a neutral intermediary between brokers, made it difficult to publicize inaccurate market information.

This trust also extended to those doing business in these specialized exchanges, because the possibility of exclusion always existed for those who failed to honor sales or purchases.

Based on this trust, the use of more sophisticated financial products emerged. These included the sale and purchase of options that gave the right of the holder to buy or sell at a fixed price at some date in the future.

Only an exchange, where both membership and trading was subject to strict controls, could provide the guarantee that those selling such contracts would deliver on their commitments. It was not the law of the land that was critical in this, but the self-regulation practiced by specialized exchanges that created the conditions under which prices could be relied on and contacts for future delivery and payment were met.

4.3 Price Determination

One consequence of the market provided by stock exchanges was authoritative and continuous price determination. Those buying and selling securities required the assurance that the price they paid or received reflected current market conditions.

Since stock exchanges imposed a charge upon those permitted to use their trading floor, determining these prices was not a free good, but one that cost money to create in the form of the infrastructure and staffing of an exchange. These costs were accepted by those using the exchange, because it gave them privileged access to the trading forum and knowledge of current prices, both of which were denied to others. These costs could also be passed onto the ultimate buyers and sellers of securities, because stock exchanges usually provided the best market for the most heavily traded stocks and bonds.

Buying and selling of securities took place on stock exchanges not simply because its members might offer the cheapest transaction cost. Membership in a stock exchange gave brokers access to the market with the greatest liquidity, allowing them to transact business for their customers quickly and with the least effect on current prices. The ability to buy and sell quickly at current prices, no matter the amount, was a service valued by the largest investors, especially institutions like banks and insurance companies.

This did not mean that stock exchanges were immune to competition. It was important for stock exchanges and their members to disseminate prices as that informed investors and banks of the market value of particular stocks and bonds, and so generated ongoing interest and repeat orders. These prices could be used by nonmembers to undercut the charges made by exchange members, since they did not pay the charges levied and need not obey the rules and regulations.

As communications technology improved with the telegraph and the telephone, this dissemination of prices became a growing issue for stock exchanges and their members. The solution adopted was to delay the dissemination of prices. By doing so, exchanges balanced the need to disseminate prices and the interests of members. The former was essential if securities were to remain widely used financial instruments. The latter was essential as the charges made on members were responsible for the continuing existence of the exchange and the market it provided.

5. The Development of Exchanges: Origins, Evolution, and Diversity before 1914

Though exchanges were all designed to fulfill a common purpose, they took many different forms. This can be seen by examining the development of stock exchanges during the nineteenth century.

5.1 Local Exchanges

In that century, numerous local stock exchanges were formed. They provided a convenient forum for trading in the securities issued by the growing numbers of local companies whose stocks were largely held by local investors familiar with their management and operations. These companies supplied basic services such as gas, water, and electricity, or were engaged in risky new ventures in mining or manufacturing. In this way, these exchanges made an important contribution to economic growth.

Local exchanges were long immune from competition, even after improved communication removed the protection of isolation. Investors long possessed a strong bias towards familiar investments. However, investors did not confine their holdings of securities to those issued by local enterprises.

5.2 National Networks

As communications improved, beginning with the telegraph in the 1840s, local exchanges were integrated into national networks, attracting orders from more distant investors because of the particular nature of the securities that could be bought and sold there. In addition, individual stock exchanges developed a national role as they became the market for particular types of securities held by investors from elsewhere in the country. The debt of the national government was such a security, and its existence contributed to the primacy of a particular location as a financial center.

In the countries of Western Europe, the stock exchanges in such cities as London and Paris acted as national hubs, and contributed to financial integration. Funds flowed to these centers to be invested in the national debt, and banks located there benefited from being able to employ temporarily idle deposits in lending to those holding these bonds.

For that reason, London in particular emerged as the central money market of the global economy, because banks from around the world increasingly directed temporarily idle deposits there. On a lesser scale, New York occupied the same position within North America, as banks from across the United States and Canada found that they could utilize the call money market located on the New York Stock Exchange to employ funds that otherwise would have remained idle.

5.3 The Position in the United States

In contrast, countries without large national debts, or where the debt was held by investors located elsewhere, lacked this high degree of national financial integration. In the United States, where the Federal government paid off the debt arising from both the War of Independence and then the Civil War, it was not until the development of the railways from the mid-nineteenth century onwards, followed by other large enterprises, that the New York Stock Exchange was able to consolidate its primacy. Even by the First World War, New York was a much less dominant financial center in the United States than was London in the United Kingdom, Paris in France, Berlin in Germany, or Vienna in the Austro-Hungarian Empire.

More generally, the fact that British and French investors held such a large proportion of the national debts issued by governments, and the stocks and bonds belonging to the world's railway companies before 1914, meant that national financial integration was generally slowed down outside Western Europe. Much of the trading on the London and Paris stock exchanges was in foreign stocks and bonds at this time, as well as in some smaller exchanges such as Amsterdam and Brussels.

5.4 Global Economic Growth

Though detrimental to national financial integration, the willingness of European investors to hold large amounts of foreign securities did foster global economic growth. Through the issue of stocks and bonds, whether by companies or governments, countries around the world equipped themselves with both railway systems and other expensive infrastructure projects, such as mass transit systems and hydroelectric schemes. Through these advances made in improved transport, there was an explosion in international trade and migration between 1870 and 1914 which, along with international financial flows, comprised the first era of economic globalization.

The markets that stock exchanges provided were central to the process in two ways. Through their very existence, stock exchanges encouraged governments to borrow to finance economic development, and companies to issue stocks and bonds, whether to construct railway lines or develop mineral and other resources. Once in existence, many of these securities were held internationally, and actively traded on different exchanges around the world.

5.5 The Influence of Telegraph and Telephone

The prices generated on each exchange were then transmitted world-wide via telegraph and telephone lines with the result that a global marketplace was created. The laying of the telegraph line between New York and London in 1866 reduced the time delay between the two cities from 5 days to 20 minutes. Further improvements shortened that to 30 seconds by the First World War, and members of the London and New York stock exchanges were among the most active users of the transatlantic cable.

When the Paris to London telephone line was opened in the 1890s, the time delay between the Paris Bourse and the London Stock Exchange was finally eliminated. Members of each market were in constant communication throughout the trading day.

What the links between members of different stock exchanges provided was a means by which money could be moved around the world in response to minute changes in supply and demand. Selling securities on one exchange established a credit in that financial center while buying in another led to a matching debit.

Though the combination of stability and growth that characterized the half-century before the First World War has long been attributed to the Gold Standard, it owed much more to the revolution in communications, the existence of internationally held securities, and the existence of stock exchanges. The rapid growth of global commerce was equally dependent on the revolution in both communications and transport, with the railway and the steamship, and the operations conducted on the world's specialized commodity exchanges such as the Chicago Board of Trade and the London Metal Exchange.

6. Exchanges Under Stress: Survival and Change, 1914–50

6.1 The First World War

All this was to change with First World War. Virtually every stock exchange closed temporarily because of the disruption caused by the outbreak of war. When stock exchanges did reopen, they were often under government supervision. Each country attempted to control national finances to assist the war effort and limit destabilizing fluctuations in prices.

The experience of the First World War left a legacy in the shape of a much greater degree of government intervention in financial and commercial markets than before. A number of stock exchanges had also disappeared, as with those in Russia following the October Revolution of 1917. Nevertheless, most stock exchanges soon recovered their pre-War position aided by the needs of governments to fund massive debts and business to finance itself, along with the resumption of international lending and borrowing. However, most internationally held securities had been sold or repudiated, so removing the assets whose flows had contributed so much to the equilibrium of the pre-1914 world economy.

6.2 The 1920s

It was thus not surprising that the 1920s was characterized by price and exchange rate instability. What emerged in that decade was an active foreign exchange market that linked banks in the world's major financial centers. Each bank now attempted to balance its assets and liabilities across different currencies as well as its current and forward commitments. To do so required dealing directly with other banks. Over all banks, it should be possible to achieve a balance as the payment to one was a debit for another.

Unlike securities, foreign exchange was not traded on formal exchanges but either directly between banks or through the use of inter-bank brokers. The largest banks had a standing within the financial community that provided some kind of guarantee that sales and purchases would be honored. Through a process of inquiry and monitoring, banks estimated the risk they ran in dealing with each other. Based on that estimate, each bank made its own decisions on which other banks to do business with and the amount that would be.

Out of this emerged some semblance of the pre-1914 international financial system. The problem was that this system had to cope with enormous imbalances between economies caused by the First World War. Neither the postwar peace conferences nor later intergovernment agreements solved these imbalances, leaving many economies highly dependent upon international borrowing to meet both imports of merchandise and payment of interest on mounting debts.

6.3 The Crash in the United States

This was all to have a major impact on the New York Stock Exchange.

Of all economies in the world, the United States had emerged as the most prosperous after the First World War. During the war, American investors redeemed the huge external holdings of US corporate stocks and bonds and then proceeded both to lend extensively to foreign banks in the 1920s and to buy foreign securities. Underpinning all this was a prolonged period of relatively low interest rates in the United States that encouraged investors to seek opportunities abroad.

These low interest rates also fuelled a stock market boom which gathered pace in the course of the decade. The number of US investors had expanded enormously during the First World War, and these investors were ready to participate in the emerging stock market opportunities offered by the issues made by large companies producing steel and automobiles or providing new services like radio and the cinema. Major US deposit banks got involved in the process through the issue of corporate stocks. Stock exchange brokers also acted as intermediaries between banks and investors, providing their clients with credit secured by the ever-rising price of stocks. As stocks rose in price, investors were able to borrow more money, which they used to buy more stocks, driving prices even higher. As long as investors remained confident that prices would rise, they continued to borrow to finance further purchases.

When credit eventually tightened, the more cautious investors began to sell, reversing the rise in stock prices and encouraging a wholesale sell-off. This happened in the course of 1929, and it became known as the Wall Street Crash. Banking collapses then followed as savers rushed to withdraw deposits because of fears that they were insolvent, having lost heavily through lending to those buying stocks at the top of the market.

The collapse of banks was more serious than the fall in the stock market, because it led to a sharp contraction in credit, which had implications for the entire US economy. As the prosperity of the US economy was now central to the successful operation of the world economy through the constant recycling of dollars, the already fragile international financial system was seriously weakened.

Crises followed in other countries, such as Austria and Germany, and spread to Britain, forcing it to abandon the Gold Standard in 1931. As Britain still played a key role in the operation of the international economy, the crisis became worldwide. Governments then compounded the problem by introducing protective measures that contributed to the collapse of international trade.

6.4 The Depression in the 1930s

By being the most visible manifestation of the financial instability present in the world economy in the 1920s, contemporaries blamed the

Wall Street Crash for the ensuing economic depression of the 1930s. There were plenty of examples of abuses and excesses to incite public anger against the New York Stock Exchange.

Some of these troubles had taken place long before the Crash and did not involve either its members or trading in stocks. One such abuse was Charles Ponzi's fraud which took place in 1920 and involved supposed foreign exchange gains to be made by purchasing postal reply coupons in foreign countries and redeeming them at face value in the United States. Nevertheless, many saw it as being symptomatic of the speculative excesses encouraged by the trading facilities provided by the Stock Exchange.

Banks that combined deposit taking with the securities business were blamed by many for creating the conditions that encouraged speculation, since they both issued stocks and lent investors money to buy them. Legislation to split up deposit and investment banking was the result.

During the collapse, the activities of short sellers also came in for criticism, as they were held responsible for driving down prices. Short sellers sold stocks they did not own in the expectation of delivering them to the purchaser by buying them back at a lower price in the future. Such an activity was a long-standing feature of stock exchange activity, as it helped to ensure that buyers could always purchase stocks.

Finally, revelations did emerge about how certain brokers and dealers had used their position to profit from inside information at the expense of clients.

6.5 The Securities and Exchange Commission (SEC)

As a result of these concerns, there was a flurry of restrictions and legislation aimed at controlling the operation of stock exchanges in the United States. In 1933–34, the US government created the Securities and Exchange Commission to police new issues and secondary trading.

Important as these actions were in making the New York Stock Exchange a safer place in which to trade, they make it less useful in terms of money market activity. Those employing funds for a short time needed access to a market where securities could be readily bought and sold. By placing restrictions on the trading techniques that members of the New York Stock Exchange could employ, the operation and development of a highly liquid market was restricted. Nevertheless, stock exchanges remained both in operation and independent in the United States, though now under a degree of government supervision for the first time.

6.6 The Second World War

Elsewhere in the world, wars and revolutions led to the temporary or permanent closure of many exchanges. Internationally, the imposition and enforcement of exchange and capital controls created major barriers between exchanges in different countries. Political and economic nationalism severed the free flow of commodities, products, and funds upon which many exchanges had thrived. Increasingly, exchange organization became a product of government intervention at the national level.

This situation was then compounded during the Second World War when many exchanges were, again, closed down or subjected to a high degree of government intervention and control. What happened to exchanges between 1914 and 1945 was but a single example of the collapse of both market liberalism and economic globalization that had characterized the years before the First World War. In its place came differing degrees of government intervention, which was at its most extreme in communist regimes. There was also a high level of economic nationalism as epitomized by the measures taken to restrict international trade and migration and the free flow of funds.

The fate suffered by exchanges in the space of the 31 years from 1914 to 1945 appeared but a minor casualty compared with the two most damaging wars the world has ever experienced, the most severe and prolonged economic depression in global history, and the worst atrocities perpetuated on mankind in human knowledge.

6.7 Post-War Regulation

Under those circumstances, it was only to be expected that those who had experienced or simply witnessed such events were intent on planning a future that would be different. In that future, exchanges were allocated either a minor role or none at all being at best regarded as marginal while, to others, they were either irrelevant or even dangerous. The Wall Street Crash had left an indelible mark on stock exchanges, in particular, as they were seen as the prime cause of the instability that had brought down the world economy, leading to mass unemployment, international tension and then renewed World War. Stock exchanges were simply too dangerous to be allowed to exist without some form of supervision.

Given the experience of the Second World War, such a viewpoint was even more entrenched in 1945 than it had been when originally formulated. Thus, even in those countries where markets were still allowed to operate, governments had a mandate for control that went far beyond the eradication of market abuse and fraudulent practices.

To exercise that control, exchanges possessed obvious attractions for governments. Through their regulatory role, exchanges had long imposed rules and regulations upon their members. By influencing the behavior of exchanges, governments possessed a means of exercising a degree of control over those using them.

Such a situation could be achieved in a variety of ways. In the United States, the mechanism used was the Securities and Exchange Commission. In the United Kingdom, there was no formal body of that kind and so the government operated through the Bank of England, which was taken into public ownership in 1946. In France, the Paris Bourse had long been an arm of the state and that position was strengthened. In those countries where new stock exchanges were formed in the late 1940s and 1950s, governments were involved from the outset.

6.8 Stock Exchange Membership Post-1945

There were attractions for exchanges and their members in complying with the requirements imposed by governments after the Second World War, as it placed them in a very privileged position.

An uneasy tension always existed between those who traded in securities as members of stock exchanges and those who did not. Sometimes this was created by the stock exchanges themselves through the refusal to admit banks, or limitations on the number permitted access to the trading floor, with both actions being driven by a desire to limit competition and enhance returns. It was also a product of a desire to control for counterparty risk and to reward those who paid for the costs of providing the market in the first place.

After 1945, an exchange could guarantee the position it occupied by cooperating with the government and becoming the regulatory authority for the national market, with all who traded being required to pay for membership or use the services of those who had. Exchanges were now able to adopt or maintain a wide range of restrictive practices on charging, access, and market behavior without fearing a loss of business.

The exchanges in existence after 1945 thus reinvented themselves. They became the allies of the state in policing the market, and this led to a growth in the rules and regulations that covered the way trading was conducted.

However, adopting this position had consequences for stock exchanges. Among the most important was to weaken further the attractions of exchange-traded securities to those whose interest was driven by money-market considerations. Measures taken to restrict speculation, as with curbs on short-selling and restrictions on the use of options, also removed some of the means used to ensure that securities could always be bought and sold whatever the volume. The greater degree of supervision also increased an exchange's costs of operation, and these were passed on to users through the higher charges levied by members.

Though the charges levied by members remained relatively modest in comparison with other property transactions, they were sufficient to drive away particular types of business. Banks and others with temporarily idle funds sought securities that could be quickly bought and sold at very close to the market price, and were only willing to pay a fee that was little more that the spread between the bid and sell price.

6.9 Conclusion

Overall, between the outbreak of the First World War and the end of the Second, exchanges underwent considerable change. Among the most marked was the changed relationship to governments around the world. Beginning with the Wall Street Crash of 1929 and then completed by the Second World War, those exchanges that still remained in operation were increasingly brought into some kind of formal or informal regulatory framework. That framework was much more responsive to public supervision and oversight than had ever been the case in the past. Where the government had long played a role, as in much of Western Europe, the degree of intervention was now much greater.

Where it had hardly existed as across North America and the British Empire, it took a number of different forms. In the United Kingdom, nothing appeared to have changed, because the London Stock Exchange was not taken into state ownership and no statutory regulatory body was established. The reality was, however, very different as the stock exchange was very responsive to any policy suggestion from the government as relayed by the Bank of England. In the United States, the Securities and Exchange Commission refined and extended its operation, becoming an accepted and established part of the way the trading in stocks and bonds was regulated. As a result, it was the US model of an official regulator for the securities market that became the model that was followed in the years to come.

7. Exchanges in a Changing World, 1950–75

7.1 Medium- and Long-Term Investors

Though the money market continued to influence stock prices and help drive turnover, stock exchanges became more and more dependent on the activities of investors who bought and sold for the medium- and long-term. Investors had long been attracted to corporate stocks, because they promised a higher income than bonds did and also had a potential capital gain, if the business prospered.

As stock exchanges became more regulated institutions than in the past, the markets they offered to such investors for the purchase and sale of stocks were also more attractive. State supervision of exchanges provided investors with an implicit guarantee that encouraged confidence, and this was particularly beneficial for stocks rather than bonds.

Corporate stocks were always regarded as involving greater risk than bonds, because their return was not guaranteed. The return generated from ownership of corporate stocks depended upon the ability of the business to generate profits greater than the amount required to pay interest on borrowings, whether from banks or via the issue of bonds. Railways and public utilities were able to do so with a high degree of regularity, because demand for the service they provided was almost constant and costs varied little.

Conversely, there were corporate stocks that involved a high degree of risk, with those dependent upon exploration for oil and minerals, developing a new product or technology or supplying a new service being at the most extreme. Such companies attracted investors because of the potentially high gains to be made if the results were successful. Between those extremes were a huge number of companies that were capable of providing investors with both income and capital appreciation in varying combinations.

7.2 Income and Capital Appreciation

The combination of income and capital appreciation in the face of growing inflation after 1950 proved to be increasingly popular among investors.

Table 1.1: Inflation Rates in the United States and United Kingdom, 1950–2008 (Annual Rate)		
Decade	United States	United Kingdom
1950–59	2.15	4.40
1960–69	2.40	3.80
1970–79	7.19	13.22
1980–89	4.65	6.23
1990–99	2.73	3.06
2000–08	2.83	2.94

Source: L. H. Officer and S. H. Williamson, "Annual Inflation Rates in the United States, 1775–2008 and the United Kingdom, 1265–2008" Measuring Worth 2009.

Inflation became a feature of most economies beginning in the 1950s, though it did vary both over time and between countries (see Table 1.1).

Inflation created a real predicament for investors, because it led to returns falling in real terms. During the 1950s, for example, the real return on bonds was negative, as the annual interest paid was less than the rate of decline in the capital value (see Table 1.2).

As investors gradually became aware of this, especially in those countries where inflation was more pronounced, they searched for assets that would retain their value as well as generating income.

Table 1.2: Real Return on Assets: World Average by Decade (Geometric Mean, Percent per Annum)		
Period	Bonds	Equities
1900–09	0.3	5.4
1910–19	−7.9	−3.7
1920–29	5.5	13.0
1930–39	5.3	1.7
1940–49	−4.8	1.0
1950–59	−0.4	17.1
1960–69	0.6	5.5
1970–79	1.6	0.9
1980–89	6.6	13.5
1990–2000	5.8	5.4
1900–2000	1.2	5.8

Source: E. Dimson, P. Marsh, and M. Stanton, Triumph of the Optimists: 101 Years of Global Investment Returns [Princeton 2002] p. 313.

Property was one such asset, whether in the form of individual home ownership or land, offices, and factories. However, property had major disadvantages as an asset, because it was neither easily divisible nor quickly transferable. In contrast, corporate stocks had the capacity to deliver the desired combination of income and capital growth in a more flexible manner. Stocks could offer the prospect of a return that would keep pace with inflation as corporate earnings grew through the ability to pass on rising prices to customers. In turn, that was reflected in the value of the business and the dividends paid, which would result in rising share prices. In the 1950s, global equity returns averaged 17.1 percent per annum compared to a loss of 0.4 percent per annum for bonds. Though these equity returns fell in the 1960s, and those for bonds rose, shares continued to be the more attractive investments (see Table 1.2).

7.3 Market Concentration

The effect of this recovery in the fortune of exchanges can be seen in the case of the New York Stock Exchange, where the turnover of shares rose from 0.8 billion in 1960 to 2.9 billion in 1970. Similar growth was observed in other leading stock exchanges like London and Tokyo.

However, not all stock exchanges benefited. Trading in stocks gravitated away from the smaller stock exchanges towards larger exchanges. By 1970, the Tokyo Stock Exchange handled 72 percent of the total volume of securities trading in Japan compared with 63 percent in 1960, and this was typical of the process taking place around the world. In the past, investors in stocks had favored both local and national exchanges. The continuing fragmentation of the market, even at a time when the transformation of communications facilitated integration, was driven by the combination of local ownership and local operation that long prevailed among companies. Investors used familiarity as a guide to purchasing securities at a time when the science of investment was still rudimentary. In addition, there remained advantages to local management, local production and local services until full economic integration was achieved.

However, that situation was transformed after the Second World War with the result that the natural tendency towards market concentration was given full reign. In addition to greater economic integration encouraging the growth of ever larger companies, the process was also responsive to the great increase in government intervention after 1945. The increased level and complexity of legal requirements and taxes imposed a growing burden of compliance on business. That burden fostered a growing scale of enterprise as only the largest companies possessed the managerial structure and staffing that could cope. Through mergers and acquisitions, businesses grew bigger as a result, and so the market for their stocks gravitated to the largest exchange.

7.4 The Rise of the Institutional Investor

Law and taxation also changed investment behavior as it encouraged collective rather than individual activity.

The rise of the institutional investor was a marked feature of the postwar years. Institutional investors had long existed in the form of the insurance company and the investment trust, but they really flourished after 1950, when there was an expansion in pension provision by both business and quasi-official bodies. In this, they were emulating the state-financed schemes that relied on taxation as well as responding to the emerging complexity of investment. In the past, an individual or institutional investor purchased government debt, mortgages or corporate bonds and then lived on the regular income they produced. In contrast, corporate stocks required both more active and more expert management, because the return was unknown and the risks greater. To minimize these risks, a diverse portfolio was required, and this was best done collectively for all but the exceptionally wealthy. The effect was to move control over the sale and purchase of corporate stocks from individuals using their knowledge and connections, often on a local basis, to trained fund managers.

The rise of the institutional investor had consequences for exchanges as finance professionals had a preference for those stocks that justified analytical research and could be bought and sold easily and quickly. These were the stocks of the larger companies. The market for such stocks was usually found in the largest stock exchange located within any country. In contrast, the market provided by the local stock exchanges was often too shallow and too narrow to cope with the buying and selling needs of institutional investors. As it was the managers of pooled funds that increasingly generated buying and selling activity, the largest stock exchanges were favored at the expense of the smaller. This phenomenon was observable across the world from 1950 onwards to a lesser or greater degree. The number of individual stock exchanges began to shrink; they either closed down or merged. In the United States, there was a steady decline in the number of exchanges, while in both France in 1966 and Britain in 1973 a single organization emerged.

7.5 Stock Exchange Mergers

These mergers were also defensive measures as stock exchanges strove to improve the quality of the market they could provide institutional investors with. The risk always existed that investors would by-pass the stock exchange. The matching of sales and purchases was made easier when investors were few and large. Such conditions had existed before exchanges came into existence when the ownership of stocks was in the hands of a few wealthy individuals. It reappeared in the age of the institutional investor, because they could trade with each other directly or use the services of inter-dealer brokers. This was already common in the foreign exchange and government debt markets. What made it more difficult in stocks was the problem of pricing compared with money market instruments. Stock exchanges were the source of the most reliable current prices for a wide range of stocks, and their members were reluctant to make these immediately available. If institutional investors had access to current prices and a mechanism for trading between each other, they could by-pass the stock exchange and save on the charges made. Stock exchanges found it difficult to prevent the leakage of current prices from their trading floor, especially with the constant advances made in information technology such as fax machines, computers, and quoting systems. Also, those members who did a large business with institutional investors were sometimes willing to pass on current market information in the hope that it would generate orders.

7.6 Tensions among Members

Within the membership of exchanges, divisions grew both between those that served institutions and those that served individuals, and between those that wanted to grow in scale and those that were content to remain small. The effect was to create tensions within exchanges as the rules and regulations that controlled the market also, in many cases, dictated who was eligible for membership, the minimum and maximum size of the unit, the scale of charges for business done, and the degree of competition permitted.

The New York Stock Exchange had a cap on membership, excluded deposit banks, and imposed a fixed scale of charges, and it was the model followed by many other exchanges around the world. Both Australia and Malaysia adopted the US model, for example, and it had been imposed on Japan after the end of the Second World War.

As the composition of investors increasingly diverged between the large institution and the single individual, this one-size-fits-all approach was increasingly unsatisfactory. Some members wanted the freedom to serve large institutional investors, and this included the ability to complete transactions internally based on current market prices. Others wanted to develop a retail business by creating an extensive branch network. Again, this would create an ability to internalize transactions. However, many among the membership of all stock exchanges were intent on using the rules and regulations of the organization to limit or prevent the growth of competition.

7.7 The Growth of Competition in the United States

In the United States, it was not possible to prevent competition between exchanges. Many separate stock exchanges remained in existence; and investors were numerous, wealthy, and spread throughout the country. Though supervised by the Securities and Exchange Commission, stock exchanges did not have a monopoly of trading in either stocks or bonds.

Under these circumstances, a specialization developed based not on location but different segments of the securities market. The New York Stock Exchange focused on that part of the securities market for which its trading facilities and rules and regulations were best suited, the market for the stocks of the largest companies. Elsewhere, a thriving over-the-counter (OTC) market developed to cater for both the securities and the brokers excluded from the New York Stock Exchange, whether it was the high-volume trading in US government debt or the low-volume transactions in the shares of smaller US companies, handled by the members of the National Association of Securities Dealers (NASD). This alternative market, however, was unregulated and so open to abuses, such as price manipulation, while many stocks issued by smaller companies could not be readily bought and sold.

In the case of trading in government debt, the lack of regulation mattered little, because trade was conducted between banks and institutional investors that possessed trained staff able to take informed decisions. However, where it involved individual investors buying and selling the stocks of small companies, regulation was required, and this was traditionally provided by stock exchanges. If these transactions no longer took place via exchanges, investors were left exposed with no recognized market price and unmarketable assets.

The use of stock exchanges as instruments to control national markets also limited their international role. The Eurobond market, which grew rapidly in the 1960s, developed both outside the United States, despite the dollar denomination, and outside established exchanges. Even in London, where it took root, the London Stock Exchange would not alter its rules and regulations to allow trading to take place, despite pressure from among its own members. They were concerned that any concession given to those trading Eurobonds would be demanded by others, especially the largest firms doing an institutional business.

7.8 The Lack of Competition in Europe and Elsewhere

Elsewhere in the world, the level of competition was either limited or non-existent. Governments had often given a monopoly of all trading to recognized stock exchanges, so forcing all transactions to be conducted through them. This was the case in the likes of France, Japan, and South Africa. Elsewhere, stock exchanges operated without any statutory authority, but were so strongly backed by their national governments or central banks that competition hardly surfaced. Such was the case in the United Kingdom where the London Stock Exchange was dominant. In Canada, growing competition from members of the New York Stock Exchange led to officially sanctioned attempts to prevent US brokers becoming members of Canadian exchanges after 1960. The justification for monopoly was that it imposed the costs and obligations of regulation on all who traded securities. Monopoly also made it easier to enforce regulations, as government or other authorities had only one or a few institutions to deal with.

However, monopoly often led to abuse. A monopoly position gave an exchange the power to charge whatever fees it wanted, while reducing any incentive to provide better service. Nevertheless, there were always powerful reasons why investors in stocks would channel their orders through members of regulated exchanges as long as the transaction costs were not made prohibitive.

In fixed-interest securities, the promised rate of return was readily comparable to the current rate of interest in the money market. This made pricing relatively easy. Also, the markets for government debt and corporate bonds were usually both deep and broad, as such assets had always been attractive to those with temporarily idle funds, as was true with banks and other financial institutions. As a result, there was always an incentive for those trading in such securities to bypass exchanges, for they could avoid paying commission charges by doing so.

In contrast, the return on corporate stocks was dependent upon the business the company was in and the quality of the management, creating major uncertainties for the investor in terms of pricing. What exchanges provided was thus not only a means through which sales and purchases could take place, but also the reference price for any particular security. By routing an order through a regulated exchange, an investor could be confident that the transaction would not only be completed quickly but at a price that reflected current buying and selling. For those reasons, investors were willing to pay a premium to a broker who was a member of an exchange, especially for transactions in corporate stocks.

7.9 Internalized Trading

The role played by exchanges also changed significantly after 1950. The greater the size of the business unit, the more buying and selling was internalized rather than passed through the market, whether it involved flows of products, commodities, or money. Multinational companies were able to do this internationally, for example. Similarly, as banks increased in size through mergers and acquisitions, they were in a position to provide more diverse financial services on an increased scale, thereby meeting the needs of ever bigger companies. Big companies themselves were also able to mobilize finance from retained earnings and then internalize the flow of funds from one sector to another, with the added advantage of minimizing the taxation that they had to pay. They had less need to raise capital from investors through new issues of stocks and bonds. Similarly, investment institutions were able to finance a direct participation in a business rather than confine themselves to only holding stocks already traded on exchanges.

These changes in the financial and business landscape removed exchanges from many of the more basic economic activities. Whereas in the past, even relatively small businesses had sought finance through an issue of stock, such a circumstance became increasingly rare. These businesses could now raise substantial funds from banks and investment institutions or grow organically within a large company. It was only at a later stage that such businesses approached the market with an issue of stock through an Initial Public Offering (IPO). That stock was then traded on a stock exchange. Nevertheless, the role of the stock exchange remained crucial for both investors in and issuers of stocks. Through an IPO, those who had backed a new enterprise were able to realize the profits they had made and so release funds for use elsewhere.

The existence of the market provided by a stock exchange was essential, because it provided the confidence that a profitable exit was possible, if the business prospered. At the exit stage, the market provided was also essential, as it allowed the participation of new investors. Many investors were not willing to finance a new enterprise because of the risks involved, but were keen to buy stock in a business with a proven track record. Essentially, what the stock exchange provided was a means of matching investors with stocks across the entire risk profile. Such a service was to become increasingly important after 1950.

7.10 Battles for Corporate Control

In this new world, stock exchanges also became the arenas in which battles for corporate control were fought. To hold assets that would cope with inflation, investors increasingly held a direct stake in the fortunes of business rather than accept a guaranteed return.

It was only when a default occurred that the ownership of corporate bonds could replace the management of the company and ensure that interest was paid and debts repaid. In the case of a sovereign default, the owners of the bonds were in an even weaker position. Often, it was only when a state wanted to borrow again that it was willing to reach an agreement with the holders of its bonds on resuming interest payments and redeeming outstanding debts.

In contrast, ownership of stock conferred control, even though investors were more concerned about the returns generated.

There was little incentive for others to pay a premium to buy control unless there were advantages to be gained, and these were limited when the commonest form of corporate stock was that issued by railways and utilities. That began to change when all types of business adopted the corporate form, as became increasingly common in the 1960s and 1970s. Management of rival companies could compete for ownership of shares and thus control, in the expectation that they would be able to generate increased profits from the combined operation. In turn, this generated increased activity on stock exchanges both through rumors about expected mergers or acquisitions and when actual bids emerged. This created a relatively new dimension to the role played by stock exchanges. The possibility of a hostile bid became a spur to management perfor-mance. Thus, added to stock exchanges' traditional role as a market for transferable assets, and their more recent function as public regulatory bodies, was one of providing a means through which the control and organization of business could be continuously challenged and changed. The result was to make stock exchanges an essential element in business from the 1950s onwards in a way they had never been before.

7.11 Underdevelopment of Exchanges Worldwide

However, the existence of active stock exchanges around the world was not universal in the 1950s and 1960s. Western Europe and North America were the main regions in which long-established exchanges continued to operate. They also existed in Japan, India, Australia, New Zealand, and South Africa. Exchanges were formed in a number of countries in the 1960s and 1970s but often very little trading was done. In Hong Kong, which was flourishing economically as a British colony in the 1960s, the stock exchange was relatively underdeveloped compared to the banks and the money market.

The reason for these differences was largely found in the attitude of governments towards both the market and corporate enterprise. Communist countries had no need for exchanges, because central planning determined the allocation of resources and dictated prices. Even in many non-Communist countries, stock exchanges were not considered to be important. After independence in 1947, the Indian government allowed the stock exchanges to continue operating, while in Pakistan they were closed. Even where governments were keen to support emerging stock exchanges, they were usually not willing to give them the freedom to operate that was necessary if they were to flourish. The financial needs of business were largely left to reinvested earnings and bank loans.

Governments themselves used both taxation and revenue generation to finance the provision of many essential services. In most countries of the world, the railways and telephones had been taken into state ownership after 1945 along with utilities supplying gas, electricity, and water. The United States was a rare exception in this.

A focus by government on the needs of those requiring finance rather than providing investors with a range and depth of opportunities meant that the role played by stock exchanges in the financial system was little considered. Instead, government was central when it came to capital-intensive projects such as the building of roads and the supply of schools and hospitals.

Similarly, when business looked for financial support beyond that available from reinvested profits, banks were on hand to provide it. Banks were seen as a substitute for markets in the mobilization and use of savings. Through direct access to the deposits of savers and an ongoing relationship with borrowers, banks were believed to be better placed to meet the financing needs of business than could companies by issuing stocks and bonds that were subsequently bought and sold on exchanges. In particular, German universal banks were held up as the ideal model, because they were able to provide their business customers with the entire range of services they required, whether it was short-term credit or long-term capital. Lost in this analysis was the need of banks to constantly balance assets and liabilities, so as to be able to repay depositors on demand if a crisis of confidence occurred.[9]

7.12 Conclusion

After the Second World War, exchanges had to reinvent themselves to survive. They did this in two ways. One was to become regulatory authorities for the securities market, acting not only on behalf of their members but also the government. The effect of that was to make them complex bureaucratic structures employing a large staff to monitor and police the market. That required considerable expenditure, which was passed onto the members and, ultimately, was met by those who bought and sold securities through an exchange.

Such a situation was acceptable as long as it delivered benefits. Governments benefited as they were able to regulate the securities market without the cost and trouble of setting up a very extensive system of supervision and enforcement. Stock exchanges benefited by being recognized by government as the means through which the securities market was regulated. Their members benefited as this enhanced position limited or removed competition, so allowing them to pass on their costs to buyers and sellers of securities. Investors benefited as they had access to a regulated market in which the risks of default or fraud were much reduced. Issuers of securities benefited as they continued to have access to a market where the stocks and bonds they created could be traded.

Unfortunately, this situation was unstable, because it also allowed members of exchanges to abuse the power they now possessed. In the interests of their members, exchanges could both resist change and impose charges, to the detriment of the evolving needs of investors. Such a situation was not sustainable, as investors would seek ways to bypass the exchange or put pressure on the government to force through reforms. By acquiring a public service function, stock exchanges placed themselves in an impossible position after 1945, but this was unknown at the time by either governments or their members.

Of more permanence was the second role that stock exchanges acquired after 1950. This role was in reality an increased emphasis on one particular type of business, which was providing a market for corporate stocks. Such a role had long been the focus of the many local exchanges as well as the New York Stock Exchange. After 1950, it steadily became the dominant activity of all stock exchanges, including both London and Paris where the bond market had long been of central importance. With this emphasis on corporate stocks, exchanges acquired a role as markets for control as well as for finance and investment.

8. May Day in New York, 1975

8.1 Return to the Markets

During the 1970s, the world economy experienced bouts of high inflation accompanied by high unemployment and governments were incapable of devising appropriate policy responses. The era of fixed exchange rates also came to an end, as governments and central banks gave up increasingly futile attempts to maintain them.

The outcome was a return to markets as the one means available to cope with volatility. It was markets that increasingly determined interest and exchange rates, as with the interbank money and foreign exchange markets located in London.

Exchanges capitalized on this changed situation by designing option and future contracts. These contracts allowed banks and businesses to cover their exposure to future changes so providing a way of reducing risk. As early as 1972, the Chicago Mercantile Exchange set up the International Monetary Market where such products could be traded.

Inflation and instability also stimulated activity on stock exchanges though the economic difficulties of that decade made it difficult for companies to return real value to investors. Depressed demand and spiraling costs were not the conditions that produced rising profits out of which dividends could be paid.

8.2 Public and Private Functions

More generally, the 1970s created increasing difficulties for stock exchanges in balancing their public and private functions. There had always existed a somewhat uneasy relationship between an exchange and its members. Unlike a bank, which was a single business, an exchange had to balance the regulation of its members with the need to attract their continuing custom.

The dynamics of that relationship was threatened in the 1970s because individual members were being replaced by a shrinking number of corporate members, in those cases where banks of differing kinds were permitted access to the exchange. When the members of an exchange were numerous, and each conducted a limited business, they relied upon an organized market in which to buy and sell. Under these circumstances, an exchange could exercise considerable power over its members, forcing them to obey the rules or risk expulsion.

In contrast, when the number of individual members was few and each operated on a large scale, the power of the exchanges was greatly reduced. Especially when the member was part of a bank, expulsion could damage the exchange. There was always the possibility that the ex-member was large enough to operate without access to the exchange's trading floor, by establishing links directly with institutional investors or other large banks.

8.3 Institutional Investors

It was not only in the relation between exchanges and members that difficulties were appearing in the 1970s. Similar difficulties were also emerging in the relation between exchanges and investors.

When investors were mainly numerous individuals, the pressure for change that they could exert was both diffused and limited. Individuals had little collective power and so could not force change to take place, other than taking their business elsewhere. Trading elsewhere was not easy, especially in those countries where exchanges had been given a monopoly.

However, by the 1970s, individual investors were being steadily replaced by institutions, and these did possess considerable influence. Institutional investors represented the interests of numerous individuals; moreover, their control over the direction of savings was of major concern to governments. As the largest of these institutions generated sufficient buying and selling to trade directly with dealers at the quoted bid/offer price, they could cut their costs if they could bypass brokers and the fees they charged.

What institutional investors wanted was the flexibility of negotiating volume discounts with brokers, and the ability to trade directly with a market-maker when appropriate. The problem faced by exchanges was that concessions of that kind would make it difficult to maintain a scale of charges applicable to all members. For many members, the maintenance of such a scale was seen as vital, because it limited competition. By eliminating price competition among members, the incentive to reduce costs, employ the latest technology and achieve economies of scale was reduced. Increasingly, it was becoming difficult to devise a scale of charges that met the needs of all investors and all members, and this was becoming apparent on some of the largest stock exchanges such as New York and London in the 1970s.

8.4 Charges

In the face of only limited concessions from stock exchanges, the largest users of their markets, such as nonmember banks and institutional investors, put pressure on governments, central banks or regulatory agencies to force through a reduction of charges or even abandon fixed fees altogether.

Governments then faced a problem. On the one hand, governments wanted to operate through stock exchanges as a way of both policing the day-to-day operation of the national securities market and influencing its operation so as to accord with policy requirements. Stock exchanges were able to finance their public regulatory role by levying a charge on their members, which was paid, because it could be passed on to customers. On the other hand, governments wanted to respond to the demands of financial institutions to pay reduced charges and to open up competition between members of stock exchanges. Increased competition between stock exchange members was seen as a simple way of reducing the cost of trading stocks for all investors.

Governments were also under pressure to regulate the securities markets further when any case of market abuse or price manipulation caught the public's attention.

It was in the United States that tensions such as these were most acutely felt within the securities market. By 1975, 75 percent of trading on the New York Stock Exchange was on behalf of institutions. Much of the rest came via the extensive retail network maintained by a small number of large brokers. Such brokers were keen to break free from the straitjacket imposed by minimum commissions.

8.5 The NYSE and NASDAQ

Though the New York Stock Exchange occupied a dominant position in the US securities market, it was only in certain types of securities, namely the stocks issued by the largest companies. The New York Stock Exchange was also facing growing competition from OTC markets, which harnessed new developments in communications and computing technologies to create alternative trading systems.

In 1971, the National Association of Securities Dealers had created their Automated Quotations system (NASDAQ). NASDAQ delivered instantaneous quotes provided by authorized market-makers on over-the-counter stocks, allowing all participants to trade by telephone on the same basis, wherever located. It thus provided a central market for those brokers and dealers who were not members of stock exchanges. Such brokers were numerous and collectively conducted a substantial business, but were scattered across the United States.

As those brokers belonging to NASDAQ challenged those belonging to the New York Stock Exchange (NYSE) for business, the result was market fragmentation in the United States. This concerned the SEC, because it was no longer certain that individual investors, in particular, had full access to a properly regulated market in which their interests would be safeguarded.

Rather than force all business back onto the NYSE, the SEC pressed for the abolition of fixed commission charges. The SEC had the expectation that by abolishing fixed charges, market fragmentation would be reversed as orders would, once again, flow to the NYSE as the deepest market. Eventually, the NYSE agreed to this and fixed charges ended on May 1, 1975.

The effect was to promote the interests of the large and efficient brokerage houses. These large firms could offer institutional clients very low commission rates or even trade commission-free, profiting from the difference between the bid/offer spread when internalizing order flow. Some even operated an extensive branch network serving numerous individual investors, which allowed them to aggregate the business they did on their behalf. As a result, there emerged a small group of large and powerful Wall Street investment banks that combined the issuing of stocks and bonds on behalf of US corporations with the retailing of these securities to investors and their subsequent trading, whether for individuals or institutions.

Wall Street investment banks were free from the competition of the large US deposit banks, including those with New York head offices. The New York Stock Exchange also excluded deposit banks from membership, which denied them direct access to the trading floor. Deposit banks were also hampered by nineteenth-century legislation, which prevented interstate banking, so that they could not create nationwide branch networks. In addition, the Glass-Steagall Act, dating from the 1933, stopped them from undertaking investment banking.

Under these circumstances, the Wall Street investment banks were able to establish a commanding position within the US securities market. Combined with the role these banks played, the ending of fixed charges, and the further measures taken by the SEC to increase competition after 1975, the NYSE recovered much of the position it had previously occupied. For the stocks that it quoted, the trading floor of the New York Stock Exchange provided the best combination of price, speed, certainty, and capacity, and so business continued to flow to it from across the country, aided by the technological revolution in communications and the nationwide connections of its members.

Even though the United States possessed the largest securities market in the world, and the New York Stock Exchange was regarded as the model from which others took their lead, the events that took place on May 1, 1975, had very limited repercussions elsewhere in the world. In many parts of the world, the entire national securities market was under the control of a single stock exchange, and it received the formal or informal backing of the government of that country. This support was delivered in return for the stock exchange taking responsibility for policing the securities market and had the effect of making it difficult for potential competitors to mount a challenge.

In addition, the continuance of exchange and capital controls by most countries insulated national stock exchanges from external competition. National stock exchanges served national securities markets and were responsive to the needs of national governments which, in turn, were supportive of them.

As a result, external business of any kind was of minor importance within national securities markets. The rapidly growing Eurobond market, where turnover rose more than tenfold during the 1970s to reach US$240 billion a year in 1980, was conducted almost entirely outside stock exchanges, for example.

Stock exchanges were willing to accept the loss of certain segments of the securities market as long as they could preserve that element that generated profits for their members, and that was largely found in the trading of stocks. Consequently, there was neither desire nor reason to emulate what had happened in New York.

Deregulation of commissions directly affected Canada, because the Wall Street investment banks already had significant operations there. However, both the Canadian government and the Canadian stock exchanges introduced measures to reduce the competitive threat.

Elsewhere in the world, little change took place in the 1970s, as the members of national stock exchanges thought that they were safely entrenched in national monopolies. Even in those countries where a number of separate stock exchanges were in existence, each possessed or acquired something akin to a monopoly, with the one located in main financial center exerting a growing influence. Nevertheless, developments in the United States provided a clear indication of the strain that was being placed on the relationship between exchanges, governments, and businesses in the 1970s.

9. Big Bang in London, 1986

9.1 Worldwide Increase in Trading Volume

Generally, in the 1980s, there was a huge increase in the trading volumes experienced by stock markets around the world, with equity turnover in New York rising almost four-fold, Tokyo nine-fold, and London seventeen-fold. Growth on this scale removed much of the incentive for change among stock exchanges. Many exchanges continued to enjoy the support of their national governments and were little exposed to competition from either domestic OTC trading or alternative markets abroad. Nevertheless, there was a gradual freeing of domestic financial markets during the decade, as governments recognized the limits of their power and sought to regulate rather than control.

Internationally, governments also recognized their inability to control financial flows and sought instead to moderate their impact. The result was to transform the world within which stock exchanges operated, as a much more competitive environment now existed, especially given the transformation in communications and trading technology.

The effect was most apparent in those countries closely connected to the United States, in terms of financial transactions and where stock exchanges were modeled on those in the United States. Canadian stock exchanges abandoned fixed commissions in 1982, while Australia followed suit in 1984 and New Zealand in 1986.

However, the catalyst for change around the world was Big Bang in London in 1986. The ending of minimum commissions in New York in 1975 had been widely followed in London but did not produce an immediate response. Even when Britain abandoned exchange controls in 1979, and so exposed the London Stock Exchange to greater competition, change did not take place. A market for the shares of the largest British companies did develop in New York, where they were traded as American Depository Receipts (ADRs). However, the loss of business was judged minor by the London Stock Exchange and insufficient to prompt a review of charges and practices. British companies were largely owned by British investors and so the London Stock Exchange remained the dominant market for their shares.

9.2 Ending of Minimum Commission Rules in London

Consequently, there was little reason for members of the London Stock Exchange to agree to reform the way the Exchange operated as most saw benefits for themselves in the lack of competition that came with minimum commissions. The only exceptions were the few large firms doing business for the biggest institutional investors. Nevertheless, the London Stock Exchange did face a problem as the government was increasingly responsive to the complaints made by institutional investors that its rules and regulations, including minimum commissions, made the whole securities market inefficient and costly, to the detriment of the City of London as a financial center.

Under these circumstances, it appeared prudent to agree to a small concession as that would leave intact all the other rules. That concession was the ending of minimum commissions, which did not appear such a serious move in the early 1980s, given the limited consequences it had in New York. The New York Stock Exchange continued to dominate the market for US corporate stocks, though the larger firms had captured a greater share of the business. Though many members of the London Stock Exchange were very resistant to the ending of the minimum commission rules, fearing the unknown, none was aware of the profound changes that would follow in its wake.

A fixed scale of charges was introduced by the London Stock Exchange in 1912 and was itself the product of another change introduced some three years before. In 1909, members of the London Stock Exchange were prohibited from operating as both brokers and dealers. This measure was introduced in response to complaints from different groups among the membership. Dealers accused brokers of trading outside the exchange, with banks and institutions, on the basis of prices being made inside. Brokers accused dealers of trading directly with major investors, and so depriving them of commission income. This dispute went to the heart of the dilemma faced by any exchange as the telephone now allowed the rapid dissemination of prices and direct office-to-office contact.

However, the measure banning dual operation proved ineffective in the absence of minimum commission rates, forcing all brokers to charge for every sale or purchase they handled. Only when that was introduced could the sovereignty of the trading floor be enforced in London. The ability of the London Stock Exchange to enforce a regime of minimum commission rates was then enhanced after the First, and especially, the Second World War, when it became the unofficial regulator of the British securities market.

Thus, when the London Stock Exchange agreed in 1983 to end minimum commission rates, it soon became apparent that the result would be a complete restructuring of the way it operated and the market it provided. Not only were fixed commission rates abandoned, but also membership was thrown open to all.

Trading also moved from the floor as the London Stock Exchange embraced the new technology that was becoming available in the 1980s. Instead of trading being reliant on face-to-face or even telephone contact, electronic networks were being introduced that allowed computers to automatically match orders entered online by users. The result was that the London Stock Exchange was transformed into a very competitive market.

9.3 Worldwide Reaction to the Changes in London

What happened in London had implications for stock exchanges located elsewhere in the world, but especially Western Europe. London was a leading international financial center and contained a dense concentration of banks and brokers from across the world, along with the communication networks and payment systems that connected them.

Nevertheless, the pace of change elsewhere in the world was both slow and modest during the 1980s. New stock exchanges did appear, but the amount of business remained low, often stifled by government antagonism towards corporate enterprise and excessive bureaucratic control over the market. Among established stock exchanges; there was a widespread resistance to change with many being self-governing institutions with a statutory monopoly over the market for corporate stocks, as in India. Others were under the control of the state, as in Peru, or heavily regulated by government, as was the case across Africa.

The 1980s did witness a number of important changes among stock exchanges that helped them to become ever more central to the operation of national financial systems. One was the creation of additional markets by established stock exchanges to cater for small and new companies, as in Amsterdam in 1982 and Frankfurt in 1986. Another was the modernization of trading through the use of computers as on the Tokyo Stock Exchange in 1982. These developments took place in a climate where the volume of business continued to grow and the gradual dismantling of exchange and capital controls permitted greater competition between different national stock exchanges.

The growing international ownership of securities by institutional investors, and the global reach now exercised by a small number of banks, also contributed to a growth of competition. Cross-border equity trading grew from US$73.1 billion in 1979 to US$1.6 trillion in 1989, with much being done in London because of the competitive rates charged by its members. The result was that during the 1980s the pressure for change intensified, forcing both national exchanges and national governments to respond.

10. Discovering a New Role, 1990–2000

10.1 Increase in Activity

In the 1990s, governments recognized that the market had a central role to play in economic activity, both domestically and internationally. During the decade, there was a mass disposal of state assets to private investors, resulting in an enormous expansion in both the number of companies and the number of investors. Between 1990 and 1999, a total of US$850 billion in state assets was sold on to the public markets, and these appealed to investors of all different types, depending upon the prospects of the business and the degree of risk involved. While many individual investors eagerly participated in anticipation of large capital gains, institutions were attracted by the opportunity to hold assets that produced both a regular and rising return over the long term.

Though many governments continued to provide their populations with benefits financed out of current taxation, there was a growing realization that these would be less generous in the future. In particular, it became important for individuals to make their own pension provision and this generated a large revenue stream for both dedicated pension funds and insurance companies.

Between 1990 and 2000, the number of companies quoted on the world's stock exchanges rose by almost 10,000 or by around 50 percent. This growth was experienced both in regions with a long established corporate culture, such as in North America and Western Europe, and in areas where it was being rediscovered as in Eastern Europe, The distribution of listed corporate enterprises remained highly skewed towards the United States, Canada, France, Germany, Japan, and the United Kingdom, but there was a noticeable diffusion to other parts of the world in the 1990s (see Tables 1.3 and 1.4).

Table 1.3: Stock Exchanges: Number of Companies Quoted*

Location	1990	2000	2007	2008
Americas				
North America	7,358	9,245	9,916	10,290
Latin/Caribbean	1,364	1,304	1,492	1,500
Subtotal	8,722	10,549	11,408	11,790
Africa				
Subtotal	769	606	916	803
Asia				
East	4,949	7,597	11,999	12,076
West	326	1,505	8,002	8,139
Subtotal	5,275	9,102	20,001	20,215
Australasia				
Subtotal	1,381	1,609	2,176	2,181
Europe				
Eastern Europe	140	753	926	1,057
Western Europe	4,698	6,881	10,865	10,660
Subtotal	4,838	7,434	11,791	11,717
World Total	20,985	29,300	46,292	46,706

Source: World Federation of Exchanges: Time Series 2009.

*The data compiled from the returns made to the World Federation of Exchanges does not include all exchanges and coverage grows over time. The effect is to produce an incremental gain as additional exchanges are added. For the geographical classification, Asia is split between India and countries to the West, and those to the East. The East Asia category contains Japan, China, Hong Kong, South Korea, the Taiwanese market, and Singapore. The Middle East is included in either West Asia or Africa, depending on the location of the individual countries. Europe: West also includes all of Scandinavia and the Baltic republics.

Table 1.4: Stock Exchanges: Distribution of Quoted Companies*

Location	1990	2000	2007	2008
Americas				
North America	84.4%	87.6%	86.9%	87.3%
Latin/Caribbean	15.6%	12.4%	13.1%	12.7%
Subtotal	41.6%	36.0%	24.6%	25.2%
Africa				
Subtotal	3.7%	2.1%	2.0%	1.7%
Asia				
East	93.8%	83.5%	60.0%	59.79%
West	6.2%	16.5%	40.0%	40.3%
Subtotal	25.1%	31.1%	43.2%	43.3%
Australasia				
Subtotal	6.6%	5.5%	4.7%	4.7%
Europe				
Eastern Europe	2.9%	10.1%	7.9%	9.0%
Western Europe	97.1%	89.9%	92.1%	91.0%
Subtotal	23.1%	25.4%	25.4%	25.1%
World Total	100%	100%	100%	100%

Source: World Federation of Exchanges: Time Series 2009.

*Within each location, the proportion is of the regional total. Each regional total is a proportion of the global total.

During the course of the 1990s, even more dramatic than the growing number of companies in existence was the growth in total market capitalization. Over that decade, the market value of the corporate stocks quoted on the world's stock exchanges grew almost fourfold, from US$8.9 trillion to US$31 trillion.

Across the world, investors discovered the advantages of corporate stocks, especially those that traded in a liquid market. Securities became the asset class preferred by all varieties of investors, ranging from the individual willing to speculate on the future value of a company developing a new product, service, technology, or resource to the institution needing to rebalance a portfolio in the light of changing circumstances. This drove up the value of quoted securities as investors searched for income, capital growth, or their preferred combination of both in different countries around the world.

Certain areas of the world did not share in this growth, most notably Africa, while for others the increase was relatively modest, as in Japan. In contrast, in North America and Western Europe, the market value of corporate stocks rose fivefold during the 1990s, as companies operating in these regions generated either steadily growing profits or promised future gains. These investment gains generated a cycle in which investors were induced to invest more, because of rising stock prices, and rising stock prices encouraged additional investment (see Tables 1.5 and 1.6).

10.2 The Dot.com Boom

One consequence of this growing investor interest in corporate stocks was a speculative boom which centered on those companies expected to profit most from new developments in information technology. Advances in computing and communications were transforming the nature of business, with enormous profits predicted for those companies supplying the equipment and software or creating new services. Unproven as these profits were, they tantalized investors who backed every new issue of stock and then drove its price up to new heights.

Table 1.5: Stock Exchanges: Domestic Market Capitalization*				
Location	1990	2000	2007	2008
Americas				
North America	3,347.1	15,980.6	22,108.8	12,771.1
Latin/Caribbean	70.3	469.5	2,211.5	1,125.2
Subtotal	3,417.4	16,450.1	24,320.3	13,896.3
Africa				
Subtotal	136.9	131.3	975.4	572.6
Asia				
East	3,290.9	4,415.0	14,959.5	7,999.5
West	76.1	255.1	4,093.5	1,589.5
Subtotal	3,367.0	4,470.1	19,053.0	9,589.0
Australasia				
Subtotal	116.8	391.3	1,345.8	708.1
Europe				
Eastern Europe	15.3	156.0	586.7	223.6
Western Europe	1,840.5	9,159.8	16,446.7	8,309.6
Subtotal	1,855.8	9,315.8	17,033.4	8,533.2
World Total	8,893.9	30,958.6	62,727.9	33,299.2

Source: World Federation of Exchanges: Time Series 2009.
*In US$ billions, current prices at year-end.

Table 1.6: Stock Exchanges: Domestic Market Capitalization*

Location	1990	2000	2007	2008
Americas				
North America	97.9%	97.1%	90.9%	91.9%
Latin/Caribbean	2.1%	2.9%	9.1%	8.1%
Subtotal	38.4%	53.1%	38.8%	41.7%
Africa				
Subtotal	1.5%	0.4%	1.6%	1.7%
Asia				
East	97.7%	94.5%	78.5%	83.4%
West	2.3%	5.5%	21.5%	16.5%
Subtotal	37.9%	15.1%	30.4%	28.8%
Australasia				
Subtotal	1.3%	1.3%	2.1%	2.1%
Europe				
Eastern Europe	0.8%	1.7%	3.4%	2.6%
Western Europe	99.2%	98.3%	96.6%	97.4%
Subtotal	20.9%	30.1%	27.2%	25.6%
World Total	100%	100%	100%	100%

Source: World Federation of Exchanges: Time Series 2009.

*Proportion of totals. Within each location, the proportion is of the regional total. Each regional total is a proportion of the global total.

The "dot.com" boom eventually peaked in 2000 as those investors with more realistic assumptions about the future level of profits sold out and fewer were drawn in to replace them. As the balance between buyers and sellers shifted towards the latter, the valuation placed on the stocks of these new companies began to fall, prompting selling by those investors who had invested merely for a quick gain on a rising market. A sharp stock market correction followed in which many of the new "dot. com" companies either collapsed, because they could not raise additional funding or struggled to establish themselves.

Despite these losses, the legacy of this speculative boom was a new generation of companies using the new technologies to supply products and services to customers. As with previous speculative booms, whether involving technologies like railways, automobiles and radio or resources such as gold, oil, and rubber, the irrational exuberance of the few did produce lasting benefits for the many. What stock exchanges now provided was a market through which investors willing to take risks were matched by entrepreneurs seeking finance for their ideas. This reflected the return of stock exchanges to the role in which the divisibility and transferability of securities was used to provide the funds required to develop new businesses rather than the conversion of existing ones.

10.3 New Exchanges

All this meant greatly increased activity on those exchanges that already existed, and the need to create new ones. Despite the growing internationalization of investment in stocks, most shares remained owned by investors resident in the country where the business was based and operated. There was thus a requirement for additional national stock exchanges where the stocks of national companies held by national investors could be traded. The result was a rash of new exchanges such as in Prague in 1992 and Botswana in 1994.

Even when there was considerable foreign interest in particular stocks, trading was often concentrated in the stock exchange where the company was based, as that was where the single greatest concentration of investors was found. Only when ownership changed did the market gravitate to another stock exchange, as happened after a merger or acquisition.

The number of dual listed companies that possessed active markets in different exchanges was rare, though there was a growing tendency for companies to have their stocks traded on exchanges located in major financial centers. By arranging to sell stocks in such centers, and then listing on the likes of the NYSE, NASDAQ, or the LSE, a company from a small or emerging economy gained access to a larger pool of investors. Investors were attracted to the exchanges with the deepest and broadest markets, as in these they could always buy and sell quickly at close to the current price.

Even within those countries where stock exchanges were long established, new ones appeared to cater for particular segments of the market, and in particular, to help float emerging companies. Exchanges had always to strike a balance between providing a market for the stocks of unproven enterprises and those issued by long-established companies. By granting a listing, the stock exchange placed its own reputation behind the stocks that it provided a market for. Especially for individual investors in corporate stocks, this listing acted like a signal that the business had good prospects and the securities could be easily bought and sold. If an exchange was too demanding in its listing requirements, it risked driving business away, as took place in New York from time to time. If an exchange was too liberal in its attitude towards listing, it endangered its own reputation among investors, as happened in London on occasion.

10.4 Increasing Liberality

One of the consequences of the outside supervision of exchanges in the postwar period was a tendency towards an increasingly conservative attitude towards the stocks for which they provided a market. In response to outside criticism and government pressure, national exchanges tended not to provide a market for the stocks of either new companies or those widely regarded as highly speculative. Instead, they confined themselves to large enterprises with most of the new additions being conversions of established businesses with a proven record of paying dividends. These appealed to institutional investors who were looking for a secure income stream and were reluctant to take risks with the money entrusted to them.

As a result of this focus on the large and proven, stock exchanges were then criticized for not providing a market for the small and enterprising ventures. Instead, these sought finance elsewhere, such as from banks and specialist funds. Where they did issue stocks, they were traded on OTC markets. An exchange also risked damaging its reputation if the companies it listed failed or its stock price experienced a rapid collapse. Reputational damage could then drive companies and investors away.

With the changed environment of the 1990s, established stock exchanges began to be more liberal in the criteria they applied to the listing of new corporate stocks with some, such as the LSE, creating separate markets for the stocks of new and risky companies. New York already possessed such a division, with the NYSE providing a market for the stocks of large and established companies, while NASDAQ catered for the newer and riskier ones, such as those in the technology field.

Overall, the result was a considerable increase in the volume of trade taking place on stock exchanges. Between 1990 and 2000, the value of transactions in corporate stocks in the world's exchanges rose from US$5.7 trillion to US$49.8 trillion, a nine-fold increase. Most of the increase took place in North America, especially on the NYSE and NASDAQ. These two exchanges dominated global transactions in corporate stocks, as they catered for the whole spectrum of investor interest, ranging from

Table 1.7: Stock Exchanges: Value of Share Trading*				
Location	1990	2000	2007	2008
Americas				
North America	1,870.3	32,440.8	59,535.3	72,363.3
Latin/Caribbean	17.8	418.5	825.4	954.2
Subtotal	1,888.1	32,859.3	60,360.7	73,317.5
Africa				
Subtotal	10.5	77.4	484.0	489.1
Asia				
East Asia	2,406.2	4,752.3	18,856.3	14,224.9
West	9.3	208.7	1,516.9	1,430.0
Subtotal	2,415.5	4,961.0	20,373.2	15,654.9
Australasia				
Subtotal	42.3	238.8	1,395.7	1,231.3
Europe				
Eastern Europe	3.8	126.7	313.3	218.3
Western Europe	1,326.7	11,520.3	30,095.8	22,741.8
Subtotal	1,330.5	11,647.0	30,409.1	22,959.8
World Total	**5,686.9**	**49,783.5**	**113,022.7**	**113,652.4**

Source: World Federation of Exchanges: Time Series 2009.
*In US$ billions, current prices.

the most speculative to the most conservative. No other exchanges could approach their volume of activity, increasing their attraction to investors because of the unrivalled depth and breadth of their markets as well as the attractions of dollar-denominated assets (see Tables 1.7 and 1.8).

The 1990s also witnessed increasing liberalization of financial activity around the world, both through the ending of exchange and capital controls and the more limited support given by governments to protect national exchanges from outside competition. Investors were able to search for and buy the assets that most suited their needs regardless of where they were to be found.

In particular, investors from around the world were attracted by the rapid growth prospects of emerging economies, many of which were emerging from decades of government control that had isolated them from international markets. The result was a large inflow of funds into emerging economies, whether in Eastern Europe or across Africa and Asia. The foreign purchases of the stocks issued by local companies directly contributed to the economic growth of these economies by

Table 1.8: Stock Exchanges: Distribution of Share Trading*				
Location	1990	2000	2007	2008
Americas				
North America	99.1%	98.7%	98.6%	98.7%
Latin/Caribbean	0.9%	1.3%	1.4%	1.3%
Subtotal	33.2%	66.0%	53.4%	64.5%
Africa				
Subtotal	0.2%	0.2%	0.4%	0.4%
Asia				
East Asia	99.6%	95.8%	92.6%	90.9%
West	0.4%	4.2%	7.4%	9.1%
Subtotal	42.5%	10.0%	18.0%	13.8%
Australasia				
Subtotal	0.7%	0.5%	1.2%	1.1%
Europe				
Eastern Europe	0.3%	1.1%	1.0%	1.0%
Western Europe	99.7%	98.9%	99.0%	99.0%
Subtotal	23.4%	23.4%	26.9%	20.2%
World Total	100%	100%	100%	100%

Source: World Federation of Exchanges: Time Series 2009.

*Proportion of totals. Within each location, the proportion is of the regional total. Each regional total is a proportion of the global total.

providing the finance required for modernization and development. Conversely, a number of these emerging economies proved so successful at selling products to Western consumers, whether oil, minerals, or manufactures, that they accumulated large trade surpluses. Surpluses were then recycled back to those countries in the West running large trade deficits, so allowing them to continue to consume imports and maintain world economic growth.

10.5 Competition between Exchanges

The other major development in the 1990s was the appearance of competition between exchanges not only domestically but also internationally. Ongoing technological developments replaced the sovereignty of the physical trading floor located in an exchange with screen-based transactions conducted on an office-to-office basis through a central computer. This forced existing stock exchanges to lower their charges, liberalize their rules and regulations, and replace floor-based markets with electronic systems. If they did not, then the result was a loss of business to these electronic rivals. In India, for example, the slowness of the dominant stock exchange, the Bombay Stock Exchange, to modernize resulted in an opportunity for the creation of an electronic platform, the National Stock Exchange, which rapidly emerged as the largest market.

Faced with an ebbing away of business to more competitive markets, exchanges around the world abandoned fixed commissions, liberalized rules and regulations, and introduced electronic trading in order to retain control over their own domestic markets. The Johannesburg Stock Exchange introduced such changes in 1996, faced with the loss of business to London. The Tokyo Stock Exchange took longer to respond, as it faced less competition, especially internationally. However, in 1999, the Tokyo Stock Exchange underwent its own revolution when the trading floor was closed, the limit on the number of members was ended, fixed commission rates were abandoned, the embargo on combining broking with banking was removed, and a market for small and emerging companies was established. By the end of the decade, national monopolies had largely been broken down, forcing exchanges to become more competitive marketplaces rather than regulatory organizations.

10.6 Consequent Mergers

In the process, a chain reaction occurred as changes in one country forced others to respond, eventually forcing further changes so as to remain competitive. The situation was particularly acute in Western Europe, where there had long existed numerous stock exchanges, each monopolizing its own national securities market, especially after the merger or disappearance of the regional stock exchanges. As early as 1989, change was taking place on both the Paris Bourse and the Madrid, Bolsa de and that was followed by Milan in 1991 and Frankfurt in 1992. These reforms led to the repatriation of much of the business that had migrated to London, as it was these national stock exchanges that possessed the deepest and broadest markets in securities listed there.

However, in many smaller European countries, the national stock exchange did not have the scale to remain competitive, once deprived of government support and protection. This encouraged mergers between exchanges, so as to provide larger and more attractive markets for both investors and companies. Out of this, for example, Euronext arose in 2000, which was an alliance between the Paris, Amsterdam, and Brussels stock exchanges, later extended to Lisbon.

10.7 Greater Freedom

What characterized the 1990s was an evolving compromise between the desire of national governments to control and regulate the markets they hosted and the desire of these markets to escape such strictures. For stock exchanges, escape meant losing the benefits they had long enjoyed as the favored means used by governments to regulate domestic securities markets, and the protection from competition that they enjoyed in whole or part. However, it also meant greater freedom for exchanges to respond to the growing competition that was present within the market for securities and to grasp the apparently limitless opportunities that now existed in a world where artificial boundaries hardly existed and technology offered instantaneous contact regardless of distance.

Pressures evident in the securities market forced those running exchanges to question the very way they were owned and organized. Though many exchanges were owned by governments, and run as branches of the state, most remained mutual organizations, being controlled by those who used them. A mutual organization worked well when stock exchanges were little exposed to competition and operated in a quasi-public role. However, mutuality was ill-suited to the increasingly competitive environment that existed in the 1990s. Competition demanded rapid and radical change and considerable investment, and that was unsuited to a continuing mutual structure. Mutuality demanded consensus, making it easy to block or slow down change. A mutual structure also made it difficult for an exchange to obtain outside capital, other than by way of a large loan. Finally, mutuality also prevented mergers between exchanges other than on amicable terms.

Given the nature of the changes taking place, especially the importance of large brokers and dealers serving the interests of institutional investors, the very organization of exchanges was preventing them from responding to challenges and grasping opportunities in the 1990s. The solution was the conversion of mutual exchanges into companies through the issue of stock to the members. As a result, the ownership of exchanges became divisible and transferable. The Stockholm Stock Exchange was the first to follow this route in 1993. In 1998 the Australian Stock Exchange went a step further, when the company that had been formed to own and run its operations was itself listed.

By converting a stock exchange into a company, members could profit directly by selling the property rights they were given on the open market. Following the success of what happened in Sweden and then Australia, exchanges around the world began to convert themselves into companies.

Many exchanges remained reluctant to convert because of fears among the members of what would happen when they lost control. Governments were also wary with several intervening to prevent foreign ownership, reflecting the continuing dilemma between an exchange's private and public function.

10.8 Conclusion

In a world where the market was growing across borders, and transaction costs were falling, the power of incumbent exchanges to resist change steadily declined. That world came into existence in the 1990s, and it demanded a new structure for the way exchanges were owned and managed. The result was that towards the end of the 1990s, it became commonplace for exchanges to be owned and run by companies.

Investors who owned their stock expected to be rewarded through dividend payments and capital appreciation generated by rising profits. The effect was to make exchanges far more responsive to the needs of all users and less to national governments than had the member-only clubs of the past. A corporate structure also created opportunities for mergers between exchanges, whether operating in different countries or across different financial products. The ability to convince shareholders, not governments, about the strategy to be followed became the overriding consideration for those managing exchanges in the 1990s.

Forced to compete for business in an increasingly global market, exchanges replaced floor trading systems with ever more sophisticated electronic trading networks. If an exchange persevered with a floor trading system, it experienced a slow but steady erosion of market share where competition was permitted, as in the United States. However, exchanges also faced another growing challenge in the 1990s beyond that created by competition among them.

During the 1990s, banks grew in scale and variety. Not only was the traditional separation between deposit and investment banking eroded in those countries where it had prevailed, but these banks also became the dominant traders on exchanges around the world. Possessing both extensive international connections and combining the whole range of financial operations, these banks became far more powerful than the exchanges to which they belonged.

The consequence was that exchanges lacked the power to police those banks that used them to buy and sell securities. That power had originally come from the fact that no member of an exchange was responsible for other than a very small share of trading. Thus expulsion damaged the member much more than the exchange. That was no longer the case in the 1990s.

After 1945, the power of an exchange had also been derived from the role it played on behalf of the national government in regulating the domestic securities market. However, the authority of national governments was shrinking in an age of globalization.

Nevertheless, these challenges were yet to fully emerge as the twentieth century came to a close. Instead, at the change of the millennium, exchanges could bask in their accomplishment of having recovered the place in the global financial system that they had possessed at the beginning, but lost in the intervening years. As transactions costs fell, for example, stocks once again appealed more and more to those investors whose actions were driven by money market considerations.

II. Post 2000

II.1 Introduction

By the beginning of the twenty-first century, markets were again as central to the operation of the world economy as they had been a century before. In turn, these markets were serviced by exchanges of all types. Stock exchanges continued to provide a market for stocks whether they were the largest such as the NYSE and NASDAQ, or smaller ones serving the growing number of countries embracing a corporate culture. Commodity exchanges also continued to expand whether for metals as with the London Metal Exchange or for oil and gas with New York Mercantile Exchange (NYMEX). Other exchanges traded complex financial instruments such as interest rate futures, currency options, and equity derivatives. Chicago was an especially fruitful center for these with the likes of Chicago Board of Trade (CBOT), Chicago Board Options Exchange (CBOE), and Chicago Mercantile Exchange (CME) and their innovations were quickly emulated elsewhere in the world. These exchanges were not a product of inertia but the outcome of a process of constant innovation and adaptation.

The world in which exchanges operated in the early twenty-first century had changed out of all recognition compared with a century before. The growing scale of business organization had internalized many of the transactions that had once taken place on exchanges, whether they involved flows of food, fuel and raw materials, or the mobilization and use of savings. No longer were exchanges central to internal and international trade as individual businesses were often in control of an entire supply chain that spanned the world. Financial intermediation had also been transformed from an activity conducted by individuals and partnerships to one undertaken by giant corporations, whose activities spanned diverse products and numerous countries. Governments also played a far greater role in the supervision and management of economic activity even in the wake of the removal of exchange and capital controls and the privatization of state assets.

11.2 Increased Regulation

By the twenty-first century, the public in developed economies expected a high degree of regulation from government so as to remove much of the risk and uncertainty of everyday life. Regulation took place at many levels, ranging from a general oversight of markets to a degree of micromanagement where abuses were exposed or even suspected. Whether through levies on particular businesses and markets, or from general taxation, government agencies financed the employment of expert staff to ensure that rules and regulations were complied with. Such a situation was very different from that before the First World War, when the burden of regulation imposed by the state was minimal. At that time the self-regulation practiced by exchanges existed because of the absence of government intervention, whereas a century later it operated in conjunction with what governments provided. Finally, the technology of information processing and communication had been revolutionized, which greatly facilitated direct contact between buyers and sellers without the need for a physical space in which to meet and conduct business or even the use of intermediaries. These issues all had major implications for the organization, structure, and role of exchanges.

Increasingly, the central role of exchanges centered around price determination and the offsetting of risk. There may have been continuing nostalgia for an earlier era of fixed exchange rates, stable interest rates, and prices that altered little, but the reality of the twenty-first century was that none of these conditions existed. Under those circumstances, exchanges played a new, equally vital role. By trading a standard product, exchanges were able to produce a current reference price that all buyers and sellers could have confidence in. That confidence extended to banks, and this was of major importance. When banks lent money or purchased assets, they needed to have some means of estimating value. The prices generated by exchanges provided that means. Banks could thus lend on commodities or securities, because these could be valued.

Similarly, banks could invest in assets not only for the return they produced, but also because of the value that could be placed upon them. As a consequence, the supply of credit and capital to governments and business was expanded and the cost reduced.

Following on from that basic service, exchanges were also able to devise other products that allowed buyers and sellers to cover risks that they ran because of fluctuations in interest and exchange rates. These products were also attractive to financial institutions as they could both cover their own risks and profit by participating in the constant buying and selling taking place.

Not all these products were suited to exchanges. Some were negotiated on a bilateral basis to meet specific circumstances, and so did not lend themselves to standardization and active trading supported by brokers and dealers. Conversely, in others trading was confined to a small number of large banks, as in the foreign exchange market, in which they constantly balanced debits and credits among themselves in terms of both currencies and time. Nevertheless, many of these products were heavily traded on exchanges, and so provided investors with a way of coping with the price volatility present in a complex and ever-changing global economy.

11.3 Comparison Between Stock and Bond Markets

There were important differences between how price determination was achieved on bond markets compared with stock markets. The bond market had always been closely connected to the money market as a means through which banks employed or accessed idle funds on a temporary basis. This took place either through direct participation or lending to those involved. With banks becoming major financial institutions with a global reach, they took command of this market. It was possible for them to bypass the facilities of a stock exchange, because the counterparties involved were a relatively small number of very large financial institutions who were capable of both generating a large amount of business and guaranteeing completion of sales and delivery or purchases and payment. The growth of specialist inter-dealer brokers like ICAP was a product of the need for intermediation between banks, as they were the major traders in money in all its diverse forms. Stock exchanges were thus left to concentrate on trading corporate stocks.

The value of corporate stocks was the product of many diverse and individual factors, with the strategy followed by individual managements often being a key feature in determining the value of a particular corporate stock. With the ownership of stock also went control, creating opportunities for the replacement of managements and a reordering of business activity through mergers, acquisitions, disposals, buy-outs, and buy-ins. Anticipation of events of these kind or of the level of profit to be declared were major drivers behind the constant fluctuations in the prices of individual corporate stocks beyond the influence of general economic and monetary conditions. Advance knowledge of company-specific information by a particular group of investors would place them in a privileged position and allow them to profit because of the ignorance of others.

Under these circumstances, it was critical to have in place regulations that ensured both equal and universal price disclosure. Exchanges played an important role in monitoring and policing the use and abuse of information using their close connection with market activity to detect unusual price movements and discover their causes. By performing this role, exchanges contributed significantly to the creation of a market in which all could have trust.

What the comparison between stocks and bonds also reveals is the precise nature of the role played by exchanges in providing markets for a diverse range of financial products. Where trading in bonds took place between a small number of banks, as they constantly adjusted their relative positions, there was little need for an exchange. Standing behind each transaction was the bank, and the transaction was a relatively uncomplicated one. Such a situation had long existed in the foreign exchange market where daily transactions were measured in trillions of US dollars. At the other end of the spectrum were transactions involving bespoke products that were difficult to price and involved expert judgment.

It was the ground in between that was the territory of the exchanges, and the demand for their services grew substantially in the early years of the twenty-first century. Between 2000 and 2007, the number of companies quoted on the world's stock exchanges rose by 17,000 or by almost 60 percent. Driving this growth was the extension of corporate enterprise in Asia at the relative expense of its traditional stronghold in North America (see Tables 1.3 and 1.4).

Across the world, business was increasingly undertaken by companies whose stocks, and thus ownership, were traded on exchanges. The market capitalization of these companies doubled between 2000 and 2007, reaching US$62.7 trillion. Again, Asia led the advance as corporate capitalism was embraced by more and more of that continent's governments, entrepreneurs and investors. Though investor confidence had been undermined by the collapse of the "dot.com" boom in 2000, it speedily revived in a climate of credit expansion and low interest rates (see Tables 1.5 and 1.6).

Matching this enormous expansion in the number and value of corporate enterprises around the world was the growth of trading activity on exchanges. Between 2000 and 2007, the value of transactions in corporate stocks in the world's regulated exchanges more than doubled from US$49.8 to US$113 trillion. Half of this turnover still took place in the United States, despite the greatly increased importance of trading on exchanges located elsewhere in the world, especially emerging economies like China (see Tables 1.7 and 1.8). The New York Stock Exchange and NASDAQ continued to provide the deepest and broadest markets for corporate stocks by virtue of the fact that the largest and most important companies in the world were still mainly from the United States. Whether investors favored long-established corporations engaged in the provision of products and services with a stable market or those at the forefront of technological change and innovation, the United States continued to possess the widest range available and valued in the world's most negotiable currency (see Table 1.9).

11.4 The Picture Post-2007

By 2007, exchanges had established for themselves a secure and permanent position at the heart of the global financial system. They had

Table 1.9: The World's Largest 100 Companies (By Market Value)		
Country	Market Value in 2006	Market Value in 2009
Total	US$11 trillion	US$8 Trillion
United States	52%	44%

Source: *Financial Times* 2006, 2009

adapted to the new world by making membership more open, developing efficient trading platforms, abandoning compulsory charges, and reforming their rules and regulations.

The conversion of many exchanges from member-owned clubs to corporate entities made them much more responsive to the needs of their largest users. It also permitted the creation of alliances between different exchanges transcending political boundaries and products traded.

Nevertheless, though financial activity was now global, national exchanges remained central, because the stocks issued by any particular company were largely owned by investors from a particular country. Under those conditions, the only way a stock exchange could capture the business done by another was through merger, as had happened nationally and later internationally. The takeover of Euronext by the NYSE gave the combined company a major stake in both the US and European securities market.

In this new scenario, in many parts of the world, exchanges were not entitled to any special privileges in the financial services sector. Exchanges had to compete for orders in an era when trading was conducted by large banks guaranteeing their own trades and using computers programmed with algorithmic models to spot minute and momentary trading opportunities.

From the standpoint of the banks, the market provided by exchanges was no longer unique. Unregulated electronic trading platforms could offer a better and cheaper service, especially if they were not required to meet the regulatory standards set for exchanges. Nevertheless, investors continued to use exchanges, especially when buying and selling stocks, because that was the only way to guarantee that transactions were completed at the universally accepted current price.

The conclusion that could be drawn from this is that, if exchanges were forced to make available these current prices, both financial intermediaries and investors would benefit, as they could access cheaper trading platforms. In theory, this conclusion appeared perfectly valid, but it failed to appreciate that it took the whole apparatus of an exchange to create a market that generated these prices and the certainty of trading that went with them. Such a situation continued to be recognized outside the United States and Western Europe because of continuing concerns over counterparty risk when trading took place outside of regulated exchanges. As a consequence, exchanges in Asia and elsewhere continued to hold onto a dominant market share in the trading of corporate stocks, because of the absence of regulatory requirements to force disclosure of current prices.

11.5 Increased Disclosure

Such was not the case in the United States and Western Europe.

As before, it was developments in the United States that drove increased disclosure in the interests of promoting greater apparent competition. In 2005, the SEC introduced a requirement that not only were current bid/offer prices to be publicly displayed, but also that all orders went directly to the market that could execute them at the best price. This was Regulation National Market System (Reg NMS).

At a stroke, Reg NMS removed one of the key advantages that regulated exchanges could offer those who paid to use their trading facilities to buy and sell, which was access to current prices in advance of those who did not. Such a situation was akin to removing copyright or patent protection, leaving the originator of the idea or the product with no reward for past effort. The outcome was increasingly intense competition between different trading platforms for the available business. A consequence was market fragmentation as Electronic Communication Networks (ECNs) became increasingly attractive to investors and their intermediaries.

Impressed by the falling transaction costs that followed in the wake of this regulation, the European Union quickly followed suit. From the viewpoint of EU regulators, the creation of a competitive pan-European market for corporate stocks would be a major contribution to market integration. The result was the introduction of the Markets in Financial Instruments Directive (MiFiD) in 2007. This emulated US practice and had many of the same consequences. New electronic markets appeared, called Multilateral Trading Facilities (MTFs). There was also a growth in "dark pools," in which trading took place away from the "lit market" provided by exchanges.

Subjected to a climate of disclosure, exchanges in the United States and Western Europe had to work hard to hold onto their share of the market in stocks. Exchanges bought up rival electronic networks, invested heavily in new technology, reduced their charges, and relaxed their rules. However, they now had to compete with electronic platforms that had access to their current prices and could offer lower transaction costs because no universal service provision was placed on them. The new electronic platforms, for example, provided a market for only the most heavily traded stocks.

In the space of 30 years, exchanges had moved from possessing a privileged position within the market to one where they were placed at a competitive disadvantage in the interests of competition. In pursuing that goal, official regulators had lost sight of the role played by exchanges in the successful operation of complex markets in advanced economies. What had been lost was the contribution made to improved regulation by those who were close to those operating in the market and so very aware of their behavior. A successful market was one that delivered an evolving balance between buyers and sellers and was sufficiently flexible to cope with their differing requirements.

Not all buyers and sellers of stocks were alike. There were individual investors looking to profit from a speculative opportunity or hoping to generate a regular income better than that available from bank deposits or bonds. Conversely, there were institutional investors faced with the need to rebalance an entire portfolio or acquire or dispose of a large holding in a particular company.

Both types of investors required full and equal access to the market, but they did not necessarily need to be subjected to the same conditions, especially with regard to immediate disclosure. For large investors like a bank, insurance company or hedge fund, the sale or purchase could be part of a strategy which it might not wish revealed until complete. A similar situation existed for a bank or broker that had committed itself to a large sale or purchase at a fixed price. Disclosure would allow others to take advantage of the situation by driving prices up or down, so jeopardizing either the entire strategy or the profitability of the deal.

For these reasons, "dark pools" flourished as well as strategies to delay the public dissemination of orders and prices. Such activity had always taken place when members of exchanges spotted an opportunity to complete a transaction by matching sales among clients, but the growth in size and reach of intermediaries had greatly increased its possibility while the developments in technology made it much easier to accomplish. When added to that were the disadvantages of using an exchange because of the disclosure rules imposed on transactions there, then trading via "dark pools" was bound to flourish, and did.

11.6 Avoidance

Any regulatory regime faces a problem of avoidance because of the costs and restrictions imposed. Consequently, those designing and implementing regulation have to ensure that it is neither too lax nor too strict. The former condones abuses and so undermines the operation of the market. The latter encourages evasion and so drives trading activity into unregulated channels.

Successful regulation does not involve absolutes. Instead, it requires flexibility and adaptation. Where regulation involves little more than a set of principles, market participants are left to interpret these to suit their own circumstances, leading some to behave in ways that endanger the whole operation of the market. Conversely, where regulation involves the adoption of unchanging rules that are strictly enforced market activity is driven into alternative channels where rules do not apply.

What had happened by the early twenty-first century is that both these situations existed. In London, the Financial Services Authority (FSA) operated a principles-based regulatory regime that was highly permissive. This attracted to London much financial activity from around the world, as it could be carried out there with little supervision or restriction. In New York, banks and markets were subject to much greater scrutiny and control, especially after the exposures following the collapse of Enron. Under these circumstances, US banks could simply divert activity from those activities that were highly regulated by conducting it away from exchanges or elsewhere than in New York, such as in London. The large banks found it relatively easy to do this, because they had operations that stretched across the globe and were engaged in a wide range of financial activities. These banks could also trade independently of regulated exchanges, because they had the scale and reputation to stand behind every transaction and give those they traded with the confidence that it would be completed.

11.7 Emerging Crisis

Thus, when these banks devised new financial products to match the needs of savers and borrowers, little thought was given to having them listed on exchanges where their robustness to different trading conditions could be tested. Instead, these products were traded in and between the banks. As long as confidence existed in these assets, this system of trading was successful and banks profited from matching buyers and sellers. However, when the inevitable crisis occurred and questions were raised about the underlying value of these assets, many became impossible to sell or even value. In turn, that had major implications for the banks that held these assets or had lent money to those who had bought them.

If such assets could not be valued, the solvency of individual banks was questioned. Under these circumstances, the situation was worse than a classic liquidity crisis, when a bank's assets outweighed its liabilities but withdrawals by depositors could not be met because of a lack of cash. Where assets could not be valued, doubts emerged whether certain banks could repay their short-term borrowings, which comprised not only retail deposits but massive obligations on wholesale money markets.

Increasingly, banks had borrowed from each other on these wholesale markets to supplement the deposits made by savers, using these funds to purchase the various financial instruments that they were themselves creating. Banks were generating new types of financial instruments and selling them to investors. These investors included banks using funds borrowed on wholesale money markets from other banks to buy them. The market for these new assets was not found on exchanges but was maintained by banks themselves, and was grounded in the trust investors had in their ability to match buyers and sellers and determine prices.

All this was taking place globally as a result of the disappearance of the exchange and capital controls that had compartmentalized the global financial system in the past. When the crisis finally broke in 2007–08, the market for many of these new financial assets ceased to operate.

Though believing these new assets to be akin to stocks and bonds, and thus liquid, banks found them to be the same as loans. Loans to finance property and automobile purchases had been packaged to resemble securities, because their divisibility and transferability would increase their attractions among investors, and thus the price that banks and other financial institutions were willing to pay. Unfortunately for those investors, such a view turned out to be an illusion when they tried to dispose of them in the crisis.

In contrast, exchange-listed corporate stocks continued to possess a market, and so they were heavily sold by those banks and investors desperately searching to improve their liquidity. The result was a massive drop in the value of listed stocks between 2007 and 2008 of almost US$30 trillion (see Tables 1.5 and 1.6). As testimony to the resilience of exchanges at a time of crisis, the value of trading remained remarkably constant over 2007–08. Decreases in volume occurred mainly on the newer exchanges, which was only to be expected, as that was where the more illiquid stocks were to be found. In contrast, the highly liquid US markets experienced a higher level of trading as banks and other investors desperately sought to meet withdrawals by selling those assets that still possessed a market or adjust their positions in the light of the new economic conditions (see Tables 1.7 and 1.8).

12. General Conclusion

An exchange is more than a market, whether it takes the form of a physical trading floor or an electronic communication network. An exchange is a place which provides a high degree of certainty to those who buy and sell in terms of completing the transaction at the price at which the deal is done. To achieve that requires both a market mechanism and rules and regulations governing those permitted to trade and the way business is conducted.

Not all trading situations require an exchange to exist. When such business is conducted between a small number of informed participants with reputations at stake and the resources to meet any commitment they make, then the market does not require an exchange. Such has long been the case in the money market where banks borrowed and lent to each other vast sums of money at negotiated rates. Such also became the case in the bond market, especially when it came to involve a relatively small number of issues generated by sovereign governments and large multinational corporations. In contrast, with trading in stocks and a variety of other financial instruments, exchanges do play an important role because of the relative uncertainty of their precise value and the constant fluctuations in prices.

The problem is to distinguish between those products and assets that benefit from being bought and sold on exchanges and those that do not. Where the use of an exchange was required, that institution needed to be allowed to finance itself by extending privileges to those who paid to transact business on it. Otherwise, it lacked the resources to provide the regulatory environment required.

Modern markets have always been the product of a tripartite system comprising government, business, and self-regulation. Government oversight of the market plays an important role in detecting and eliminating general abuse, especially that running contrary to the law of the land. The role of the individual business is to police its own employees and take responsibility for the consequences of its own actions. That leaves exchanges with a collective responsibility for the day-to-day operation of the market in which participants vetted their peer group. The key to success is the balance between them.

In the nineteenth century, governments were reluctant to intervene in exchanges in the belief that full self-regulation was best. In the wake of the Wall Street Crash and the Second World War that belief changed, and government supervision of exchanges became commonplace. Neither situation was perfect, but simply reflected the expectations that prevailed at each time.

Each also has lessons for the future direction of regulation and the balance between governments, business, and exchanges. Such lessons are vital as the world within which exchanges operate is one that continually changes. Over the last 100 years, the role of government has been transformed. The public has come to expect a far greater degree of government intervention in everyday life. Exchanges have had to respond by imposing a far higher standard of market behavior to meet externally imposed rules and regulations. No longer is the maxim "let the buyer beware" sufficient to prevent intervention in a market if the public are agitated over regulations of abuse. That situation is likely to prevail and even intensify.

In the course of the twentieth century, the nature of business, including banking, was also transformed, with major implications for exchanges. Banks have grown in scale both horizontally, through the development of extensive branch operations, and vertically, to cover the whole range of financial activities. Exchanges thus have had to cope with a situation in which their main users grew to surpass them in scale if not only in reputation. Such a situation is likely to continue into the future. Though crises have occurred, banks have learnt to cope with the risks they run in their own way, including the use of the active markets provided by exchanges. Though concerns have been expressed that banks have become "too big to fail," it has been US banks that have the greatest tradition of instability and, failure because legislation long prevented the creation of large nationwide institutions. In contrast, the Canadian banking system has proved remarkably stable even though it has long comprised a very small number of very large banks.

Exchanges are regulated marketplaces that reduce or eliminate risk and uncertainty, whether in terms of trading or in pricing. This made them Janus[10] institutions, as they faced two ways simultaneously. On the one hand, they acted as the interface between markets and governments or those acting in their name. On the other hand, they were also the interface between businesses and the market.

The consequence was that exchanges cannot be judged from simply one angle, as that fails to appreciate what they actually do. They have often been portrayed, correctly, as an essential link in the process through which governments and later companies raised finance. Without the market they provided, both would have had difficulty raising the finance they required at the price they were willing to pay. For companies, this made them arenas where battles for corporate control took place, so facilitating the constant reshaping of business as failing managements were replaced and new enterprises were created or shaped.

By virtue of these functions, exchanges became central components of advanced economies, contributing to the efficient mobilization and use of available savings both nationally and globally. However, exchanges were also places where investors either employed their savings or realized their assets, though this angle is often forgotten and downplayed. By providing a means through which those with idle funds could readily employ them in full knowledge that the process could be easily, quickly, and cheaply reversed was essential if a complex economy was to maximize its available savings and avoid repeated crises.

The value of such a service was only too apparent in 2007–08 through its absence in most off-exchange areas of the capital markets. As a report by the McKinsey Global Institute concluded, in the wake of that financial crisis, "Deep financial markets helped foster the significant productivity growth of the 1990s and gave many borrowers unparalleled access to credit. Public equity listings can improve corporate governance. Debt capital markets serve as an important alternative to bank credit, particularly in times of financial system distress." [11]

Along with both governments and banks, exchanges are part of the solution to the world's financial difficulties and have been so for centuries.

Notes

This chapter is based on a lifetime's research into securities markets and stock exchanges that is still ongoing. It has appeared in the form of books, articles, chapters in edited volumes, and conference papers. For a general overview of the history of securities markets see, R.C. Michie, *The Global Securities Market: A History* [Oxford 2006].

1 J.M. Keynes, General Theory of Employment, Interest and Money [London 1936].

2 For evidence of the public's enduring negative perception of finance in general and the stock exchange in particular see, R.C. Michie, Guilty Money: The City of London in Victorian and Edwardian Culture [London 2009].

3 P. Jorion and W.N. Goetzman, "Global Stock Markets in the Twentieth Century," Journal of Finance, 54 (1999).

4 "Global Stock Exchanges," The Banker, May 2008, p. 2.

5 See C.M. Reinhart and K.S. Rogoff, This Time is Different: Eight Centuries of Financial Folly [Princeton 2009].

6 For these origins see, G. Felloni and G. Laura, Genoa and the History of Finance: A series of firsts? [Genoa 2004].

7 London Stock Exchange Commission, Report, 1878.

8 Twentieth Century Fund, Stock Market Control [New York 1934] pp. 163–4.

9 For more on the role played by banks compared to markets see, D.J. Forsyth and D. Verdier (eds) The Origins of National Financial Systems: Gershenkron Revisited [London 2003].

10 Janus, The Two-faced God of Doors in Western Mythology.

11 McKinsey Global Institute, Global Capital Markets: Entering a New Era [September 2009] p. 31.

The Economics of Trading and of Regulated Exchanges

LARRY HARRIS

This chapter is about trading, the central activity of exchanges. Trading facilitates investment, risk management, and capital formation. Well-functioning markets thus are essential to economic well-being and growth.

Liquidity, informative prices, and transaction costs depend on how exchanges organize trading, and upon the traders that operate there. Good public policy therefore requires that regulators understand well the determinants of market quality, and in particular why people trade, how they trade, and how exchange rules affect their trading.

Academics, among many others, have contributed extensively to understanding regulated exchanges and the environments in which they operate. Their studies of market microstructure have helped regulators and practitioners better understand what exactly happens in exchange markets.

Academic research into trading and exchanges has advanced substantially during the last 50 years. Researchers have carefully considered the determinants of transaction costs; the role of information in the markets; how trading rules affect liquidity, price efficiency, and volatility; the competition among exchanges, brokers, and dealers; and how to regulate the markets to make them fair, liquid, and price efficient.

Academic research has occasionally led to very substantial changes in market structures. A notable example was the 1994 *Journal of Finance* study by Bill Christie and Paul Schultz, "Why do NASDAQ Market Makers Avoid Odd-Eighth Quotes?" This study showed that bid/ask spreads were wide relative to what market observers and participants might have expected. In response to this study, the US Securities and Exchange Commission commenced enforcement actions and ultimately changed order-handling rules and reduced tick sizes. These regulatory actions substantially lowered transaction costs for investors.

Other studies have focused attention on the importance of transaction cost measurement, and on differences in execution costs among exchanges. These studies led to the development of a small consulting industry that measures transaction costs for traders working at brokerages and investment firms throughout the world, enabling them to demonstrate quantitatively that they are fulfilling their fiduciary obligations on behalf of their clients. The result again has been substantially lower transaction costs as exchanges and brokers compete for order flow.

Still other academic studies have identified the importance of quote-matching strategies; determinants of dealer behavior, bid/ask spreads, quotation sizes, and volatility; implications of network externalities for the competition among exchanges; problems associated with internalization and other off-exchange trading; how tick sizes affect market quality; the roles of intermarket order routing systems, clearinghouses, and crossing networks; and how contract design affects liquidity; to name just a few.

This chapter provides a brief overview of academic insights into regulated exchanges, their trading processes, and those of their competitors. The discussion addresses most of the aforementioned issues and many others as well.

Many of the perspectives presented here are familiar to practitioners, though they often may not be consciously aware of them. That is understandable. Practitioners are often busy working in the markets, and much of their knowledge is intuitive. Much of what academics know about the markets has come from practitioners who generously shared their practical knowledge. Academics organized this knowledge to help people recognize and better understand the issues important to them. The resulting body of knowledge provides a "big picture" that helps practitioners make better trading decisions and helps exchanges and regulators better understand how to organize and oversee trading.

Most empirical studies that academics have undertaken of the markets would not have been possible without the generous cooperation of exchange managers who provided data and explanations of how their data were produced. Exchanges such as the Paris Bourse, New York Stock Exchange, Chicago Board Options Exchange, Toronto Stock Exchange, and Korea Exchange, to name just a few, have generously provided data to academics over the years. Without these data, we would know much less about trading than we presently do.

The discussions in this chapter present the essentials of the knowledge that academics have organized about exchanges and about trading in general. To ensure that the presentation reads easily, the text discusses only the principles of each contribution and not the history of the contribution. Readers who wish to learn more should consider reading my introductory text, *Trading and Exchanges: Market Microstructure for Practitioners*. For excellent surveys of theoretical and empirical studies in market microstructure, readers also may consider consulting Maureen O'Hara's book, *Market Microstructure Theory*, Joel Hasbrouck's book, *Empirical Market Microstructure: The Institutions, Economics, and Econometrics of Securities Trading*, and Ananth Madahvan's August 2000 *Journal of Financial Markets* survey article, "Market Microstructure, a Survey."

Practitioners and academics are very interested in various dimensions of market quality, the most important of which are liquidity, price efficiency, and volatility. Liquidity refers to the cost of trading. Markets are liquid when traders can easily arrange a trade without affecting prices much. Price efficiency refers to the extent to which prices reflect information about fundamental security values. Although difficult to define, fundamental values generally are the security and contract values that rational analysts would calculate if all information—data and theories—about future values were common and undisputed knowledge. Prices are efficient when traders cannot use publicly available information to predict future price changes. Volatility refers to the rates at which prices change. Prices are volatile when fundamental values change quickly, when traders trade foolishly, or when exchange mechanisms do not work well.

Market quality depends primarily on traders. Traders make markets liquid when they give other traders opportunities to fill their orders. They make prices efficient when they trade securities based on analyses of information that they conduct. They make prices excessively volatile when their demands to trade are excessive relative to the normal capacity of the market to provide liquidity. Accordingly, our discussion starts with an identification of the major reasons why people trade. These reasons ultimately determine whether exchanges will be successful, whether their markets will be liquid, and whether the prices discovered at exchanges will be informative. The first half of this essay addresses these questions.

Market structure—how exchanges, brokers, and dealers arrange trades—helps determine market quality by shaping the opportunities and incentives that different types of traders face. The second half of this essay describes how different market structures affect market quality.

▬▬ I. Traders

Economists identify three broad groups of traders when describing the origins of various market quality dimensions: Utilitarian traders, informed traders, and dealers. Utilitarian traders expect to obtain some benefit besides trading profits from their transactions. Informed traders seek to profit from accurate predictions of future prices. Dealers sell liquidity to other market participants. Although people trade for many different reasons—and often for more than one reason at a time, these three types of stylized traders represent most trading strategies.

1.1 Utilitarian Traders

Utilitarian traders include many different types of participants whose market activity generally is unrelated to fundamental security values. The best-known utilitarian traders are investors and borrowers who trade to move wealth from the present to the future or vice versa. Financial markets allow investors who have money now that they expect to spend in the future to connect with borrowers who need money now that they can repay in the future. Examples of such investors and borrowers are workers who save for their retirements, and corporations who need funds to execute new productive projects.

Other utilitarian traders include hedgers who trade to offset or insure against risks that scare them; gamblers who trade for entertainment; tax avoiders who arrange trades to lower or defer their taxes; and asset exchangers who exchange one asset for another that is of greater immediate value to them.

In each of these cases, utilitarian traders trade because they hope to obtain some benefit besides trading profit. Investors and borrowers move money through time. Hedgers reduce their net risk exposure. Gamblers obtain entertainment. Tax avoiders lower the present value of their tax liabilities, and asset exchangers obtain assets of greater immediate value to them. In all cases, these traders hope to profit from their trading, but if they trade purely for the reasons noted, they do not expect to earn more than the normal expected returns associated with holding (or shorting) securities and contracts.

Economists often call these utilitarian traders "noise traders," because their transactions are unrelated to fundamental values. Accordingly, if their trading pushes prices around, prices will be less informative. Statisticians say that such prices are noisy estimates of fundamental value.

Regulated exchanges and clearinghouses facilitate their transactions by:

- Substantially lowering the costs that utilitarian traders must incur to find each other, either directly or through the intermediation of dealers
- Requiring timely and material disclosure of corporate financial information that allows traders to fairly value securities
- Regulating trading practices and corporate capital structures to reduce fraud
- Creating contracts that encompass the risks that concern hedgers
- Ensuring that traders settle their trades and contracts

1.2 Informed Traders

Informed traders collect information that allows them to predict futures prices. They buy when they expect prices to be higher and sell otherwise. Although they often are wrong, successful informed trades are right more often than they are wrong, and therefore profit from their efforts. Well-informed traders base their orders on careful analyses of data that they believe will help them predict future values. Their information may include data about fundamental security values, or it may include information or predictions about the orders that other traders will likely send to the market in the future.

Informed traders employ three main trading strategies. They may base their trades on estimates of fundamental values, on news about changes in fundamental values, or predictions about what other traders will do.

Value-motivated traders estimate fundamental security values. They then buy if their value estimates are sufficiently greater than market prices, and they sell if their value estimates are sufficiently lower. They estimate fundamental values by collecting and analyzing all information that their research budgets allow them to obtain. Since data collection and analysis are expensive, value-motivated traders can only profit if their trading gains are greater than their research costs. Many equity and commodity exchanges reduce data collection costs by mandating financial disclosure by their listed companies, by collecting and publishing information about commodity supply and demand conditions, and by disseminating market prices and volumes.

News-traders trade on news about events that change fundamental values. They buy when they believe that values will rise in response to an event, and they sell when they believe that values will fall. Since the effect on values of many events are quite obvious, news-traders must trade very quickly to profit from freshly released information and news reports. They therefore invest in systems that allow them to obtain and act upon information quickly. Since these systems can be expensive to build and operate, news-traders can only profit if their trading gains are greater than their information collection costs.

Order anticipators try to predict the trades that other market participants will arrange. If they expect that other traders will buy substantial quantities of securities or contracts and thereby increase prices, order anticipators try to buy first to profit from the price increases to come. They likewise try to sell before other traders sell. Order anticipators generally increase the costs of liquidity for the traders before whom they trade. When order anticipators trade in front of orders that they know about, they are front-runners. Fiduciary duty prevents brokers from front-running their clients' orders or from knowingly allowing others to do so. Regulated exchanges make front-running illegal to protect public traders and to reduce their costs of trading. However, order anticipators often try to anticipate the orders that other traders intend to submit by analyzing trading patterns and related psychological models. These other traders must be utilitarian traders, because by definition, traders cannot predict the trades of value-motivated or news traders without the information upon which these informed traders base the orders that they send to the market.

1.3 Dealers

Dealers supply liquidity—the ability to trade when you want to trade—to other traders. They generally post quotes or limit orders that give buyers and sellers opportunities to transact. Dealers profit by selling to buyers at offer prices that are slightly higher than the bid prices at which they buy from sellers. If the average spreads that they obtain between the prices at which they sell and the prices at which they buy are sufficiently large, their dealing will be profitable.

Dealers run the risk that prices will fall after they have bought, or that prices will rise after they sell, before they can unwind their positions. When such adverse price changes occur, they may not be able to trade out of their positions at a profit. They therefore hope to sell immediately after they buy and vice versa.

Dealers generally do not know much about fundamental values. They do know that if they set quotes too low, they will receive many buy orders and few sell orders. Likewise, if they set their quotes too high, they will receive many sell orders but few buy orders. Since they want to sell after they buy and buy after they sell, they try very hard to find the prices at which buyers and sellers are willing to trade equal volumes. These prices are called market clearing prices. Market prices differ from fundamental values when traders do not know fundamental values well, as is generally the case.

1.4 Adverse Selection

Dealers and other traders who supply liquidity lose on average to well-informed traders. When well-informed traders expect prices to fall, they sell. The dealers who buy from them lose if prices fall before they can sell their positions. Dealers likewise tend to lose to well-informed traders when the informed traders expect prices to rise.

Economists call this problem the adverse selection problem. The problem results because informed traders do not trade at random. Rather, their trading is correlated with the future price changes that they anticipate: They buy when they expect prices to be higher, and sell when they expect prices to be lower. If they realize their expectations, whoever traded with them loses. Dealers often obtain adverse results—trading losses—when trading with well-informed traders because the latter more often than not can select the profitable side of the market.

Dealers must quote bid/ask spreads large enough to recover from utilitarian traders what they lose to informed traders. Utilitarian traders thus lose to informed traders through the intermediation of dealers, because they must pay wide spreads.

Adverse selection makes liquidity expensive. Utilitarian traders can avoid these losses by trading infrequently. When few utilitarians trade, informed traders will be responsible for a substantial fraction of the order flow, and bid/ask spreads will be very wide. Informed trading will be difficult and expensive, which will reduce informed trader profits, decrease the resources that they spend on research, and thereby make prices less informative.

In the extreme, if informed traders dominate the order flow, the spreads that dealers must quote to survive may be too large to support a viable market, and the market will fail to operate. Adverse selection thus explains why small stocks for which information is not widely disseminated tend to trade in less liquid and less informationally efficient markets than do larger stocks.

Many equity exchanges that have started special markets for emerging companies have discovered that these markets often do not operate well due to the adverse selection problem. Some exchanges therefore provide dealers with special incentives to make markets in these small company nurseries with the hope that these companies will grow larger with time. They also provide various warnings to those who would trade these stocks.

The adverse selection problem has pervasive effects throughout all aspects of trading. Consider some examples of how adverse selection affects trading strategies, exchange design, and the design of financial products:

- Dealers try to avoid trading with well-informed traders if they can do so. Since dealers generally believe that retail traders are uninformed, many dealers choose to fill only retail order flows away from exchanges in a process called internalization. They thereby avoid the losses that they would incur by trading with well-informed institutions at exchanges.
- Dealers rarely offer to trade large size with traders that they do not know well. They want to know their counterparties so that they can avoid losing to well-informed traders.
- Since dealers who can avoid adverse selection offer more liquidity, exchanges are very keen on creating trading mechanisms that protect dealers from trading with well-informed traders. For example, many exchanges have trading halt rules that stop market operations in a given security when dealers would be most vulnerable to informed traders. These halts may occur when information releases

are pending, when market prices change quickly, or when prices clearly would change substantially if permitted.

- Many block brokers permit their clients to specify with whom they are willing to trade, so that they do not find themselves opposite actors such as hedge funds that are likely to be well informed.
- Regulated equity and equity options exchanges ban trading on inside information. These bans protect dealers and other market participants from losing to well-informed traders. With these protections, the exchanges hope that traders will offer more liquidity to the marketplace. These bans also promote a sense of fairness among market participants that increases their confidence in the integrity of the markets, which promotes liquidity.
- Equity exchanges maintain and enforce listing standards that require listed firms to disclose material financial information on a timely basis. Likewise, many commodity exchanges collect and publish information about market supply and demand conditions. These information programs reduce adverse selection by leveling the playing field for all participants.
- Exchanges and others have created many index products that help investors purchase exposure to market-wide risks through a single transaction rather than through multiple transactions in many individual securities markets. Liquidity is cheaper in markets for index products than in individual security markets, because adverse selection is a smaller problem in index markets than in security markets. Generally, few people ever have deep insights into market-wide valuations, whereas some traders often are well informed about individual security values.

1.5 The Zero-sum Game

Trading is a zero-sum game with respect to trading profits. The profits that buyers make are profits foregone by sellers, and the losses that buyers incur are losses avoided by sellers.

If traders were motivated only by expected trading profits, no rational traders would be in the market. The least well-informed traders would recognize that they would lose on average when trading, so they would simply stop transacting. The least well-informed traders among the remaining traders also would not trade, because they also would recognize that they would lose on average. The logical end to this argument is that no traders will trade with each other if expected trading profits were their only motivation. In this case, markets would have no liquidity, and prices would not be informative.

Fortunately, trading is not a zero-sum game when utilitarian traders are included. Utilitarian traders come into the market, because they obtain benefits besides expected trading profits. As noted in the foregoing section, these benefits include moving money through time, risk management, tax avoidance, and entertainment. The losses that utilitarian traders sustain when trading with informed traders are the costs they bear to obtain the various services that they seek from using the markets. The equivalent gains that the informed traders make fund their efforts to acquire information. Their trading on that information makes prices more informative. Utilitarian trading thus indirectly funds price efficiency. Markets exist only when traders are interested in trading for reasons besides trading profits. Without utilitarian traders, markets fail.

Accordingly, exchanges devote substantial resources to identifying products that will interest utilitarian traders. Examples of such products include investment vehicles such as exchange-traded funds (ETFs) that allow investors to move money easily through time; futures and options contracts that allow traders to offset risks that scare them, or take on risks that tempt them; and levered vehicles such as contracts for differences, options, and levered ETFs that attract gamblers as well as many other types of market participants.

Regulated exchanges generally structure their trading rules to protect the interests of the utilitarian traders without whom the markets would not exist. Efforts to prevent front-running, insider trading, market manipulation, and financial fraud reduce the costs that utilitarian traders bear when they use the markets. When successful, these programs strengthen markets and thereby facilitate the exchange of capital and risk among traders, and between corporations and the public investors that finance them.

Markets that have many utilitarian traders tend to be liquid markets with informationally efficient prices. Ironically, although utilitarian trading can make prices less informative in the short run, it ultimately provides the resources that informed traders need to conduct and act upon their research, and thus indirectly makes price more informative in the long run.

1.6 Informative Prices

When informed traders base their trades on their best assessments of fundamental value, their market operations tend to push prices towards their estimates of value. If their value estimates are higher than current prices, they buy and push prices up towards their estimates. Conversely, if their value estimates are lower than current prices, they sell (or sell short) and push prices down towards their estimates. Their trading thus causes prices to reflect their value estimates so that prices become informative.

Informed traders often estimate different values for the same securities and contracts. Variation in value estimates occurs when traders analyze different information or when their analyses of the same information differ. Such variation is common and often leads to trading among well-informed traders. The resulting market prices reflect the average of their value estimates and not the assessment of any one informed actor. Such averages generally reflect values better than do individual value estimates.

When prices come to reflect all available information about values, market prices are close to fundamental values, and value-motivated traders and news traders cannot profit from additional trading.

Although many traders hope to trade successfully by carefully analyzing information, few are able to profit consistently. Those who rationally expect to profit on average are truly informed traders. Traders can rationally expect to profit from trading on information when they are confident that their information is not already in the price.

Economists call the other traders pseudo-informed traders. Pseudo-informed traders think that they are trading on information, but either their information is already in the price, or they are not able to properly analyze its implications for future prices. In either event, their trading is futile, since it does not produce trading profits on average over time. If their trading pushes a price around, that price will be less informative, and they will ultimately lose money when prices return to values. Pseudo-informed traders thus are actually noise traders.

1.7 Market Efficiency

Economists say that markets are informationally efficient with respect to some set of information when traders can no longer profit by using that information to predict future prices. They say that prices are weak-form efficient when traders cannot predict future price changes based on past price changes. Prices are semi-strong form efficient when traders cannot predict future price changes based on any public information. Strong-form efficiency holds that prices cannot be predicted with any information, public or private. Few people believe that markets are strong-form efficient, since insider trading on private information can be exceptionally profitable if insiders know material nonpublic information about values.

The efficient markets hypothesis is a conjecture that the markets are semi-strong form efficient. Many studies indicate that this hypothesis is correct. This result is not surprising. If many traders knew that they could trade profitably using widely available public information, they would do so. Their efforts to profit from the information would cause prices to reflect that information, which would ensure that no one could then profit from the information. The competition among informed traders to profit ensures that prices are quite informative. It also makes being a successful informed trader very difficult.

Successful informed traders must trade on information that is not widely available to others. Such information is either privately obtained, or it is created through private analyses of publicly available information. Since both processes are expensive, the trading profits that informed traders generate must cover the expenses of generating their predictions.

Rational traders who cannot obtain valuable insights into future prices do not speculate on future values. Instead, they confine their market operations to only that trading which is necessary to attain other objectives such as risk management or investment. As market structures have evolved over recent decades, such traders have typically come to rely increasingly on index products.

Although empirical evidence suggests that the efficient market hypothesis is essentially true, logically it cannot always be true for all traders. If it were always true, prices would always equal fundamental values, so that informed traders could never profit from research into fundamental values. In which case, informed traders would not invest to obtain information, and they would not trade. However, if informed traders do not trade, prices would not be informative. The efficient market hypothesis therefore cannot always be true: Prices prevailing at a given moment do not always equal fundamental values.

Informed trading ensures that prices generally are near their fundamental values so that further informed trading is not profitable. In that case, when is informed trading profitable? Fortunately, for informed traders, fundamental values and market prices tend to move together, though often not in lockstep. Informed trading becomes profitable either when values change but prices do not, or when prices change and values do not. Both ways, market prices differ from fundamental values, and informed traders will have an opportunity to trade.

How does this work in practice? Values change in response to material events. Traders who are aware of these events and their implications for value profit if they can trade before others recognize that values have changed, to what extent, and in which direction. These traders are the news traders described earlier.

Market prices often change while fundamental values remain the same when utilitarian traders trade substantial volume on the same side of the markets. Their efforts to fill their trades cause prices to move independently of fundamental values. The traders best able to recognize this situation are value-motivated traders who estimate security values, and who come into the market when they perceive that prices differ from their estimates.

Since value-motivated traders act in response to the demands for liquidity made by utilitarians, they supply liquidity to the market. Value-motivated traders generally are willing to provide more liquidity than dealers are, because their unique skills and information enables them to do a better job of assessing fundamental values. As well-informed market participants, they are much less afraid of trading with other better-informed traders than dealers typically are. Dealers generally know only market values well and not also security values. Accordingly, value-motivated traders are the ultimate suppliers of liquidity. Dealers frequently trade with value-motivated traders when they are uncomfortable with their inventory positions.

Public disclosure programs mandated by exchanges or by regulatory agencies increase price efficiency by reducing the costs of research for informed traders. With lower costs, informed traders require less liquidity to obtain a given level of profitability. Prices therefore will be more informative in illiquid markets when material information about security and contract values is readily available.

2. Implications of Liquidity Search Problems for Market Structures

Traders face two significant problems when trying to fill their orders. First, and most obviously, traders must find others willing to trade with them. Second, while searching for counterparties, they must be careful that their actions do not adversely affect the prices at which they ultimately trade: Other traders may front-run their orders or withdraw liquidity from them. These problems are most severe for large traders.

To help traders solve these problems, exchanges, brokers, and alternative trading systems have added various features to their trading systems. Understanding how these problems affect trading is essential for comprehending why markets are structured as they are.

2.1 The Search of Liquidity

The problem of finding traders with whom to trade is most easily solved when all market participants transact in the same trading system. When willing buyers and sellers are present at the same time and price, exchanges or brokers can easily match them together.

Exchange and brokerage trading systems facilitate the search for liquidity by concentrating order flow at a single place. Traders who want to buy or sell seek out these systems, because that is where sellers and buyers generally go when they want to trade.

Call markets further concentrate liquidity by bringing together all traders to transact at the same point in time. The resulting markets can be very liquid at the times of their calls, but they are completely illiquid between calls. The call sessions that open and close many exchange trading sessions are usually the most liquid periods of the day.

In a continuous trading environment, traders can arrange transactions at any time that the market is open. However, buyers and sellers often are not present at the same time. Dealers commonly offer liquidity in such conditions. They may buy from a seller in the morning and sell to a buyer in the afternoon or vice versa. The effect of their trading is to connect buyers and sellers who come to the same place to trade, but who arrive at different times. Many exchanges cultivate relationships with dealers to ensure that their continuous markets will be liquid.

Large trades are particularly difficult to arrange because traders who can take the other side of a large trade may not be present in the market. Many traders who ultimately prove willing to transact do not consider whether they would be willing to trade until they are asked. Economists call such traders latent liquidity suppliers.

Block brokers facilitate large trades by keeping track of who owns large blocks of securities that they might sell, and who might be interested in purchasing large blocks of securities. When asked by a client to buy or sell a block, they then consider who might be willing to take the other side. Successful block brokers therefore must have many clients whom they know well. Block brokers generally run their businesses away from exchanges, because the information that they must collect and communicate rarely appears on exchange floors or in exchange trading systems.

2.2 Informed Trading Issues

Concerns about informed trading also make trading large blocks difficult. Most market participants presume that large traders are well informed, because well-informed traders tend to trade large orders and because large traders generally can afford the research necessary to become well informed. Consequently, dealers and other traders are unwilling to fill large orders without a substantial price concession if they suspect that the large trader on the other side may be better informed about value, market interest, or both.

Block dealers and brokers help solve this problem for large utilitarian traders by confirming that the large traders are indeed utilitarians and not well-informed traders. They make these determinations by knowing their clients and understanding the reasons why they trade.

Block dealers and brokers must always consider whether their clients have based their trading decisions on material information that is not yet in the price. Dealers who facilitate client trades stake their wealth on the quality of these analyses. Block brokers stake their reputations on the quality of these analyses when they introduce a large trader to their other clients who might take the other side of the trade. These research activities generally take place away from exchanges, because exchanges usually cannot provide the information resources that would allow traders to determine who is well informed and who is not.

2.3 Quote-matching Issues

Large traders who expose their limit orders risk a response from others in the market employing a strategy called "quote-matching." An example best explains this strategy. Suppose that a large trader places a limit order to buy at 20. A clever trader may see this order and immediately try to buy ahead of it, perhaps by placing an order at 20 at another exchange or by placing an order at a tick better at the same exchange. If the clever trader's order fills, the clever trader will have an interesting position in the market. If prices subsequently rise, the trader will profit to the extent of the rise. However, if values appear to be falling, perhaps because the prices of correlated stocks or indices are dropping, the clever trader will try to sell his position to the large trader at 20. If the clever trader can make trade decisions faster than the large trader can revise or cancel his order, and faster than others competing for the same opportunity can, then the clever trader will be able to limit his losses. The clever trader thus profits on one side, but loses a little on the other side. The large trader has the corresponding opposite position: If prices rise, he may fail to trade and wish that he had. If prices fall, he may trade and wish that he had not. The profits that the clever trader makes are lost opportunities to the large trader.

The quote-matching strategy is profitable when very fast traders can extract the option values of standing limit orders. Standing limit orders have option values, because they give traders opportunities to trade at fixed prices in markets that are constantly moving.

Large traders avoid quote-matching losses by limiting the exposure of their orders. Exchanges, brokers, and alternative trading systems have developed many systems to help traders manage their order exposure. On floor-based exchanges, large traders trust their orders to floor brokers with the understanding that their brokers will only display the orders to traders who the brokers expect will fill them and who the brokers trust will not front-run them. Off-floor brokers likewise carefully manage the exposure of the orders entrusted to them.

Most electronic exchanges and alternative trading systems now permit traders to hide all or a portion of their orders. The orders are either hidden at their limit price, or they display at their limit price and provide for a specified degree of discretion to trade at a better price that is not displayed. Practitioners call systems that do not expose orders to the public "dark pools."

Traders discover these orders by submitting limit orders at the prices at which they hope to find hidden liquidity. They usually mark these limit orders as immediate or cancel (IOC), so that their own efforts to find liquidity remain hidden if they do not find liquidity at the given price. Using electronic systems, traders routinely sweep many markets with IOC orders as they try to fill their orders at improved prices and sizes. Some brokerage systems submit more than 100 IOC orders for each filled order as they sweep various markets and prices searching for hidden liquidity. This process occurs very quickly in today's electronic environment, since the roundtrip time between submission and the report of an unfilled order is often less than 30 milliseconds. Hidden order facilities protect traders from front-runners, because traders can only learn about hidden orders by committing to trade with them, and then only to the extent that they are willing to trade. Hidden liquidity in some form or another has always existed, whether electronic or otherwise.

Repeated trade reports at prices or quantities that reveal hidden liquidity often predict additional liquidity at that price. Some traders monitor the market for these situations, and they then try to trade ahead of orders that they suspect are hidden. Such traders risk that no liquidity may remain where they expect it to reside, or that the order submitter may cancel the order.

2.4 Other Front-running Issues

Traders with large orders often must move prices substantially to obtain the liquidity necessary to fill their orders. These price concessions are especially large when other traders believe that the large traders are well informed, but they may still be quite significant even if the large trader is a utilitarian trader. The concessions are necessary to encourage traders who otherwise would not be willing to buy or sell on the other side to participate to the extent required. Practitioners say that large traders exert price pressure as they try to fill their orders.

Expectations of these price changes make filling large orders very difficult. If other traders become aware of a large buy order, some may immediately buy in front of the order to profit from the expected price change. Such trades increase the ultimate costs of filling large orders.

In addition, if traders who have posted limit orders or quotes are aware of these large orders, they may withdraw their offers of liquidity so that they can re-price them further from the current market in anticipation of the price pressure to be exerted. These traders are said to "fade" their orders from the market, so that once again, large traders ultimately pay more to complete their transactions.

Both problems—front-running by traders on the same side and fading by liquidity suppliers on the opposite side—understandably make large traders very reluctant to disclose the full size of their orders. To mitigate or avoid entirely these problems, large traders use the hidden order facilities described earlier when posting limit orders. If they are using marketable limit orders, they attach immediate-or-cancel instructions to their orders to ensure that they do not display after they have taken all liquidity at a given price. They may also simultaneously submit orders to all markets at the same time to collect as much liquidity as they can at a given price or prices before liquidity suppliers realize that a large trader is present.

2.5 Price Discrimination

Traders generally will break their bigger orders into smaller pieces, so that they can fill the first pieces at the best available prices, and then only fill the remaining pieces at inferior prices. Since traders who offer liquidity are aware of this price discrimination problem, they tend not to post much size at the best-quoted prices. Those who do post large sizes fail to earn the price concessions that large traders typically must pay to fill their orders.

As discussed in the preceding section, traders seeking to transact substantial size often can find suitable counterparties at better prices if they use the services of a block broker or dealer. However, dealers do not want to offer liquidity, and brokers do not want to arrange for liquidity, if a large trader intends to price discriminate. Doing so would produce immediate losses for the dealers or the brokers' contra-side clients when the large trader executes more size at inferior prices. To avoid this problem, block dealers and brokers want to know the full size of an order, so that they can price it accordingly.

One of the more important functions of the block trading market is to determine the true size of large orders. Dealers and brokers ask their clients what the full sizes of their orders are. They attempt to keep them honest by paying close attention to their clients' subsequent trades and by making it clear that they will not arrange trades again for clients who prove to be dishonest. Those traders who can credibly convince others that they will not price discriminate often obtain better average prices for their orders than they would if they tried to price discriminate.

Front-running—legal or otherwise—and price discrimination are related. By trading ahead of large orders, front-runners take the benefits of price discrimination that large traders would otherwise obtain. In many cases, they then sell the blocks that they have aggregated to the large trader at the market clearing price.

2.6 Informed Trading

Informed trading is most profitable when informed traders can execute substantial size with little market impact. Since no one wants to trade with a well-informed trader, informed traders must employ stealth trading strategies. In general, they try to appear to be utilitarian traders. Practitioners often say that they are "wolves in sheep's clothing."

Informed traders prefer to trade in anonymous markets. In those markets that reveal trader identities, they may use brokers as "beards" behind which they can hide, if regulations and exchange rules permit.

Informed traders often break their orders into small pieces that they dole out over time to avoid recognition. This strategy works only when they are in sole possession of material information that will not soon become public. If the information will soon become public, or if many other traders also have the information, they must trade quickly to capitalize on their information advantage.

Dealers pay close attention to the urgency with which traders seek to act. If they believe that many traders all want to trade quickly on the same side of the market, they fade from the market and adjust prices rapidly to restore a two-sided order flow.

As mentioned earlier, exchanges often help protect dealers from informed trading by halting markets when a material corporate disclosure is pending, or by halting trading when prices have (or would) move substantially in response to a one-sided surge of orders. These trade halt rules protect liquidity suppliers from losing to informed traders and to large traders who seek to price discriminate. With such protections, dealers are more willing to offer liquidity to other market participants.

Dealers must be very careful when trading with anonymous counterparts. Since informed traders can break their orders up and send their submissions to the market over time, they must be careful to recognize that small persistent short-term order imbalances may turn into long-term order imbalances. Accordingly, they must adjust their expectations of value in response to every order that they see, since any anonymous order may come from an informed trader. When their expectations change sufficiently, they change their quotes.

Dealers also must take care to change prices uniformly in response to small and large orders to avoid losing to market manipulators. For example, if a dealer believes that large traders are well informed and small traders are not, a market manipulator may increase prices with several of large purchases that change prices substantially, and then sell out with many small trades that collectively do not change prices as much. If the cumulative price impact of the large trades is greater than that of the small trades, the average sales price will be greater than the average purchase price, and the manipulator will profit.

Exchanges and the governmental bodies that regulate trading generally make market manipulation illegal to protect dealers and other traders. However, enforcement of anti-manipulation regulation is extremely difficult in practice, because manipulators invariably claim to be informed traders who bought because they thought prices were low and sold to lock in their gains when prices rose. Dealers thus must protect themselves against such manipulations by ensuring that the cumulative impact of buy and sell order flows of the same size are similar regardless of how they arrive in the market.

3. Exchange Rules Affect the Provision of Liquidity

Exchanges and other trading systems choose their trading rules carefully to meet the needs of traders and thereby attract them. Their rules typically affect the incentives to take or supply liquidity that various types of traders face.

Order precedence rules determine for which traders the exchange matching system will first arrange trades. The first order precedence rule is price priority. Exchanges invariably give precedence to those traders who offer the best prices since such prices will most likely attract traders on the other side of the market. Accordingly, impatient traders who wish to transact quickly must bid higher prices when buying or offer lower prices when selling.

The remaining order precedence rules are secondary precedence rules, because they determine who has precedence at a given price. Trading systems vary in their secondary precedence rules. In those systems that permit hidden orders, displayed orders (or the displayed component of a partially hidden order) have precedence over those orders that are not displayed. This rule encourages traders to display their orders, which helps the exchange attract order flow.

The next secondary precedence rule usually is some version of time precedence. Time precedence rules give precedence to orders that arrive earlier than other orders. Exchanges vary in their time precedence rules. Strict time precedence gives precedence to orders at a given price in the sequence in which they arrived. No order can be filled until all earlier orders have filled. In contrast, floor-based exchanges and some electronic exchanges give time precedence only to the first order to arrive at a given price. At such exchanges, once that order is filled, all other orders are generally filled on a *pro rata* basis. Time precedence rules encourage traders seeking to transact to submit their orders as early as possible. They also direct order flow to those traders who improve prices, thereby encouraging traders to improve price.

Pro rata allocation schemes give traders who post large orders a greater share of the allocation of incoming marketable orders. In such systems, traders often post much larger orders than they intend to fill with the hope of filling their desired order size. However, they must be careful, because this strategy gives very large traders opportunities to transact. *Pro rata* allocations rules favor large traders and fast traders who can quickly cancel their orders in response to changing market conditions. These rules discriminate against small retail traders for whom posting liquidity is unwise, because their orders will only fill when nobody else is willing to trade at that price. Exchanges adopt *pro rata* allocation rules to maximize displayed total order size.

Secondary trading rules are not meaningful when the exchange tick size—the minimum variation by which prices can change—is small. If the tick size is small, traders who do not have precedence at a given price will obtain it by improving price by a trivial amount. A small tick size thus favors price competition and deemphasizes incentives to post and display orders early.

However, a small tick size also reduces the costs of front-running and quote-matching strategies. Giving traders precedence over large orders without requiring that they substantially improve prices allows quote-matchers to extract more option value from large orders, since they gain more if prices move in their direction and lose less if they have to trade out of their positions.

Many exchanges give special privileges to dealers whom they may call specialists, designated market makers, or designated dealers. The special privileges often allow the dealers to take precedence over standing orders for some of the incoming order size, or allow them to improve price based on information that other traders may not have, or allow them to guarantee execution with the option to not participate in the trade should another trader come along. Exchanges give these valuable privileges in return for special services that they expect from their designated dealers. In particular, they generally expect that the dealers make markets when others will not so that some market for each security will always exist at the exchange. These special privileges generally hurt limit order traders who offer liquidity, because the special privileges give dealers precedence that otherwise would have gone to their limit orders. The special privileges may also hurt traders who take liquidity by limiting the opportunities for price improvement that they otherwise might have.

Many exchanges also have public order precedence rules. A public order precedence rule gives precedence to public traders over member traders at a given price. These rules help prevent front-running and generally increase public confidence in exchanges. They are less common now that most exchanges use electronic trading systems to arrange trades.

▆ 4. The Cost of Liquidity

Liquidity too often is a poorly defined concept. It often means different things to different people. The confusion undoubtedly is due to its many dimensions, all of which are related to characteristics of the bilateral search among traders for the best price. Perhaps the most all-encompassing definition of liquidity is that liquidity is the ability to quickly buy or sell substantial size at low cost when you want to trade.

This definition hints at several liquidity dimensions. "Low cost" refers to a dimension called width. Width usually is measured by bid/ask spread, market impact, and commissions. "Size" refers to a dimension called depth, the ability to trade a quantity at a given price. Width and depth are closely related. Width is cost for a given quantity whereas depth is quantity for a given cost. "Quickly" refers to a dimension called immediacy. Immediacy usually is measured by the time required to arrange a trade of a given size at a given cost.

These various dimensions of liquidity are related. Traders generally can trade more size if they are willing to provide greater price concessions: Depth increases with width. Likewise, at a given cost, traders generally can find more size if they search longer. In addition, traders often can trade a given size at lower cost if they search longer.

These dimensions are related, because they all characterize aspects of the same search problem. In general, "ability to trade" depends on how much the trader wants to transact, how much the trader is willing to pay for the trade, and how long the trader looks for counterparties. One market is more liquid than another if the probability of trading a given size at a given cost within a given time period is greater.

Several factors determine market liquidity. The most important factor is the interest of utilitarian traders. If utilitarians are not interested in trading, the market simply will not exist, because rational profit motivated traders cannot all expect to profit when trading with each other.

Volatility is the next most important determinant of liquidity. Volatile markets tend to have wide spreads as dealers and other traders try to control the option values in their orders. The value of a fixed price limit order or quote increases with volatility because volatility increases the potential benefits from the quote-matching strategy. It also increases the costs associated with limit orders that have become stale. Accordingly, volatile markets tend to have wide spreads.

Adverse selection also increases bid/ask spreads, because dealers must ensure that they can obtain enough profit from utilitarian traders to cover their losses to informed traders. Exchanges try to control adverse selection by mandating substantial financial disclosure by their listed firms. These disclosures reduce information asymmetries and thereby reduce informed trading.

5. Order Submission Strategy and Equilibrium Bid/ask Spreads

Traders manage their transaction costs by carefully choosing their search strategies. At organized exchanges where limit orders are matched with marketable orders, the main order submission decision is whether to take liquidity with a marketable order or to offer liquidity by posting a standing limit order. The tradeoff depends on several factors, foremost of which are the bid/ask spread and the cost of time. All other things being equal, traders post orders when spreads are wider, and they take liquidity when spreads are smaller. Among traders, those who most value their time or who most need to trade quickly (because material information upon which they are trading will rapidly become better known) use marketable orders, because such orders execute quickly. Those who can wait for a better price, post limit orders and wait for the market to come to them.

Traders say that the bid/ask spread is the price of liquidity. When that price is high, traders offer liquidity. When the price is low, traders take liquidity.

The bid/ask spread represents the summed cost of trading two orders: a market order to buy and a market order to sell, both simultaneously submitted. These trades will accomplish nothing on net, but they will lose the half the bid/ask spread for each share traded. Accordingly, the cost of trading a small market order is one-half the bid/ask spread.

Trading is most efficient when traders submit equal aggregate volumes of posted limit orders and of marketable orders on each side of the market. These balances occur only when the bid/ask spread—the price of liquidity—is set at the right level. Fortunately, market forces determine the proper bid/ask spread, which economists call the equilibrium spread. The following argument outlines how spreads are determined.

If spreads are too wide, most traders will post standing orders and little trade will take place. In which case, some traders will narrow their spreads to improve price in the hope of encouraging other traders to switch from posting liquidity to taking liquidity. In contrast, if spreads are too narrow, most traders will try to take liquidity and few will post liquidity. Those who post will quickly have their orders filled so that bid/ask spreads widen. The wider spreads will discourage some traders from taking liquidity in favor of offering liquidity. These two arguments indicate that markets will find an intermediate bid/ask spread that just balances the demand for liquidity with the supply of liquidity.

Understanding how spreads are determined in equilibrium provides tools for predicting what effects the make-or-take exchange fee pricing model has on bid/ask spreads. Some exchanges charge a simple transaction fee for arranging trades. The fee may be borne by the seller or the buyer, or split among them. In contrast, other exchanges charge an access fee to traders who trade by taking markets (hitting bids and taking offers) with marketable orders. These exchanges also pay a liquidity rebate to traders who are hit or taken when making markets with posted buy and sell limit orders. The difference between the access fee and the liquidity rebate is the net revenue earning by the exchange for arranging trades. This difference is generally approximately equal to the transaction fees charged by exchanges that use the transaction fee model.

Since the access fee makes using market orders expensive and the liquidity rebate makes using limit orders attractive, an increase in both rates would cause traders to shift from submitting market orders to limit orders (if spreads remained constant). However, in equilibrium, equal volumes of marketable orders and limit orders must match. This condition will be met only if bid/ask spreads decrease. Since traders generally care only about net prices, the net price of liquidity (half the bid/ask spread plus the access fee) will be the same regardless of how high the access fee and liquidity rebate are set, as long as the difference is constant. Accordingly, any equal increase in the access fee and in the liquidity rebate will produce twice the decrease in equilibrium spreads.

Make-or-take pricing thus distorts quoted bid/ask spreads. This result is extremely important to understanding the competitions among dealers and exchanges, and among exchanges.

▇▇▇▇▇ 6. The Competitions to Supply and Organize Liquidity

Many traders compete to supply liquidity. Dealers compete with public limit order traders, and both compete with arbitrageurs.

Public limit order traders often can push dealers out of a market, because the public traders generally quote prices to fill their orders whereas dealers quote prices to trade profitably. Public limit order traders offer liquidity with the hope of improving the average fill prices of their orders. Their greatest risk when doing so is that they will fail to trade when informed traders move prices away from their orders. They minimize this probability by pricing their orders aggressively. In contrast, dealers trade to profit from offering liquidity. Since they ultimately must reverse their trades, their greatest risk is that informed traders will cause prices to move before they can trade out of their positions. They minimize the losses associated with this adverse selection risk by moving their orders away from the market. The different risks that these two types of traders perceive in response to informed trading cause the public limit order traders to be more aggressive and the dealers to be less aggressive. If enough public traders are in the market, pure dealing strategies become unprofitable and dealers quit.

Arbitrageurs also compete with dealers to profit liquidity. As discussed earlier, dealers match buyers to sellers arriving in the same market at different points in time. In contrast, arbitrageurs match buyers to sellers arriving at different markets for essentially the same risks at the same time. For example, an arbitrageur may offer to buy in one market with expectation that he can sell the same security in another market at a higher price. This often happens when a large seller depresses prices in one market, but not in another market. The arbitrageur thus competes with the dealer to provide liquidity to the seller.

To protect their member dealers from this competition, some exchanges have tried to place limits on traders conducting arbitrage. Such limits are problematic, because identifying arbitrage trade is difficult, and because regulators generally support equal and fair access for all traders.

Dealers also compete with brokers and exchanges to fill orders. Dealers fill orders for their own accounts whereas brokers and exchanges fill orders by matching their clients. Although many dealers make markets at exchanges, they generally prefer to make markets away from exchanges where information is not so widely available to their clients. Exchanges and dealers thus often have conflicting objectives with respect to how exchanges operate, and in particular with respect to the dissemination of information about prices.

Finally, brokers and exchanges often compete with each other to arrange trades. When permitted by regulatory authorities, many brokers first try to match orders among their clients before sending unmatched remainders to an exchange.

Since brokers and exchanges both complete to arrange trades, functional distinctions between exchanges and brokers often are subtle, especially for brokers who maintain electronic limit order books and automated order matching systems. The primary distinction is regulatory. Many exchanges regulate their members' business activities and their listed firms' capital structures and information disclosures. In contrast, brokers only regulate trading in their trading systems.

The various competitions to supply and organize liquidity help reduce transaction costs for traders and provide them with innovative exchange services. The competitions among dealers, arbitrageurs, and brokers to fill orders ensure that their customers obtain liquidity at the lowest cost possible. The competitions among brokers and exchanges have led to the creation of diverse trading systems designed to serve the special needs of various types of traders. Most dark pools exist, because exchanges were unable or unwilling to meet the needs of large traders in an increasing electronic environment.

The competition among regulated exchanges and less-regulated trading systems has created two serious problems. First, the regulated exchanges often must seek approval for changes to their trading systems and fee structures before they can implement them. Their competitors generally face no such constraints. Accordingly, delays in obtaining these approvals can be very costly to regulated exchanges.

Second, regulated exchanges often provide regulatory supervision over their participants, and in the case of equity exchanges, over their listed firms. These services, which include surveillance, dispute resolution, and the promulgation of standards for capital structure and information disclosure are expensive to provide. They rarely attract order flow, because the benefits of these regulatory services accrue to the public as a whole and not only to the customers of the exchange. Exchanges that provide these services thus have a cost disadvantage with respect to their competitors that do not provide these services.

7. The Two Mostly Incompatible Competitions

Two competitions occur in securities markets: the competition among traders for the best price, and the competition among exchanges and brokers to host the first competition. Unfortunately, these two competitions generally interact with each other poorly. Most policies that would promote one competition hurt the other and vice versa.

The competition for best price works best when traders or their brokers bring all orders to a single market so that buyers and sellers can most easily find each other. This observation suggests that regulation should consolidate all trading to a single market. Indeed, many countries have adopted such policies. For example, US law allows exchanges to consolidate trading in a given futures contract to a single exchange. Likewise, several Asian countries consolidate equity trading in local equities to a single national exchange. However, such consolidation is imperfect if traders can arrange trades outside of the country.

Such regulatory consolidation completely rules out competition among exchanges to provide exchange services. That competition works best when traders are free to route their orders to whatever exchange they believe best serves them. Where such freedoms exist, exchanges and brokers compete to provide high-quality, low-cost services. In many cases, these services are tailored to meet the special needs of various clienteles. However, the resulting fragmentation often concerns regulators who wonder whether the diversity of exchange platforms significantly impairs the competition for best price.

In practice, most trading generally consolidates to a single exchange (if exchanges can wrest trading away from dealers), because most traders and brokers send their orders to the most active market since that market most often offers the best opportunities to trade at favorable terms. Practitioners say that "liquidity attracts liquidity." Economists call this phenomenon the "order flow externality." It exists because traders are attracted to the many free trading options provided by limit orders posted in an active market.

The order flow externality places a severe burden upon innovative execution platforms that try to compete with established exchanges.

Even though many—perhaps all—traders may believe that an innovative system would provide higher-quality exchange services than an incumbent exchange, few traders will send their orders to the new system because they must execute their orders, and the incumbent exchanges at which orders are already posted are the only exchanges where they can trade quickly and at favorable terms. The order flow externality ensures that an innovative new platform will thrive only if the innovation provides very substantial advantages, if everyone coordinates a common move to the new system, or if government intervention changes the rules of the game.

The order flow externality will not consolidate all trading to a single venue when the needs of traders vary substantially. For example, large traders support different trading systems than do retail traders, and informed traders favor different systems than do uninformed traders. In general, large traders prefer systems that allow them to control order exposure and protect them from trading with informed traders; retail traders generally prefer markets that provide narrow bid/ask spreads and quick turnaround; informed traders prefer continuous consolidated markets in which they can trade anonymously; and uninformed traders often prefer call markets that only permit order matching among similar traders. When needs are sufficiently diverse, so will be the trading systems that exchanges and brokers develop to satisfy them.

Although the resulting fragmentation complicates the search for best price, at least three considerations suggest that the problem may not be large. First, traders often will route their orders to markets that do not provide them with the services that they most desire when trading opportunities at those markets are most attractive. Second, traders who are aware of better trading opportunities in other markets will adjust their orders to reflect those conditions, even if they cannot or will not route their orders to those markets. Third, arbitrageurs will move liquidity from one market to another market when prices differ enough to make their trading profitable. The costs of a fragmented system thus depend on the costs of routing orders, the costs of building and maintaining consolidated information systems, and the resources spent by arbitrageurs in pursuit of trading profits.

Most regulatory bodies oscillate between favoring the competition for best price and the competition for exchange services. Their decisions often depend on changing political philosophies and upon changes in technologies that facilitate the creation of new and compelling trading systems.

Lobbyists intent on influencing public policy in favor of their clients invariably argue that the policy that they favor is the pro-competitive policy. One side argues to improve or maintain the competition for best price while the other side argues to improve or maintain the competition for exchange services.

8. Some Current Regulatory Issues

Chapter 3 of this volume provides a broad survey of regulatory issues in exchange markets. This section provides a short discussion of the economics underlying a few current regulatory issues.

8.1 Make-or-take Pricing

In the United States and in many other countries, principles of best execution require that dealers fill small orders at the best prices quoted at any accessible exchange when internalizing order flow (trading off an exchange). Exchanges and alternative trading systems known as electronic communication networks (ECNs) that collect their fees using the make-or-take pricing model cause quoted bid/ask spreads to be smaller than they otherwise would be, because their liquidity suppliers compete to receive liquidity rebates. However, the narrower spreads do not provide a net benefit to customers who must pay access fees to access them. At a minimum, make-or-take pricing creates a transparency problem, because quoted bid/ask spreads do not represent the true costs of trading.

The smaller spreads disadvantage dealers who must fill orders at best quoted prices, because regulations or business norms prevent dealers from charging their customers an access fee for trading with them. The make-or-take pricing model thus favors exchanges over dealers. To remain profitable, dealers most post their quotes at exchanges so that they can receive liquidity rebates when trading.

The make-or-take model also distorts the competition among exchanges. When brokers must route orders to exchanges based on the best-quoted price and not best net price, make-or-take exchanges have an advantage over transaction fee exchanges, because the former tend to have more aggressively priced orders.

Finally, the make-or-take model causes brokers to send their limit orders to the exchanges that offer the highest liquidity rebates. Such exchanges invariably also have the highest access fees. When two exchanges quote the same bid or offer prices, market order traders send their orders to the exchange with the lowest access fee. Limit orders at exchanges with high access fees thus are the last to trade at a given price. By this time, they are often stale, because price is moving against them. The make-or-take pricing model hurts limit orders that are posted at those exchanges with highest access fees, since the limit order traders often fail to trade when prices are moving away from their orders. Brokerage customers generally do not realize that their orders are disadvantaged as they do not understand the problem and because standing limit orders have delayed executions under the best of circumstances.

Since brokers will route limit orders to the exchanges with the highest liquidity rebates, exchanges compete to have high rebates, which requires that they have high access fees. No natural economic process limits this competition to provide the highest liquidity rebates. Accordingly, regulators must limit it before it gets out of hand. In the United States, the Securities and Exchange Commission limits access fees to 0.3 cents per share for equities and 30 cents per contract for 100-share options contracts.

Since the make-or-take exchange pricing model creates a transparency problem and since it does not improve market quality, this author believes that regulators should prohibit access fees.

8.2 Flash Orders

Exchanges often receive orders that are not marketable at the receiving exchange but that are marketable at other exchanges. Rather than routing those orders to where they can immediately trade, some exchanges flash them to a set of designated traders for a short period of 30–150 milliseconds, depending on the exchange. During the flash period, the first dealer willing to fill the flashed order at the best price available at another exchange, or at a better price, then fills the order. If no designated trader is willing to fill the order, the exchange then routes the order to the other exchange.

Flash orders benefit the traders who submit them, because they often obtain a quick execution that is sometimes at a better price or for more size than is displayed elsewhere. Since the competing price is often at a make-or-take exchange, traders of marketable orders also often benefit by avoiding the other exchange's access fee.

Flash orders also benefit the exchanges that flash them by allowing them to fill orders that otherwise would go to other exchanges.

Finally, flash orders benefit the traders who fill them by allowing them to decide whether they want to trade in response to an opportunity rather than by forcing them to commit to trade whenever the opportunity arises. The option not to trade is valuable to them, especially when they can quickly determine that market conditions have suddenly changed.

The most obviously disadvantaged party is the trader offering the aggressively priced liquidity at another exchange. If the receiving exchange fills the flashed order, the aggressive trader at the other exchange will not be rewarded for posting an aggressive market. Worse, that trader may lose if the dealer filling the flash order is pursuing the quote-matching strategy. The problem arises because exchanges do not give time precedence to orders posted at other exchanges.

The arguments for and against flash orders thus boil down to opposing arguments for the two types of competitions discussed preceding section. The affirmative argument favors the competition among exchanges to provide exchange services by allowing them to innovate to serve the needs both of their clients and of their primary liquidity suppliers. The negative argument favors the competition for best price by protecting the interests of the traders who improve markets.

8.3 Market Data, Fast Access, and High-frequency Trading

Access to market data and the ability to act upon it quickly is a key determinant of profitability for traders. Those traders who are immediately aware of prices and volumes, both before and after trades are arranged, have a substantial advantage over those who have less timely information or no information at all. The greatest advantage goes to those who can act on timely information before others can. Not surprisingly, questions of who has quick access to data and order processing systems are quite contentious.

Traders who already have the best access to market information generally are most interested in restricting access to others. For example, bond dealers throughout the world have resisted publication of bond trade prices. Their superior knowledge of trade prices gives them much greater negotiating power than their clients have. The dealers are always willing to trade at prices favorable to them, but they will not trade at unfavorable prices. Their clients, who are less able to distinguish between favorable and unfavorable prices, often unknowingly trade at unfavorable prices.

Historically, regulated exchanges have been at the forefront of efforts to make prices more transparent, both before and after the trade. Transparent prices attracted customers to their markets by providing them a basis for ascertaining whether their trades occurred at fair prices.

Now that many exchanges are for-profit organizations, the potential for selling market data has encouraged them to make more data available to the public. Many exchanges now derive a substantial fraction of their revenues from sales of market data. These data include ultra-fast data feeds that broadcast quotes, changes to limit order books, trade information, and changes in indices as they occur. The prices for these services are often quite high so that the only purchasers are those professional traders who can most profit from the market information. Through the data revenue that they collect from these traders, exchanges effectively obtain a share of their clients' trading profits.

Many exchanges now also sell superior access to their order routing systems to proprietary traders. In particular, they allow traders to colocate their computer servers in the same facilities in which they locate their exchange servers. Proprietary trading systems running on colocated servers can respond much more quickly to new market information than can systems running on remote servers.

The speed advantage depends on the distance between computers, the speed of light, and the number of routers through which messages must pass before arriving at their destination. These differences can be quite significant. For example, at the speed of light, a message takes a little more than 4 milliseconds to travel the 800 miles between Chicago and New York. If it passes through only four routers on the way, each of which delays the message by 1 millisecond, the total time to complete a round trip would be 16 milliseconds. During this time, a computer processor running at three gigahertz can do 48 million operations. Obviously, when two traders compete to exploit the same trading opportunity, the one that is closer to the information and closer to the means of acting upon it will be the first to profit from the opportunity. The closer traders can always respond first, and they may respond more intelligently if they use their time advantage to more thoroughly analyze market conditions.

Many market participants believe that allowing some traders superior access to information is unfair. Many also question whether exchanges should even have the right to sell data, none of which would have any value were it not for the traders who use the exchange.

Others simply note that even on a level playing field, better players will always have an advantage.

The profits that high-frequency traders make come from many trading strategies. The most important of these strategies involve supplying liquidity to utilitarian traders either as dealers or arbitrageurs. Many commentators recognize that these profits must come from utilitarians without recognizing the value of the liquidity services that the high-frequency traders provide. In fact, since high-frequency trading is very competitive and the marginal cost of operating trading systems once built is low, electronic high-frequency trading has substantially reduced the liquidity costs for utilitarian traders. The real losers have been traditional dealers and arbitrageurs who have not build electronic systems that can compete with the proprietary traders who have.

8.4 Internalization, Payments for Order Flow, and Best Execution

Many broker–dealers fill their client orders in a process called internalization. Acting as dealers, these brokers fill their client orders off exchange.

Many brokers also route client orders to dealers in exchange for payments from the dealers in a process called preferencing. The dealers then fill these orders off exchange.

The potential for abuse in these internalization and preferencing arrangements is very high. Acting as agent for their clients, brokers must seek the best prices for their clients' orders. However, when also acting as a dealer to fill those orders, they profit most when the fill prices are least favorable to their clients. If they sell order flow to dealers, the payments that they can obtain depend on the profits that the dealers make, which are greatest when the clients receive poor prices. In both cases, the immediate incentives to obtain best execution for their orders are small.

In principle, these problems would not arise if clients could easily determine whether their brokers were obtaining best execution for their orders. If not, they would demand better service from their brokers or send their orders to other brokers who would provide better service. Best execution is generally understood to be good execution prices for marketable orders, though it may also include other dimensions of execution quality such as quick execution.

In practice, brokerage clients, and especially retail clients, cannot easily determine whether the prices that their brokers obtain for their orders are as good as they could have obtained. To do so, they must know what market conditions prevailed when they submitted their orders, and they must compare their execution prices with the prices that they would have expected to receive, given those market conditions. This process is very data intensive, and reliable results require analytic modeling skills that are substantially beyond the expertise of most clients. At best, retail clients only have a weak sense of whether their executions occur at favorable prices, and then only to the extent that their execution prices are at or within the bid/ask prices that their brokers may or may not present to them, and even then, only if the clients are paying attention. In contrast, institutional clients generally employ consultants to analyze the executions of their orders.

Concerns about the quality of execution in these relationships have led brokers and the authorities that regulate them to require that small orders executed off-exchange be executed at the best prices quoted on the regulated exchanges, or at better prices. To meet their best execution requirements, brokers increasingly demand that the dealers to whom they route orders provide improved prices.

These guarantees provide some assurance of execution quality in instruments that are exchange traded. Not surprisingly, when decimalization and increased automation of exchange systems and of proprietary dealing systems decreased bid/ask spreads in these markets, payments for order flow decreased as internalized dealing revenues substantially decreased. However, payments for order flow and internalized dealing profits remain high in instruments such as fixed income for which viable exchange markets rarely exist.

Dealers only pay for order flow that they believe comes largely from uninformed traders. In particular, they will not pay for order flow that comes from informed traders since such order flow is too costly for them to fill. Broker–dealers likewise only internalize those orders that they believe are benign and pass the remaining orders on to exchanges. Since retail traders generally are not well informed, most internalized orders come from retail traders.

The diversion of order flow from exchanges decreases market quality at the exchanges by removing utilitarian order flow. The remaining order flow is better informed and thus harder to fill profitably. As order flow is diverted from exchanges, exchange bid/ask spreads widen. In the extreme, exchange markets fail and no public bid/ask spreads are available. In which case, the markets trade strictly over-the-counter and dealer profits generally are high. Exchange markets for corporate bonds are very hard to establish in large part, because brokers are preferencing order flow to dealers in return for payments.

These issues greatly concern many practitioners and regulators who value the transparency of the regulated exchange markets and the role exchange transparency plays in regulating best execution for off-exchange trades. They also note that widening of bid/ask spreads from order flow diversion makes off-exchange trading more profitable, which will lead to a further diversion of order flow.

Although payments for order flow and internalized dealing profits would seem to directly benefit brokers, brokers only benefit if they can obtain order flow from their clients. When payments for order flow are high or internalized profits are high, brokers compete fiercely among themselves to obtain order flow from which they can profit. Their competition lowers the commissions that they charge their clients, and it improves the quality of services that their clients value and can easily recognize. Since most brokerage markets are quite competitive, brokers presumably compete away the benefits that they obtain from valuable retail order flows so that they just earn normal economic profits.

Since broker–dealers try to internalize and sell only order flow from utilitarian traders, the profits that they earn on that order flow are higher than the profits that they would earn if they traded a similar quantity of order flow at an exchange, where they would be exposed to more adverse selection from well-informed traders. With competitive broker-age markets, these additional profits return to the clients that generate the order flows. Thus, if the competition for order flow is efficient, inter-nalization benefits utilitarian clients by providing them with better net prices than they otherwise could obtain if their orders were mixed with those of informed traders and not processed separately.

No competition is perfect, however. As market structures become more convoluted, more profits stay with the intermediaries, and brokers generate more waste, as they provide customers with services to attract their order flow that the clients may not fully value. These issues undoubtedly will long concern regulators and practitioners.

9. Conclusion

The ideas presented in this chapter come from academic studies of market microstructure. Academics, along with many others, have identified the essential forces that structure exchange markets and that ultimately produce market quality characteristics such as liquidity, price efficiency, and volatility.

Some of the more important principles include:

- **Asymmetric information and adverse selection**. Well-informed traders profit from those who are less informed. Dealers in particular lose to well-informed traders and must always consider whether their quoted prices reflect current values. Their quotes must be wide enough that the profits that they earn from trading with utilitarians cover the losses that they incur to well-informed traders.
- **The zero-sum game**. Rational profit-motivated traders only trade if they expect to profit. Other traders transact, because they obtain other benefits besides trading profits. The most important of these utilitarian traders are investors, borrowers, hedgers, tax avoiders, and asset exchangers. Markets exist only when utilitarians are willing to trade.
- **Price efficiency**. Well-informed traders cause prices to reflect information. They profit only because utilitarians are willing to trade and accept their losses to informed traders. The interest of utilitarians thus ultimately determines how informative prices are. Public disclosure programs increase price efficiency by reducing the costs of research for informed traders. Prices cannot always be efficient. Prices differ from value when values change in response to news but prices have not changed, or when prices change in response to trading by uninformed traders but values have not changed. These events allow informed traders to profit.
- **Liquidity**. Trading is the successful outcome of bilateral searches conducted by buyers and sellers. Exchange systems that reduce the costs of conducting these searches reduce transaction costs. By concentrating order flow to a single place and often to a single point in time, exchange trading systems help buyers find sellers and vice versa. Liquidity is the ability to quickly buy or sell substantial size at low cost when you want to trade. Liquidity has many related dimensions, the most important of which are width, depth, and immediacy.
- **Order exposure.** Large traders and their brokers must be very careful when exposing their orders, since large orders give away significant trading options and often tend to move the market. Clever traders who are aware of large orders will trade ahead of them to extract the option values of these orders or to exploit their expected

price impacts. Both activities can significantly increase the costs of trading.

- **Rules affect liquidity**. Exchanges design their trading systems to provide incentives to traders to offer liquidity. The rules generally reward traders who offer the most aggressive prices, who display their orders, and who arrive early.

- **Liquidity costs**. Transaction costs ultimately depend on whether utilitarians are willing to trade, the degree of information asymmetries among traders, and the volatility of the underlying instrument.

- **Equilibrium bid/ask spreads**. The primary decision that traders must make when choosing an order submission strategy is whether to post limit orders and wait for other traders to come to them or to use marketable orders to transact with those traders who have posted orders. In general, traders take liquidity when their time is valuable or when they trade on information that will soon become public. Other traders offer liquidity. These decisions are regulated by the cost of liquidity, which bid/ask spreads often represent well. When spreads are large, offering liquidity is attractive. Order submission decisions affect bid/ask spreads. Markets find an equilibrium spread that maximizes the volume of trade.

- **Make-or-take pricing**. The make-or-take exchange fee pricing model distorts quoted equilibrium spreads, but does not change bid/ask spreads net of access fees. Traders who offer liquidity at exchanges that use this pricing system post more aggressive quotes, because they receive liquidity rebates. Net pricing remains the same, since spreads must adjust to obtain a balance between traders making and taking liquidity. Otherwise, traders would switch from taking to making or vise versa.

- **Competition**. Dealers, arbitrageurs, public traders, brokers, and exchanges compete to provide and organize liquidity. Their competitive efforts reduce the transaction costs and produce innovative trading systems and products.

- **The two competitions**. The competition among traders to obtain the best price and the competition among exchange service providers to provide exchange services often are incompatible with each other. Policies that would improve one competition typically harm the other. The pro-competitive position on any issue affecting both competitions—which includes most issues—therefore is rarely unambiguous.

- **Access to information and trading systems**. The proprietary trading profits of high-frequency traders increase with superior access to information and to exchange trading systems. The high prices that for-profit exchanges place on these services effectively allow the exchanges to participate in the profits that high-frequency traders obtain from their trading. Although these high-frequency traders profit from utilitarian traders, they also serve them by lowering liquidity costs. The primary losers are traditional dealers who have not created proprietary electronic trading systems.
- **Internalization and payments for order flow**. Broker–dealers internalize or sell retail order flow to dealers to profit from filling order flows that are less informative than those that institutions submit to exchanges. These processes are particularly profitable when bid/ask spreads are wide at exchanges. Unfortunately, the diversion of benign order flow from exchanges increases exchange bid/ask spreads, which makes internalization and preferencing more profitable. Competition among brokers for the customer order flow from which they profit returns much of the profits to the customers in the form of lower commission and better services. However, competition is never perfect so that brokers and dealers undoubtedly benefit from the system.

The importance of well-functioning exchanges to the efficient allocation of capital in market-based economies has led to their regulation in almost every country. Good regulatory policies help ensure that exchanges continue to provide fair markets in which traders can meet to exchange assets and risks. The formulation of good public policy depends on a deep and thorough understanding of what exchanges do, how they create liquid markets and informative prices, and how alternative market structures can promote or damage these market qualities.

The contribution of academics to our understanding of how exchanges operate, and thus to the effective regulation of trading, has been very significant. Unlike many practitioners, academics generally pursue knowledge for the sake of better understanding, and not for the sake of private gain. Accordingly, academic perspectives on public policy questions often best promote public welfare, and not just the welfare of practitioners with special interests.

Academic interest in regulated exchanges remains very strong due to the importance of high-quality markets to our economic well-being, and to the significant changes that markets experience as new communications and information processing technologies lead to valuable trading system innovations. We undoubtedly will continue to learn more about trading from academics and from all others who study trading.

Capital Markets Regulation Revisited

KAREL LANNOO AND PIERO CINQUEGRANA

▬▬ 1. Overview

The regulation of capital markets—of markets, products, and institutions—is a multifaceted concept.* It evolved rapidly with market and technological developments before the 2007–09 Financial Crisis came to the fore. It will continue to evolve in its wake. Regulation distinguishes regulated exchanges from other unsupervised markets, and it is a central feature of their business operations.

This essay considers the regulation of the markets, products, and institutions that are the building blocks of our financial system. We provide an overview of the economic problems that regulators attempt to solve, and the principles underlying their regulations. We also provide our expectations about future regulations that we believe governmental authorities will adopt in response to the crisis.

Many of these issues are quite controversial, and market participants will undoubtedly long debate them. While we recognize that not everyone will agree with the conclusions offered in this essay, including the World Federation of Exchanges (WFE) and its members, we hope that our treatment will advance the discussion. We appreciate the opportunity that WFE has given to the Centre for European Policy Studies to explore its thinking in this important field.

Before starting the discussion, consider the diversity in markets, products, and institutions:

- Trading takes place in several types of markets: auction markets such as stock, commodities, futures and options exchanges, multi-lateral trading facilities (MTFs) and electronic communication networks (ECNs); crossing markets such as broker-sponsored crossing networks and systematic internalizers; and over-the-counter (OTC) markets in which traders or their brokers negotiate bilateral transactions with dealers.
- Within products, one can distinguish different segments. In declining degree of regulatory intensity they are: equity, fixed income, on-exchange derivatives, commodities, OTC derivatives, and foreign exchange. OTC derivative markets have attracted much attention as a result of the crisis, and can be expected to be more heavily regulated in the future along with bond markets. In contrast, foreign exchange may remain largely unregulated.
- Within institutions, one can distinguish different levels of regulation, going from highly regulated entities such as deposit-taking banks, insurance companies, pension funds, mutual funds, to less tightly regulated entities such as broker–dealers, financial holding companies, hedge funds, private equity firms and off-balance-sheet entities—the so-called "shadow banking system." These last categories have so far escaped most, if not all, prudential business of conduct and governance rules.

The basic objectives of capital market regulation are efficiency, fairness, and transparency. These principles are not applied with the same intensity and weight to all objects of regulation because financial products and systems are tailored to meet the needs of different types of users. For example, thus far, regulators generally have not intervened as heavily in bond or OTC derivative markets as compared with equity markets, under the assumption that professional investors do not need the same level of protection as do retail investors. (Regulators, of course, are now reconsidering this assumption.) In all areas, the impact of technological progress on capital market activity, often not well understood, poses a fundamental challenge for policymakers in the analysis and application of the basic objectives.

Equity markets are extensively regulated because of their central role in corporate finance and the widespread trading and ownership of equities by retail investors. The question today is whether the regulatory model presently used in the equity markets should be extended to other markets and products.

More transparency may be useful in other capital market segments, and stricter prudential, conduct and governance regulation also may need to focus on the institutions active in these markets. Regulators also should consider extending rules to the "shadow banking system" and should assess whether additional product regulation is appropriate. Moreover, self-regulation—now discredited but so crucially important in capital markets—should continue to play a role in standard setting and codification.

The Financial Crisis turned upside down rationales behind the regulation of financial markets. Regulators are reconsidering the liberalization of trading venues—one of the cornerstones of the European Union's Markets in Financial Instruments directive (MiFID)—because increased fragmentation potentially may threaten market integrity. They are now considering the advantages of mandating more centralized trading, clearing, and settlement. Restrictions on trading practices that seemed out of touch with market liberalization, such as the ban on short selling, are reemerging in response to demands for systemic stability. Furthermore, although the dramatic growth in OTC derivative markets before the crisis was seen as a healthy sign of the markets' ability to innovate and expand, now regulators are considering more centralization of trading, mutualization of losses due to counterparty failures, and standardization of products. A radical shift in policy is emerging, which will impact future market structure and development.

This essay focuses mainly on the regulation of products and markets for tradable securities (including derivatives[1]) with longer maturity, that is, capital markets regulation. The discussion does not consider nontransferable and short-term instruments such as time and retail deposits, commercial paper, and repurchase agreements. Although the general concepts presented here have wide geographic application, the analysis of specific rules is mostly confined to the European Union and the United States. These jurisdictions have the most extensive sets of rules, and they often provide benchmarks for other countries.

The essay does not discuss prudential regulation. In the aftermath of the Financial Crisis, the debate on prudential rules has overshadowed discussions on product and market regulation, though the latter are as critical for the sound functioning of financial markets as are the former. We aim, with this essay, to refocus the debate away from prudential rules.

This essay argues that too little capital markets regulation is as intolerable as too much intervention. The economic and social havoc that unbridled financial markets can wreak on the global economy clearly demonstrates the risks of too little regulation or of regulators who are unwilling to exercise powers already granted to them. However, one should not forget that excessive government intrusion and nationalistic rules obstructed global economic integration in the 1950s and 1960s. We believe that a bias toward free markets must be tempered with the knowledge that unregulated markets can spin out control, especially when financial and technological innovations take markets into unfamiliar realms.

This essay starts with a discussion the regulatory issues associated with events that contributed to the 2007–09 Financial Crisis. Our presentation then provides some concept definitions followed by a brief historical survey on how and why governments have intervened in the capital markets. The discussion next traces the rationale behind government intervention, and then pinpoints failures. We then analyze how EU and US regulators have applied these objectives in practice. We end the essay with some final conclusions.

2. Reflections on the 2007–09 Financial Crisis

Can effective capital markets regulation be devised? Can regulation prevent or mitigate bubbles, manias and crashes? Was the crisis the result of market failure, regulatory failure or bad enforcement? Can insider trading be properly regulated? Is there an optimal level of disclosure? These and other questions will haunt scholars and commentators for years to come, while policymakers rush to implement new, more stringent rules under the pressure of the public opinion.

Before the global 2007–09 Financial Crisis, in spite of an ample microeconomics literature on market failures and behavioral finance, the dominant view in macro- and financial-economics assumed rational agents, efficient markets, and perfect information. While knowing the limitations of these assumptions, central bankers, commercial and investment bankers, financial regulators, courts, and market participants conducted monetary policy, devised models, calculated capital requirements, and designed regulations, enforced rules, and traded in the markets as if they were efficient (Akerlof and Shiller 2009; Authers 2009; Langevoort 1992).

Dissenters and critics of the dominant view have always been vocal. However, before the Financial Crisis, many leaders in the private and the public sectors were at best skeptical of regulation, at worst wary of any involvement of governments in financial markets. In the words of an academic:

> . . . one can seriously question the extent of systemic risk in today's banking system, at least in most advanced economies . . . the entire system of banking regulation is predicated on the possibility of systemic risk as a result of a substantial fear of the unknown, the supposed lessons of the past, and the bureaucratic imperative to preserve power (Scott 2005, pp. 5–6).

A former Chairman of the Commodity Futures Trading Commission (CFTC), Philip McBride Johnson, shared this view when speaking about the Commodity Futures Modernization Act of 2000, legislation that deregulated over-the-counter (OTC) markets in the United States:

> Congress has substantially deregulated commodities markets for sophisticated investors. This deregulation is based on the premise that our country's larger institutions and wealthier individuals can operate safely without stringent regulatory system micro-managing their market activity. This was a remarkably refreshing development, especially in the regulatory world where all instincts are to control events so tightly that nothing bad can happen (Johnson and Hazen 2004, p. 315).

These opinions were not only common in the United States, but they were mirrored on the other side of the Atlantic, especially in the United Kingdom. When talking about the Financial Service Authority's (FSA) approach to financial regulation, the director of Strategy and Risk recently argued: ". . . we should place responsibility on senior management wherever possible rather than trying to intervene as regulators ourselves" (Ross 2007). The Chairman of the FSA, Callum McCarthy was clear:

> . . . in a complex world, regulators should—and will—look increasingly to industry for assistance . . . I hope [the industry] will

often provide the solution without the need of any regulatory intervention. That is by far the best outcome . . . there are many, and better, means of solving problems than new regulations (McCarthy 2006).

Dissenting opinions were treated respectfully, but they never wielded much influence on policy during the previous decade. In consequence, capital markets regulation largely reflected the principles that:

- Financial markets are generally informationally efficient
- Self-interest and market discipline would police and govern institutions
- Risk and uncertainty can be modeled with technical skills
- Capital transactions between sophisticated users should be left to private contracts and the enforcement of courts
- Unfettered product innovation is welcome
- Regulators are less motivated, skilled, and knowledgeable than private players
- Systemic risk is decreasing and derivatives contribute to disperse and contain it
- Markets would naturally provide an optimal level of transparency

The Lehman Brothers bankruptcy on September 15, 2008, definitively shattered the consensus that pronounced government intervention in the capital markets is undesirable, undermining the ideological foundations of the edifice that guided policy-makers for more than 30 years. Alan Greenspan, perhaps the single most influential policy-maker in the deregulation era, claimed:

those of us who have looked to the self-interest of lending
institutions to protect shareholder's equity (myself especially)
are in a state of shocked disbelief . . . a vast risk management
and pricing system has evolved . . . this modern risk management
paradigm held sway for decades. The whole intellectual edifice,
however, collapsed in the summer of last year . . . (Greenspan
2008).

The policy actions taken since have been created in an intellectual and academic vacuum. Much like the 1930s, when actual events and policies predated new thinking, the global Financial Crisis of 2007–09 will be remembered as a watershed in new theories and policies.

Formerly marginalized voices criticizing the dominant view such as James Tobin, George Soros, Joseph Stiglitz, Nassim Nicholas Taleb, Adair Turner, Nouriel Roubini, Robert Shiller, and William R. White are now more carefully considered.

In one of the best depictions of the crisis, Professor Shiller argues:

> Classical theory tells us that financial markets will be stable. People will only make trades that they consider to benefit themselves . . . What this theory neglects is that there are times when people are too trusting. And it also fails to take into account that if it can do so profitably, capitalism produces not only what people really want, but also what they think they want . . . It will produce snake oil. Not only that: it may also produce the want for the snake oil . . . it is the role of the government . . . to see that these events do not occur . . . [the government] has the duty to regulate asset markets so that people are not falsely lured into buying snake-oil assets (Shiller 2009).

No new, emerging consensus is yet forthcoming, however. Substantial fringes of the financial industry and of academia resist the notion that the Financial Crisis was the product of too little regulation and market failures. Instead, they place the blame squarely on government and regulatory failure (see for instance Wallison 2009). This is, at the same time, true and misleading. On the one hand, regulators and experts had not properly assessed the risks inherent in certain markets and products, and regulation had gone missing in the "shadow banking system," which was one of the main causes of the crisis. In this respect, the crisis was also the result of regulatory failure. On the other, the dominant academic and political discourse and successful lobbying efforts pursued by parts of the financial services industry left regulators unwilling or toothless to play a significant role in capital markets (Leight 2009).

Some also contend that new regulations would do little to address the causes of the crisis and would—on the contrary—prevent market discipline to operate (e.g. Calomiris 2009). Indeed, substantial risk exists that more regulation would place more barriers to entry and stifle competition and innovation, and hence economic growth. However, market discipline and competition function correctly only in markets with complete information, rational agents, and no externalities—a far cry from today's financial markets. We develop these themes in more depth in Section 4.

The 2007–09 Financial Crisis supplies interesting examples of market-damaging behaviors that regulations should prevent. The perspectives offered in this section raise many theoretical and empirical questions concerning the present and future shape of capital market rules. How can we devise efficient and fair capital markets regulation? What are its fundamental principles and core objectives? What are the appropriate instruments to achieve those outcomes? Are markets to be regulated for the benefit of existing users or a broader constituency, taking into consideration a wider social sweep?

3. Definitions

The following definitions help clarify our discussion of the regulation of markets, products and institutions:

- **Markets** are procedural and organizational structures, that can be physical or virtual, created to facilitate the exchange of products. Markets can be divided into *primary* (when the issuer is raising capital or debt through issuance of securities) or *secondary* (where the trading of financial instruments takes place). Market regulation comprises rules regarding the trading, clearing, settlement, and custody of securities, and the governance of the institutions active along this chain (stock, futures and option exchanges, clearinghouses, and central securities depositories).
- **Products** are financial instruments, both tradable and non-tradable, characterized by investment objectives, external management of assets, and horizontal commonality (pooling). They include debt and equity securities, on-exchange and OTC derivatives, structured products, and funds.
- **Institutions** include intermediaries such as depository institutions (banks, credit unions, and savings banks) that collect deposits and funds from the public and loan these monies to borrowers, as well as nondepository institutions such as investment banks, insurance companies, pension funds, brokers, underwriters, and investment funds. Rules regarding institutions encompass *prudential regulation* (capital requirements designed to absorb different risks), *conduct of business regulation* (requirements concerning the interaction between institutions and their customers) and *organizational requirements* (rules regarding the governance structure of the financial actor).

Product and primary markets regulation concerns the manufacturing and underwriting of financial goods. In other sectors of the economy such as packaged food, pharmaceutical, electronics, and others, consumer safety concerns led to the establishment of regulatory agencies to inspect goods before their release on the market. Rules on financial products have not been as stringent or generalized. Regulators presume that institutional governance mechanisms and market discipline are sufficient to prevent the distribution of harmful products, and that excessive product regulation would slow innovation.

Conduct of business regulation mandates that financial firms treat their customers fairly, honestly and professionally, in accordance with the best interests of their clients (e.g., best execution) and prohibits them from engaging in fraudulent activities (e.g., churning, mis-selling, and front-running). This branch of regulation originates in the common law principle of fiduciary duty of agents towards principals.

Conduct of business regulation can lead to *organizational* and *governance requirements* that require financial institutions to separate functions or to structure in certain ways to avoid conflicts of interest and perverse incentives. These regulations may impose structural separations between divisions in banks. The structure of capital markets regulation is shown in Figure 3.1.

Secondary markets regulation concerns trading in publicly registered securities. Capital markets provide a price-discovery function that is essential for the well-functioning of the capitalist economy and is at the same time vulnerable to manipulation. Exceptions to immediate price discovery are made for specific transactions, in well-determined circumstances.

Hence, secondary markets regulation must ensure that the price formation process is well monitored to maintain confidence in fair and orderly markets. The degree to which these objectives are enforced differs importantly across securities markets and jurisdictions, with tight regulation of equity, on-exchange futures, and options markets, but less regulation of fixed income markets, and almost no regulation, at least until today, of OTC derivative and foreign exchange markets.

The next section identifies the conflicting forces of regulation and deregulation of the capital markets. The importance of these forces has varied through time in response to historical and political circumstances. Governments have reacted to popular pressure during times of crisis, but were constrained by the facts on the ground.

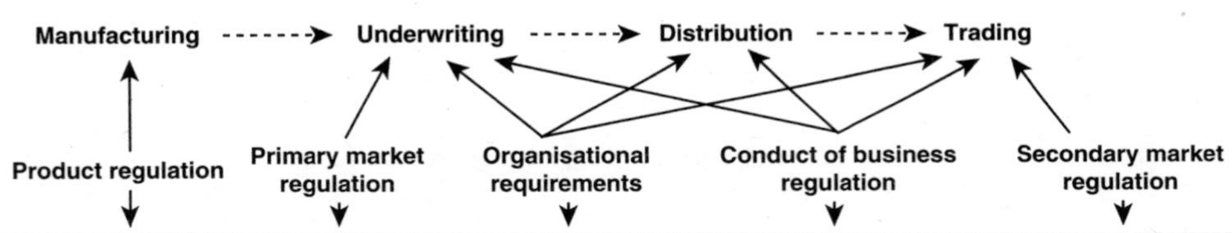

Manufacturing ------> Underwriting ------> Distribution ------> Trading

	Product regulation	Primary market regulation	Organisational requirements	Conduct of business regulation	Secondary market regulation
Rules	Investment fund rules (UCITS, mutual funds)	Prospectus, registration, rules on initial public offerings (IPOs)	Governance criteria, separation of functions, remuneration, internal controls, reporting	Best execution, suitability, appropriateness, transaction reporting	Market access, price transparency, market abuse rules, short selling rules
Rationale for Intervention	Investor protection, systemic stability	Disclosure, investor protection, asymmetries, agency problems	Conflicts of interest, ex post verification, moral hazard	Information asymmetries, agency problems	Market efficiency and integrity, information asymmetries
Examples of Misconduct	Churning, front-running,	Spinning, market timing, laddering	Biased advice, biased incentives, excessive risk-taking, welfare-reducing retrocessions	Churning, mis-selling, front-running	Insider trading, bang the close, corner and squeeze, phantom stocks

Figure 3.1 The Structure of Capital Markets Regulation
Source: Authors' elaboration.

4. Origins of Capital Markets Regulation

Broadly speaking, the first traces of government intervention in the securities markets in the modern era can be found in England at the end of the seventeenth century. In previous centuries, kings and princes around Europe had repeatedly failed to pay coupons on bonds issued, or defaulted on their obligations altogether, undermining their very efforts of borrowing from private investors long-term at low interest rates. In 1694, William III established the Bank of England to restore confidence in the gilt market.

The Bank of England served as an intermediary between investors and the government by attracting private capital and allocating it to the government with a guaranteed interest of 8 percent annually. This solution ensured the protection of private investors, and it was emulated in France, with the establishment of the General Bank in 1716 (Michie 2006, pp. 29–35). In 1697, under the pressure of growing public hostility towards speculation, the British Parliament enacted a piece of regulation—expiring in 1708—limiting the number of brokers, capping their fees, and forbidding them to trade on their own account (Banner 1998, pp. 39–40).

In 1719–20—in spite of these institutional changes—the first Europe-wide speculative financial bubble developed and burst (the "South Sea bubble" in England and the "Mississippi bubble" in France). In 1721, in the wake of the public outrage following the bursting of the bubble, the British Parliament acted to regulate securities contracts entered into, but not yet settled in two ways, leaving contracts unregulated going forward. First, it mandated registration of equity derivatives—in the modern terminology—on the book of the corporation whose underlying stock was in question; and, second, it invalidated any contract that was the result of covered or naked short selling (*ibid*, p. 80).

In 1724, the French government—convinced that uncontrolled trading contributed to inflating stock and bond prices—quickly seized the opportunity to control access to trading by establishing the first floor for government securities in Paris. Similar rules were put into place in Austria. However, in both jurisdictions trading continued outside official exchanges, despite the efforts of governments to control it. In 1734, the British government banned the use of options, contracts for difference, covered and naked short selling, and, finally, mandated that brokers keep a record of all transactions. Evidence that these rules were enforced is scarce, however, and the bill was finally repealed in 1860 (*ibid*, p. 106).

Throughout the eighteenth century, attitudes towards exchange markets were ambivalent. On the one hand, public opinion considered speculation morally and politically lamentable; on the other, a growing part of the population enjoyed the benefits of new investment opportunities. In consequence, new draconian proposals for limiting "stock jobbing" frequently made their appearance during economic downturns, but they were always rejected. It was not until the French Revolution in 1789 and the US stock market crash in 1792 that new measures were enacted.

In 1791, the French revolutionary government closed down the Paris Bourse and banned all joint-stock companies (Michie 2006, pp. 52–54). In 1789, the act establishing the US Treasury Department included rule against conflicts of interest and insider trading regarding public debt (Banner 1998, pp. 161–3). The state of New York passed a bill in 1792 forbidding covered and naked short selling and prohibiting public auctions for securities. As it was the case in England, the statute had limited impact, and it only drove contracts outside the official legal system.

In 1801, the London Stock Exchange formally came into existence as a prime example of self-regulation, followed in 1817 by the New York Stock and Exchange Board. These examples of self-regulation were highly successful, in the sense that—in modern jargon—the prices at these stock exchanges served a price discovery function for off-exchange transactions (*ibid*, p. 256).

In the nineteenth century, laissez-faire policies and self-regulation were dominant on both sides of the Atlantic. In the United States, a mistrust towards the federal government led to the repeal of two attempts to establish a central bank. It was only in 1911 that Kansas enacted the first Blue Sky Law—a state law regulating securities offerings. However, market participants largely ignored these state regulations.

The origins of twentieth century securities market regulation can be traced to the US Securities Act of 1933 and the Securities Exchange Act of 1934 following the 1929 Stock Market Crash. Similar acts also followed in some European countries, but not all. General statutory securities market regulation in Europe arrived much later and can be traced back to the action of the European Community in the late 1980s and early 1990s, with rules covering offerings, broker-dealers, and insider trading.

After having briefly reviewed the history of government intervention in the capital markets, the next section enquires about the rationale behind such rules.

5. Why is Regulation Needed?

One might legitimately ask why capital markets rules are needed. Some might say "let the buyer beware" (*caveat emptor*)—a principle that place the responsibility of supervision on the investor. Why should we entrust government bureaucrats with the supervision of securities markets and financial firms? Why cannot individuals look after their own interests when purchasing financial products? Do not market discipline and reputational incentives suffice to prevent damaging behaviors?

The reality is not so simple. Historical experience suggests that different forms of intervention are justified. Markets require private and public institutions to address market failures and to reduce transaction costs. Debates based on ideology rather than empirical evidence assume a stark dichotomy between *regulated* and *unregulated* markets, with government intervention completely missing from the latter. In reality, unregulated markets rely on judiciary enforcement *ex post* of private contracts, whereas regulated markets rely on an administrative system of direct control (Posner 2003, p. 383). The enforcement of contracts lowers transaction costs in private transactions, which would be hardly feasible without the implicit threat of legal suit (Coase 1960).

Securities law embraces the concept of fiduciary duty as a contractual basis for the relation between the customer and the professional investor. In the face of negligence, misconduct or fraud, customers can have recourse to courts to have their rights enforced. It is clear that this protection is far too weak on its own. Even in the presence of courts to enforce contracts, when left to private transactions, individuals and firms have a tendency to exploit positions of power, commit fraud for personal gain or just fail to co-operate in a way that would be socially optimal. Consider some recent examples from around the world of behaviors that are detrimental to the functioning of capital markets:

- In the period 2001–08, the UK mortgage giant HBOS—subsequently taken over by Lloyds TSB with the British government's support—encouraged systemic fraud in mortgage applications to expand its balance sheet.
- European and South American retail investors purchased bonds issued by Parmalat—a multinational Italian dairy company—marketed by financial advisors as safe assets, before the firm collapsed in 2003 under the weight of its financial shenanigans.

- In 2006, the hedge fund Amaranth Advisors LLC controlled as much as 80 percent of the open interest in US natural gas futures markets and attempted to manipulate the price of that commodity before imploding.
- Gome Electrical Appliances had its shares suspended for trading on the Hong Stock Exchange in 2008 after Huang Guangyu, the company's Chairman, was investigated for stock manipulation.
- Bernard Madoff ran a pyramidal scheme based in New York, totaling over US$64 billion, to defraud investors for over 15 years, which was uncovered at the end of 2008.
- The French bank Société Générale incurred €4.9 billion in losses in 2008 after Jérôme Kerviel, a trader, engaged in unauthorized trading activities.

Deviant behaviors are inherent in the nature of human beings and their institutions. The creation of supervisory and regulatory entities (as opposed to courts) specialized in capital markets attempts to remedy to these problems by direct supervision, improving the overall quality of markets. Among the possible preventive solutions to detrimental behaviors are:

- **Disclosure** aims at informing investors about the characteristics of products, the financial position of firms, and, broadly, reducing information asymmetries. Disclosure is the least intrusive mode of regulation, but it also assumes that those who receive the information understand it, are able to process it, and can make informed decisions based on it. Those who prepare the disclosures must also do so honestly and clearly.
- **Transparency** aspires to enhance market efficiency by providing price-sensitive information. It can be divided in pre- and post-trade. Pre-trade transparency forces market operators to publicize bid and ask orders for securities, aiming at improving price discovery and reducing bid-ask spreads. Post-trade transparency mandates the publication of security sales prices within a certain time limit to allow for verification of best execution.
- **Conduct of business rules** (covering, for example: conflicts of interest and short selling). The formulation of the rules is crucial, however. A very specific restriction may be more easily evaded, since technological and market developments can make a rule obsolete. On the other hand, principle-based rules can be more long-lasting, but they may be harder to pin down and enforce.

- **Mandates** force firms to do something they would not otherwise do (e.g., best execution, suitability, and appropriateness). Again, the specificity of the rule/principle impacts its effectiveness, durability, and enforceability.
- **Structural/functional restrictions** restrict firms from owning or operating some economic activities (e.g., Glass-Steagall Act of 1933, US restrictions of bank ownership by private equity, and the Volcker Rule currently being considered). The legislature may recognize that there is an inherent conflict in two economic activities and therefore impose ownership or functional restrictions.

What follows are a more specific discussions of the situations where capital markets, without direct or indirect statutory supervision (through regulated exchanges), have a tendency to fail because of information or coordination problems or wrong incentives.

5.1 Financial Products are Unlike Other Products

Financial products are unlike other goods and services on the market. When purchasing a financial product, investors buy something they cannot touch or evaluate directly. They effectively lend their money to unknown entities or individuals. Several factors make this category of products more prone to fraud and manipulation:

1. The uncertainty in putting a price on the value of the managers' present and future performance
2. The difficulty in pricing immaterial assets such as goodwill and intellectual property
3. The liquidity of financial products in comparison to transactions in material goods and services
4. A large part of a company's performance depends on unpredictable macro-economic factors such as monetary and fiscal policy, regulation, market sentiment, and technology
5. Both buyers and suppliers are bounded in their cognitive capacity in understanding complex risks and products

Primary markets regulation such as securities registration and prospectus compliance is designed to reduce this uncertainty. Securities authorities ensure that securities offerings do not constitute swindles based on fictitious companies or imaginary assets. Moreover, prospectuses provide some level of disclosure to potential investors. However, this regulation applies mainly to listed plain vanilla products (mostly equity and bonds), and to a lesser extent, or not at all, to complex financial instruments.

Because regulators deem professional investors able to obtain sufficient information when trading in complex financial instruments such as OTC derivatives and structured products, they do not require mandatory disclosure for such segments. As a result of the 2007–09 Financial Crisis, some have argued that *all* financial products should have the same form of controls as packaged food or pharmaceuticals, with a formal authorization process before they are brought to the market.

Regulated exchanges provide a function similar to a formal authorization process in which they stand behind the products listed on their markets. When companies list their stock or bonds on an exchange of good repute, they enjoy a reputational advantage over firms whose stocks or bonds trade over-the-counter.

5.2 Adverse Selection

The particular features of financial products and services give rise to a set of further problems. Managers hold more information than investors do because of their expertise and superior knowledge of the inner workings of their companies. This information structure is different from uncertainty (which affects both counterparties to the same degree), and it is known in the economics literature as information asymmetry (Akerlof 1970). Financiers tend to offer the worst securities to the market while retaining the best for themselves. This selection undermines confidence in the entire system. If buyers are unable to distinguish good from bad companies, they are unwilling to pay a price high enough for good companies to stay in the market, because "lemons" drive down the market-clearing price. Adverse selection takes place when the market is dominated by bad companies and investors lose confidence, stopping to transact in a gridlock-like situation.

Regulation and self-regulation can maintain minimum quality standards, reducing the information asymmetry between buyers and suppliers. Only external entities can provide signals about the quality of the products. Exchanges constitute entities that mandate the provision of information necessary to produce such meaningful signals. Through mandatory disclosure of well-defined price-sensitive information, the listing rules of regulated stock exchanges do much to reveal the quality of the company whose securities trade on that exchange.

This aspect generally makes on-exchange products more liquid than off-exchange ones.

5.3 Agency Problems

During the contract period, when buyers (*principals*) purchase a financial product, they entrust the supplier (*agent*) with the management of their assets. However, the interests of principals and agents rarely align. For instance, a company's management may want to maximize current earnings and favor short-term growth prospects, while equity holders may prefer to maximize long-term firm profits and dividends. Likewise, an investment advisor who gets a commission over certain products is very likely to give biased advice to customers. When the commission induces advisors to favor one product over another, advisors breach their fiduciary duty, as they no longer work in the best interests of their clients.

Principals have difficulty monitoring their agents because information is costly to collect. The combination of information asymmetries and conflict of interests create principal/agent problems (Mitnick 1973; Ross 1973). The European Union and the United States have defined fiduciary duties and set organizational requirements to contain the impact of agency problems. For instance, in the United States, investment advisers, broker–dealers, and regulated exchanges must disclose and manage conflicts of interest. In Europe, the Markets in Financial Instruments Directive (MiFID) requires investment advisors to disclose conflict of interests and to adopt clear policies towards clients.

However, a general fiduciary duty is hardly sufficient, and it is difficult to enforce. Thus, MiFID also mandates that the financial firm verify that the product being sold is *suitable* (for advised transactions or discretionary portfolio management) or *appropriate* (for execution-only services) for the customer, shifting the responsibility of supervision from the buyer to the supplier.

Moreover, as a result of the 2007–09 Financial Crisis, some have questioned the validity of the distinction between sophisticated and unsophisticated investors. Some pension funds, municipalities, and regional banks—generally considered sophisticated investors have purchased financial products whose underlying risks they did not fully grasp. Emblematic of this is the case of Italian municipalities that entered in derivative transactions with financial firms, losing large sums of money with repercussions to the public purse. The issue is whether they should be granted the same level of protection as retail investors.

Table 3.1 Market Failures Originating from Information Asymmetries

Root Cause	Information Asymmetries		
Time frame	*Ex ante*	**Contract period**	*Ex post*
Market failure	Adverse selection Hidden information	Agency problems Hidden action	Verification Hidden outcome
Outcome	Market breakdown, gridlock, mis-selling	Breach of fiduciary duty, conflicts of interest	Breakdown in confidence
Possible solution	Mandatory disclosure, suitability and appropriateness	Business of conduct regulation	Standards for professional auditing, class action procedures

Source: Adapted from Spencer (2000).

5.4 Coordination Problems

In the provision of public goods, economic agents are willing to shoulder less than a fair share of their cost of production. Collective action or coordination problems arise as a result. Market integrity and market confidence are public goods, because all participants reap the benefits, but few are willing to bear the costs of providing them. Without integrity and confidence, financial markets do not function correctly.

Investors must have faith that asset managers are looking after their interests. While they are aware of the inevitable tension between their interests and those of the agents, investors should not fear mis-selling, bad management, manipulation, or large fraud. If market confidence is not widespread, individuals, institutional investors, and even institutions will be reluctant to invest, lend to each other, and even transact.

Although a gross simplification, we can interpret the Financial Crisis of 2007–09 as a generalized collapse in confidence. The markets of securitized issuances, for instance, seized up as principals doubted the integrity of the products after default rates unexpectedly started to climb in the underlying pool of loans. For the same reason, liquidity in the interbank lending market dried up, because institutions did not know whom to trust. In short, confidence is part of the critical infrastructure of global capital markets.

Delegating the supervision of markets to an independent government agency or a liable self-regulatory organization (SRO) can remedy the problem of free riding. Through mandatory fees, agencies or SROs can bear the cost of monitoring agents, ensuring that appropriate rules are enforced and that managers do not misappropriate funds or act irregularly.

Self-regulation has its limits, however. Although more attuned to the needs and innovations of markets, SROs are more subject to capture and lenient supervision than are regulatory agencies. One way to make self-regulation more stringent is to render it enforceable in courts and thus avoid more burdensome administrative supervision. Another way is to make SROs liable for their decisions. We return on these themes in the next section.

Another type of coordination problem arises in the provision of price discovery. Liquid and centralized markets contribute to the formation of prices, which serve as signals to guide overall economic activity. Prices are public goods for which actors are not necessarily willing to shoulder the costs of preventing market manipulation and providing liquidity. That is partly why regulated exchanges charge higher fees than alternative trading venues such as MTFs, ECNs, systematic internalizes and OTC markets. There has been a tendency, at least for US-regulated markets, to externalize in part the market surveillance function towards Financial Industry Regulatory Authority (FINRA) to attempt to remedy to the free riding problem.

In the past, order concentration rules aimed at keeping trading activity centralized, fearing that dispersion of trading would diminish the significance of prices discovered on regulated exchanges. Slowly, preferences of competition over centralization and technological breakthroughs have allowed dispersed liquidity over different venues, while maintaining orderly price formation.

5.5 Systemic Risk

From a securities regulation perspective, systemic stability risks may arise from harmful financial innovation.[2] Proprietary product development may lead to market illiquidity, originating from the inability of other players to correctly price the issues. Illiquidity also affects the perception of the solvency of financial institutions because markets react unpredictably to uncertainty in the balance sheet.

Market participants argue that regulation should not force them to disclose the pricing of structured products and other exotic or complex derivatives, because these rules would discourage innovation and market making. They draw a parallel with intellectual property law, whereby product developers have a legal safeguard against reproduction of the product to provide an incentive to innovate.

However, this parallel is misleading. Prices of securities should not be subject to legal protection. Markets for books and pharmaceuticals can hardly become illiquid, whereas markets for complex securities can. Illiquidity cause prices to fall, with serious repercussion for the balance sheets of firms (a condition compounded by mark-to-market accounting). In short, monopolistic pricing of securities aggravates the fragility of the financial system, as the risk of illiquidity reduces the transparency of the balance sheets of financial firms and hurts price-discovery during times of turmoil.

Equity and futures exchanges have remained open and liquid during times of distress, when compared with other segments such as OTC derivatives, bonds, and foreign exchange, which experienced widening bid-ask spreads and illiquidity. Regulated exchanges have functioned as important outlets, letting investors liquidate open positions in the face of uncertainty. This last point poses a fundamental question: should regulators force more products on-exchange to make them more resilient? Alternatively, would standardization and multilateral clearing of certain complex products such as bespoke OTC derivatives be enough to reduce counterparty risk and address questions about the solvency of financial institutions?

5.6 Non-economic Rationales

Other rationales beside strict market failure can provide a sound basis for intervention. One can portray market irrationality as a special case of coordination problems, whereby self-interested rational agents cause a collectively irrational outcome. However, the literature of behavioral finance suggests that these patterns of behavior may be systematic. Mimicry, irrational exuberance and pessimism, limited investor attention, and noise trading are recurrent features of financial markets, which lead us to believe that agents' irrationality is more than just a deviation from normal behavior.

6. Why Does Regulation Fail?

Markets are imperfect, but so are public institutions. Countless stories of incompetence, bad faith, or risk aversion can be told about civil servants.

To paraphrase Queen Elizabeth II, one can pose the question to regulators: why did they not see the 2007–09 Financial Crisis coming? In a precrisis world, the consensus view was that the glass was half full rather than half empty. The unparalleled expansion in credit and derivative markets was on a sustainable path, most regulators may have thought. This subjectivist interpretation of reality and the herd behavior that from time to time characterize markets can also be applied to regulators.

6.1 Technical Failure

The first element to consider when looking at regulatory failure is its technical nature. Technical failure arises from poor information, poor rule-design, or poor enforcement. Bounded rationality affects market actors and regulators alike. Nevertheless, the precrisis assumption that markets have more information than government officials is valid. By definition, the decentralized structure of market activity produces and processes large amounts of data, and officials can be easily overwhelmed.

In consequence, government agencies do not have enough information, are not able to process it or are unable to find it when most necessary. Securities prospectuses often span hundreds of pages and the risks are buried in the avalanche of legal language. Moreover, complicated corporate structures of financial firms defy regulators' skills and jurisdiction, hiding risks where they are least likely to be uncovered. Finally, prior to the crisis, rapid financial innovation created new products and legal structures (such as synthetic collateralized debt obligations, credit-linked notes, and structured investment vehicles). Regulators did not fully understand their consequences and functions and often acted incorrectly or did not act at all.

Rules may also be responsible for technical failure, and the law of unintended consequences looms large when producing new rules. Poorly designed rules may encourage financial players to devise ways around them or provide perverse incentives that are detrimental for the correct functioning of the market. For instance, burdensome rules in public markets can drive activity in private markets or foreign jurisdictions, diminishing overall transparency or efficiency (so-called *regulatory arbitrage*). In that case, the net effect of regulation may be negative.

The final element in technical failure is poor enforcement. Absent strong enforcement mechanisms, financial regulation is unlikely to work. Officials need to be competent and committed to the existing rules. Too often bureaucrats operate in a culture of a checklist approach to compliance rather than looking at the rules' underlying objectives. Furthermore, political ideology can make regulators' lenient towards the firms they are supposed to oversee.

6.2 Regulatory Capture

In highly specialized sectors of the economy such as finance, regulatory capture is an ever-present danger. The fast pace of innovation and the specialized knowledge of the inner workings of financial markets make public officials reliant on private sources of information. Further, regulators spend a lot of time with the industry they should be regulating, and they are often confused about whose interests they are trying to protect.

The dilemma of independent securities regulators is that they have a tendency to protect the interests of the industry they regulate. Revolving doors between regulatory agencies and the financial industry are widespread, because without market experience regulators can hardly do their jobs correctly. Further, politicians are unsuitable to oversee the financial sector, given the populist pressure and their lack of technical expertise.

6.3 Lack of the Macro-picture

A clear lesson of the 2007–09 Financial Crisis is that although financial players may have not acted illegally at the micro-level, the enormous and rapidly growing scale of activity in financial markets was creating dangerous exposures at the macro-level. Before the crisis, financial supervision moved away from central banking towards integrated supervisory authorities, a process underway in many EU countries and elsewhere. This phenomenon stimulated legalistic supervision, missing the macro-picture. The creation of macro-prudential supervisory authorities in both the United States and the European Union addresses this shortcoming, but many questions remain on how they will function. At the global level, the Financial Stability Board (FSB) is now charged with coordinating this function.

In the future, these new authorities thus are expected to warn and take action against bubbles and imbalances. They should identify, monitor and prioritize all macro-financial risks. In doing so, they may be subject to heavy pressures from interest groups, they may be criticized for stifling economic growth and job creation, or they may be accused of missing the real bubble. It is far from certain that regulation will fail less in the future, even after the 2007–09 Financial Crisis.

7. The Present Debate on Securities Market Regulation

The previous sections presented how capital markets regulation is structured, its origins, rationale, and failures. In this section, we look at how regulators have applied these principles in practice in the EU and the US regulatory jurisdictions. We focus primarily on the regulation of secondary securities markets where important changes are taking place. Our discussion employs the concepts developed in the preceding section to evaluate the present debate on the future shape of capital markets regulation.

7.1 Fragmentation and Liquidity

The Financial Crisis reoriented the debate on the regulation of securities markets trading towards liquidity and transparency issues, and the advantages of mandating centralized solutions versus open competition between market infrastructures. Before the 2007–09 crisis, market participants and regulators in the European Union and the United States were involved in intensive debates on the balance between liquidity and fragmentation. In legislation adopted just before the crisis, the two jurisdictions left scope for a large degree of competition for the markets to work out the most appropriate solutions. It is very likely that in the post-crisis world, the pendulum will swing back towards mandating more centralized solutions, essentially for the sake of transparency and systemic stability. This preference will be strengthened by the debate still to come on the role of investment banks in the financial system.

The core pieces of market regulation in the EU and the US equity markets are MiFID and Regulation National Market System (NMS), respectively. MiFID (Markets in Financial Instruments Directive, EC 2004/39) intended to complete the process started with the 1993 Investment Services Directive (ISD) and further liberalized Europe's capital markets by abolishing order concentration rules in various European countries. Reg NMS aimed at modernizing and strengthening the NMS of 1975 for equity securities trading. Although Reg NMS is more limited in scope than MiFID, an in-depth comparison reveals the core issues in the debate of the regulation of securities trading: how to find a balance between efficient price formation and competition.

Too much fragmentation of order venues can lead to lower liquidity and a decline in the quality of the price formation process, leading to higher bid-ask spreads and higher prices for investors, as the Securities and Exchange Commission (SEC) argued in its case in favor of Reg NMS. Regulatory interventions on both sides of the Atlantic strike a balance between providing the public good of price-discovery by resolving the coordination problem of traders and favoring competition of trading venues, which lowers prices for end-users. Also, in the debate preceding the adoption of MiFID, safeguards were added to maintain some degree of concentration in trading, but these may need to be clarified, as the actual functioning of the new directive becomes more evident.

Research does not provide a satisfactory answer to the question of the potential harm of fragmentation. In a review of both US- and non-US-based empirical research, Levin (2003) finds no conclusive answer. Network externalities tend to make trading activity gravitate toward the most liquid markets, but at the same time markets have to cater to a variety of demands coming from traders. A balance must be struck between the benefits of a fragmented marketplace, where the diversity of structures meets the different needs of the traders, and the benefits of an integrated marketplace, where the information content of centrally discovered prices may well be maximized (Levin 2003, p. 58). Conflicting forces are at work in securities markets.

Incentives also come into play: a monopoly exchange will not be forced to adapt its pricing structure or technology, which reduces market efficiency. In addition, specialized venues may only be interested in the most lucrative trades or most actively traded stocks (*skimming*), leaving the others to the traditional market, all of which affect the quality of the price formation process in the markets overall.

The choice between off- versus on-exchange trading also raises conduct of business issues. Conflict of interest problems arise as a result of internalization of trading, where the intermediaries' interests are not necessarily similar to those of their clients. Exchanges, on the other hand, may also face conflicts of interest, if their pricing structures favor large clients or if intermediaries dominate their boards.

Faced with these questions, the European Union and the United States have taken comparable but differing approaches. While overall the fiduciary duty of acting in the best interest of the client has long been enshrined in legislation, its practical application and implementation varied widely and market developments differed importantly. At the same time as the US authorities thought it necessary to reduce fragmentation in securities trading, EU legislators pushed for more liberalization. A closer comparison of the approaches and experiences in both jurisdictions, which total approximately 74 percent of annual global equities markets turnover at the end of December 2009 according to the World Federation of Exchanges, is indicative of global trends in securities trading regulation.

Reg NMS is based on the 1934 Securities Exchange Act. It reinforced the best execution principle enshrined in the National Market System (1975) by prohibiting "trade-throughs" in automated markets, and abolished the trade-through rule for manual quotations that protected the manual trading floors of the established exchanges.[3] While the NMS had strengthened competition among trading venues, this process had—according to the SEC—led to declining price quality.

MiFID, and its predecessor—the 1993 (ISD)—are based upon the EU Treaty, and their objective is to create a single market. EU directives or regulations flesh out and detail the relevant freedoms set forth in the EU Treaty, namely the free provision of services and the free movement of capital. MiFID abolished order concentration rules, which was still in force at the time of its adoption in 2004 in several member states, and mandated that trades be executed following detailed best execution principles. Banks can internalize trades, but need to follow strict transparency rules for trades of standard market sizes in liquid shares (Art. 27 MiFID). Banks or exchanges can also create alternative, less-regulated multilateral trading facilities (MTFs). MiFID and Reg NMS were both implemented in the second half of 2007.

Although a consolidated pan-European trade reporting system for equity transactions does not exist, we cite the most reliable source of information that the Centre for European Policy Studies (CEPS) could identify. The detailed numbers are much debated, but that does not change the overall picture. As a result of MiFID, new trading venues have managed to capture increasing market shares, forcing exchanges to adapt their tariff structures. However, so far, liquidity fragmentation has not deteriorated orderly price formation. Spreads at the larger European exchanges have further narrowed.[4] However, exchanges have highlighted that the new trading facilities piggyback on the price formation process of the traditional exchanges, and only trade the most liquid shares, which entirely conforms with the argument about skimming developed earlier.[5] In addition, it seems that best execution is not uniformly applied across the European Union, according to the data of one trading platform, Equiduct. Hence, it is too early to draw far-reaching conclusions set by the European example.[6]

Figure 3.2 shows how the European share trading market has drastically changed in its composition over the last years. The market shares of the established exchanges shrank radically, whereas new entrants managed to capture a growing part of the market. The market share of the main regulated securities exchange in the European Union, the London Stock Exchange (LSE), declined from 35 percent to 24 percent from 2008 to 2009. Within the local stock market index, the FTSE 100, the LSE has a market share of about 60 percent, down from about 80 percent the year before. The most successful new entrant, the Multilateral Trading Facility (MTF) Chi-X, grabbed a 12.5 percent market share in 2009 of the total European reported trading volume. In addition, as a result of the technological developments discussed in the following section, the number of trades on the order book has sharply increased, reducing OTC trades as a share of total turnover. In the case of LSE, the number and value of trades off order book halved between 2006 and 2009.

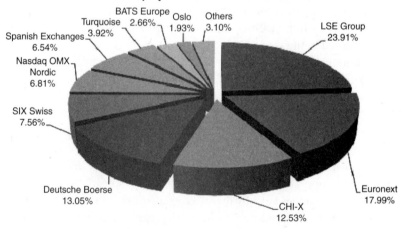

EU Equity Markets - 2009 Market Shares

Figure 3.2 Trading Centers and Estimated Market Shares of the Most Important Trading Venues in Europe, by Reported Trading Volume (2009)
Source: Thomson Reuters

A similar trend has been observed in the United States, where the abolition of protection for manual quotations in Reg NMS led to a dramatic reduction in the market share of the New York Stock Exchange. In January 2005, New York Stock Exchange (NYSE) executed 79.1 percent of the consolidated share volume in its listed stocks, compared with 27.4 percent by end 2009 (see Figure 3.3). At the same time, NYSE's speed of execution for small immediately executable orders was 10.1 seconds in January 2005, compared with 0.7 seconds in October 2009, its daily turnover in terms of number of transactions increased tenfold, and the value of trades threefold (SEC 2010). As with the European Union, fragmentation does not seem to have harmed market quality. In a detailed analysis, O'Hara and Ye (2009) find that fragmentation in US markets generally reduces spreads and transaction costs and increases execution speed.

Hence, the evolution in securities markets in the European Union and the United States has started to move in parallel. Whereas the main European trading centers had automated trade matching in place since the early 1990s, the United States continued to have the protection of manual quotations until Reg NMS came into force. On the other hand, the European Union still allowed concentration rules until MiFID came into force in November 2007, whereas in the United States, various Automated Trading Systems (ATSs) had been competing with the main markets since the mid-1990s.

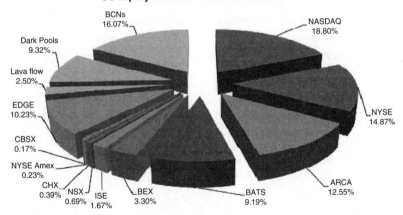

US Equity markets - 2009 Market Shares

BCNs 16.07%
NASDAQ 18.80%
Dark Pools 9.32%
Lava flow 2.50%
EDGE 10.23%
NYSE 14.87%
CBSX 0.17%
NYSE Amex 0.23%
CHX 0.39%
NSX 0.69%
ISE 1.67%
BEX 3.30%
BATS 9.19%
ARCA 12.55%

Figure 3.3 Trading Centers and Estimated Share Volume in NMS Stocks (2009)
Source: Tabb Group.

Other developed markets are following the liberalization trend set by the European Union and the United States, though market shares of new entrants are not yet significant. Japan followed the examples of the European Union and the United States in abolishing concentration rules, and introducing best execution rules, but Japanese equity markets are not as fragmented (Osaki, 2004). In Canada, fragmentation is just starting. China and most Asian markets, on the other hand, strictly prohibit off-exchange trading. IOSCO, the International Organization of Securities Commissions, has not taken a clear position yet on the issues of fragmentation and liquidity, though it analyzed them some years ago (IOSCO 2001).

7.2 Transparency

A policy issue on both sides of the Atlantic concerns the role of dark pools of liquidity on the order book of exchanges and in banks. In essence, these issues regard the appropriate level of transparency. Although markets may provide a suboptimal quantity of information, regulators should be careful about forcing participants to disclose too much. Protecting small investors and reducing information asymmetries are worthy objectives, but they should not be pursued at the expense of reducing the overall quality of the price formation process. The debate boils down to finding a balance between fairness, efficiency, and market confidence.

Dark pools offer anonymous trading services to institutional investors and others seeking to execute medium to large trading orders (though the order size accepted has been declining down to 100 shares). They minimize the movement of prices against the trading interest, reducing overall trading costs. Exchanges have been at the forefront in getting more order flow on exchange, but they delay pretrade reporting of big orders with so-called "iceberg orders."

Exact data on the size of dark orders in the European Union and the United States are difficult to come by: There is no single definition of dark pools, and most of these trades are reported to the established exchanges and should be reflected in their data on volume. The SEC data, as reported in Figure 3.3 earlier, estimate the share of broker dealer internalization and dark pools at about 25.4 percent. In Europe, formal internalization—as defined by MiFID—is extremely limited (thought to be around 1–2 percent), the share of dark pools is estimated at about 2–3 percent.

As a result of the Financial Crisis and the demand for more transparency, the share of off-exchange trading will likely decline. In the European Union, the MiFID legislation on the subject seems not well implemented or is subject to differing interpretations. Small trades should follow the rules on systemic internalization (Art. 27 of MiFID), but it is unclear how the rules apply to the splitting of order flow over different venues. In the United States, the 2010 SEC Concept Release seeks views on the fairness of dark pools and on whether undisplayed liquidity undermines the quality of the public price discovery process (SEC 2010, p. 68). The question boils down to whether the reduction in trading costs has benefited end-investors and whether investors have still confidence in the fairness of markets. A strict enforcement of best execution and more transparency of costs along the whole trading chain should prevail in both jurisdictions.

7.3 Conduct of Business and Secondary Trading Rules

In the United States, conduct of business rules regarding equity, bond, and on-exchange derivatives markets date back from the Great Depression. The Securities Act of 1933 and the Securities Exchange Act of 1934 regulated primary and secondary markets, respectively, for "securities" defined as stocks, bonds, and debentures by subjecting them to registration, antifraud, and antimanipulation provisions. The 1934 Act also created the Securities and Exchange Commission (SEC) to enforce the new rules. After a few years, US legislators strengthened the existing, parallel regime for physical commodity and commodity derivatives markets in 1936 with the Commodity Exchange Act, which was extended to financial derivatives in 1974 together with the creation of the Commodity Futures Trading Commission.

In 1962, the SEC first enforced the best execution principle in a litigated enforcement case against a broker. However, it was not until later—when competition among trading venues arose—that this concept acquired greater significance. Also in the 1960s, the principles of "know-your-customer" and "suitability" emerged to battle against brokers pursuing high-pressure sales tactics. These legal mandates aim at reducing information asymmetries and protecting investors from fraud and manipulation, adapting the concept of fiduciary duty to the context of capital markets.

Unlike in the United States, in the European Union, detailed conduct of business rules for securities trading are a recent phenomenon.

Even in the most developed capital market, the United Kingdom, conduct of business rules were the domain of self-regulatory bodies until the mid-1990s. The European Union's 1993 (ISD) only set some general fiduciary duty principles, but left the implementation and the enforcement to the member states with large differences across the Continent.

The first EU rule on insider trading (Council Directive 89/592) came into force in 1994. Unlike in the United States, a charge of illegal trading under EU law was not based on a breach of fiduciary trust but only on the possession (and use) of nonpublic information or information that if made public would have a significant impact on the stock price (Karmel 1999). Primary insiders are prohibited from either trading or giving tips to others, and secondary insiders are prohibited from trading, but are not subject to provisions against providing information. Before, several member states placed no statutory restraint against insider dealing, and the regulations that did exist differed widely. As with the Major Holdings Directive (88/628/EEC), which set rules for disclosure of acquisition of major stakes in listed companies, implementation did not come about smoothly. Germany, for example, only implemented the Insider Trading Directive in 1995, four years after the required date.

The Market Abuse Directive (2003/6/EC) replaced the former Insider Trading Directive, detailing the measures and extending it to market manipulation. However, the directive deals with market manipulation and insider dealing in financial instruments listed on EU-regulated markets only, but does not apply to instruments listed on alternative markets, or nonlisted products. In the case of insider dealing, it also covers financial instruments not admitted to trading on a regulated market, even though the value depends on financial instruments admitted to trading on a regulated market. Hence, the directive clearly omits an important part of the possible malpractices. The Commission is currently consulting for the extension of the Directive.[7]

MiFID implemented some conduct of business principles already present in the United States (though adapted to the European context) such as best execution and suitability, while creating some anew such as appropriateness. Suitability and appropriateness shift the burden of responsibility from retail investors to investment firms to check that the financial products sold are suitable (for advised transactions or discretionary portfolio management) or appropriate (for execution-only services) for the client. Best execution, on other hand, aims at ensuring investors get the best price for their orders. Moreover, MiFID sets stringent rules for management or disclosure of conflicts of interest, devised to overcome or mitigate principal–agent problems. These rules can be waived for eligible counterparties, that is, institutional and professional investors (we have seen in the foregoing section how ill-suited these categories may be).

Overall, the conduct of business and securities trading rules are more clear-cut in the United States than in the European Union. However, both regimes have failed to properly enforce the rules, as exemplified by the Crisis, and are trying to reform their institutional structure. The implementation of MiFID across the European Union is not homogenous, for example, and much work remains to be done to ensure proper enforcement of its provisions.[8] The creation of European supervisory authorities, as further to the proposals of the de Larosière report, should improve this situation.

Although the US regulatory regime has extensive rules, certain regulatory loopholes proved crucial in run up of the Financial Crisis. The US Commodity Futures Modernization Act of 2000 exempted OTC derivatives (including credit default swaps and collateralized debt obligations) from reporting requirements and market monitoring. One has to wonder to what extent financial history would be different, had this segment of the market been under the supervision of public officials.

7.4 Technology

The primary driver and enabler of transformation in equity trading has been the continuous evolution of technologies for generating, routing, and executing orders. Smart order routing is the key technology of the process, providing access to multiple exchanges, MTFs, dark pools, and broker pools to allow buy- and sell-side firms to achieve best execution of trades while minimizing market impact.

Another fundamental technological advance is algorithmic trading, which uses computer programs for entering trading orders with the algorithm deciding on aspects such as the timing, price, or quantity, and in many cases initiating orders without human intervention. Institutional traders use algorithmic trading to divide large orders into several smaller orders to manage market impact and risk. Sell-side traders, such as market makers and some hedge funds, provide liquidity to the market, generating and executing orders automatically.

"High-frequency trading" (HFT)—as the term suggests—employs algorithmic trading to trade with high frequency to profit from small spreads and price changes across markets in fractions of seconds. In the United States, high-frequency trading accounts for about 50 percent of total volume or higher (SEC 2010, p. 45). In Germany, algorithmic trading volume stood at 43 percent in 2008 (Engelen and Lannoo 2010, p. 37).

The fact that exchanges want to be as close to the trading community as possible, and vice versa, illustrates the importance of trading technologies. Euronext moved its trade matching engine from Paris to London to reduce the latency in transmitting orders for trades. In the United States and elsewhere, exchanges offer colocation services that enable exchange customers to place their servers in close proximity to the exchange's matching engine.

The central role of technology raises fundamental regulatory problems related to its accessibility, and more generally, the role of regulation. In the United States, the SEC launched a consultation on the subject in early 2010 to examine whether this evolution meets its objectives, and in particular, the interests of long-term investors and smaller institutions. Can smaller institutions still afford such systems and compete successfully? Do these new technologies enhance market quality? The SEC also questions the impact on market structure, specifically on very liquid versus small stocks (SEC 2010, p. 35).

In a recent study on the US market, Angel, Harris, and Spatt (2010) analyze these questions and argue that the impact of information technology has been very positive overall. "Virtually every dimension of US equity market quality is now better than ever. Execution speeds have fallen, which greatly facilitates monitoring execution quality by retail investors. Retail commissions have fallen substantially and continue to fall. Bid-ask spreads have fallen substantially and remain low. . . . Market depth has marched steadily upward" (Angel, Harris and Spatt 2010, p. 5). According to the authors, the introduction of computerized trading systems and high-speed communications networks allowed exchanges, brokers, and dealers to better serve and attract clients. The authors warn against ill-conceived responses to recent changes in the trading environment, which could lead to deterioration in market quality. However, they also call for action on broker–dealers with poor risk management standards, which could enchain systemic risks, and against front-running practices.

A similar debate on the impact of technology has started in Europe in the context of a possible revision of the MiFID directive. Considering the specialized literature on the subject, it is clear that the impact of

MiFID on technological change has been very positive. The question remains whether end clients perceive these changes positively and are confident in the fairness of markets and whether EU rules have to be reinforced following the US example.

7.5 Non-equity Markets

Most of the aforementioned rules are applicable to equity markets and not, or not to the same degree, to other segments of the securities markets. Since the Financial Crisis, a consensus is emerging that more transparency is needed in bond and OTC derivative markets, but the discussion is still on how to implement change.

Under the European Union's MiFID directive, general conduct of business provisions apply to provision of services in all financial instruments, but the pre- and post-trade transparency requirements now only apply to equity markets. A clause for extending the transparency provisions to non-equity markets is foreseen. In the United States, a system has been in place for years for mandatory reporting of over-the-counter secondary market transactions in eligible fixed income securities. All broker dealers are obliged to report transactions in corporate bonds to the Trade Reporting and Compliance Engine (TRACE). These prices then are reported to market participants with a 15 minute lag. Nevertheless, the securities trading rules of Reg NMS, discussed in the foregoing section, apply to equity markets only.

Before the crisis, banks and other intermediaries profiting from spreads argued against more transparency in bond and derivative markets because of the lack of evidence of market failure. In addition, they argued that bond and derivative markets are, unlike equity markets, composed of a multitude of different contracts, which are mostly traded among professional investors. Regulators generally bought this argument and went along. Indeed, more price transparency may hurt market making, and thus reduce liquidity in these markets (Casey and Lannoo 2009, p. 167). It is clear that, with the crisis in hindsight, but also with the initial experience of Reg NMS and MiFID, that these arguments no longer hold.

Initiatives discussed in the European Union and United States envisage a set of measures to achieve greater transparency and a safer, more stable market infrastructure, to mitigate counterparty risk and encourage a more responsible use of derivative financial instruments. The European Union intends to push for a high degree of standardization of these products that would be centrally cleared and possibly traded on exchanges. Higher capital requirements would apply for transacting OTC derivatives that cannot be centrally cleared.

The United States will only request that eligible contracts be centrally cleared. The industry is also taking initiatives to create central data repositories of derivative financial instruments. The question of how regulation defines eligible contracts remains, however. Ambiguous wording of the rules may lead market participants to devise non-standardized contracts with the purpose of avoiding regulation.

Hence, although there is a tendency to question the applicability of equity securities trading rules to OTC markets, more securities may be traded on exchanges following the Financial Crisis. Regulators probably should also draw conclusions from the crisis on which regulatory tools are the most effective: the regulation of markets, institutions or products. It seems that regulated markets have continued to function correctly, notwithstanding huge upheaval, that further product regulation will be needed, certainly on the derivative side, but that the biggest problem remains in the supervision of institutions. The European Union, and above all the United States, has a very extensive regulatory system covering the conduct of business of institutions. It includes rules to enforce the fiduciary duty towards clients, which are crystallized in the "best execution" concept and "know your customer" provisions, rules on price transparency and reporting, rules battling conflicts of interest, market manipulation and insider trading. The Crisis Revealed that much work remains to be done to make these rules work in practice.

8. Conclusion

The debate on the scope and appropriate degree of capital markets regulation, already in *"perpetuum mobile"* before the 2007–09 Financial Crisis, was reinvigorated by events in this Crisis. This essay provides an overview of the regulation of capital markets and supplies normative and conceptual tools to debate the future development of regulation. Further, this essay provides a sketch of the emerging consensus about new regulatory initiatives.

We believe that the Crisis will cause the domain of capital markets regulation to be further extended. How far remains to be seen. Principles common to equity market regulation, such as pre- and post-trade transparency, strict best execution requirements, more concentration of central multilateral clearing and trading platforms, tighter conduct of business requirements for the operators in the markets, and stricter product rules, will likely be applied to other markets.

Equity markets have remained liquid in the face of an enormous slump in turnover, with spreads declining even during times of distress. However, because the equity markets regulatory model requires a high degree of product standardization—affecting market development and product innovation—it cannot be extended indefinitely. The key question in the coming years is devising an appropriate response for other markets.

Technological developments in securities markets require regulators to continuously adapt their regulatory frameworks to ensure that the basic principles of transparency, efficiency and fairness continue to apply. At the same time, the need to continuously adjust regulations suggests that a higher level of abstraction in regulation is missing. Should not the principles survive technological progress and be generic in their application? How can regulators devise principles that are not so vague as to be insignificant but general enough to pass the test of time? In the end, this issue turns on the question of principles-based versus rules-based regulation. While many believe the former approach is the best to follow, the present trend is clearly towards the latter.

The Financial Crisis was a life test for our markets-based economy, in which regulated exchanges play central roles. The financial market upheaval revealed inefficiencies in our regulatory framework. Clearly, regulators must think carefully about how to restore the public trust in our financial system.

▰ 9. References

Acharya, Viral and Matthew Richardson (eds) (2009) *Restoring Financial Stability: How to Repair a Failed System*, Hoboken: John Wiley & Sons.

Akerlof, George A. (1970) "The market for 'Lemons': Quality uncertainty and the market mechanism," *Quarterly Journal of Economics*, Vol. 84, No. 3, August, pp. 480–500.

Akerlof, George A. and Robert J. Shiller (2009) *Animal Spirits: How Human Psychology Drives the Economy, and Why It Matters for the Global Capitalism*, Princeton: Princeton University Press.

Algorithmic Trading and Smart Order Routing (2009) *A Buy-Side Handbook*, London: The Trade, 2009. *www.thetradenews.com*.

Angel, James J., Larry Harris and Chester Spatt (2010) *Equity Trading in the 21st Century*, Knight Capital Group.

Authers, John (2009) "Wanted: New model for markets," *Financial Times*, September 29.

Banner, Stuart (1998) *Anglo-American Securities Regulation: Cultural and Political Roots, 1690–1860*, Cambridge: Cambridge University Press.

Bator, Francis M. (1958) "The anatomy of market failure," *The Quarterly Journal of Economics*, Vol. 72, No. 3, August, pp. 351–379.

Benston, George J. (1973) "Required disclosure and the stock market: An evaluation of the Securities Exchange Act of 1934," *American Economic Review*, Vol. 63, No. 1, pp. 132–55.

Black, Bernard S. (2001)"The legal and institutional preconditions for strong securities markets," *UCLA Law Review*, Vol. 48, pp. 781–855.

Brunnermeier, Markus et al. (2009) "The fundamental principles of financial regulation," *Geneva Reports on the World Economy*, Preliminary conference draft, No. 11, International Center for Monetary and Banking Studies and Centre for Economic Policy Research, January.

Calomiris Charles W. (2009) "Financial innovation, regulation and reform," *Cato Journal*, Vol. 29, No.1 (Winter), pp. 65–91.

Casey, Jean-Pierre and Karel Lannoo (2009) *The MiFID Revolution*, Cambridge: Cambridge University Press.

CFA Institute (2009) "Market microstructure: The impact of fragmentation under the Markets in Financial Instruments Directive."

Coase, Ronald (1960) "The problem of social cost," *Journal of Law and Economics*, Vol. 3, No. 1, October, pp. 1–44.

European Capital Markets Institute (2010) "Restoring Investor Confidence in European Capital Markets," *Report of the European Investors Working Group*, February.

European Commission (EC) (2009) "Call for evidence: Review of Directive 2003/6/EC on insider dealing market manipulation," June.

Engelen, Peter-Jan and Karel Lannoo (eds) (2010) *Facing New Regulatory Frameworks in Securities Trading*, Antwerp: Intersentia.

Greenspan, Alan (2008) "The Financial Crisis and the role of federal regulators," Hearing before the Committee of Oversight and Government Reform, US House of Representative, 111th Congress, October 23, 2008. Available at http://oversight.house.gov/images/stories/documents/20081023100438.pdf.

International Organization of Securities Commissions (IOSCO) (2001) "Transparency and market fragmentation," November.

International Organization of Securities Commissions (IOSCO) (2003) "Objective and principles of securities regulation," May.

Johnson, Philip M. and Thomas L. Hazen (2004) *Derivatives Regulation*, New York: Aspen Publishers.

Karmel, Roberta (1999) "The case for a European Securities Commission," *Columbia Journal of Transnational Law*, Available at SSRN: http://ssrn.com/abstract=178228.

Langevoort, Donald C. (1992) "Theories, Assumptions, and Securities Regulation: Market Efficiency Revisited," *University of Pennsylvania Law Review*, Vol. 140, No. 3, pp. 851–920.

Lannoo, Karel (2007) "MiFID and Reg NMS: A test-case for substituted compliance," *ECMI Policy Brief No. 8.*

Leight, Jessica (2009) "The crisis of old models: Theories of regulation post-2008," Paper presented at the Tobin project's conference on "Government and markets: Ferment in the face of the crisis," Yulee, Florida, April.

Levin, Mattias (2003) *Competition, fragmentation and transparency: Assessing the ISD review*, Brussels: CEPS.

Llewellyn, David (1999) "The economic rationale for financial regulation," Occasional Paper Series No 1, April, London: FSA.

McCarthy, Callum (2006) "IOSCO Conference—opening speech," IOSCO Conference, November 16, 2006, available at http://www.fsa.gov.uk/pages/Library/Communication/Speeches/2006/1116_cm.shtml.

McCormick, Robert E. (1981) *Politicians, Legislation and the Economy: An Inquiry into the Interest-Group Theory of Government*, Hingham: Martinus Nijhoff Publishing.

Michie, Ranald C. (2006) *The Global Securities Market: A History*, Oxford: Oxford University Press.

Mitnick, Barry M. (1973) "Fiduciary rationality and public policy: The theory of agency and some consequences," Paper presented at the 1973 Annual Meeting of the American Political Science Association, New Orleans, Louisiana, September 1973.

O'Hara, Maureen and Mao Ye (2009) Is Market Fragmentation Harming Market Quality?, March, available from: http://ssrn.com/abstract=1356839.

Ogus, Anthony (1994) *Regulation: Legal Form and Economic Theory*, New York: Oxford University Press.

Osaki, Sadakazu (2004) "The enactment of the amended securities and exchange law (in Japan)," *Capital Research Journal*, Vol. 7, No. 3.

Palmiter, Alan R. (2008) *Securities Regulation*, New York: Aspen Publishers.

Phillips, Susan M. and J. Richard Zecher (1981) *The SEC and the Public Interest*, Cambridge: The MIT Press.

Posner, Richard A. (2003) *Economic Analysis of Law, 6th Edition*, New York: Aspen Publishers.

Ross, Stephen A. (1973) "The economic theory of agency: The principal's problem," *The American Economic Review*, Vol. 63, No. 2, Papers and Proceedings of the Eighty-fifth Annual Meeting of the American Economic Association, May, pp. 134–39.

Ross, Verena (2007) "London's financial markets and the FSA's approach to financial regulation," FSA Economist Conference, December 4, 2007, available at http://www.fsa.gov.uk/pages/Library/Communication/Speeches/2007/1204_vr.shtml.

Scott, Hal (ed.) (2005) *Capital Adequacy Beyond Basel: Banking, Securities and Insurance*, New York: Oxford University Press.

Securities and Exchange Commission (2010) Concept Release on Equity Market Structure, January.

Shiller, Robert J. (2009) "A failure to control the animal spirits," *Financial Times*, March 9, 2009.

Spencer, Peter D. (2000) *The Structure and Regulation of Financial Markets*, New York: Oxford University Press.

Stigler, George J. (1971) "The theory of economic regulation," *The Bell Journal of Economics and Management Science*, Vol. 2, No. 1, Spring, pp. 3–21.

Stiglitz, Joseph E. (2009) "Government failure versus market failure: Principles of regulation," in Balleisen, Edward and David Moss (eds.) *Government and Markets: Toward a New Theory of Regulation*, Cambridge: Cambridge University Press.

Taleb, Nassim Nicholas (2007) *The Black Swan: The Impact of the Highly Improbable*, New York: Random House.

Wallison, Peter J. (2009) "Regulation without reason: The Group of Thirty report," Financial Services Outlook, American Enterprise Institute for Public Policy Research, January 2009.

Notes

* Comments by Diego Valiante are gratefully acknowledged.

1 From a legal perspective, in spite of being tradable instruments, derivatives generally do not fall under the definition of "securities." For instance, in the United States, the legal definition of "commodity" defines most derivatives. In the European Union, derivatives and securities are lumped under the definition of "financial instruments." In this chapter, we use the definition of "securities" to encompass derivatives because they share many characteristics with narrowly defined "securities" such as stocks and bonds.

2 For an excellent discussion of systemic risk from a prudential perspective, please refer to Acharya and Richardson (2009).

3 A trade-through is the execution of a trade at a price inferior to a protected quotation for a NMS stock. A protected quotation must be displayed by an automated trading center, must be disseminated in the consolidated quotation data, and must be an automated quotation that is the best bid or best offer of an exchange, SEC (2010) p. 26.

4 See CFA (2009) for an extensive overview of the impact of fragmentation under MiFID.

5 An illustrative example is the breakdown of the IT infrastructure of the London Stock Exchange (LSE) on November 27, 2009. For the duration of four hours when the trading system was down, the most well-known MTFs could not price trades in LSE-listed stock.

6 Equiduct found that 33 percent of the trades could have achieved a better price (or extra cost of € 30 million in one month), see www.equiduct-trading.com.

7 European Commission (2009), Review of Directive 2003/6/EC on insider dealing and market manipulation.

8 The European Commission will review the application of the MiFID rules in the course of 2010.

PART II

FIVE DEFINING INNOVATIONS

4

A Retrospective on the Unfixing of Rates and Related Deregulation

ROBERTA S. KARMEL

▬ I. Overview

Traditional stock exchanges were membership organizations where stock exchange members dealt with one another on a preferential price basis. Fixed minimum commissions were the glue that held the New York Stock Exchange (NYSE) and other exchanges together, while members of the National Association of Securities Dealers (NASD) dealt with one another at an inside trading price. Commission price regulation similarly was the norm in Canada, Australia, London, Japan, and elsewhere. In addition, NYSE rules required members to bring all of their orders to the NYSE floor for execution, prohibited access to the exchange by non-members, and required member firms to be engaged primarily in the securities business. NYSE member firms could not incorporate or become public companies.

In the late 1960s, however, the fixed minimum commission structure came under pressure in the United States due to the institutionalization of the public securities markets. Although the NYSE resisted the deregulation of commission rates, various rebate practices developed that put pressure on the fixed commission structure and eventually assured its demise. In the mid-1970s, the NYSE finally abolished fixed minimum commission rates. Further deregulation flowed from negotiated commission rates. The Securities and Exchange Commission (SEC) dismantled the prohibitions against off-board trading. Brokerage firms incorporated and many became public corporations in the years that followed. In time, these public corporations became financial services conglomerates. In the 1990s, a spread fixing scandal ultimately forced the NASD to abandon the one-eighth trading spread convention, and the SEC subsequently mandated trading in decimals rather than fractions.

Canada and Australia followed the US lead and deregulated commission rates in 1983 and 1984, respectively. In London, the trading markets were similarly deregulated by the 1986 "Big Bang" mandating negotiated commissions and ending the separation of brokers and jobbers. Fixed minimum commissions eventually ended in other trading venues as well, although Japan did not deregulate exchange commission rates until after the Japanese "Big Bang" announced in 1997.

Deregulated commission rates not only changed the organizational structure of securities firms, but also of stock exchanges. Beginning in 1993, stock exchanges demutualized in many countries and became public corporations. Furthermore, stock exchange floors disappeared and electronic communications networks or alternative trading systems (ATSs) formed to compete with regulated exchanges.

These changes were precipitated both by developments in the trading markets, especially the growth of institutional trading and technological innovations, and a political preference for competition over regulation. In addition, to compete internationally, once the United States unfixed commissions, other jurisdictions had little choice but to follow suit. The philosophical impetus for a changed view of the role of economic regulation can be traced back to Alfred Kahn, and such deregulation was initiated in industries other than the securities industry. Yet, considerable new regulation of the trading markets accompanied deregulation of the securities industry in the United States, in the form of national market system regulation and in Europe, in the form of European Union (EU) directives and regulations. In the United States, the Securities and Exchange Commission (SEC) focused on making transaction costs as cheap as possible, but at the same time, limiting the extent of market fragmentation. The Europeans focused on dismantling of protectionism and on the creation of a European securities market as part of the internal market program.

Although the unfixing of commission rates and related deregulation of the trading markets were successful in bringing down the costs of execution, the substitution of a trading culture for an investing culture is troubling to many. Public investors wonder whether securities intermediaries have been looking after their own interests to the detriment of retail investors.

This chapter will describe the unfixing of commission rates and related deregulation of the trading markets in the United States and a number of other countries. It will pose, although not answer, the question of whether this response to institutionalization and computerization of the trading markets has benefited all participants in the public securities markets.

In any event, the broad political consensus favoring deregulation in the securities field probably ended with the financial meltdown of 2008. The SEC and the European Union are currently worried about fragmentation and a lack of transparency in securities trading. These concerns were raised in the mid-1970s, but later submerged in the rush to deregulate the trading markets. Whether the private markets of today will be the public regulated markets of tomorrow is a good question. Alternatively, perhaps trading on these ATSs will return to traditional regulated markets—stock exchanges—because of a return to a political philosophy favoring regulation.

2. Developments in the United States

2.1 Unfixing of Commissions

From the time the NYSE was organized in 1792 until 1975, exchange members charged fixed minimum commissions. The exchange required members to charge the minimum commission set by the exchange on all transactions with nonmembers, and members were not permitted to lower the commission through rebates or discounts.[1] All purchasers or sellers of listed securities were charged a set commission per share, regardless of order size. In addition, nonmember brokers who were members of regional exchanges had to pay the full minimum commission. This system did not adequately take into account the costs of executing a trade, volume discounts were not allowed, and economies of scale were not recognized. Furthermore, institutions could not avoid fixed minimum commissions by joining exchanges or trading off exchanges.

This highly regulated cost environment had many advantages. Small firms were able to maintain exchange memberships so that the securities industry had many players, spreading risk widely, and obviating the need for enormous capital requirements. The public had confidence in the viability of exchange members and the fairness of exchange trading. Following the enactment of the Securities Exchange Act of 1934 (Exchange Act), the SEC started to regulate the NYSE and other US exchanges, but the exchanges were able to continue to regulate listed companies and exchange trading and thereby maintain high standards for both. This constrained trading culture was undermined by the growth of mutual funds, insurance companies, pension funds, and other investment institutions. Retail investors executing 100-share orders no longer were the primary customers of member firms. Instead, the firms began competing for large institutional orders that cost much less to execute per share than 100-share orders. This change in the business model of broker-dealers had two immediate effects.

First, Wall Street could not efficiently handle the huge increase in volume that took place in the 1960s that led to the "Paperwork Crisis" of that decade. Firms began to computerize their books and records to meet these challenges, but some did so badly and essentially lost control of their record keeping systems. This back office chaos, combined with the 1969 stock market break, led to a financial crisis on Wall Street in which many firms failed. Although the NYSE had a trust fund to insure customer funds and securities in brokerage accounts, the trust fund proved inadequate to the crisis, and the federal government was required to step in and create the Securities Investor Protection Corporation (SIPC) to insure such accounts.

Second, traditional exchange trading could not accommodate the needs of institutional large order traders. Instead, block-trading desks developed to do so. Nevertheless, these block-trading facilities required more capital than had been necessary to run small order execution brokerages on the exchanges. Furthermore, institutions, realizing that the execution of large orders at the same fixed minimum rates as for 100-share orders produced huge profits for brokers, began to demand large commission rebates. Prohibited from providing explicit rebates, the brokers delivered rebates by way of practices that distorted the trading markets, for example, through "give ups," and through the provision of goods and services disguised as "research." In addition, institutions began trading listed securities at over-the-counter "third market" firms and even in a "fourth market" among themselves.

The growth of institutional trading was instrumental in the unfixing of commissions. Between 1940 and 1975, open-end funds grew in total dollar value from approximately US$448 million to approximately US$49 billion. Pensions funds similarly grew from approximately US$18 billion in 1950 to almost US$400 billion in 1975.[2] Thanks to technological innovation, institutional portfolio managers traded in relatively large blocks, and the execution costs per share for these trades was substantially lower than the execution costs for retail trades.[3]

Although economic and business developments began to place extreme pressure on the fixed minimum commission rate structure, the paperwork crisis and the need for profits at a time of economic stress on Wall Street drove the NYSE to staunchly defend the fixed commission rate structure. This collision between the needs of broker–dealers and the needs of their large customers resulted in the emergence of a number of economic distortions and questionable practices. Creative rebates were developed, including: (1) providing analytical and statistical services; (2) providing reciprocal business; (3) proving research services; and (4) emphasizing the sale of the client's shares to obtain that client's brokerage business.[4] Some brokers even used inside information as a form of rebate for their preferred customers. Many obtained inside information by performing investment banking or advisory services for issuers, through representation on boards of directors, or though other means.[5] SEC Chairman William J. Casey condemned this practice in 1972 and stated that any professional who has inside information must not act on it or share it.[6]

One of the most common types of rebates was the customer directed give-up. Although the NYSE prohibited commission rebates or discounts for nonmembers, the exchange allowed a member to split its commission with other NYSE members as directed by the customer, regardless of whether the other members were engaged in the same transaction. Therefore, an institutional investor could execute trades through a NYSE member and direct the member to "give up" a part of the commission it received. Frequently, the give up was directed by a mutual fund to a member firm that sold its shares to the public, or by a fund or other institution to a member firm that provided the customer with research.[7] In 1968, NYSE members gave up 38 percent of the US$243 million in commissions they received from investment companies.[8] At about this time, the SEC observed that "[m]utual fund give-up practices have been tolerated and have spread in the exchange markets only because of exchange minimum commission rate schedules, which do not take into account the nature and cost of providing brokerage services to large institutional investors."[9]

Smaller, regional exchanges also allowed give-ups in order to compete with the NYSE for institutional business. These regional exchanges permitted members to give up a part of their commission to broker–dealers who were not members of the same exchange, such as any member of the NASD, or even any registered broker–dealer.[10] Large institutional investors engaged in schemes to circumvent the high commission rate by executing orders away from the NYSE, or by creating vehicles, such as captive broker–dealers that could have direct access to exchanges for the sole purpose of receiving give-ups. Although all orders in NYSE exchange listed securities handled by exchange members were required to be executed on the exchange,[11] institutions were not members and so were able to execute transactions in the over-the-counter (OTC) third market, or form broker–dealer subsidiaries and join regional exchanges. These practices were opposed by the NYSE, which argued that regional securities exchanges were "nothing more than rebate mechanisms to get commissions to those who do not qualify or to return them to institutions."[12] Shareholders of mutual funds, however, argued in favor of these practices.

In Moses v. Burgin,[13] a stockholder of Fidelity Fund, Inc. brought a derivative action against a mutual fund, its directors, its investment advisor, and its underwriter alleging that the Fund could, and should, have recovered a portion of its brokerage commissions it was obligated to pay on its portfolio business because customer-directed give ups were paid to brokers who sold shares of the fund. In essence, the plaintiff contended the fund should have formed a broker–dealer subsidiary and joined a regional exchange to recapture its commissions. The court held that directors had no duty to pursue such recapture but the management defendants were guilty of gross misconduct by failing to disclose the possibility of NASD recapture to the unaffiliated directors.

These developments led the SEC and Congress to question securities industry rate regulation and ultimately to move the securities industry to a negotiated rate structure. The groundwork for a political philosophy of substituting competition for regulation had been laid in other regulated industries, most notably by Alfred E. Kahn. Kahn believed that direct regulation suppresses competition, or at least severely distorts it, and that competition free of restraints is a preferable system of economic control.[14] He asserted three broad propositions for economic deregulation: whenever even imperfect competition is feasible, it is superior to command-and-control regulation; for competition to work well, government regulation to remedy imperfections and market failures should not be economic rate making; and regulation is deficient in information and incentives and suppresses competition.[15] Kahn was the moving force behind the deregulation of the airlines, and he regarded the deregulation of stock exchange brokerage commissions as a major milestone.[16]

The Antitrust Division of the Department of Justice also weighed in by instigating litigation to abolish the fixed commission rate structure. Gordon v. New York Stock Exchange, Inc.[17] was an assault on the fixed commission rate structure that ultimately failed in the Supreme Court only because the Court held that the SEC exercised direct and active supervision of rate fixing by securities exchanges, and the SEC had the authority to abolish fixed rates. Under Section 19(b) of the Exchange Act, the SEC had the power to order exchanges to alter or supplement their rules with respect to certain matters, including the fixing of reasonable rates of commissions.

The SEC began pressuring the NYSE to alter its fixed commission rate structure as early as 1968, but the exchange strongly resisted moving to negotiated rates. On January 26, 1968, the SEC proposed Rule 10b-10 under the Exchange Act, designed to prohibit give-ups unless the benefit of the give-ups accrued to fund shareholders.[18] On May 28, 1968, the SEC sent a letter to the NYSE, requesting it to amend its commission rate schedules by either conforming to a schedule provided by the SEC or eliminating minimum commission rates on orders of greater than US$50,000. The SEC also requested the NYSE to reduce the current intra-member rate for non-executing firms or to eliminate requirements for minimum intra-member charges to such non-executing firms.[19] The President of the NYSE accepted the SEC's commission schedule and proposed to eliminate customer-directed give-ups all together.[20] The SEC accepted the NYSE's counterproposal on August 30, 1968, and on December 5, 1968, the NYSE adopted the proposal to prohibit give-ups.[21]

Between 1968 and 1975, the SEC pressured the NYSE to allow volume discounts for certain orders. In addition, the NYSE interpreted its anti-rebate policies with some flexibility. However, the industry at this time was financially too stressed to adjust easily to the demands of its institutional clients. On January 16, 1973, the SEC promulgated Rule 19b-2 under the Exchange Act requiring all national securities exchanges to make their memberships available to any broker–dealer otherwise qualified, provided the member utilized its membership to conduct a predominantly public securities business.[22] Although the SEC was gradually moving the NYSE and other exchanges to a negotiated rate environment, albeit in a rather convoluted fashion, Congress stepped in and mandated the unfixing of commission rates in the Securities Act Amendments of 1975. The SEC then unfixed the rates by rule on May 1, 1975. This event was called May Day on Wall Street "as if it were some communist plot."[23]

For better or worse, Congress also bowed to the competing demands of institutional investors, exchange members, OTC traders, and others by adding the national market system mandate to that statute and leaving it to the SEC to fill in the blanks of what that securities trading system should be. This legislation substituted a new regulatory framework for the traditional exchange system of regulation. The SEC obtained much greater authority over exchange and NASD rulemaking. Moreover, the legislation required the SEC to include an evaluation of the anticompetitive aspects of such rules in approving or disapproving them. Although, as a very general matter, competition was substituted for regulation in securities trading, the implementation of the national market system was intensely regulatory. Congress was able to impose this new regulatory system on the securities industry, in part, because it was very difficult for exchange member firms that had operated under a regulated rate system for so long to adjust to a negotiated rate system, and many had failed. Congress provided financial support to the industry by creating SIPIC in 1970, but then proceeded to replace trading market self-regulation with government regulation.

2.2 Off-board Trading

The maintenance of fixed commission rates required a number of ancillary constraints, the most important of which was a ban against the trading of exchange-listed securities off the exchange board by exchange members. Although negotiated commissions relieved some of the pressure for institutions to be free from rules requiring orders to be executed on exchanges, institutions wanted more leverage to negotiate lower rates. As described in the foregoing section, the off-board trading rule did not apply to institutions executing orders on regional exchanges or between themselves in the "fourth market." Before the SEC tackled the elimination of the off-board ban, however, it believed it had to deal with the threat of fragmentation of the price setting mechanism for equity securities. The SEC feared that the disintermediation of exchanges would seriously impair the pricing mechanism for equities.

In a 1978 Policy Statement, the SEC asserted that Congress supported three major principles when mandating the creation of a national market system. These were: (1) creating an ideal auction type market by implementing a nationwide system according to price and time priority for all limit orders of public investors over all professional orders; (2) the types of securities qualified to be included in a national market system should depend primarily on their characteristics rather than where they were traded; and (3) a refusal to achieve a nationwide centralized auction-type market for qualified securities by abolishing over-the-counter trading in listed securities.[24]

The SEC viewed fragmentation, or "the existence of multiple, geographically separated forums in which trading in the same security occurs. . . ."[25] as a major problem in a deregulated trading market. To combat this threat, the SEC proposed a composite quotation system, the development of comprehensive linkage and order routing systems, a public limit order book for public agency orders, and a consolidated transaction reporting system. In this context, in 1980, the SEC then adopted Rule 19c-3, which permitted exchange members to trade off-board as agents for their customers, except in agency crosses, and abolished off-board trading restrictions as to stocks listed after April 26, 1979. However, remaining off-board trading restrictions were not removed until May 2000.

2.3 Going Public

Under US law, general partners are personally liable for the debts of a partnership. In contrast, shareholders are not liable for a corporation's debts. Under NYSE rules, until 1953, only individuals could be members of the exchange, and all exchange member firms were required to do business as partnerships.[26] The rationale for NYSE rules requiring member firms to be private partnerships was rooted in the mutual form of exchange organization, and the notion that when making a trade, an exchange member could be trusted to stand behind any trade over the exchange. In addition, as described earlier, the NYSE used this rule to keep institutions off the exchange.

In the late 1950s, the partnership form of organization began to break down because of the need for additional capital to function as a modern securities house. Two of the first firms to incorporate exemplify different types of organizations. One was Merrill Lynch, Pierce, Fenner & Smith, a large wire house catering to retail customers that incorporated in 1959.[27] Another was Donaldson, Lufkin & Jenrette, a firm that catered to the execution of trades by institutional investors such as banks, insurance companies, mutual funds, and pension funds. It incorporated in 1959, and then became the first NYSE member firm to go public in 1971.[28] To skirt stock exchange rules, it formed a holding company that had a public offering, so that the operating broker–dealer company was not technically a public company. When faced with the threat of losing large and important member firms, the NYSE changed its rules to allow member firms to become public companies. On March 26, 1970, the NYSE changed its rules to allow its member firms to go public.[29] In 1971, Merrill Lynch, Reynolds Securities, and Bache & Co. all went public.[30] The economic problems of the 1970s and the unfixing of commission rates precipitated numerous mergers of Wall Street firms, and the ability of NYSE members to raise public capital accelerated the consolidation pursuant to which many old line firms went out of business.

In 1975, when commission rates became negotiable, the Glass-Steagall Act still separated investment banking from commercial banking. Further, federal law also fixed interest rates paid by banks. After interest rate deregulation in 1980, investment banks and commercial banks began to push into one another's traditional lines of business. Negotiated rates, technological innovation, a search for increased capital and global competition from universal banks in Europe eventually led to the creation of giant financial services holding companies and the repeal of the Glass-Steagall Act. Although this story is beyond the scope of this chapter, it is an important footnote to the unfixing of brokerage commission rates, not only in the United States, but also in other countries, especially the United Kingdom. When commission rates were unfixed, ancillary restrictive regulations also fell and allowed access to trading markets by institutional customers. The lifting of activity restrictions allowed consolidation in the financial services industry that ultimately resulted in gigantic "too big too fail" banking and investment banking firms that have been a focus of regulators in the current financial crisis.

2.4 Soft Dollars

When Congress passed the Securities Act Amendments of 1975 which unfixed commission rates, institutional money managers were concerned that they would be forced to execute transactions at the lowest execution cost available and that paying more than the lowest cost would constitute a breach of fiduciary duty.[31] They were also concerned that obtaining research would be more difficult. At the same time, broker–dealers were concerned that they would no longer be compensated for research, because orders would be directed only to the broker–dealers that charged the lowest commissions. As a result of these concerns, the Securities Acts Amendments of 1975 included Section 28(e) of the Exchange Act, which provides that a money manager does not breach its fiduciary duty if it pays more than the lowest available brokerage commission as long as the money manager determines in good faith that the commission paid is reasonable in relation to the brokerage and research services provided by the broker–dealer.

In 1976, the SEC issued an interpretive release in which it specified that give ups do not fall under the Section 28(e) safe harbor. The SEC stated that in order for research services to fall within the safe harbor, they must be "provided by the particular broker which executed the transactions."[32] Additionally, whereas Section 28(e) might include research services that are provided by a third party, "the money manager should be prepared to demonstrate the required good faith determination in connection with the transaction." Similar interpretative advice was reiterated in 2005 and 2006.[33] Soft dollars are a throwback to the era of fixed commission rates. They demonstrate the persistence of economic distortions in the pricing of securities transactions which flowed from the new regulatory structure imposed by the Securities Act Amendments of 1975.

2.5 Decimalization

Traditionally, the trading of stocks in the United States occurred in one-eighth increments. Exchange and OTC trading was conducted in eighths and the transactions were reported in eighths. This trading convention ended following an antitrust investigation of the NASDAQ Stock Market ("NASDAQ"). The Department of Justice and SEC investigated anti-competitive practices by OTC market makers, and the SEC criticized the NASD for its regulatory deficiencies in failing to uncover these practices.[34] The end of the one-eighth trading convention was comparable to the unfixing of stock exchange minimum commission rates in its effect on the profitability of certain segments of the securities industry, as well as in the market structure issues it triggered.

NASDAQ began trading in one-sixteenth increments on June 2, 1997,[35] a development that led to compressed trading spreads in actively traded stocks. Concurrently, some members of Congress pressed to change trading conventions to decimals. The Common Sense Pricing

Act of 1997, had it passed, would have required stock trading in dollars and cents within a year of its enactment.[36] While Congressional pressures to effect such a change were frequently justified as lowering trading costs and modernizing trading, they were resisted by the securities industry, and to some extent the SEC, for two reasons. First, many anticipated that the move to decimalization would be costly for broker–dealers, because it would greatly increase stock market volume. Increased volume was one effect of the unfixing of commission rates, and it had disastrous results, as many securities firms were unable to adjust their systems to deal with this increased volume. Second, many feared that trading increments could drop to a penny or less. As the unfixing of commission rates also demonstrated, once charges for the trading of stocks are deregulated, predicting how low such charges will descend or what collateral consequences will ensue is difficult.

Accordingly, the move to decimalization was slow due to worries about operational capabilities. Although the NYSE voted to trade stocks in decimals in June 1997, such trading did not begin until January 2001, and NASDAQ did not change over to decimals until April 2001.[37]

Contrary to expectations, the change to decimal pricing strengthened the position of the NYSE as a central marketplace but had some adverse consequences with respect to liquidity. Electronic communications networks, or ATSs, had not reached the critical mass necessary to become a genuine source of pricing discovery rather than a derivative pricing mechanism.[38] Further, institutional investors complained that the shift to decimals permitted specialists to step in front of large orders and therefore reduce liquidity.[39] Although governmental pressures forced the US exchanges to convert to decimal trading, it did not appear at the time that the change enhanced competition between the NYSE, NASDAQ, and ATSs, although subsequently the exchanges and NASDAQ confronted competition from ATSs.

3. Unfixing of Commissions in Non-US Jurisdictions

3.1 Canada

Under the Canadian Securities Act, the Ontario Securities Commission (OSC) has the authority to rule on every Toronto Stock Exchange bylaw that it considers affects public policy. Since Canada is the economy most closely tied to the United States, between 1967 and 1981, the OSC held public hearings on whether to unfix commission rates.[40] However, after the United States unfixed brokerage commission rates in 1975, Canada did not immediately follow suit. The OSC decided that it did not have sufficient evidence to determine whether the public would benefit from such a change. The OSC believed that fixed commissions were a method to subsidize small retail investors and worried about their fate if rates became negotiated. Furthermore, the OSC was concerned that brokerage commissions set by competition would decrease the profitability of securities firms. At the same time, the TSE also opposed the elimination of fixed brokerage commissions.[41] In 1983, when negotiated commissions were adopted in Australia and the United Kingdom, the OSC decided that fairness required that competition set commission rates. On April 1, 1983, TSE's commission rates were unfixed. On the same day, the Quebec Securities Commission unfixed commission rates on the Montreal Stock Exchange.[42]

3.2 Australia

Australia unfixed commission rates on April 1, 1984.[43] Before that time, the brokerage industry in Australia had a fixed scale of fees and if a broker gave a discount to anyone other than immediate family or staff members, the broker could be heavily fined.[44] In 1979 and 1980, brokerage fees accounted for 86 percent of brokerage firms' revenues. Brokers argued that this system allowed them to offer customers advice and other services.[45] As in the United States, stock exchange membership in Australia was subject to restrictive regulations.[46] In the late 1970s and early 1980s, the Campbell Committee conducted studies that resulted in recommendations to deregulate the financial industry to increase the efficiency of the financial system and to promote competition between banks.[47] The Committee's final report argued for a financial system based on market forces and the lessening of government regulation.

Accordingly, the Committee recommended the deregulation of brokerage fees.[48] The Australian financial industry also pushed for the abolition of fixed commissions. As large brokerage firms expanded into underwriting and began to offer a fuller variety of services, merchant banks had an incentive to push for the unfixing of commissions, because they were unable to become stock exchange members.[49] They argued that the Trade Practices Act of 1974, which dealt with collusive pricing and other restrictive practices, made fixed commissions illegal. At first, the Trade Practices Commission determined that public benefits derived from fixed commissions exceeded the harm caused by them, but in the early 1980s, the Trade Practices Commission adopted a rule against restrictive regulations on stock exchange memberships and brokerage fees.[50] These developments led to the unfixing of commissions and a deregulation of the securities industry in Australia.

3.3 London

Although the London Stock Exchange did not deregulate commission rates until the Big Bang on October 27, 1986, the forces leading to this unfixing of commission rates go back to the development of the Eurosecurities market in the 1960s. A developing global market in the top 500 equities of international companies by foreign (including US) securities firms resulted in an erosion of business on the London Stock Exchange, and pressures for change.[51] The unfixing of commission rates in the United States was a response to institutionalization, but the Big Bang was a response to the internationalization of the equity markets.[52] It was an effort to capture trading share in international equities for the London Stock Exchange. As was the case in the United States, deregulation in London was a process with several components. The most important elements were: (1) changing the membership structure of the London Stock Exchange so that major British and foreign investment and commercial banks could join; (2) changing the exchange's trading system by, among other things, eliminating single capacity trading; and (3) encouraging the London market to freely compete with the United States and other negotiated commission markets.[53]

This process of deregulating commission rates in London began in 1977 when the Director General of Fair Trading instituted an action against the London Stock Exchange for anticompetitive conduct, charging that the exchange's fixed commissions and membership rules were illegal.[54] At this time the fixed commissions on the London Stock Exchange were twice that of those on the NYSE.[55] In July 1983, the competition case against the stock exchange was settled by a commitment from the Exchange to unfix commissions. This Big Bang took place on October 27, 1986. At the same time, the Financial Services Act was passed to impose new regulations on the London market in anticipation of the changes that would be wrought by the Big Bang.

The UK government had several goals in mind in forcing the Big Bang on the Exchange. Securities trading was beginning to bypass

London, and the government wanted London to become more competitive. The government also wanted to change the way in which the gilts market operated, where only three firms were authorized to trade. After the Big Bang, the gilts market was opened up to other UK and foreign firms. The unfixing of commissions led to the end of single capacity trading under which a firm was either a dealer or jobber. It also led to the end of the separation of British banks into commercial lenders and merchant banks.

In retrospect, it seems that the City of London was surprisingly unprepared for the changes that would flow from the unfixing of commission rates, even though New York had gone through these wrenching changes only a decade earlier. Industry consolidation, the need for increased capital, the pressure on back-office systems, and the differentiation of the wholesale and retail markets were unanticipated.[56] One consequence of this lack of preparedness was that foreign banks swarmed into London, buying up British firms and universal banking became the norm.[57] As a result, London became the center of a globalized capital market, but old line British securities firms disappeared.

In particular, small firms disappeared and financial conglomerates began to dominate the securities markets. Institutional investors benefited from lower commissions, but retail investors were hurt, because their commission rates increased.[58] Ironically, US banks came to dominate the London capital market, in part, because they were able to escape from restrictive US regulations prohibiting the combination of investment banking and commercial banking in a single firm when operating abroad.

In response to London's Big Bang, other European markets also became deregulated. France unfixed commission rates in 1989, the Netherlands in 1990, Switzerland in 1991, and Spain in 1992.[59] Other deregulatory developments accompanied negotiated commission rates in Europe, in particular the opening up of stock exchange membership and access.[60] Accordingly, in addition to competing with New York, London became subject to competition from money centers in Europe and had to deal with EU directives aimed at reducing protectionism in Europe and protecting investors, but pushed forward by Continental countries unhappy with London's hegemony in European financial services. As a result, reams of new regulation were produced in Brussels. The most important of these from a market structure perspective was the Investment Services Directive,[61] ultimately replaced by the Market in Financial Instruments Directive.[62] Although it is hard to say that these market regulation initiatives were a direct result of the unfixing of commissions, like the national market system regulations in the United States, European governments were concerned about the adverse affects of unbridled competition on fragmentation and fairness.

3.4 Japan

Until the late 1990s, heavy regulation of the Japanese financial markets limited competition in at least three ways. The regulation was based on changes mandated by the post-Second World War occupation of Japan by the United States aimed at dismantling the Japanese zaibatsu or industrial holding companies. First, banks were not allowed to participate in the securities markets, and the entire financial sector was rigidly compartmentalized.[63] Second, price and nonprice competition was restricted through the regulation of deposit rates, stock brokerage commissions, and insurance premiums.[64] Third, the range of available securities was severely restricted.[65]

In November 1996, Japan's Prime Minister proposed a fundamental deregulatory shift in the country's economic policy in response to the bursting of a bubble economy in late 1990 and 1991 and the loss of Japan's international financial competitiveness.[66] The goal of Japan's Big Bang was to revitalize the Tokyo market into a financial center comparable to New York and London according to three principles: free, fair, and global.[67] "Free" meant achievement of a market based on principles rather than regulation. "Fair" meant greater transparency in financial regulation. "Global" meant reforming and modernizing the market to make it international.[68]

The unfixing of brokerage commission rates was only one component of a much broader reform of financial services regulation. The reforms included: elimination of controls on foreign exchange transactions; liberalization of the organizational structures of financial institutions; deregulation of securities derivatives; upgrading the market settlement system; mark to market accounting; and a new securities disclosure system.[69] Structural impediments to the reform process, including administrative guidance as a regulatory technique, the keiretsu system, and cultural and political forces made the realization of the Big Bang reforms slow and difficult.[70] Nevertheless, on April 1, 1998, 19 types of fees and commissions of over-the-counter equity transactions were liberalized, and brokerage commissions on stocks listed on the Tokyo Stock Exchange and other exchanges were also liberalized and unfixed for all large trades.[71]

3.5 Summary

The unfixing of commission rates around the world was driven by similar forces—institutionalization, automation, and globalization. To maintain market share, even in the trading of their own nation's equities, exchanges had to become competitive with regard to execution costs. This generally meant that institutional orders could no longer subsidize the costs of smaller trades. It also meant that many smaller brokerage firms could no longer maintain their independence. Therefore, a long-term effect of competitive rates was securities industry consolidation and increased institutionalization of trading markets.

Furthermore, regulators as well as exchanges had to adopt to changed market dynamics. Self-regulation by exchanges, made effective partly because of the mutual ownership of exchanges and fixed rates, gave way to greater government regulation. This development led to the creation of new government securities commissions in the Netherlands, Germany, and elsewhere. This government regulation frequently attempted to impose order and transparency on trading markets that extended beyond discrete national exchanges, and therefore was possibly more stringent than self-regulation, because it had the force of law. A good example of such new government regulation is the Market in Financial Services Directive of the European Union, a far-reaching regulation designed to eliminate national rules that concentrate trading on official stock exchanges and enable competition between different market execution centers, through pre- and post-trade transparency rules.

4. Demutualization of Exchanges

Demutualization is the process of transforming an exchange from a cooperative or mutual form of business organization to a for-profit, shareholder-owned corporation. After commission rates were unfixed in many jurisdictions and the rules requiring orders to be executed on exchanges were abolished, exchanges became confronted with competition from over-the-counter (OTC) markets, or automated trading systems (ATSs). The need to become more efficient and customer-focused and to modernize generally led to a widespread movement for stock exchanges to demutualize and then become public companies. The process of demutualization often coincided with the move to electronic trading from floor-based trading. The World Bank and regional development banks often recommended demutualization as a way to reform securities regulation as well as securities trading. This recommendation was based in part on a view that exchanges should be operated in the public interest under the supervision of government regulators, rather than for the benefit of traders as self-regulatory organizations.

The first stock exchange to demutualize was the Stockholm Stock Exchange in 1993. By 1999, of 52 exchanges present at a meeting of the Federation Internationale des Bourses des Valeurs, now the World Federation of Exchanges (WFE), 15 had demutualized, 14 had member approval to demutualize, and 15 were actively contemplating demutualization. This phenomenon is discussed and analyzed in another chapter, but it is part of the story of the deregulation, and re-regulation of securities market structure and trading that followed the unfixing of commission rates. The changes experienced by stock exchanges between 1975 and today were due to technological innovation, institutionalization, and international competition. To remain viable, exchanges, like their member firms, had to change their organizational form and their business models, and to adjust to new regulatory paradigms. Demutualization was a means of cashing out floor traders and moving to electronic markets.

One of the consequences of the changes in the securities markets was that significant trading of equities migrated from exchanges to ATSs. To some extent, this migration was a foreseeable consequence of the deregulation of exchange markets that began in the United States in the mid-1970s and then spread around the world, but the future was only dimly perceived by market participants and their regulators.

▬▬▬ 5. Regulation of Fragmented Markets

In the 1970s, when the SEC ordered the unfixing of commission rates and began to eliminate the rules that required orders in listed securities to be brought to the NYSE for execution, the agency worried about market fragmentation and the damage deregulation could cause to the pricing mechanism for securities trading. Many of the national market system regulations put into place then and later were designed to address this problem. Similar concerns animated the Investment Services Directive, the Market in Financial Services Directive, and Market Abuse Directive in the European Union. Despite these regulatory efforts to create a transparent, central pricing mechanism for securities trading, pressures from institutional investors, technological advances, and the competition to exchanges from ATSs have created fragmented trading markets for equities that are not necessarily transparent. Although today's markets may be more efficient, especially as to cost and speed of execution, than the markets that existed in 1975, they are not necessarily fair, especially to retail investors.

The SEC is now embarked on rulemaking to address the lack of transparency in equity trading by "dark pools" of liquidity in ATSs that are able to circulate indications of interest to selected market participants without including such trading interest in the public consolidated quotation system for national market system securities.[72] The SEC's proposals would amend current regulatory requirements in three ways: first, indications of interest would generally be treated as firm bids and offers for purposes of the requirements of the consolidated quotation system; second, the trading volume threshold would be lowered for the requirement that an ATSs display its best-priced orders for a listed stock and nondiscriminatory access to such orders to nonsubscribers would have to be provided in certain circumstances; and third, real-time disclosure of the identity of each ATSs that executes a trade would be required. Since the adoption of Regulation ATSs by the SEC in 1998, ATSs trading has grown dramatically. OTC trading is approximately 38 percent of total market volume, and dark pool trading represents 7.2 percent of the total share volume in listed stocks as of the second quarter of 2009.[73]

The European Commission is also preparing to review the Market in Financial Services Directive to determine whether dark pools create "unfair commercial advantages."[74] In addition, the WFE has expressed its concerns about dark pools to the Financial Stability Board, arguing that dark pools prevent a level playing field between exchanges and nonexchange entities that perform similar functions and hamper price discovery.[75] This is because dark pools create information fragmentation in the market.

The concern about dark pools is related to the concern about flash orders that allow some traders to see orders for one second or less before the orders are displayed to the public, and to trade with these orders within that time frame. The SEC therefore has proposed to prohibit all flash orders.[76] The SEC recognized that flash orders offer liquidity benefits to market participants who do not wish to display their interest, and may also make executions cheaper.[77] However, the SEC is concerned that flash orders will create a two-tiered market in which the public will not have access to the best price for listed securities, because a flash order can be set at a price better than the published national best offer or bid price.[78] Thus, flash orders are another instance of market fragmentation that advantage certain institutional traders but disadvantage others, especially retail traders.

The concerns about dark pools and flash orders are not new, but are simply an update of concerns about market fragmentation and the time and place advantages that some institutional traders would enjoy after the unfixing of commission rates and the abolition of rules requiring orders to be sent to regulated exchanges for execution. The general deregulation of markets and the improved technology that enables orders to be executed faster and more efficiently have simply transferred the concerns about market fragmentation to new execution venues and techniques. These new ways of executing orders have escaped from the regulatory constraints of the national market system in the United States and the Market in Financial Services Directive in the European Union, just as executions on regional exchanges and in the fourth market escaped from SEC and exchange regulation in the 1970s.

6. Conclusion

Negotiated commissions were forced on exchanges and their owners by institutional customers, technological advances in trading mechanisms, and globalization. Antitrust or competition authorities struck the death blow to fixed commission rates in the United States and the United Kingdom, but in both money centers, business exigencies were forcing the exchanges to unfix commissions by the time legal action mandated negotiated rates. As a young associate in a law firm in the late 1960s and early 1970s, I spent many hours on the telephone, advising clients whether a particular rebate practice could pass muster under NYSE rules. Although I hardly saw the big picture of the changes rocking the markets, I sensed that the permitted rebate exceptions were swallowing the rule mandating fixed commission rates. As a practicing lawyer, I also witnessed the bankruptcy of many brokerage firms that were unable to adjust to negotiated rates or that had lost control of their books and records during the paperwork crisis, and I worked on some of the consolidations of firms that occurred during this period.

A few years later, when I became a Commissioner of the SEC in 1977, I was confronted by the off-board trading or Rule 390 issue, and I worried about the fragmentation of the markets that might accompany further deregulation of the exchanges and the adverse effects of a market dominated by institutional traders on public investors. In retrospect, I am still not convinced that deregulation of exchange trading and the creation of giant financial industry holding companies was entirely positive. In 1975, no firm was too big to fail, although the adverse consequences of the failure of a large bank or brokerage firm worried regulators who tried to ward off such collapses.

Modern securities trading markets are more efficient than they were in 1975, and the fixed commission rate schedule had become untenable, but today's markets seem insufficiently regulated. Competition has not proved a sufficient check on trading conduct. In addition to questions about trading abuses, the systemic risks in the markets that became evident in 2008 are a danger to all investors and the real economy. While it is hard to blame these systemic risks on the unfixing of commission rates, the failure of the OTC markets to appropriately value securities (including derivatives) trading in those markets was a key component of the asset bubble that burst so disastrously. When the SEC was struggling with the decision to abolish Rule 390, Harold Williams, who was then the Chairman of the SEC, remarked to me that if we abolished Rule 390, some day the SEC would have to impose a new similar regulation on the entire public securities market. That seems to be the pass we have reached currently, and it is an interesting question as to how exchanges will fit into the regulated securities marketplace of the future.

In 1975, institutional investors held 35 percent of all US stocks. They now own and control almost 70 percent of the shares of US corporations. Mutual funds own the largest amount (26 percent), and private pension plans and government pension plans own another 20 percent. Whether the deregulatory changes discussed in this chapter are the cause or effect of these changes in the profile of stock owners is hard to say. Many public investors have lost confidence in the equity markets as a repository for their savings. Whether regulatory reforms to restore faith in financial markets should include changes in the rules for trading stocks is a good question. Since 1975, the prevailing wisdom had been that competition, rather than regulation, should govern the public trading markets. However, these markets continued to be subject to extensive regulation, even as they became more global, competitive, and efficient. The question confronting regulators today is whether less-regulated markets, and more competition is always good public policy, and if not, how the markets of the future should be regulated.

Notes

1 *The Stockbroker's Minimum Commissions and the Securities and Exchange Commission*, 37 U. MO. KAN. CITY L. REV. 69, 70 (1969).

2 D. Bruce Johnsen (1994) *Property Rights to Investment Research: The Agency Costs of Soft Dollar Brokerage*, 11 YALE J. ON REG. 75, 81.

3 *Id.*

4 James F. Jorden (1975) *"Paying Up" For Research: A Regulatory and Legislative Analysis*, 1975 DUKE L. J. 1103, 1106–07.

5 Stanislav Dolgopolov (2008) *Insider Trading, Chinese Walls, and Brokerage Commissions: The Origins of Modern Regulation of Information Flows in Securities Markets*, 4 J. L. ECON. & POL'Y 311, 328.

6 *Id.* at 330. *See also* Cady Roberts & Co., 40 S.E.C. 907 (1961).

7 SEC Inspection Report on the Soft Dollar Practices of Broker–Dealers, Investment. Advisers and Mutual Funds, § 2, pt. B, ¶ 2 (September 22, 1998), *available at* http://www.sec.gov/news/studies/softdolr.htm.

8 Dologopolov, *supra note* 5, at 331.

9 Report of the Securities and Exchange Commission on the Public Policy Implications of Investment Company Growth, H.R. Rep. No. 89-2337, at 17 (1966).

10 Proposal to Prohibit Give-Ups, Exchange Act Release No. 8239 (1968), at 3.

11 Former NYSE Rules 394, 390.

12 Robert W. Haack, President, NYSE, Remarks at the Economic Club of New York: "Competition and the Future of the New York Stock Exchange," in 77 Sec. Reg. & L. Rep. (BNA), November 17, 1970, at J-1.

13 445 F.2d 369 (1st Cir. 1971).

14 Alfred E. Kahn (1990) *Deregulation: Looking Backward and Looking Forward*, 7 YALE J. REG. 325, 328.

15 *Id.* at 340–41.

16 *Id.* at n. 2.

17 422 U.S. 659 (1975).

18 Proposal to Prohibit Give-Ups, Exchange Act Release No. 8239 (1968), at 11.

19 Letter from Manuel F. Cohen, Chairman, SEC to Robert W. Haack, President, NYSE (May 28, 1968) *reprinted in* Order for US Securities and Exchange Commission Investigation and Public Investigatory Hearing on Commission Rate Structure, Securities Exchange Act Release No. 8324 (May 28, 1968) *available at* http://www.sechistorical.org/museum/papers/1960.

20 Indep. Broker–Dealers' Trade Ass'n v. SEC, 422 F.2d 132, 136 (D.C. Cir. 1971).

21 *Id.*

22 This meant that 80 percent of the business of a member had to be conducted with nonaffiliated persons. *See* PBW Stock Exchange, Inc. v. SEC, 485 F.2d 718, 720 (3rd Cir. 1973).

23 William C. Freund, *First the Big Board, Now the Big Bang,*
WALL ST. J., October 27, 1986.

24 Development of a National Market System, Exchange Act Release
No. 14,416, 43 Fed. Reg. 4354 (February 1, 1978). I was a Commissioner of
the SEC at this time.

25 *Id.* at 17.

26 *See* Jay F. Coughenour and Daniel N. (2002) Deli, "Liquidity
Provision and the Organizational Form of NYSE Specialist Firms," 57
Journal of Finance 843.

27 Merrill Lynch & Co., Inc.: 2007 Factbook, at 11, available at
http://www.ml.com/media/92209.pdf. The first corporation to be
admitted to NYSE membership was Woodcock, Hess & Co. in 1953.
New York Stock Exchange: Firsts & Records, available at http://www.
nyse.com/about/history/1022221392987.html.

28 Donaldson, Lufkin & Jenrette, Inc. Company History. *See also*
Interview with Richard Jenrette, at 10 (2002), available at http://www.hbs.
edu/entrepreneurs/pdf/richardjenrette.pdf.

29 "Big Bang Brief: New York's dummy run," *Economist*, August 16,
1986, at 54.

30 Allan D. Morrison and William J. Wilhelm, Jr., *The Demise of
Investment-Banking Partnerships: Theory and Evidence,* at 1, available at
http://gates.comm.virginia.edu/wjw9a/Papers/ibdemise2.pdf.

31 Commission Guidance Regarding Client Commission Practices
under Section 28(e) of the Securities Exchange Act of 1975, Release
No. 52635, at *3 (2005).

32 Interpretation of Section 28(e) of the Securities Exchange Act of
1934; Use of Commission Payment by Fiduciaries, Exchange Act Release
No. 12251, at *2 (1976).

33 Sec. 28(e) Release, *supra* note 31; Commission Guidance Regarding
Client Commission Practices Under Section 28(e) of the Securities
Exchange Act of 1934, 71 Fed. Reg. 41, 41,993 (2006).

34 See In the Matter of Nat'l Ass'n of Securities Dealers, Exchange Act
Release No. 37,542 (August 8, 1996).

35 Deborah Lohse, "Nasdaq to Start Trading All Stocks in Sixteenths,"
Wall St. J., May 29, 1997.

36 Common Sense Pricing Act, H.R. 1053, 105th Cong. (1997).
This bill never became law.

37 *See* Kate Kelly and Jeff D. Opdyke, "Nasdaq to Complete its Shift to
Decimals With All Stocks Priced in Dollars, Cents," *Wall St. J.*, April 9,
2001, at C9; Jeff D. Opdyke, "NYSE Adds Decimals, Subtracts Fractions,"
Wall St. J., January 29, 2001, at C1.

38 See Greg Ip, "If Big Board Specialist Are an Anachronism, They're
a Profitable One," *Wall St. J.*, March 12, 2001, at A1.

39 Jeff D. Opdyke and Gregory Zuckerman, "Decimal Move Brings
Points Of Contention From Traders," *Wall St. J.*, February 12, 2001, at C1;
Unger, *Exchange Officials Testify Decimals Have Affected Depth, Liquidity of
Trading*, 33 Sec. Reg. & L. Rep. (BNA), at 803 (May 28, 2001).

40 I. Krinsky and W. Rotenberg (1989) "The Transition to Competitive Pricing on the Toronto Exchange," *Canadian Public Policy*, Vol. 15, No. 2, p. 135.

41 During this time, brokerage commissions were regulated by a TSE by-law and brokers were not permitted to charge a commission that was lower than the amount stated in the bylaw, although they were free to charge a higher commission. Stephen L. Harris, *Financial Regulation and the Influence of Non-State Actors*, 15 Nat'l U. Of Singapore Lee Kuan Yew Sch.of Pub. Pol'y, Research Paper SPP-13-02), available at http://www.spp.nus.edu.sg/Handler.ashx?path=Data/Site/SiteDocuments/wp/2002/sp13.pdf.

42 J. Peter Williamson, *The Investment Banking Handbook* 515 (1988).

43 Edna Carew (2007) National Market, National Interest: The Drive to Unify Australia's Securities Markets 149.

44 *Id*. at 122.

45 *Id*.

46 *Id*. at 123.

47 Adam Boyton, *Liberalisation of Foreign Investment in the Australian Financial Sector*,at 95, available at http://www.treasury.gov.au/documents/202PDF/Article07.pdf.

48 Carew, supra note 43, at 158–59.

49 *Id*. at 123.

50 *Id*. at 125, 149.

51 Norman S.Poser, *International Securities Regulation* 24 (1991).

52 *Id*. at 17.

53 *Id*. at 28.

54 *Id*. at 26.

55 *Big Bank Brief*, ECONOMIST, August 30, 1986, at 72.

56 Eric C. Bettelheim, *Book Review: The Transformation of Threadneedle Street: The Deregulation and Reregulation of Britain's Financial Services*, 14 NW. J. INT'L L. & BUS. 231, 234–35 (1993).

57 "See Five Years Since Big Bang B After the earthquake," *Economist*, October 26, 1991, at 23.

58 *Id*.

59 Norman Poser, "Automation of Securities Markets and the European Community's Proposed Investment Services Directive," 55 *Law & Contemp. Probs*. 29, 32–33 (1992).

60 *Id*.

61 Council Directive 93/22/EEC on Investment Services in the Securities Field (1993) O.J. (L.141/27).

62 Directive 2004/39/EC on Markets in Financial Instruments, of the European Parliament and of the Council of April 21, 2004, amending Council Directives 85/611/EEC and Directive 2000/112/EC of the European Parliament and of the Council and repealing Council Directive 93/22EEC, 2004 O.J. (L. 145/1).

63 Ernest T. Patrikis, "Japan's Big Bang Financial Reform," 24 BROOK. J. Int'l Law 577, 581 (1998).

64 *Id.*

65 *Id.*

66 Jessica C. Wiley, "Will the 'Bang' Mean 'Big' Changes to Japanese Financial Laws?," 22 *Hastings Int'l & Comp. L. Rev.* 379, 379–82 (1999).

67 *Id.* at 393.

68 Shingi Fukukawa, *Development of Japanese Big Bang and Its Impact* 1, available at http://brie.berkely.edu/research/forum/fukukawa.html.

69 *Id.* at 2–4.

70 *See* Wiley, *supra* note66, at 401–04.

71 *Japan to Liberalize OTC Fees from April,* BNA Securities Law Daily, March 23, 1998.

72 Regulation of Non-Public Trading Interest, Exchange Act Release No. 60997, 74 Fed.Reg. 61208 (November 23, 2009).

73 *Id.*

74 Jeremy Grant, *Dark Pool Review to Focus on "Unfair Commercial Advantages,"* September 20, 2009, available at http://www.ft.com/cms/s/0/a903e5ae-a5d4-11de-8c92-00144feabdc0.html.

75 Letter from William J. Brodsky, Chairman, WFE to Mario Draghi, Chairman, Financial.

76 SEC Rule Proposal: Elimination of Flash Order Exception from Rule 602 of Regulation Stabililty Board (September 21, 2009), available at http://www.worldexchanges.org/files/file/WFE%20Board%20 statement%20to%20G20%-2021-09-09.pdf.NMS, Exchange Act Release No. 60687, 74 Fed. Reg. 48633 (September 18, 2009).

77 *Id.* at 48638.

78 *Id.* at 48636.

5

Chicago's Decade of Innovation: 1972–82

HAL WEITZMAN

"The Chicago system was so dynamic. There were days when there'd be guys fighting—fistfights. It was just great drama. It was wonderful. It made for an aura that said: 'We're going to trade these things; we're going to price these things; and I'm going to do better than you.' That's the Chicago story."

—Wayne Luthringshausen,
Options Clearing Corporation
Chief Executive since 1975

If anyone in Chicago in the 1960s had suggested that, within a few decades, the city would establish itself as an international financial center, they would have been laughed out of town. To be sure, Chicago was to some degree a center of money management, a banking hub for the US Midwest. It was also a town whose biggest markets had international significance: the settlement prices for corn, oats, wheat, and soybean futures at the Chicago Board of Trade, the world's biggest futures market, set prices for the whole world. However, agricultural commodities were simply not part of mainstream finance. Wall Street was largely indifferent to futures trading, which was looked at as an exclusive domain of farmers and industrial food producers.

Yet, between 1972 and 1982, Chicago's futures exchanges effectively created modern financial derivatives markets. In a decade-long burst of radical innovation, the Chicago Board of Trade and the Chicago Mercantile Exchange—its younger and smaller rival—introduced a string of new financial derivatives that completely transformed the city, its exchanges and the entire world of finance. Beginning with the creation of the International Monetary Market in 1972, followed by the birth of the Chicago Board Options Exchange in 1973, through the introduction of Government National Mortgage Association ("Ginnie Mae") futures in 1975, futures on US Treasury bills in 1976, US Treasury bond futures in 1977, Eurodollar futures in 1981 and capped by the creation of index-based derivatives and options on futures in 1982, this decade of innovation laid the foundation of modern finance. It marked a critical paradigm shift, opening up the world of derivatives to the power of trading financial instruments and making the broader financial world aware of the importance of derivatives.

The new products the exchanges introduced in those ten richly creative years would help establish Chicago in the subsequent decades as America's—some would say the world's—capital of risk management. They would come to form the backbone of today's markets. Derivatives markets, which four decades ago were purely agricultural in nature, are now dominated by the trading of financial products. More fundamentally, the very contracts launched between 1972 and 1982 continue to make up the bulk of today's futures markets. Volumes may have grown exponentially, trading may have become speed-of-light fast, open outcry may be breathing its last gasps, but the most traded derivatives in the world remain products such as interest-rate futures, index-based contracts, and exchange-traded options. Not only did Chicago attract the world to its markets, it also exported its methods internationally: today, scores of exchanges around the world trade futures and options on the Chicago model.

Why Chicago? How did this city on the edge of the Midwestern prairie make the leap from trading corn and soybean oil, cattle, and pork bellies to international currencies and equity options, interest rates, and Eurodollars? What enabled Chicago to transform itself into an international financial center and, in turn, to change the way the entire world traded? And why did the basis for this transformation occur in one explosive, decade-long burst of innovation? Another question lurks implicitly beneath all these: what did Chicago have that New York—the undisputed capital of American finance—lacked?

With hindsight, Chicago's advantages over its eastern counterpart are clear: its experience of creating new products and the liquidity to trade them; the vitality and dynamism of its trading floors; its culture of hedging and risk-taking; its political savvy; its evangelism for derivatives markets. However, at the time, there was little sense in New York that Chicago was a potential competitor. If anything important were to happen in finance, New Yorkers simply assumed it would happen in New York. Within the city's financial community, the products traded in Chicago were even not referred to as "futures," but more derisorily as simply "commodities." "They thought of them as something farmers played around with," recalls Bill Brodsky, the World Federation of Exchanges (WFE) Chairman and Chicago Board Options Exchange (CBOE) Chairman and Chief Executive, who was working at the time for Model, Roland and Co., a New York securities firm that became a charter member of CBOE.

This snootiness only aided Chicago's efforts. For one thing, it obscured the marked difference between New York and Chicago at the level of the exchanges themselves. Creativity was at the heart of the Chicago exchanges. Over the years, they had learned not only how to create new products, but also how to create the liquidity needed to make them successful.

Such creativity was alien to mainstream New York finance. Product innovation was simply not part of operating a stock exchange. Rather than actively seeking business, the large New York stock exchanges operated in a world in which they were used to being approached by companies seeking to secure a share listing. Historically, the route to success for a stock in New York usually progressed through a predictable sequence. When a company first went public, it would trade on the "pink sheets." When it achieved more volume, it graduated to the American Stock Exchange. The pinnacle of success was a listing on the New York Stock Exchange. The system worked, and the exchanges themselves had little need for innovation or the creation of liquidity.

This difference was to prove critical to the transformation of the Chicago trading world. Necessity had often been the mother of innovation in Chicago: in the face of falling trading volumes in existing contracts, the exchanges frequently turned to new contracts, with varying degrees of success. In response to slumping trade in its traditional contracts, the Board of Trade looked to soybean futures in 1936, soybean oil contracts in 1950 and soymeal futures the following year. The Chicago Mercantile Exchange—"the Merc"—meanwhile, tried to diversify during the Great Depression with cheese futures and potato contracts. In 1942, when the Second World War put a low limit on trading volumes, the Merc launched onion futures and an experimental contract in hides. In 1949, when trading volumes in egg futures slumped, the Merc had introduced apple, dressed poultry and frozen egg contracts.[1]

A similar motivation gripped the Chicago exchanges in the late 1960s. The catalyst that led to the creation of financial derivatives was really the search for diversification. Trading volumes had slumped at the Board of Trade as government-controlled agricultural surpluses drove down grain prices. The soybean market, which had become one of the exchange's most promising growth areas, went through a series of short periods in which markets went very quiet, prompting the senior of Chicago's two main trading venues to start to look once again for new contracts to trade. "People were sitting on the edge of the bean pit reading the newspaper, for lack of anything else to do," remembers Joe Sullivan, CBOE's first president, who was then director of the Board of Trade's planning and market development department and who—along with Eddie O'Connor, the exchange's vice Chairman and a member of the new products committee—would lead the effort to develop the new options market.

Meanwhile, although the recently introduced cattle and pork belly contracts had really taken off at the Merc, many at that exchange remained somewhat shell-shocked from the Congressional ban on onion futures in 1958, the first time a futures market had been closed by fiat from Washington.[2] Moreover, the markets for butter and eggs had been transformed by new technology, effectively making obsolete the corresponding futures contracts. These developments reinforced the notion that contracts could both be killed and die naturally. On one hand, this legacy spurred an even greater desire to diversify. On the other, the success of the new contracts—which were growing much faster than the Board of Trade's grain futures—put a spring in the step of the Merc, with the idea that the younger exchange might finally challenge its big brother on LaSalle Street for the limelight.[3]

Financial futures were not the first or the last contracts that were tried out in the energetic pursuit of diversification. The Board of Trade launched beef futures in 1965 and followed the Merc in introducing live cattle futures in 1966 (the Merc had introduced them in 1964). In 1968, the exchange launched futures on iced broilers (processed chickens packed in ice), followed by plywood futures and silver futures in 1969. Throughout the 1960s, as well as live cattle, live hogs and pork bellies, the Merc had launched a host of new contracts—futures on apples, potatoes, shrimp and turkeys—none of which really took off. The Merc also launched lumber futures in 1969. There was much that was innovative in these new products. Live hog and cattle contracts for the first time eliminated the problem of storage, while plywood, lumber, and silver futures took the exchanges away from their dependence on agricultural products. However, the aim was not necessarily to develop a novel breed of futures so much as to create a successful new trading vehicle that would extend the exchanges beyond their traditional products. "Basically we were looking for another pit, another contract," recalled Corky Eisen, by then a senior and active member of the Board of Trade. "We weren't thinking in terms of a new exchange. We weren't out to create a whole new world. We just wanted a little pit in the corner of the trading room."

It was in this context that financial futures emerged—as yet another possible route to diversifying the range of contracts being traded. The idea did not pop up in Chicago out of thin air. For some years, there had been discussions among traders, lawyers, and academics about how to craft financial derivative contracts. There was talk about the possibility of futures on bankers' acceptance notes, a type of commercial paper.[4] Milton Friedman, the University of Chicago economist, had publicly complained about retail investors being shut out of trading currency forwards after a series of US banks blocked him from selling short US$300,000-worth of British pounds in 1967. As a graduate student, Mark Powers, who went on to become the first economist at the Merc in 1969, had heard Friedman discuss foreign exchange futures in a public debate.[5] In 1968, Murray Borowitz, a former trucker and a member of the New York Produce Exchange, had proposed to launch futures on the Dow Jones Industrial Average on the newly formed National Product Exchange—a plan vetoed by the SEC.[6] That same year, senior members of the Board of Trade discussed and rejected the idea of a cash-settled futures contract on the Dow.[7] In 1970, Richard Sandor—then a professor at Berkeley and later the Board of Trade's chief economist—wrote a paper about futures on catastrophe risk for the Journal of British Finance.

Even such talk may not have been as novel as it seemed. Several years earlier, Elmer Falker, a spats-wearing, cigar-chomping, oyster-eating diminutive floor trader, had talked on the floor of the Merc about stock-index futures being the "ultimate" futures contract, but had lamented that "it will never happen 'cause you can't take delivery."[8]

Falker's comment suggests that such ideas had for some time been the subject of casual conversations in the futures world.

The hunt for new products took the two exchanges in different directions. Although the Board of Trade considered stock futures, the exchange ultimately decided to use its license with the Securities and Exchange Commission—the only one of its kind among the US commodities exchanges, it had been acquired in 1929 in order to trade stocks but had lain dormant since 1939—to trade equity options. The Merc decided to develop currency futures. Markets for both already existed—in the case of options, an OTC business run by put-and-call dealers in New York; while an inter-bank market operated for currency trading. Rather than reinventing the wheel, the Chicago exchanges were aiming to put their floor-trading expertise to work on bringing transparency, price discovery and openness to markets that were hitherto deeply inefficient (options) or highly restricted (currencies).

The lack of openness in the currency market had been exposed by Milton Friedman's repeated public expressions of frustration at having been locked out of trading in 1967. Another economist with a growing interest in derivatives—Myron Scholes—recalls being similarly irritated when trying to trade the OTC put and call options whose prices were advertised in Sunday editions of the *New York Times*. "I would price them all and call a dealer on Monday morning to make a trade," says Scholes. "He would tell me they were sold out and try to offer me something else. That's when I learned about 'bait and switch.'" The market was informal, inefficient and unorganized. Put and call dealers would gather in Michaèl's, a New York restaurant, working at the tables and the telephone booths.

Chicago was not alone in recognizing there was an opportunity in introducing exchange-trading to these markets. In April 1970—several years before financial futures traded in Chicago—the International Commercial Exchange (ICE), another project spearheaded by Murray Borowitz at the New York Produce Exchange, launched futures trading on nine currencies. The ICE's efforts would seem to have justified the paranoia of Leo Melamed, the Merc Chairman at the time, who spearheaded the effort to establish the International Monetary Market (IMM). "I thought it was such a good idea that someone would steal it—the Board of Trade, or if not them, those bastards in New York," he recalls.

However, Melamed and other Merc officials were calmed on a two-day visit to the ICE shortly after its launch. "It was like being in a library," he says. "There was no sound." The contracts he saw were quite unlike those he had in mind—sized at US$10,000-worth lots, they were more aimed at small businessmen traveling to Europe than at tapping into the interbank market. "They had it all wrong," he says. "If this was a good idea, it was a big idea and you needed the dealers to be involved, so the size of the contracts had to make sense." More critically, the ICE effort was introduced while the Bretton Woods system was still in place, denying the new market the volatility it needed to flourish.

Within two years, Bretton Woods had collapsed and the Merc launched IMM, whose success in the wake of ICE's failure suggested an instructive lesson—to succeed, Chicago did not have to be the first; it had to be the best. First-mover advantage was obviously important, but it did not guarantee success. Ultimately, it did not matter where the idea for financial futures originally came from. As Murray Borowitz had demonstrated, there was no profit *per se* in dreaming up the idea. What mattered was if the idea could successfully be put into practice. First-mover advantage only applied if the move itself was viable. Financial futures may not have been born in Chicago, but they certainly grew up there.

That lesson was reinforced at the tail-end of Chicago's "decade of innovation," when the Chicago exchanges were beaten by the Kansas City Board of Trade (KCBT) in the race to introduce index-based futures. KCBT launched Value Line stock index futures in February 1982 (it had first proposed them in 1977), two months before the Merc introduced Standard and Poor's (S&P) futures. Two years earlier, the world's first cash-settled futures contract had been launched not in the United States but at the Sydney Futures Exchange—a US dollar currency future.[9] In the United States, Kansas City received first approval in 1982 from the Commodity Futures Trading Commission for the first cash-settled index futures contract.[10] Nevertheless, ultimately the contracts thrived not in Kansas or in New York—where the New York Futures Exchange also launched a cash-settled index-based futures contract—but in Chicago, which contained by far the biggest pool of experienced futures traders. Within five months of being launched, the Merc's S&P contract had overtaken the combined trading activity of its rival products in New York and Kansas City.[11] To be sure, New York had a futures-trading community—particularly at the New York Produce Exchange, which had also spotted the opportunity offered by expanding into financial contracts—but it was not in the mainstream of Wall Street. The New York Produce Exchange had also been severely weakened by the US$150-million DeAngelis salad oil scandal of 1966. The result was that while the brightest and best minds in Chicago were completely focused on futures, their counterparts in New York were concentrated on equities.

With IMM, the Merc had launched the first viable market for financial derivatives, a record that might have gone the way of the Board of Trade were it not for the SEC's tortuous approval process. In fact, the Board of Trade's board first discussed the idea of an options exchange in 1969[12]—a year before the Merc's board began considering currency futures,[13] but securing the regulatory go-ahead proved a long road. The SEC's opposition to the proposal was embodied in Irving Pollack, then director of the agency's division of trading and markets (and subsequently an SEC commissioner), who Sullivan remembers as "an old-guard, throw-back regulator, bound and determined to stop us in our tracks." Pollack's attitude to the plan was encapsulated in a remark he made to Sullivan, in which he told the Board of Trade employee he had "never seen a market manipulation in which options weren't involved."[14] When the exchange first met the SEC staff to discuss the idea, Pollack told them "not to waste a nickel on this. There are absolutely insurmountable obstacles to doing what you're proposing, so forget it."[15] At times, SEC staff seemed willfully ignorant that what was being proposed was quite different to an equity exchange, insisting that exchange-created options have an "issuer," that margins be set at the same level as equities, that investors should receive prospectuses and that options should be traded through specialists rather than open outcry.[16]

By the early 1970s, attitudes in Washington began to change, as a more business-friendly tone filtered down through the agencies of the federal government following Richard Nixon becoming president in 1969. William Casey, who became SEC Chairman in 1971 (and subsequently went on to run the CIA under Ronald Reagan), was much more sympathetic to the Board of Trade's proposal and helped overcome the resistance of SEC staff.[17] By October 1971, Pollack himself gave the go-ahead in a letter written in fluent legalese. "Based on the material presented to date, the Commission finds that in principle the proposed options exchange does not appear to be inconsistent with relevant statutory requirements and standards," he wrote.

Although this marked a severe about-face for the SEC official, Joe Sullivan recalls that perhaps the only part of the CBOE proposal Pollack favored from the start was the plan to separate brokers and dealers and to give priority to public orders. In Pollack's view, this was far superior to the trading system at the New York equity exchanges, whose specialists the SEC staffer regarded as "a bunch of thieves," Sullivan recalls.

This difference was another critical reason why IMM and CBOE succeeded—the dynamism, camaraderie, and meritocracy of the trading floors of the Chicago exchanges stood in sharp contrast to their counterparts in New York. At the New York Stock Exchange and the Amex, liquidity was based on the specialist system. The specialists effectively had a monopoly on making markets in individual shares, while the rest of the market was made up by traders employed by brokerages. As Myron Scholes remembers: "The specialists had the keys to the city, they had the mantra, they had fixed commissions. They didn't have to innovate. They were selling securities in a securities-based world."

The Chicago system of trading had evolved very differently. Members of the exchange could trade in the pit either on their own account, as a broker for others, or both. This system had inherent conflicts of interest, but in Chicago no one had the "right" to be the marketmaker in a particular product. There was no concept of monopoly or franchise. Traders were not limited to any one pit, and often went from one to another, creating both genuine competition and a thirst for new trading opportunities. That made the Chicago exchanges the most vibrant, lively, competitive, and aggressive in the world, with the biggest pool of independent professional risk-bearers anywhere.

The distinction made a tangible difference to the market. For example, when the Amex launched options trading in 1975 and started to compete with CBOE, the spreads were tighter in Chicago. In 1977, *The Economist* noted that CBOE "has a superior form of market mechanism to conventional American stock exchanges; instead of one, occasionally two, 'specialists' who trade both as agents and as principals, there are several designated market-makers who trade only for their own account. The competing market-makers account for the higher volume of trading and for the finer spreads on CBOE."[18]

If the New York financial community tended to look down its nose at the Chicago trading style, the traders on the floors of the Merc and the Board of Trade reciprocated the sentiment, plus interest. "We thought New York was stodgy," recalls Charlie Carey, who began trading in the 1970s and went on to become Chairman of the Board of Trade in 2003. "We thought it was run by brokers and specialists. We thought that's what led to their inability to capture new ideas like the CBOE. It was run by the large New York firms. In Chicago, we were proud that what we did was open and honest. Anyone who wanted to had an equal chance of making money. You didn't feel that way about New York. It was a closed game, rigged against the customer."

There was also a strong sense of community among the Chicago traders. Many had little or no formal education, and the pit was their classroom. In Chicago, futures trading was a way for those with limited opportunities elsewhere to become wealthy and successful. Typically, people often began their lives at the exchanges as clerks before moving on to the trading pit. They grew up on the trading floor, both personally and professionally, with cohorts maturing under the watchful eyes of senior traders. They were often loud and brash, dressed sharply, used colorful language and socialized together after trading hours. "There was a very clubby atmosphere," recalls Charlie Carey. "It was a small grain-trading club. There were 1,400 members but only about 600 or 800 came to work every day—you'd be surprised how many of the guys down there you'd end up knowing. It was kind of clubby by pit."

Younger traders were often mentored by older patrons who gave or lent them the start-up money they needed for membership or trading. Corky Eisen recalled a conversation with his mentor in 1950. "He said: 'You've been given an opportunity here. You owe the same opportunity to those who come behind you.' That was the difference between Chicago and New York. There, you were born to it, here you aspired to it and you worked your way up."

The mentor gave Eisen US$15,000 to help him become a clearing member at the Board of Trade. "He said: 'here's how you get started,'" Eisen said. "I said: 'how do I thank you?'. He said: 'you don't. You owe somebody else a chance.' That was the culture here. Years later, after he retired to Florida, he came to visit Chicago and I took him to the market-makers' lounge and introduced him to a young trader sitting there. The young guy threw his arms around him and hugged him. 'I owe my start to you,' he said. 'Corky told me you wrote him a check to get him started, and he in turn has got me started. I owe my career to you.'"

Chicago was not entirely meritocratic, however. As in New York, where specialist positions often passed from father to son, having a relative on the floor was a big help, particularly at the Board of Trade. "It was difficult to break in to the Board of Trade unless you knew somebody, you had an entrée or someone shepherded you along," says Les Rosenthal. "I was lucky. The person who sponsored me didn't have a family of his own and he took me under his wing and sort of adopted me. Were it not for someone who was willing to sponsor me through the membership process, I wouldn't have been able to join." Ethnic ties also helped. Within Chicago, the Board of Trade was often known as "the Irish exchange" and the Merc "the Jewish exchange"—a caricature, albeit one with a grain of truth.[19]

The sense of community reflected the fact that there was an enormous amount of member control in Chicago, a structure that made members very interested in the institution of the exchange itself. Member control was reflected in their attitude to even the most senior exchange employees, who the traders regarded as their employees. The members had in mind not only what the exchange presented them in terms of opportunities to trade but also what was "best" for the institution. Corky Eisen and other traders of longstanding at the Board of Trade would deliberately trade newly launched contracts to try to ensure they would be a success. He recalled a colleague's reaction when Eisen rushed to participate in trading a new futures contract for live chickens. "He said to me: 'what do you know about trading chickens?' I said: 'Absolutely nothing, but I don't care if it's horseshit or hay—it's a contract and I'll trade it.'" Soon after Eddie O'Connor had helped establish CBOE, he returned full-time to the soybean pit. "I got involved in the options only because we were in expansion mode," he says. "I was doing it for the exchange, but my livelihood was trading soybeans."

Member control could also be a burden—particularly when it came to trying to secure internal approval for launching financial futures. The Board of Trade faced a more serious hurdle in this regard. As the more established exchange, it had a more conservative culture. Even after the SEC gave the CBOE proposal the initial nod, Sullivan and O'Connor still faced considerable opposition among the members. Some of the naysayers were motivated by business considerations. The membership of the Board of Trade could be broadly divided into "locals"—independent traders—and "commercials" working for the big food-processing companies. The locals were more keen on the idea, while the commercials, in general, were not. "The Board of Trade was an agricultural exchange," recalled Corky Eisen." It was run by the Cargills, the Continental Grains and the Bunges, and that was their world. It was very difficult to sell them on the concept of coming up with a new trading vehicle. They liked it just the way it was." These companies with long institutional memories were also aware of the part options—in their former guise as "privileges"—had played their part in the Great Wheat Collapse of 1932, when speculators tried to corner the wheat market using calls and futures, a scandal that led to commodity options trading to be banned under the 1936 Commodity Exchange Act. Equity options had almost been banned as well two years earlier.

Other opposition was more down to internal politics, led by a trader named Ford Ferguson, whose faction had not only backed the idea of trading Dow Jones futures but also strongly disliked the leaders of the CBOE effort. "Whatever O'Connor tried to do, Ferguson was against it," Eddie O'Connor recalls. Another problem was that by early 1970s, the commodity markets had taken off again, and the need for diversification seemed less urgent. The interminable dealings with the SEC meant most Board of Trade members saw no progress for at least two years. On a few occasions, only the Chairman's casting vote kept the project alive.[20] At times, Sullivan and O'Connor pulled the wool over the members' eyes in order to hide the spiraling costs.[21]

As the up-and-coming exchange, the Merc was more open to new ideas.[22] In the late 1960s, a group of "young Turks" had seized control of the Board. However, Leo Melamed recalls that there was some initial opposition to the plans for IMM. "There were former egg traders, agricultural traders who opposed the move into financial futures," he says. "Cattle and pork bellies were doing well and hogs were coming up. The cost of membership had gone up from US$3,000 to US$100,000. They thought it would be a risk, that it would blow up and destroy the exchange or make us a laughing stock."

Even in the mid-1970s, when CBOE had demonstrated success, the Board of Trade membership was far from convinced about Ginnie Mae futures. "Whatever programme you came up with, there was always 49 percent of the group that was against it," says Les Rosenthal. When it came to the proposal to issue special-purpose seats to trade the new contracts, the member ballot was only won by two votes—one of whom had to be dragged back from O'Hare Airport to participate in the vote.[23] One recurring argument was that new contracts would take away business from established ones, recalls Richard Sandor. "First they argued the bonds would take liquidity from the Ginnie Maes. Then they argued the 10-year T-notes would take liquidity from the bonds. Then they argued the bond options would take liquidity from the bonds. None of it was true. In fact, they created liquidity because people wanted to speculate on the yield curve," Sandor says.

The ability to overcome such opposition was another aspect that set Chicago apart. The city's exchanges were blessed with extraordinary leaders—both political leaders and thought leaders—who collaborated to bring new ideas to fruition in the face of internal and external obstacles. Leo Melamed, Joe Sullivan, Eddie O'Connor, Richard Sandor, Les Rosenthal—these men were extraordinary visionaries, risk-takers, unafraid to use their intellectual imagination, determined to bring their ideas to fruition and devout believers in the future of their industry.

The Merc—which was to overtake the Board of Trade in size and eventually to acquire it—also had tremendous continuity of leadership, which saw Leo Melamed and Jack Sandner in powerful positions for decade after decade. That continuity provided a long-term vision that enabled the exchange to flourish.

In spite of this leadership, the opposition to IMM and CBOE suggested that even though Chicago had established liquidity and dominance in futures trading, it would not necessarily be a straightforward task to transfer it over to the newly listed products. The exchanges responded ingeniously. At the Merc, rather than depending on the existing members to move from their established pits over to the untested markets, the exchange created a new institution with its own membership.[24] Every full Merc member received an IMM seat, but the exchange also created 150 new memberships, which went on sale to the public at the relatively low price of US$10,000. This innovation overcame both the problem of depending on veterans to provide the bulk of liquidity and—because membership was very affordable—tapped the pool of young would-be futures traders for whom the cost of a full membership was prohibitive. As a result, the exchange attracted young blood—a tranche of new, youthful traders, including professionals attracted by the prospect of making serious money; fresh college graduates; sons, relatives, and friends of Merc members; and "runners" or others in low-level positions at the Merc. "They were different because they were hungry, they were in their twenties and thirties and they had something to prove," recalls Leo Melamed.

CBOE was also established as a separate entity. In part, this was because opponents at the Board of Trade took the view that it should shoulder its own debts rather than foist them on its parent. Moreover, for regulatory reasons it also made sense not to make equity options simply another pit on the established trading floor.[25] As its own exchange, CBOE also had its own sale of seats—which, like those at IMM, were priced at US$10,000. However, in order to ensure liquidity, CBOT, as the founder exchange, gave all of its 1,302 members a perpetual right to trade at CBOE, inadvertently creating a problem that would later came back to haunt the options exchange in a series of lawsuits that delayed its demutualization and were only resolved in 2009. CBOE's trading hours were longer than those of the grain pits, staying open until 3 PM to allow them to cross over to the options floor when trading finished at 1.15 PM on the main exchange. (When it came to launching financial futures, the Board of Trade similarly stratified the trading hours to accommodate grain traders who wished to cross over after the main pits had closed for the day.) In line with the collegial sentiment of helping new contracts along, a group of senior traders also created "the lunch bunch"—up to 40 people who would move over to trade options when the grain pits were quiet between 11 AM and 12.30 PM.[26] Both the longer hours and the "lunch bunch" helped create instant liquidity at CBOE and added to its success.[27]

Chicago's other great built-in advantage over New York was in clearing. The weakness of the settlement process in New York was exposed in the late 1960s and early 1970s in the paperwork crisis, which overwhelmed back offices and forced the New York Stock Exchange to reduce trading hours, extend the settlement cycle by one day and shut its doors every Wednesday. Rather than genuine clearing houses, New York had mechanisms for physically delivering stocks after each trans-action. By contrast, the nature of a future or option was different, so clearing was more efficient in Chicago, where futures trading and clear-ing functioned effectively throughout the paperwork crisis (albeit on lower volumes). When New York subsequently succeeded in immobi-lizing stock certificates by creating the Depository Trust Company and the National Securities Clearing Corporation, "they recreated the Chicago system," says Wayne Luthringshausen, who was put in charge of CBOE's clearing house at its inception.

CBOE's clearing house—modeled on that of the Board of Trade's Clearing Corp—began as a wholly-owned subsidiary of CBOE. However, in 1975, when the Amex was seeking to launch options trading, negotia-tions at the SEC between the exchanges produced two possible solu-tions: interfaced clearing houses—essentially recreating the stock model—or one common clearing house. Luthringshausen convinced Sullivan to push for the latter option. "If Amex came in with its own clearing, it wouldn't be long before the New Yorkers moved all their business there," he recalls. "So I said: 'Let's control clearing as much as we can.' I convinced him we needed to fight to keep it in Chicago. If we hadn't, the New Yorkers would've overwhelmed it." What emerged was the Options Clearing Corporation (OCC), still based in Chicago and now the world's biggest derivatives clearing house.

With the creation of IMM and CBOE, the dawn of financial deriva-tives had arrived. Both of the Chicago exchanges had established sepa-rate trading institutions dedicated exclusively to the buying and selling of financial products, the first time such a thing had happened outside New York. Building on its long history of futures trading, the city had moved beyond agricultural products and into a new era. A few big names on Wall Street came to Chicago to trade for the first time. The dawn of a new era was not immediately evident, however. The general attitude in New York to IMM was one of dismissive indifference or incredulity, although some of the more progressive thinkers on Wall Street showed more interest initially in CBOE—including Robert Rubin, then a partner at Goldman Sachs, who was a founding director of the exchange. The transformation of Chicago into an important financial hub was not truly recognized until after the "decade of innovation." Some in Chicago would say today that the leaders of Wall Street have still yet to recognize the city's status. Nevertheless, within a few years of the launch of IMM and CBOE, financial derivatives seemed to be on the verge of fulfilling Leo Melamed's uncharacteristically modest boast to Richard J. Daley, the legendary mayor of Chicago, that they would "move the centre of gravity of finance in the country a couple of feet west of New York."[28]

Having created new memberships through the creation of IMM and CBOE, the Chicago exchanges repeated the trick throughout the decade. When the Board of Trade launched interest rate futures, it created another class of memberships to trade the new contracts. In 1976, the Merc further expanded its membership by offering 300 seats at the relatively cheap price of US$30,000 each to nonlivestock traders in what was to become the Associate Mercantile Market Division. In 1982, the Merc did the same when it secured a license to trade Standard and Poor's index futures, creating 1,300 new seats in its Index and Options Market (IOM) for all members (at a cost of US$30,000 each) and sold more seats to the public (for US$60,000 each). The Board of Trade did the same with the Index, Debt and Energy Market (IDEM) and the Commodities Options Market (COM) in 1982. Each new development became an opportunity to create more memberships, tied to trading particular new products. The system ensured that the contracts would be successful and freed them from any dependence on veteran traders. As Les Rosenthal puts it, the seat expansions were

> ". . . designed to attract "cannon fodder" for the new contracts . . .
> It was very difficult to get an established corn trader to trade US
> government bonds. We designed memberships that could only
> trade government bonds and couldn't trade corn, so the corn
> trader wouldn't be worried about creating competition for
> himself."

The result was that from 1972 to 1982, the number of exchange memberships tripled to about 6,000. The net effect was that capital and liquidity poured into the new markets.

Although this was a further step for the exchanges, they had always understood the importance of creating liquidity in new products—something their New York counterparts had never had to deal with. As far back as the 1850s, the Board of Trade had tried luring traders with a free lunch of cheese, crackers, and ale when trading was slow.[29]

In the 1930s, the Merc enthusiastically solicited new members with newspaper ads, educational pamphlets, and by cold-calling commodity brokers. In the late 1960s, the Merc had hired Martin Cohen, a daring young advertising executive, who had created eye-catching ads that even ran in *Playboy* magazine. Being naturally more conservative, the Board of Trade was slower to dive in to modern advertising, but by the time Ginnie Mae futures were launched, the exchange made up for it with an ad in *Forbes* that promoted the new contract by personalizing Ginnie as a beautiful young woman, winking one lash-rich eye at the reader with an enticing look. "We're not plain grain any more," the ad stated. As an industry with a shady reputation, about which many investors were either ignorant or had a negative opinion, the futures and options industry was forced to market its products in a way that stock markets did not. The Chicago exchanges set out on these campaigns with a missionary zeal. To promote IMM, the Merc sent its top executives on a European road show to drum up support from investors across the Atlantic. Since volumes at IMM built up slowly, the exchange was forced to promote it even harder. In 1980, the Merc went on to become the first US exchange to open an office in the City of London. Such efforts not only helped build liquidity for the exchanges themselves, but also had a positive effect on the entire industry. The success of options in the United States, for example, in large measure depended on CBOE's efforts in direct education to both brokers and customers.

The Chicago exchanges understood, then, that new products had to be explained, that investors and traders needed to be educated. As the "lunch bunch" demonstrated, within the exchanges, a sense had also developed that liquidity had to be created, with exchange leaders and senior members prodding their fellow traders to help provide volume. When the Merc came to launch S&P futures in 1982, Jack Sandner and Leo Melamed ran a highly effective campaign that saw them standing at the door of the exchange and handing out lapel badges to every trader with the motto "Fifteen minutes, please" on them, to try to encourage traders to spend some time each day trading the new contracts. Such efforts came after many contracts over the years had fallen by the wayside. For much of the history of the Chicago exchanges, product development had been akin to throwing mud at a wall and trading whatever stuck, with committees of traders coming up with ideas for new contracts without a great deal of preparatory research.

In the late 1960s, both the Merc and the Board of Trade started to take a more professional approach, hiring teams of economists to research new products and potential markets. Mark Powers, an agricultural economist at the University of Wisconsin who had written his doctoral dissertation on pork belly futures, went to work for the Merc in 1969, where he played a critical role in the development of IMM. Richard Sandor, a professor at Berkeley, joined the Board of Trade in 1972, where the departure of Joe Sullivan—not an academic but a former financial journalist—to CBOE had left a research void. The recruitment of academic economists was another difference between Chicago and New York. Some veteran members did not see the need to recruit academics. "What do we need a doctor for?" Izzy Mulmat, a Jewish émigré who retained a strong Central European accent, asked rhetorically when the Merc hired Powers. "Are we a hospital?"[30] However, such appointments were a natural corollary to the need of Chicago's exchanges to create new products to trade. Because the markets were innovative, experimental and valued financial engineering, they were attractive to the top minds in cutting-edge financial research—among them, Nobel laureates Milton Friedman, Myron Scholes (whose collaborator Fischer Black had died by the time Scholes was awarded the Nobel) and Robert Merton. "Here was a live, real market that people came to study," says Sandor. "It was a laboratory for economists."

For example, a 1968 study of the options market, led by Burton Malkiel and Richard Quandt at the Financial Research Center at Princeton University, encouraged the Board of Trade to try to bring exchange trading to the options market. (Quandt, Malkiel and their Princeton colleague William Baumol, along with James Lorie and Merton Miller of the University of Chicago and Paul Cootner of MIT, also helped write the Nathan Report, the CBOE feasibility study submitted to the SEC.) Milton Friedman, then a professor at the University of Chicago, wrote the feasibility study for IMM and teamed up with Melamed to promote the idea.

The academics were not just a source of ideas. The exchanges used the support of Friedman and Malkiel and Quandt to add an air gravitas and respectability to undertakings that met with a great deal of skepticism and deprecation, particularly in New York. When the Black-Scholes formula was published—by happy coincidence, a few months after CBOE launched—it not only helped traders in the fledgling market to price options accurately, but also added to the status of the new exchange, with the idea that some of the youngest and brightest economists of the day were interested in how the market functioned.

As Sandor was to find out when he made the move from San Francisco to Chicago (a move initially made as a one-year sabbatical) however, having good ideas only got you so far. Together with Warren Lebeck, the Board of Trade's executive vice president and secretary, Sandor drafted the first contract for Ginnie Mae futures in April 1972,[31] one month before the launch of IMM. Although the contract needed to be reshaped no fewer than 23 times before it was ready to trade, the most serious hurdle the Board of Trade faced was regulatory. Under the US regulatory framework of the early 1970s, interest-rate futures would have been viewed as securities and thus subject to the jurisdiction of the SEC. Given the hoops, the Board of Trade had been forced to jump through to gain approval for CBOE, that was not a prospect the exchange relished repeating. At the same time, it became clear that with the futures sector's expansion into financial contracts, the industry's continued regulation by the US Department of Agriculture's flaccid Commodity Exchange Authority[32] was becoming unsustainable. Political action to enhance oversight of the futures industry was also spurred by the widespread outrage in the early 1970s at the rising cost of food—a phenomenon many consumers blamed on the phantom of "speculation" at the Board of Trade and the Merc. In response, Congress recommended a new watchdog designed specifically for futures markets, including financial futures. The Board of Trade—which had spent a considerable amount of time developing ties and educating staff at the Agriculture department—initially balked at the idea, but quickly came to see that it could shape the new agency to its benefit. The Merc was also enthusiastic.

Chicago's main point man in the negotiations in Washington over the new agency was Philip McBride Johnson, the Board of Trade's outside counsel. During two years of hearings, Johnson practically lived in the capital, explaining time and again the role of the futures markets and rebutting accusations of excessive speculation. The Board of Trade had sent Johnson to Washington to secure two main objectives. First, to ensure the new agency would have sole and exclusive authority over the futures markets. Secondly, the young lawyer was tasked with the aim of making sure "that the definition of a commodity would get broadened out to include just about anything that the mind could imagine," Johnson recalls. This broadening out had to be done without using the word "security." There was a concern that the interest-rate futures the Board of Trade was developing would be deemed in Washington as instruments on securities, raising the prospect that the exchange would once again become entangled in a drawn-out approval process at the SEC. To Johnson's credit, he fulfilled his mission on both counts, in spite of the efforts of some at the SEC—who feared the erosion of the distinction between securities and commodities—to thwart the Chicago lobby.

The creation of the Commodity Futures Trading Commission (CFTC) in 1975 was a milestone for the futures industry. For the first time, futures markets were regulated according to contract type rather than the underlying commodity. This cut across the existing regulatory framework, however, setting up a perennial turf war between the new agency and the more powerful SEC. Moreover, the creation of the CFTC allowed futures trading on intangibles such as interest rates for the first time. By providing a clear and unambiguous regulatory framework, it set the legal foundation for the futures industry to become largely financial. Ironically, it also represented an important moment of recognition for an industry that had so often been overlooked. As Richard Sandor notes: "You know you've arrived in Washington when you get your own regulatory agency."

In the wake of the ban on onion futures, the Chicago exchanges had talked about stepping up their visibility in Washington, but the creation of the CFTC made that a more urgent need. The Board of Trade set up a political action committee in 1976 and the Merc did the same the following year. They raised money quickly: in his first address to the membership as Merc Chairman in 1980, Jack Sandner was able to boast that the exchange's political action committee was second only to Standard Oil's, with a war chest of US$340,000.[33] Both exchanges set up permanent offices in Washington to work with the CFTC and lobby Congress. The exchanges also looked to the US Department of Agriculture when recruiting new staff, such as the Merc's appointment of Clayton Yeutter, a former Assistant Secretary of Agriculture (and subsequent Agriculture Secretary) as its Chief Executive in 1978.

As soon as the CFTC was up and running, the Board of Trade secured approval for Ginnie Mae futures, the first financial futures launched on the exchange. Like IMM and CBOE, Ginnie Maes sought to standardize and transfer over to exchange-trading forward contracts from an OTC market. When Richard Sandor began researching Ginnie Mae futures after arriving in Chicago, he soon learned that the Federal Home Loan Bank Board, the Citizens Federal Savings and Loans Association in San Francisco and "Freddie Mac"—the Federal Home Loan Mortgage Corporation—had all been working on the same idea.[34] These organizations provided important political support in Washington during the debates around the creation of the CFTC.

When the Board of Trade launched Ginnie Maes in 1975, there was no long bond market in the United States. "If there was a long bond, we probably would've done that first," says Sandor. However, once the US federal government started to issue long-term debt, the exchange instantly recognized it would be more volatile than Ginnie Maes and had the potential to be a far bigger market. "We figured we were in the right church but the wrong pew," recalls Les Rosenthal. In the meantime, the Merc—which had been advised that Ginnie Mae futures were unfeasible and that there would be more business on the short end of the Treasury curve than the long—responded rapidly to the Board of Trade's entry into interest rate contracts by launching futures on 90-day Treasury bills in 1976. The Board of Trade countered with 20-year T-bond futures in 1977, the most successful futures contract in the history of the industry. The Merc hit back with futures on one-year T-bills in 1978 and 4-year T-notes in 1979. In 1982, the Board launched futures on 10-year T-notes.

This exchange of contract gunfire suggested another reason why Chicago's futures industry was so dynamic: there was competition between the exchanges. It was rarely the kind of head-to-head competition that led to them listing similar contracts, however, and more the kind of rivalry between two exchanges both trying to assert themselves as the top trading venue in the futures world. Although the Board of Trade had historically looked down on the Merc and continued to do so for much of the 1970s, it could not ignore how the younger exchange had grown very fast, taking an increasing slice of market share and overtaking by some measures. "The Merc had gone from nothing to a major exchange in a few years," says Eddie O'Connor. "That was an impetus for the Board of Trade to get into an expansion mode." For its part, the Merc had a point to prove and a rival to catch up with. "We would try to beat them to the punch on a product design," says Jack Sandner. The exchanges had tended to dance around each other, even when they competed, although in the 1960s the rivalry had intensified around live cattle and beef contracts. There was no direct tussle in the interest rate products both launched in the 1970s, but there was a general sense of competition to be the "best" exchange in Chicago. This spirit was another advantage Chicago had over New York, where the relations between the exchanges were very different.

In spite of Chicago's increasing presence in Washington, the exchanges could not insulate themselves from the broader political climate. Just as the Nixon administration had been good to the futures world, President Jimmy Carter looked on it less favorably. In 1978, Carter even floated the idea of scrapping the CFTC. James Stone, Carter's choice as CFTC Chairman in 1979, was seen by the industry as hostile, and product approval under his leadership slowed to a sluggish crawl. Stone, a former Massachusetts insurance commissioner and brother of Oliver Stone, the Hollywood director, clashed with both Chicago exchanges in 1980—struggles that the exchanges were able to win by using their new lobbying might on Capitol Hill. Although the Stone years were challenging, industry lobbying was able to block the appointment of Hugh Cadden, Stone's special assistant, and Jamie Wade, another Stone protégé (known in Chicago as the "Stone Clone") to seats on the Commission.

When Ronald Reagan became president in 1981, a more benign environment prevailed towards the Chicago exchanges. Reagan named Philip McBride Johnson to be the new CFTC chief. For the first time, the agency had a Chairman who knew the industry from the inside—and from the perspective of Chicago. Within several months, the Chicago exchanges would be thankful for having their own "man on the inside." In 1981, CBOE applied to trade options on Ginnie Maes. The Board of Trade—fearful of any damage to its lucrative futures contract—first objected to the SEC and then sued when the Commission approved the contract, bringing the CFTC–SEC conflict into a federal courtroom. The resolution of this case ultimately enabled the creation of index-based futures, finally severing the exclusive link between derivatives and physical assets. The great hurdle between the futures exchanges and the juicy opportunity of index-based contracts—long a dream of the futures industry—was deliverability. The obvious solution was cash settlement, yet this was the very issue that in the minds of many had long drawn the line between "legitimate" commercial trading and "illegitimate" financial speculation. In the nineteenth century, the Board of Trade had successfully waged a legal war against "bucket shops," which took bets on what prices the markets would quote, even persuading the state of

Illinois to change its gambling laws to outlaw cash-settled contracts.[35] By 1981, for decades only a tiny fraction of contracts had been physically settled (most were settled by offsetting the trade by buying or selling an "opposite" contract), but the underlying commodity was always deliverable. On the face of it, Eurodollar futures—another highly successful contract, developed by Fred Arditti, the Merc's chief economist and launched in 1981—were cash-settled, but the underlying commodity was itself US dollars. That was not the case for stock index-based contracts, which for the first time required that an underlying asset be translated into cash for settlement. John Shad, then Chairman of the SEC, and Philip McBride Johnson both understood the market disruption that would occur in securities markets if they were to insist on delivery in index-based futures.[36]

The 1982 Shad-Johnson Accord that emerged from negotiations between the chairmen formally established two critical principles: that securities were within the CFTC's jurisdiction when futures trading was involved; and that cash-settlement was valid for futures (even though the CFTC's statute referred time and again to a delivery right). This brought the idea of cash-settlement out of its 80-year-old exile, finally "legitimizing" the practice and paving the way for the introduction of index-based derivatives. Once again, Johnson—backed up by the exchange's powerful lobbying arms—had secured Chicago's interests in Washington. Bill Brodsky, who was the Amex's executive vice president at the time, remembers feeling that in the negotiations, the Chicago exchanges "ate our lunch," outwitting and outmaneuvering both the SEC and the New York exchanges, who felt that politics and lobbying were somehow beneath them and underestimated how good the Chicago exchanges had become at the Washington game.

The advent of cash-settlement and the increasing strength of Chicago's voice on Capitol Hill did not mean that arguments about speculation were over. The bankruptcy of the Hunt brothers, which caused ructions in silver, gold, and cattle markets in 1980, forced the Chicago exchanges to make their case much more widely than to the agriculture committees on Capitol Hill with whom they were used to dealing. There had been such hearings on the futures markets before, but the Hunt scandal caught the public's imagination, shining a bright, accusatory light on the industry. Jack Sandner remembers testifying in front of Senate banking committee presided over by William Proxmire, the Wisconsin Democrat. Butting in ahead of Sandner's opening statement, Proxmire began the hearing saying: "Before you speak, I want to tell you what I think about what you do: what you do is like Klondike fever at the Indianapolis 500." The mixed metaphor may have been hostile, but at least by calling the Merc to give evidence, Congress was recognizing that the exchanges had become important financial institutions.

The Shad-Johnson Accord enabled the exchanges to launch the stock index-based derivatives that Elmer Falker, Murray Borowitz, Joe Sullivan and Eddie O'Connor had dreamt of but been unable to trade. Kansas City had just beaten Chicago to the starting line, but with the vibrancy of their trading floors, the Merc and Board of Trade knew they could do better. The Board of Trade misstepped, listing a contract based on the Dow Jones Industrial Average without first consulting Dow Jones. "We thought it was like the word 'aspirin,' that it had become generic," says Sandor. The exchange had to withdraw the contract. The Merc had tried to collaborate with Dow Jones but was rebuffed, which propelled it into the arms of Standard and Poor's. The exchange negoti-ated an excellent deal for use of the S&P 500—one so favorable to the Merc that it voluntarily reworked the agreement two years later to give more revenue to S&P. The year after the Merc launched S&P futures, CBOE launched options on what was to become the S&P 100, the first cash-settled index option.

As they moved into the world of stock indexes, the Chicago futures exchanges needed to tap expertise from Wall Street—especially since New York was becoming increasingly aware of the potential for financial futures and threatening head-on competition. The Merc acted boldly in 1982 by poaching Bill Brodsky from the Amex to be its executive vice president and Chief Operating Officer. It was the first time the Chicago exchanges had gone to New York to find a senior executive with expertise in stocks and options. "It's a sign of the times that William Brodsky doesn't know beans about pork bellies," the *Chicago Tribune* observed wryly.

A year that had already proved its place in futures history was capped when later in 1982, the Board of Trade launched options on Treasury bond futures, a move that would be echoed throughout the 1980s with the launch of options on a wide range of financial and agricultural futures.

In terms of new products, industry growth and the wider use of derivatives, the "decade of innovation" marked just the beginning for the financial futures and options industries. However, much of the ground-work for that future expansion was already set. The growth of financial products was so explosive that it was clear by 1982 that they represented the industry's future. The most popular products of subsequent decades would be contracts launched between 1972 and 1982: equity options, Treasury futures, Eurodollars, and index-based derivatives. In subsequent decades, these contracts would provide entire suites of products, with a host of new contracts based around the original building blocks put in place during the "decade of innovation." They became part of mainstream finance, widely used by companies, money managers, financial institutions, and trading houses as an integral part of their investment strategies. In 1979, Salomon Brothers made news by hedging part of a US$1 billion IBM bond offering using T-bond futures. Morgan Guaranty Trust set up Morgan Futures Corp in 1981, becoming the first big commercial bank authorized as a futures commission merchant.[37] The US government rapidly came to depend on the Treasury futures market, to the extent that a few days before Christmas in 1982, the government held an auction for US$3 billion of 20-year bonds one day ahead of schedule so as to allow the Board of Trade to close at noon on December 23 as usual.[38] The arguments about speculation did not disappear (they were to reemerge a few years later after the 1987 crash) but the futures industry had its own Washington watchdog and a clearly defined legal framework.

Chicago's need to promote the futures and options industry and its belief in its value to modern financial markets also prompted a willingness to share its intellectual capital. CBOE helped the European Options Exchange launch in Amsterdam in 1978. Not only was EOE modeled on CBOE, but traders also used the same kinds of jackets as their counterparts in Chicago and conducted business in English. Veterans of the Chicago exchanges also helped launch the London International Financial Futures Exchange in 1982. Chicago would go on to aid the launch of the Singapore International Monetary Exchange in 1984 by providing clearing services through an electronic link. Some in financial circles wondered why Chicago would give away its secrets, but in the Windy City the belief was that the more people that understood the value of derivative instruments, the more the Chicago exchanges would ultimately benefit. By contrast, the New York stock exchanges lacked both the same kind of know-how to share and the proselytizing ethos of their Chicago counterparts.

Chicago's exchanges had shrugged off their purely agricultural past and created a brave new world, one in which the city was an important international center. They had succeeded because they had experience of developing new products and liquidity; because their trading floors were vibrant and aggressive; because they had built a presence in the corridors of political power; because they possessed energetic, entrepre-neurial, and determined leaders; because they attracted the brightest theoretical minds; because of cross-town rivalry; because they believed in spreading the word about derivatives markets; because they took nothing for granted.

Good timing, prescience, and luck also played their part. A prime example was the Black-Scholes formula, which had little to do with Chicago's efforts. Rather, it sprang from what Myron Scholes regarded as the "interesting academic exercise" of trying to value options based on OTC data collected by his students. Black and Scholes had first pre-sented their ideas in a 1970 paper, but had difficulty publishing it until 1973, shortly after CBOE launched. By coincidence, around the same time, handheld calculators were introduced, proving extremely valuable to options floor traders—so much so that Texas Instruments hard wired the formula into their models specifically to be sold to traders at CBOE. While the story of CBOE, Black-Scholes and the handheld calculator marked the unique confluence of three unrelated events, broader trends also helped other Chicago markets to flourish. IMM capitalized on the collapse of Bretton Woods. Ginnie Maes were born out of the creation of the CFTC. Treasury futures benefited from the 1979 "Saturday Night Massacre," when Paul Volcker, then Chairman of the Federal Reserve, decided to target the money supply instead of interest rates, and the issuing of huge amounts of government debt. Index-based futures had the Shad-Johnson Accord. Portfolio theory was increasingly coming into play, making derivatives more attractive to financial institutions.

Innovation did not cease after 1982. The Chicago exchanges still launched new products and made them successful. However, the "paradigm shifts" of the kind that IMM, CBOE, Treasury futures, and index contracts represented became much fewer and further between. CBOE's Volatility Index, introduced in 1993, was a genuinely "basic invention" of the same kind. Other attempts at new products—such as weather (also developed by Fred Arditti), real estate, and carbon emis-sions contracts (championed by Richard Sandor)—have not yet attracted large trading volumes. In the years after the "decade of innovation," organic growth in the new financial markets meant there was simply no need for exchanges to look aggressively at "blue sky" inventive activity. There was the entire yield curve on Treasuries to be filled in, indices to be added, and options on futures to be rolled out. By the 1990s, the exchanges' attention turned to issues such as demutualization, electronic trading, and infrastructure building to accommodate the massive new markets. Later on, a good deal of product innovation began to move from exchanges to electronic trading firms, which developed their own algorithms rather than depending on the exchanges to launch new instruments. The Chicago Mercantile Exchange's (CME) purchase of the Chicago Board of Trade (CBOT) in 2007 put an end to cross-town rivalry and created the largest financial exchange in the world, an institution that could easily afford to buy innovation.

Today, thanks to the "decade of innovation," Chicago is comfortably among the world's financial centers. However, that period demonstrates that incumbency can slide into inertia; and Chicago cannot afford to become complacent. In the days of electronic markets, rivals can as easily emerge from Atlanta or Kansas City as from New York. As competition becomes ever more global, new competitors are springing up in emerging economies, which have the power to develop their relatively untapped markets in innovative directions. In the 1970s, Wall Street and securities markets operated in a quite different world from derivatives. The "decade of innovation" transformed finance by changing the very idea of what capital markets could become. Nowadays, barriers between asset classes have largely been eliminated—at least, outside the United States—opening up the world of finance to new trading possibilities. The experience of Chicago suggests that to take advantages of these new opportunities, exchanges around the world would do well to think more imaginatively than simply mimicking products that have already been established elsewhere. With electronic trading dominating markets and most exchanges no longer owned by traders, they cannot depend on the pits to generate ideas. That makes it even more important for exchanges to maintain open lines of communication with their customers, both as a sounding board for the new kinds of financial instruments they are trying to develop and to encourage liquidity when it comes to launching them. Moreover, as the "decade of innovation" showed, a good sense of timing is everything. As the global economy continues to become ever-more interwoven, international trends will throw up new opportunities for trading as-yet-unthought-of financial instruments. In an age in which financial markets are truly global, the competition is furious, but the rewards are vast and the possibilities endless.

Notes

All quotes are from interviews with the author unless otherwise footnoted. The author thanks those who gave time to be interviewed for this chapter: Bill Brodsky, Charlie Carey, Corky Eisen, Scott Gordon, Philip McBride Johnson, Wayne Luthringshausen, Leo Melamed, Eddie

O'Connor, Les Rosenthal, Jack Sandner, Richard Sandor, Myron Scholes, and Joe Sullivan. Corky Eisen sadly passed away in April 2010, shortly after a second interview with the author.

1 Tamarkin, Bob, *The Merc: The Emergence of a Global Financial Powerhouse* New York: HarperBusiness, 1993, p. 61, 86.

2 The 1958 Onion Futures Act was prompted by lobbying by the National Onion Growers Association, which argued that speculation at the Merc had driven down onion prices. The law was introduced into Congress by Gerald Ford, at the time a Republican representative from Michigan who went on to become US president. It has never been repealed.

3 By 1969, Everette Harris, CME Chairman, was boasting that pork belly futures at the Merc had overtaken corn futures at the Board of Trade in August of that year as the world's most traded futures contract, with cattle futures a close third. Volume at the Merc was also ahead of the Board of Trade's in August 1969 (see "History of the Chicago Mercantile Exchange" by Everette B. Harris, available to download on www.cmegroup.com).

4 Comment by Richard Sandor, in interview with author.

5 Tamarkin, p. 179.

6 Falloon, William D., *Market Maker: A Sesquicentennial Look at the Chicago Board of Trade* Chicago: Board of Trade of the City of Chicago, 1998, p. 209; Tamarkin, p. 157; Lothian, John, "Who is Murray Borowitz?," John Lothian Newsletter, September 16, 2004.

7 Falloon, p. 210.

8 Cited in Tamarkin, p. 99.

9 Tamarkin, p. 270; author correspondence with Matthew Gibbs, Manager Corporate Relations at ASX, March 16, 2010.

10 Tamarkin, p. 429.

11 Sandner, Jack, address to the Financial Times World Financial Futures Conference, London, September 14, 1982.

12 Falloon, p. 211.

13 Tamarkin, p. 183.

14 Cited in Falloon, p. 220.

15 Interview with Joe Sullivan.

16 Interview with Philip McBride Johnson.

17 Interview with Joe Sullivan.

18 Cited in Falloon, p. 226.

19 "Before World War One, the Board of Trade was very WASPy, but then the Irish started to take clerk jobs at the exchange," said Corky Eisen. "Later, there was a three-pronged membership: Irish, Jewish and WASP." Certainly, many senior leaders and traders at the Merc had been Jewish immigrants.

20 Falloon, p. 221.

21 Falloon, p. 218.

22 Eddie O'Connor recalls that it was easier selling CBOE memberships to CME members than to getting support for the idea at CBOT, because "they were used to backing new concepts."

23 Recollection by Richard Sandor, in interview with the author.

24 IMM subsequently became a division of the Merc in 1976.

25 Sullivan recalls that this would have made CBOT traders subject to regulation by the SEC.

26 Joe Sullivan remembers this group as "the McDonald's lunch bunch," as they would tend to trade McDonald's options, whose post was the closest to the main CBOT trading floor.

27 Most of the active options traders were new members, however. Eddie O'Connor recalls that only about 20 traders made the move from trading in CBOT pits to CBOE.

28 Tamarkin, p. 166.

29 Tamarkin, p. 12.

30 Interview with Leo Melamed. Richard Sandor, who was charged with organizing the research department at the Board of Trade, recalls that there was also opposition to the professionalsation of staff among the members there.

31 Falloon, p. 241.

32 The 1966 DeAngelis salad oil swindle had exposed the Commodity Exchange Act's (CEA) weakness when the General Accounting Office and the United States Department of Agriculture (USDA) both found evidence that the CEA had known of illegal activities but had failed to act. By 1973, the USDA was openly criticizing the CEA for exercising only "minimal surveillance" over exchanges. Moreover, the CEA was unready for a world of financial futures. Leo Melamed recounts that to win approval for currency futures, the Chicago Mercantile Exchange (CME) had to fill out a form that requested information about the size, location and condition of the warehouses in which the underlying commodities would be stored.

33 Sander, Jack, Address to the Membership, 1980.

34 Falloon, p. 238.

35 In popular imagination, cash-settlement and illegal betting became synonymous, painting the notion of financial contracts as immoral: bucket shops figured in the Congressional debates of the early 1930s that led to the establishment of the SEC.

36 As the sociologist Yuval Millo notes: "in a market where index-based contracts are traded, an obligatory delivery would be equal to calling for a market crash. Therefore, what was a condition of the legal existence of trading in the 'real assets' world became unbearably dangerous in the world of index-based contracts." (Millo, Yuval, "From Green Fields to Green Felt Tables and Back: The Origins of Index-Based Derivatives," Centre for Analysis of Risk and Regulation Discussion Paper No. 44, 2007).

37 The bank received regulatory approval in 1982, shortly after the North Carolina National Bank in Charlotte was also approved. Morgan's Futures Commission Merchants (FCM) application met with stiff resistance from some commodity brokers and dealers, who feared the banks would lure away their customers.

38 Falloon, p. 252.

6

The Long, Promising Evolution of Screen-based Trading

MICHAEL GORHAM

▆▆▆▆ I. In the Beginning

As exchanges were created, they adopted the technology of the time. Early on, the technology available was relatively primitive. The first stock exchange began in Amsterdam in 1603, and the earliest modern futures exchanges began in the 1860s. In those years, the human voice was the main mechanism for executing a trade. Pen and paper were the tools used to record trades, and chalk and chalkboards were the basic technology to display quotes.

Of course, as technology developed, it was embraced by the exchanges, though only up to the point that it did not interfere with a member's attempt to make a living in his occupation. For remember that exchanges were generally member-owned associations, and their major purpose was to ensure and support the ability of members to conduct their business of broking trades. Therefore, technology was embraced in the pursuit of communicating prices and transactions to the rest of the world. When the ticker tape was developed in 1867, it was quickly adopted by exchanges first in the United States, and then later in Europe. Likewise, when technology made it possible to display clear, readable, and easily updatable prices to large numbers of members on the trading floors, electronic wallboards quickly pushed the chalkboards aside.

However, exchange members jealously guarded the honey pot of trading, that process where traders yell their bids, offers, and acceptances of deals. Exchange members stood at the center of every trade and received a commission for their role in representing outsiders who wished to have their orders executed. They were not keen to give this role up to machines. They would gladly cede to machines the role of bringing orders to the trading floor, of confirming executions, and of disseminating market data to the public. Thus, technology was fine as long as it was confined to a supporting role at the existing, floor-based, member-owned exchanges.

The story of electronic trading narrated here is separated into three sections. First, we look at the evolution of electronic trading by focusing on the pioneers and the problems they were trying to solve by creating fully automated exchanges. We contrast the new fully automated exchanges with the existing exchanges which resisted changes that might prove unpopular with their member–owners and made very limited use of the new technology. Second, we look at the changes wrought by electronic trading, including the increase in transparency, the precipitous decline in the cost of trading, the proliferation of new order types, the drivers behind and issues involved with customers having direct access to exchange matching engines, and the merger and acquisition frenzy driven by electronic trading. Third and finally, we present a brief assessment on where we currently stand in this transition to screens and the value of the major changes that has flowed from this transition.

2. The Screen-based Pioneers

Most of the early efforts to create fully electronic exchanges took place in derivatives during the 1980s. With a single notable exception, which we will explore shortly, stock exchanges did not show up in full electronic clothing until the very end of that decade. Hence, we will look at the derivatives exchanges first and then examine the stock exchanges. However, the first fully electronic financial marketplace was created for trading neither equities nor derivatives. As best we can tell, the first fully electronic market was the New York Stock Exchange's Automated Bond System (ABS), which after several years of development went live in 1977. The New York Stock Exchange (NYSE) noted at the time of the launch that "...trading in corporate bonds has traditionally been a tedious, time consuming and mostly manual operation that involved nine different steps and hour-long searches through cabinet files for possible matches on bonds, prices, quantities."[1] ABS simplified bond trading by listing bonds with bids and offers, allowing remote access to the system and "suggesting" matches. The suggested matches did not become binding, however, until a printed version was circulated on the floor of the bond room and approved by the relevant brokers.

2.1 Derivatives Pioneers

It should be no surprise then that the earliest electronic exchanges were generally not conversions of older floor-based exchanges, but were rather de novo events, creations of brand-new exchanges. On the derivatives side of the business, most of the new electronic exchanges were successful. In fact, of the first ten screen-based derivative exchanges, created during the pioneering period from 1984 to 1993, all but two got traction. In fact, these eight, either in their original form or after one or more mergers, have become highly successful. The first attempt was actually a North American exchange camouflaged as a Bermuda exchange. The second was launched in New Zealand by a group of wool traders; the third in Sweden by an entrepreneur who had fallen in love with options while living in New Jersey; the fourth and ninth in Tokyo; the fifth and sixth in Europe; the seventh and eighth in Australia and South Africa; and the tenth in China. Every one of these, except for the two Japanese exchanges, was created from scratch. See Table 6.1 for a list of the first 20 derivatives exchanges to become fully electronic.

2.2 The First, Failed, and Forgotten Pioneer—INTEX[2]

The first electronic derivatives exchange, called INTEX, is one that no one remembers. It was launched over a quarter century ago, and it failed, and only historians remember failures. Nevertheless, it is an interesting case study, because it is essentially a story of how a small group of people who believed that screens were better than floors worked hard to create the first electronic derivatives exchange, in a jurisdiction where they could gain quick regulatory approval, but were beaten back by entrenched floor-based interests on the mainland. In the early 1980s, a retired Merrill Lynch futures broker named Eugene Grummer had grown tired of what he felt were abuses on the trading floors in Chicago and New York,[3] and he felt that the time was right for an electronic solution to the problem. A venture like this needed capital and Grummer teamed up with a Texas

	Fully Electronic	Partially Electronic	Exchange
1	October 1984	Never	Intex
2	January 1985	Never	NZ Futures and Options Exchange
3	June 1985	Never	OM
4	April 1988	Never	Tokyo Grain Exchange
5	June 1988	Never	SOFFEX
6	January 1990	Never	DTB
7	1990	October 1987	Australian Stock Exchange
8	August 1990	Never	SAFEX
9	April 1991	N/A	Tokyo Commodity Exchange
10	May 1993	Never	Zhengzhou Commodity Exchange
11	1997	1990	BOVESPA, Brazil
12	December 1997	N/A	Wiener Boerse AG
13	June 1998	April 1998	MATIF
14	September 1998	Never	Eurex
15	November 1998	N/A	Budapest Stock Exchange
16	January 1999	1982	Tokyo Stock Exchange
17	February 1999	1998	OSLO Exchange
18	1999	Never	Shanghai Futures Exchange
19	July 1999	October 1988	Osaka Securities Exchange
20	July 1999	Never	Taiwan Futures Exchange

Source: Mondo Visione, exchange websites, emails from exchanges, assorted news clips.

oilman named Wallace Sparkman. He also needed someone with significant market experience to run the company and he selected Junius Peake, a former partner in a major securities firm.

The group actually wanted to start the exchange in the United States. However, after informal meetings with the Commodity Futures Trading Commission (CFTC) staff, they realized that there would be huge delays in approval because of anticipated serious pushback by the big floor-based exchanges. Therefore, they began to put down roots in Bermuda. While this may seem like a strange choice, Grummer and Peake had already decided on the London Commodity Clearing House (LCCH) to clear the new exchange's trades and LCCH already had a presence in Bermuda. In addition, the British territory was sufficiently close to the United States to make it easy for the US-based officers of the exchange to travel there.

Building an electronic exchange in the early 1980s was not easy. This venture was complicated by the fact that the customers of the new exchange were almost 800 miles away in New York City and could be connected only by transatlantic cable. INTEX tried to create the perfect system for the time and attempted to incorporate all the suggestions that were given by potential participants. Launch dates were announced a number of times, but had to be canceled continually, because the technology was not quite ready. At the time of the exchange's opening in October 1984, less than half of the memberships and terminals had been sold. In addition, INTEX made the strategic mistake of choosing gold futures as its first new product. It was a mistake, because the conventional wisdom is that new products do best in a bull market when there is a strong inclination to buy. Gold had been in a long bear market for almost five years and continued in that same trend for another six months.

Nevertheless, the biggest factor in the failure of INTEX was the pressure exerted by the big, floor-based exchanges in United States on their member firms. Members of floor-based exchanges were understandably afraid of the rise of electronic trading and the fact that this could very likely put them out of business. Therefore, the Chicago exchanges did everything they could to discourage brokerage firms from doing business at the new electronic INTEX. This included suggestions that firms could lose prime booth space on the Chicago exchange floors, should they send any trades to INTEX. On opening day, October 25, 1984, the exchange saw only 142 gold contracts trade, and it never got any better.[4] This first attempt to create an electronic derivatives exchange was a failure, and the floor-based exchanges could breathe a little easier, at least for a while.

2.3 Screens Solve the Location Problem Down Under

New Zealand's is a short story. It is a story of seven wool traders spread over four different wool trading centers in New Zealand, who wanted to create a local futures market in New Zealand wool, but found themselves quibbling about which city would host the new exchange. Each trader, of course, wanted the new exchange to be in his city. They then did two smart things. First, they decided to make the exchange screen-based so that no one would have any particular advantage and they all would be equally happy or unhappy. Second, they recruited ten financial institutions to join them in the project. The two groups pooled their funds, intelligence, and energy to create the world's second screen-based derivatives exchange. On January 20, 1985, the New Zealand Futures Exchange opened its doors with government bonds, commercial paper and US dollar futures followed a few months later by wool futures. The exchange got off to a slow start—200 contracts represented a big trading day in the early years. However, they kept at it, later added options and merged with the much larger Sydney Futures Exchange (SFE) in 1991, which itself merged with the Australian Stock Exchange in 2006. The lesson from the New Zealand wool traders was that an electronic exchange solved the "where-to-locate" problem; and with adequate backing (from the bankers) and product diversification (by including both commodity and financial products), the effort became the first successful electronic derivatives exchange.

2.4 Options and Northern Lights

Electronically traded options were the original foundation for the Swedish OM Exchange that opened its doors in 1985 as the world's third screen-based derivatives exchange. Unlike the first two, OM was successful out of the gate. The force behind OM was a Swedish entrepreneur named Olaf Stenhammer, who first learned options as a broker in New Jersey shortly after the founding of the Chicago Board Options Exchange (CBOE) in 1973. When he returned to Sweden, he got involved in other ventures, but he could not get options out of his head and he began designing a system for the electronic trading of options by small retail customers. A very effective marketer, he signed up Sweden's largest bank, Enskilda and its biggest industrial conglomerate, the Wallenberg Group, as his major backers. The exchange made a splash and was profitable from the very first year, a rare event.[5] Within two years, the exchange was trading 30,000 contracts per day. As might be expected, the success created competitors and OM was in fact faced with a serious competitor during its second year of business. Luckily for OM, the competitor was a floor-based options exchange, and OM was so far ahead, and its transparency and cost advantages were so great, that the new competitor could never gain traction and quickly disappeared.

Not only was OM one of the very early pioneers in screen-based trading, in 1987, it became the world's first publicly listed exchange; and after a long string of mergers, in 2007, it became half of the giant, trans-Atlantic exchange NASDAQ OMX.

2.5 The Pivotal Event in the Battle between Screens and Floors

The defining event in the transition from floors to screens took place in Europe and involved a battle between a floor-based Goliath and a tiny screen-based upstart. The London International Financial Futures Exchange (LIFFE) was the largest derivatives exchange in Europe ever since its creation in 1982, which was consistent with London's position as the world's most prominent financial center. In 1988, LIFFE listed futures on Europe's leading sovereign debt instrument, the German government bond or Bund. Traditionally, exchanges listed derivatives chiefly on their own country's assets (stock indexes, government debt, and agricultural commodities). However, Germany had not yet started a derivatives exchange to list the German products. This was due to German law that viewed futures as gambling and futures contracts as nonenforceable. Hence, LIFFE decided to list Bund futures, a smart move as trading in the product grew rapidly and by the early 1990s, the Bund had become LIFFE's most actively traded product.

About the same time that LIFFE was launching Bund futures, a group of German banks began discussing the creation of a German derivatives exchange along with the change required in German law. They hired Jorg Franke, the head of the Berlin Stock Exchange, to set one up. Just like the wool traders in New Zealand, the banks sponsoring the exchange were spread around the country, in this case in Berlin, Hamburg, Stuttgart, Munich, and Hanover, and each wanted the exchange to be in its city. As in New Zealand, they solved the problem by locating the exchange in cyberspace. Moreover, to speed up time to market, instead of building a new electronic matching engine from scratch, they bought one from their neighboring Swiss Options and Financial Futures Exchange (SOFFEX). In its first year (1990), the Deutsche Terminbörse (DTB) listed three products—futures on the German stock index (DAX), the German equivalent of Eurodollars (FIBOR), and LIFFE's crown jewel, the German Bund.

In the futures markets, once an exchange has attracted a reasonable number of buyers and sellers, built solid trading volumes, and established good liquidity in a product, it has been virtually impossible for another exchange to successfully list the same product. This principle of liquidity-driven monopoly ensured that each exchange generally held a portfolio of monopoly products. Therefore, when DTB listed the product in which LIFFE had already built one of the most active markets in the world, seasoned observers expected the DTB to fail, just like virtually all other exchanges that had gone after a liquid market at another exchange. After all, here was the newest and smallest exchange in Europe trying to compete with Europe's biggest and oldest financial derivatives exchange. The competition is shown in Figure 6.1.

However, there was an interesting difference in this contest. The little German challenger was a screen-based exchange, while the exchange being attacked was floor-based. This meant that DTB was more transparent and cheaper than LIFFE, but it was also quickly building an international following by pursuing the establishment of remote memberships and terminals in Paris, London, and the United States. In its first year, thanks in part to its banker owners that directed their trades to the new exchange, DTB traded 5 million German Bund contracts, and it continued growing almost every year thereafter. Nevertheless, LIFFE continued to grow just as rapidly and maintained a two-thirds market share. Then things started to look up for DTB. In 1996, the CFTC gave it permission to place terminals in the US market. In 1997 and 1998, DTB cut fees and made its terminals free for foreign participants. With growing participation from traders in Chicago, London, and Paris, DTB volume began to soar at the expense of LIFFE. By the end of 1998, volume at LIFFE had fallen virtually to zero and DTB had traded over 140 million

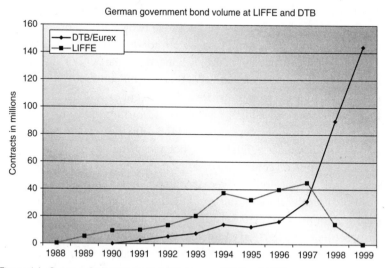

Figure 6.1 German Government Bond Volume at LIFFE and DTB
Source: Futures Industry Association, Volume Reports, 1988–1999.

contracts for the year—almost five times the level of two years earlier. It took eight years to do it, but a brand new electronic exchange had captured 100 percent of the market share of Europe's biggest contract at Europe's biggest floor-based exchange. Never again would the floor-based exchanges of the world be able to sleep peacefully. Moreover, to further underline the importance of the victory of the electronic exchange, in that same year, 1998, the German DTB merged with the Swiss Options and Financial Futures Exchange (SOFFEX) to form Eurex, creating the largest derivatives exchange in the world. For over a century, the floor-based Chicago Board of Trade (CBOT) had been the world's largest derivatives exchange. It was now clear that the future belonged to screens.

2.6 The Dangerous Phase Between Floor and Screen

What DTB's capture of all of LIFFE's Bund volume points out is that the transitional phase is especially dangerous for floor-based exchanges. This lesson was brought home again in 2006, when a large US exchange almost had its cornerstone product stolen by a new all-electronic exchange. While the New York Mercantile Exchange (NYMEX) did have an electronic platform, it was not robust and the exchange was not pushing it. In fact, in 2005 and 2006, NYMEX was still pursuing a floor-based expansion strategy in Europe, Asia, and the Middle East at the behest of its member–owners. It actually set up floor-based subsidiaries in Dublin and London and was planning to do the same in Singapore and Dubai. Meanwhile, the Intercontinental Exchange (ICE) had established liquid over-the-counter (OTC) and exchange-traded markets on a solid electronic platform. In February 2006, ICE listed a clone of NYMEX's benchmark West Texas Intermediate (WTI) crude oil contract. Within a few months, ICE went from zero to a 30 percent market share. It then launched clones of NYMEX's gasoline and heating oil contracts. What was playing out was a repeat of the DTB–LIFFE story. There were two important differences. First, it is not clear that ICE really wanted NYMEX's crude oil contract to disappear. NYMEX's WTI contract was a traditional, physically—delivered contract, where anyone left with a position after the close of trading at the expiration of the contract either delivered or received actual crude oil. The ICE product, by contrast, was cash settled (often referred to as financially settled) based on the NYMEX price. If the NYMEX contract vanished, the ICE contract would lose its settlement mechanism. More importantly, NYMEX saw the folly of its floor-based orientation and quickly made a deal to use

CME's battle-tested GLOBEX electronic platform. Therefore, CME saved NYMEX from possible extinction at an undisclosed cost. Two years later, CME bought NYMEX.

2.7 Baby Steps—Floor-based Exchanges Try After Hours Electronic Trading

While new exchanges were being created in an electronic format, existing floor-based exchanges took a much more cautious route. Several futures exchanges established electronic systems, but exclusively for after-hours trading, so as not to intrude on or compete with the regular trading hours of their members. Securities exchanges often would allow electronic trading only in lightly traded issues, again so as not to seriously impinge on the business of their members. This approach allowed the exchanges to take small steps toward competing electronically, while preserving for the exchange members exclusive rights to trade during regular daytime trading hours or in the most liquid markets.

Leaders of futures exchanges knew they must recognize the technological revolution that was engulfing the world, but they also knew that their members would have their heads if they began to shift their floors to screens. Hence, they adopted electronic trading in a very limited way to solve a very different problem. The problem, especially in the United States, had to do with the rise of Japan as a trading power. The Japanese, and to a lesser extent other Asian countries, had jumped into derivatives with both feet. Many Japanese brokerage firms decided to become members of US derivatives exchanges, so many in fact that CME hired away a Northwestern University professor of Japanese to act as a full-time liaison with these Japanese firms. At the same time that Japanese trading was growing rapidly on US derivatives exchanges, it was also growing rapidly at home in Japan. What US exchanges worried about was whether the Japanese would soon list on their own exchanges the same products they were now supporting on the US and European exchanges. In addition, the US exchanges realized that they were not exactly being customer friendly by requiring the Japanese wishing to trade on the Chicago exchanges to stay up all night to do so. There was absolutely no overlap between Chicago or New York trading hours and Japanese trading hours. Moreover, there was only a very slight overlap between the opening on European exchanges and the closing times on Tokyo exchanges.

While some products were protected by exclusive licensing agreements, like the S&P 500 and all other branded stock indexes, most futures products were generic and could be started by any exchange at any time. For example, the contracts based on interest rate products, currencies, and physical commodities had absolutely no intellectual property protection. In the United States, exchanges feared that the Japanese and others in the Asian time zone would establish their own versions of all of the big blockbuster contracts that the Japanese were trading in Chicago and in New York. Of course, there were also low-tech approaches to protecting Western markets. For example, the Chicago Board of Trade was sufficiently committed to floor trading that it decided in 1987 to extend its hours into the Japanese trading day by having an evening session staffed with members making markets on the trading floor. This approach did not last long. The New York Cotton Exchange also had a floor-based evening session beginning in 1992 that actually went on for 15 years, but again the volumes were never very large.

The other approach, most successfully pursued by the CME, but also by the CBOT, NYMEX, and the London International Financial Futures Exchange (LIFFE) was to set up screen-based systems for trading products after the trading floors closed in the afternoon. LIFFE was first, launching its Automated Pit Trading (APT) system in 1989. The system catered to pit traders and was sufficiently nonrobust that LIFFE did not call on it when faced with the 1997–98 DTB attack described earlier. The most strategically important of these systems was CME's GLOBEX. It was not an easy thing for any of these exchanges to sell electronic trading to their member–owners. Leo Melamed, long-time CME leader, was Chairman of the Strategic Planning Committee that came up with GLOBEX. He needed to convince CME members that after-hours electronic trading was in their interest.[6] Therefore, he and then Chairman Jack Sandner tried to reduce fear by promising members that GLOBEX would never be open during regular daytime trading hours unless the members voted to do so. They also created a financial incentive by committing to give 70 percent of GLOBEX profits to the members. Finally, to convince members that the project had a high probability of success, they chose to collaborate with then technology pioneer Reuters Holdings PLC. The plan was unveiled to members in the fall of 1987. A few weeks later, the members approved the plan with a landslide vote, though the system would not actually light up until five years later, in June of 1992.

Industry approaches to after-hours screen-based system took two major paths. One was to focus on making floor-trading members happy by creating a screen that resembled as much as possible the traditional trading floor. The other approach was to create trading screens that would appeal most to outside traders who had no particular familiarity with, and certainly no deep love of, the traditional trading floor. The "let's appeal to the floor trader" path to electronic trading was pursued by both CBOT and LIFFE. CBOT unveiled its floor-trader-friendly Aurora system at the annual Futures Industry Association Conference in Boca Raton Florida in March 1989. Aurora had a beautiful, colorful screen and was much more interesting than the CME GLOBEX screen. It was a collaboration between Apple Computer Inc., which supplied the colorful Macintosh icons; Texas Instruments, which supplied the artificial intelligence; and Tandem Computer, which supplied the raw processing power. Pit traders loved Aurora. The rest of the world was not so crazy about it, and the product never came to market. CBOT spent several years pretending to join CME and Reuters in their GLOBEX system, but ultimately, in 1994, it broke ranks and returned to developing its own pit-trader-friendly, proprietary system renamed Project A. While Project A did have some advantages over its predecessor Aurora, it never really caught on, and CBOT abandoned the system for a more robust and battle-tested system created by Eurex of Frankfurt. That relationship lasted only a few years before CBOT switched from Eurex's system to LIFFE's system, and then finally to CME's GLOBEX after the 2007 merger of the two giant Chicago exchanges.

One thing that CBOT's continuous swapping of trading platform partners points out is just how modular exchanges have become in the electronic age. In the floor-based days, exchanges were generally self-contained, having pretty much all functions in house—trading floor operations, product development, marketing, legal, regulatory, and often clearing and settlement (in the case of futures exchanges). Today, exchanges can and do outsource many, and in some cases all, of these functions. This is especially true with trading platforms and related technology. The Swedish exchange OM, one of the early pioneers in electronic trading, was also early in leasing its trading platform to other exchanges. Today, in the form of NASDAQ OMX, it has leased technology to support trading and clearing in more than 50 countries. The London-based LIFFE, now part of NYSE Euronext, created a widely respected trading platform called LIFFE CONNECT in 1998, which it has leased out to exchanges in the United States, Canada, and Japan and which is used for all the European derivatives exchanges that have become part of the Euronext half of NYSE Euronext.

2.8 Automating the World's Stock Exchanges

As we have seen, the early pioneers of electronic derivatives trading created brand new exchanges starting in the mid-1980s. It took almost another decade before existing floor-based exchanges began fully converting to screens. Aside from the fact that conversions from floors to screens met stiff resistance from member–owners whose livelihoods were threatened, derivatives trading, especially in financial products, was still in its infancy and many countries did not yet have derivatives exchanges. New Zealand, Sweden, Switzerland, Germany, South Africa, and China all had no derivatives exchanges. Therefore, during the mid-1980s and early 1990s, all these countries created new derivatives exchanges, and they were all electronic right out of the box.

Stock exchanges, on the other hand, were relatively mature institutions, and most countries of any size already had one or more stock exchanges and were not generally building new ones. Moreover, given the natural resistance of member–owners, the existing stock exchanges, just like the existing derivatives exchanges, were not likely to quickly convert to screens. Consequently, early electronic activity on the securities side was carried out on an experimental basis, typically only for stocks that were relatively inactive. Hence, in Figure 6.2, we see that except for the isolated event of the Cincinnati Stock Exchange becoming electronic in 1980, it was not until 1989 that stock exchanges began to start converting to electronic trading in earnest.

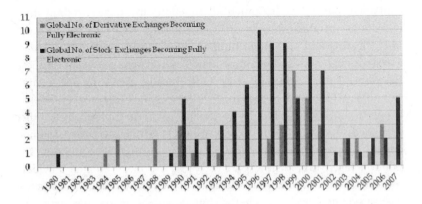

Figure 6.2 Comparison of Global Number of Derivatives and Stock Exchanges Becoming Fully Electronic: 1980-2007

Many partial steps were taken toward creating electronic trading platforms even in the 1970s and 1980s. In 1977, the Toronto Stock Exchange became the first exchange to create an electronic matching system.[7] NASDAQ, of course, had even earlier in 1971 created an electronic quotation system, whereby dealers could enter and view bids and offers for all NASDAQ stocks. However, the matching, the deals, the actual trades, were still done over the phone, to preserve the dealers' role and ensure that they were able to earn the bid-ask spread for their market making contribution. Six years after NASDAQ lit up its quotation screens, Toronto lit up CATS (for Computer Assisted Trading System), an electronic limit order book in which brokers could match market orders against the limit orders in the book. Nevertheless, this new system was used only for inactive stocks. This was not threatening to the floor traders who found it much more profitable to focus their attention on the more actively traded issues.

Its innovation in electronic matching put the Toronto exchange on the map. As other exchanges explored the possibilities of computerized stock trading and began looking for models and mentors, Toronto became a compulsory stop on their world tours. In 1982, the Tokyo Stock Exchange introduced an automated system modeled on CATS. They altered the name to Computer Assisted Order Routing and Execution System, so CATS became CORES in Japan. One curious thing about the Japanese adaptation of CATS was that even though all the limit orders were placed in an electronic file, trades were actually matched manually by order clerks, called "saitori members." It was less efficient, but was a way to preserve jobs, to make Schumpeter's "creative destruction" a little less destructive. In addition, while CATS revealed the limit order book to all market participants, Tokyo restricted it to exchange members only. Many exchanges have licensed Toronto's CATS—the Brussels Bourse, the Paris Bourse and the Madrid, Bolsa de as well as three other stock exchanges in Spain, to name a few.[8]

Even though the Toronto Stock Exchange was the first to create an electronic matching engine, it took another 20 years before trading became fully electronic in Toronto. As can be seen in the Figure 6.2 (and Table 6.2), the first fully electronic exchange of any kind was created in 1980 and involved the conversion of the 95-year old Cincinnati Stock Exchange into a fully automated marketplace. However, it took almost a decade for the trend to really start. In 1989, there was an electronic exchange created in Chile, and then in each subsequent year, there was at least one and sometimes as many as nine or ten fully electronic stock

Table 6.2: First 20 Stock Exchanges to Become Fully Electronic

	Exchange	Established	Fully Electronic	Location
1	National Stock Exchange*	1885	1980	Chicago, United States
2	Bolsa Electrónica de Chile	Nov 1989	Nov 1989	Santiago, Chile
3	Paris Bourse	Jun 1802	1989	Paris, France
4	OMX Nordic Exchange in Helsinki	1912	Apr 1990	Helsinki, Finland
5	Saudi Stock Exchange (TADAWUL)	1930	Apr 1990	Riyadh, Saudi Arabia
6	OMX Nordic Exchange in Stockholm	1863	1990	Stockholm, Sweden
7	Australian Stock Exchange (ASX)	1861	Oct 1990	Australia
8	Shanghai Stock Exchange	Nov 1990	Dec 1990	Shanghai, China
9	Warsaw Stock Exchange	1817	1991	Warsaw, Poland
10	Stock Exchange of Thailand	May 1974	1991	Bangkok, Thailand
11	New Zealand Exchange (NZX)	1915	Aug 1992	Wellington, New Zealand
12	Shenzhen Stock Exchange	Dec 1990	1992	Shenzhen, China
13	Prague Stock Exchange	1850s	Apr 1993	Prague, Czech Republic
14	Vilnius Stock Exchange	Sep 1992	Sep 1993	Vilnius, Lithuania
15	HKEx	1891	Nov 1993	Central, Hong Kong
16	National Stock Exchange of India	1992	Jun 1994	Mumbai, India
17	Tehran Stock Exchange	1936	Sep 1994	Tehran, Iran
18	Istanbul Stock Exchange	Oct 1984	Nov 1994	Istanbul, Turkey
19	Borsa Italiana	1808	1994	Milan, Italy
20	Indonesia Stock Exchange	1912	May 1995	Jakarta, Indonesia

*Originally Cincinnati Stock Exchange

Source: Mondo Visione, exchange websites, communications with exchanges, assorted news clips.

exchanges lighting up screens. About 80 percent of these were conversions, like Cincinnati, and the other 20 percent were brand new ventures, like the Bolsa Electronica de Chile.[9] The most intensive activity took place between 1995 and 2001. Of the 85[10] fully electronic stock exchanges that came on line between 1980 and 2007, most occurred in Europe (33 percent), the Asia-Pacific region (29 percent), and the Middle East (11 percent).

However, the question remains: why was the Cincinnati Stock Exchange the first to become fully electronic in 1980, and why did it take almost a decade for another stock exchange to follow its lead?[11] Cincinnati converted to screens via a serendipitous combination of desperation and ingenuity. By the 1970s, most of the US regional stock exchanges had disappeared, and those remaining were looking for some way to survive in the shadow of the New York Stock Exchange. At the same time, there were broker/dealers who felt squeezed between falling commissions (the SEC eliminated fixed commissions in 1975) and the high costs they faced dealing with the NYSE specialists. The Weeden brothers, Don and Frank, who had their own broker/dealer, approached Cincinnati with an electronic matching system they had developed. If they and others could become specialists on a regional exchange like Cincinnati, they could avoid the NYSE specialists altogether.

With revenues and membership values falling, the Cincinnati board felt they had nothing to lose. They began experimenting with the system in 1976 and designing a new exchange. By 1980, the exchange was ready to darken its floors and light up its screens. There were two things that Cincinnati did that helped them to succeed. First, they created a system of multiple dealers for each stock, more like NASDAQ than NYSE. Second, they established a rule that allowed the dealers to trade against their own customers if they did so at a price that was better than the best bid or offer. Initially they did well. Tom Peterffy, who started Timber Hill and Interactive Brokers, was making markets in 35 stocks for as many as 3,000–4,000 shares at a time and was offering better prices than the NYSE.

Why did no other exchange follow suit? No member-owned exchange really wanted to convert to screens. Moreover, in the United States, there was tremendous resistance in New York to Cincinnati's strategy, especially when Cincinnati's share began to push up to 5 percent. In fact, the pressure was so great that no other American exchange appeared among the world's first 20 stock exchanges to become fully screen based. The Asia-Pacific region and Europe accounted for 75 percent of the first

20 and both South America and the Middle East had more electronic stock exchanges than the United States by 1995.

3. How Electronic Trading Has Changed the World

3.1 Transparency for All

Transparency used to be for a very limited group. In the old world, the public never saw the limit order book. The best that traders and investors could see was the last trade, and they might be told the current bid and ask in the pit. Of course, specialists at stock exchanges held the order books for their stocks, which meant that they were the only market participants who could see them. Big floor brokers in the futures markets would see the portion of the order book created by their own customers' orders, so again they had an exclusive view of at least the piece of the order book for the futures contracts they filled orders for.

However, in the new electronic world, there is a lot more transparency and the public knows much more about resting limit orders than it did in the floor-based world. In fact, the exchange itself holds the entire limit order book,[12] and it is technically feasible for it to show the entire book to the public. Largely due to bandwidth costs, exchanges have chosen not to reveal the entire order book, at least not for free. More data takes more space and wider pipelines so exchanges will often charge higher fees to supply deeper looks into the limit order book. In addition, the real time book has great value to traders, and exchanges are trying to get traders to pay for that value. As a concrete example, firms that wish to see the entire NYSE order book updated in real time can do so for US$60,000 per year, and firms wishing to gain access to the full limit order book for the Euronext half of the trans-Atlantic exchange can do so for €40,000.

Illustrating the bandwidth problem, CME began its electronic trading venture by showing the best five bids and best five offers, along with quantities. When it acquired CBOT in the summer of 2007, that rival exchange was showing twice the depth—the best ten bids and offers. Due to congested pipelines, CME had to reduce the view of CBOT order books from ten bids and offers to five, as it migrated these products on to its electronic trading platform, GLOBEX. However, at the end of 2008, CME required its market data vendors to switch over to the FIX FAST protocol, which compresses market data by 70 percent and allows more data to be distributed with the same bandwidth.[13] This enabled it a few months later to begin converting all of its products, beginning with CBOT products whose order book views it had previously reduced, back to the ten-best-bid-and-offer-CBOT standard.

3.2 Speed—Algo Trading and Co-location

There was a time when customers were delighted to have a trade executed within a minute of placing an order. Computer-based trading has made such an exercise about 900 times faster. While numbers are not generally published, insiders will tell you that it currently takes about 30 ms (milliseconds, that is, thousandths of a second) to get an order from the box to the CME exchange matching engine. It takes about 5 ms for the matching to take place and then another 30 ms to get the confirmation back to the box, or about 65 ms total for the round turn.[14]

Mark Gorton, cofounder with fellow engineer and Scotsman Alistair Brown, of Lime Brokerage LLC, says that at 6,000 orders per second, his Chinatown-based firm trades faster than any other company on Wall Street.[15] While it is difficult to verify who is fastest, in 2008, the firm was trading about 175 million shares per day and on peak days more than twice that. It claimed to be able to grab price quotes in 0.1 milliseconds and then do the trade in another 0.1 milliseconds. These speeds, which will soon seem like an eternity (discussions of speed are beginning to shift to microseconds—millionths of a second) are gained largely by improving network architecture. One way to do this is to minimize the number of nodes that a message passes through between the customer and matching engine, which is why customers insist on direct market access, which will be discussed in the following section. If there are two or three intermediary nodes, this doubles or triples the time it takes to reach the matching engine.

One of the major effects of electronic trading has been the inevitable trend toward algorithmic trading, that is toward having computers replace humans in deciding on and executing trades. Since the successful exploitation of an arbitrage opportunity depends upon a trader seeing the opportunity and getting her order in before others, speed becomes very important. It is clear that lines of efficiently written code resident on a server can recognize and exploit trading opportunities much more quickly than a human watching a screen and moving a mouse or pressing keys. While a scary thought to some, the vision of computers trading with one another is fast becoming a reality. With everyone looking for speed, algorithmic trading has spread rapidly.

According to a September 2009 survey by the Tabb Group, algorithmic trading jumped from 30 percent to 70 percent of all US equity trades between 2005 and 2009. Because algorithmic trades tend to be of smaller sizes, the 70 percent of trades in 2009 translates into 60 percent of volume.[16] Penetration in other countries is generally lower but on the rise. One surprising result is that the firms that are doing much of this trading are often new start-up proprietary trading firms rather than the traditional investment banks. For example, a New Jersey hedge fund called Tradeworx, which employs mainly twenty-something physics and computer science grads, started high-frequency trading in January 2009 and by the end of the year was doing 3 percent of the volume in the Standard & Poor's Depositary Receipt (SPDR), one of the world's most popular Exchange Traded Funds (ETFs).[17] While Tradeworx is a hedge fund, many of the high-frequency firms are simply trading their own capital. Getco, for example, is a little known proprietary trading firm founded in 1999 by a couple of former floor traders from CME and CBOE. Trading about 1.5 billion shares a day, the firm accounts for about 15 percent of equity trading volume in the United States.[18]

Everything about markets is faster, and traders are continually looking for ways to trade faster. More efficient computer code, greater bandwidth and closer proximity to the exchanges' matching engines are all pursued. The extreme case of getting closer is co-location, which involves the placement of the servers containing the black-box software in a room either close to the exchange's matching engine or connected by extremely fast cable to that matching engine. High-frequency trading and co-location go hand in hand. Again, co-location is simply the electronic version of a practice engaged in by floor traders for decades. Futures trading floors had a species of trader known as the scalper or local. They made their living by buying and selling all day long, always ready to buy a little lower and sell a little higher than the last price. In essence, they were market makers, supplying liquidity and trying to profit from the bid-ask spread. They found that the closer they could stand to the big order fillers, the more likely they would get to trade opposite large orders coming in. Being right next to the big order filler also allowed the local to build a relationship (floor traders chat during slow periods) that can lead to more favorable treatment. In fact, physical co-location on the trading floor was so important that some traders would arrive long before the opening to grab their little piece of real estate in the pit, and at times, disagreements over where one stood resulted in arguments and even fistfights. In the electronic world, you do not have to arrive early or fight to colocate; you simply have to pay for the service of locating your server in a place near the exchange's matching engine.

3.3 The Price of a Trade

The shift to screens has dramatically reduced the cost of trading in three ways. First, it has ushered in huge increases in volumes in many assets, resulting in smaller bid/ask spreads. Second, it has resulted in substantially lower trading fees, and third, it has slashed the price of market data, especially for small traders. We will deal with the second and third of these sources of cheaper trading.

Brokerage firms have dropped their commissions drastically as the electronic revolution has pushed down costs and increased competition. Back in the early 1980s, it was not unusual to pay a 1.25 percent commission to trade stock at a full service brokerage firm in the United States. For 300 shares of a US$50 stock, the commission ran US$187.50. Today, the cost of that same transaction would be between US$1.50 and US$10—from 95 percent to 99 percent lower.[19] The bid-ask spreads have narrowed considerably as well. In the 1990s, it was not unusual for a NASDAQ stock to have a bid-ask spread of 25 cents. Today that same stock, following new order handling rules imposed by the SEC along with decimalization, would easily have a one cent bid-ask spread— a 96 percent decline.

Exchange fees did not have as much room to drop, since most exchanges were not-for-profit entities. The biggest change is that fees have gotten more complex. A combination of electronic trading, clearing, and a newfound concern over profitability that comes from being a publically traded company has resulted in a plethora of prices. Fees on new products being promoted can be reduced, while products in which the exchange has a secure dominance or incurs greater costs can be increased. Let us take CME as a case in point. Before CME went public and had any serious degree of electronic trading, it had a single price for all futures customers—70 cents per contract.[20] It did not matter whether the customer traded one or 10,000 contracts, or whether the product was pork belly or Eurodollar futures, the price was 70 cents to be long or short one contract.[21]

While 70 cents was the fee received by the exchange, the customer also had to pay the floor broker US$1 to execute the trade on the trading floor (an expense that disappeared with screens). Therefore, the total cost of dealing with the exchange was the sum of these two fees or US$1.70 to either buy or sell. Today, the exchange fee depends upon the product traded and there are 13 different fees ranging from 16 cents for micro-foreign exchange contracts (one-tenth regular size) to US$2.30 for full-size equity futures, like the S&P 500. Hence, equity futures cost 30 percent more, interest rates 30 percent less and commodity and foreign exchange futures within 10 percent of the US$1.70 cost a decade back. CME has to pay McGraw Hill and others undisclosed payments for the exclusive right to list the S&P 500 and other stock indexes, so it is logical to see equity index fees higher. The smaller fees for mini and micro-products are proportional to the smaller product sizes. Weather products are innovative creations that have generally not found significant traction and need lower fees to make them more attractive. Based on February 2010 volumes, the mean CME fee is about US$1.23, or 27 percent lower than the US$1.70 fee charged before it went public and became substantially electronic. This is a much smaller drop than that seen in brokerage fees. The difference is that the brokerage industry is fiercely competitive, whereas the futures exchange world is characterized generally by exchanges with exclusive products and thus much less competition. Table 6.3 lists the CME total customer fee per side.

Table 6.3: CME Total Customer Fee Per Side	
US$2.30	Equity
US$1.89	Commodity Futures
US$1.60	Foreign Exchange Futures
US$1.29	Commodity Options
US$1.19	Interest Rates
US$1.14	E-mini Equity Futures
US$0.85	E-mini Foreign Exchange
US$0.85	Foreign Exchange Options
US$0.55	E-mini Equity Options
US$0.54	Weather
US$0.35	ETF
US$0.18	E-mini Eurodollar Futures
US$0.16	E-Micro Foreign Exchange

Source: CME Fee Schedule, January 1, 2010

3.4 The Price of a Price

While trading fees have fallen tremendously following the advent of electronic trading, the price of real time quotes has fallen much faster and helped to fuel the growth of online trading by retail clients. As can be seen in Table 6.4, the monthly cost to a retail trader of receiving unlimited quotes on bid/ask and last price on NYSE stocks fell from US$168.50 in 1983 to US$1 today. To be fair, in 1983, a retail trader had to pay the same amount as a professional, US$168.50, and virtually no one did. Most retail traders had full service or discount brokerage accounts and conveyed their orders over the telephone after their brokers told them the bid-ask and last price available on the brokers' screens. The nonprofessional category was added in 1984 and resulted in a 92 percent reduction in monthly costs. Over the next four years, as a result of unrelenting pressure from online brokers trying to build their businesses, the monthly fee for real time bid-ask and last prices dropped another 95 percent for nonprofessional traders and helped to attract a huge increase in clients to the online brokers.

The price battle was tough and fascinating. Despite the fact that exchanges had relied on sales of market data for a significant share of their revenue, the online brokers argued that charging for prices was sort of like Wal-Mart charging for a price list as you walked into the store. Nevertheless, the issue was even more interesting in that it raised the question of who really owned these prices. It was clear that the exchange was the entity capturing the market data resulting from transactions on its floor or electronic platform, but it was often the customers

Table 6.4: Monthly Fee to View Bid/Ask and Last Prices	
(For Non-Professionals)	
1983	US$168.50
1984	US$13.50
1987	US$4.00
1992	US$4.25
1997	US$5.25
1999	US$1.00
2010	US$1.00

Note: Non-Pro category introduced in 1984

Source: Appendix D, Network A in Perspective: 1975–2000, of NYSE Comments to the SEC Concept Release on "Regulation of Market Information Fees and Revenues" (Release No. 34-42208; File No. S7-28-99) with current price from NYSE.

of the brokerage firms who were parties to the transactions, so, shouldn't they be considered part owners of the prices, since it was their actions that created the prices? As a practical matter, when quote vendors and brokers entered into contracts with exchanges to receive the market data, they had to sign a document saying that the exchange owns the data. However, this did not fully settle the issue. Ownership of prices has been hotly contested in the United States, but at present, the courts are saying that exchange settlement prices are not the intellectual property of the exchange and others are free to make use of them as they wish.

3.5 New Order Types

Many observers would argue that electronic trading has resulted in an explosion of order types. To others, there was nothing quite like the human broker, who could do virtually anything a computer could do and much more besides. The truth, as it often does, lies somewhere in between. One longtime floor broker told me of a customer who would tell him to sell eggs when pork bellies went above a certain price. This was not a normal CME order type, and it required monitoring two markets, but he was young and hungry at the time and would bend over backwards to please customers.[22]

There is little doubt that the number of order types in the electronic world is much larger than it was during the floor years, but some new orders are not actually all that new. Throughout the development of electronic trading platforms, many old timers quipped that the human floor broker could never be replaced by a computer. A case in point is when a customer would give a floor broker a large order and tell the broker to work the order gradually so that it could get executed with the least amount of market impact. Such orders were called "Disregard Tape," "Not Held" or "Take Your Time." This was considered the kind of value added that only an experienced human broker could supply.

In today's electronic world, that same order is known as an iceberg order, which essentially allows the trader to display only a small portion of his bid or offer while hiding below the surface the much larger total size of the order. For example, if a trader wishes to buy 50,000 shares of stock, but does not want to signal this size to the market and allow other traders to lie in wait for him, he may enter an iceberg order to show only 1,000 shares at any given time, hiding the remainder for gradual release to the market. Only after the visible portion gets hit by market orders does more of the order become visible. Such order types can be provided by the exchange, the broker, software licensed from a third party (called Independent Software Vendors or ISVs) or by proprietary software created by the trader. There is an irony in the iceberg order and the other new hidden order types. While the limit order book has become more transparent, and traders have a much better sense of the depth of the displayed market, the hidden order types actually make the limit order book less transparent.

In the old world of floor trading, the number of order types varied by exchange but generally there may have been a dozen at most—"market," "limit," "stop," "market on open," "market on close," "not held," "good till cancelled," "all or none," et cetera. The number of order types is today truly larger. One large, retail brokerage firm that handles both securities and derivatives offers 50 different order types and algorithms to its customers.[23] Some of these 50 are the traditional orders available in floor trading, but many are new and possible only in an automated trading environment. One of these is the VWAP, or volume weighted average price, which allows the customer's order to be gradually executed throughout the day to capture something close to the average of all the day's trades weighted by volume. Such a price can be easily programmed, but really could not have been executed before the advent of electronic trading.

3.6 The Wonders and Worries of Direct Market Access

In the floor world, if a trader wanted direct access[24] to the matching engine, which in those days was the trading pit or specialist's post, there was only one way to do it: purchase a membership and stand in the pit or around the specialist's post. In other words, only exchange members had direct market access. The closest that customers got to direct access in those days was to call down to their brokerage firm's booth on the trading floor and have their order carried into (or later as markets sped up, hand signaled into) the trading pit. This allowed the clerk on the floor to notice if an order was ridiculously large or otherwise unreasonable and take appropriate action. In the new screen world, many electronic exchanges initially preserved this common sense risk management by allowing only exchange members to have access to trading terminals. Customers continued to phone their orders into their brokers, who would in turn enter them into the electronic system, after checking trading or position limits that had been established for each account. Even as customers were allowed to enter orders via their own computers (or PDAs and cell phones), it was a simple matter to block orders that exceeded pre-established trading limits.

Nevertheless, as speed became more important, some customers, such as hedge funds and proprietary trading shops (prop shops), demanded direct links to the exchange's matching engine, without being slowed down by passing through the firm's risk management system. Given the amount of business such traders brought to the firm, it was difficult to refuse them, and firms would allow these customers to trade directly at the exchange in the name of the brokerage firm, without any risk management filter. Of course, the brokerage still had to guarantee the trades and make good on them if the customer failed to do so. In these circumstances, the best they could do was to carefully examine the customer's risk management system prior to allowing direct access, and to monitor all orders submitted in real time. Therefore, instead of looking at the order before it hit the exchange's limit order book, as in the past, the brokerage firm got out of the way and saw the order a fraction of a second after it had hit the exchange. This small delay was caused by the order going to the exchange on an express route (which was quite expensive) and coming to the firm via back roads (that is, the free Internet). If the firm saw something terribly wrong, it had the right to go in and cancel the order if it had not already been executed. However, this kind of best practice followed by the big firms was not necessarily followed by all their smaller brethren. The trade-off between giving customers the fastest possible access to the exchange's matching engine and protecting the firm from losses resulting from algorithms gone wild is one that will continue to require thoughtful attention by exchanges, firms, and regulators.

A number of people worry about the risk of this direct market access. It is a fact that algorithms can be buggy. A colleague of mine lost US$258,000 in 11 seconds as a result of a poorly written program. It could have been much worse had he not been staring at the screen at the time. Another, better-known firm lost US$4 million in a very short time due to a bad program. Another firm actually went bust in 16 seconds after an employee inadvertently turned on a program.[25] In addition, there are many such examples like these, which are not reported, because of the need for secrecy and the fact that the firms are privately owned. Nevertheless, the fear is not that firms lose money. None of us should care if a firm that was taking speculative positions with its own capital does damage to itself. That is the nature of the business. The fear is that bad code could result in a program going crazy and selling huge quantities of stock, triggering another crash.

While some argue that direct access customers are smart enough to design well-written programs and the brokers could stop something gone awry quickly enough, errors do happen.[26] NYSE Euronext fined a Credit Suisse Group subsidiary for slowing down trading by jamming the system with hundreds of thousands of cancel and replace requests when the original orders had never been sent. The US SEC is sufficiently concerned that in January 2010, it proposed a ban on naked access.[27]

3.7 Out Trades Out, Fat Fingers In

In the old world of trading floors, traders would shout out bids or offers and shout out an acceptance of a bid or offer.[28] They would then record the details of these trades on special trading cards, if trading for their own account, or on the customer order if they were acting as a broker. They would write down quantity and price and commodity involved in the trade, along with the time or time bracket in which the trade took place. They would also jot down the opposing trader's floor name and the number of his clearing firm, both of which appeared on every floor trader's badge. This information then would be keypunched into the exchange's clearing system. If any one of these trade descriptors did not match, the system rejected the trade as an out trade, a trade that did not match and did not stand until the two parties resolved the differences. There were many out trades during the floor years, especially in very active markets. Sometimes a trader would simply make a mistake in writing down a trade description. Sometimes there would be a miscommunication. One trader says she is selling 60 contracts and the other trader hears 16. Sometimes there would be a keypunch error by the exchange employee.

Back in the 1980s, there was a period when as many as 25 percent of all trades done in certain pits at CME had errors in them and had to be resolved by the human intervention of special outtrade clerks after the trading session or the next morning before the market opened. Each broker had such a clerk to represent him in negotiating a settlement to such an out trade. In some cases, it was clear that one of the two traders was at fault and he would eat the error. In other cases, it was unclear and the two parties would simply split the cost of the error. Out trades were just considered one of the costs of trading and regulators did not much like them, because they gave the traders the opportunity to change certain dimensions of the trade after the fact. Some exchanges would impose penalties on clearing firms if the percent of their trades that resulted in out trades exceeded a certain level.

Screen-based trading eliminated the traditional out trade along with the hordes of out-trade clerks needed to resolve these mismatched trades. Electronic trades match instantly and all relevant data to the trade is gathered automatically, so there is no room for misunderstanding. This does not mean that human traders did not make mistakes in entering orders, but the misunderstandings due to not properly hearing a counterparty or sloppily writing down the wrong name for the counterparty or clearing firm was essentially eliminated.

With the out trade being dead, where do we channel human error? Into fat finger errors. There are not as many of them, but they can be quite large. A fat finger error refers to a situation where a trader hits the wrong button—a buy instead of a sell, a wrong price or a wrong quantity. When the head of an exchange has to resign over the embarrassment created by a fat finger error, it is clear that the error is a shocking one. And that's just what happened in 2005, when an employee of Mizuho Securities entered an order backwards. He sold 610,000 shares of J-Com at ¥1 per share, instead of selling one share at ¥610,000, which is what he intended.[29] The firm only had 14,500 shares of J-Com in its inventory. But of course, traders took advantage of the cheap shares and took the other side of the order. The Nikkei 225 closed down 2 percent for the day. In 2001, a Lehman Brothers trader accidentally sold US$300 million instead of US$3 million worth of a UK company, sending the FTSE 100 down 120 points and taking US$50 billion off the value of the FTSE. And then there was the London Salomon Smith Barney trader who accidentally sat on his keyboard, submitting orders to sell 10,607 contracts, sending the value of the Notional bond down 149 basis points.[30,31]

Early on, when their customer bases were growing rapidly, there were also a number of cases where broker–dealers created shoddy systems that resulted in big headaches for customers. For example, a customer at one of the largest online brokerage firms complained back in 2000 that while his account showed that he had turned his original US$12,000 investment into US$2.3 million, in fact he had actually been losing money.[32] Another had a US$71,000 position created in a stock he did not want and suffered a US$53,000 loss that the broker insisted he pay, because he did not report the error quickly enough. A third customer claimed that he entered an order to sell his 5,000 shares of a company and the online system executed the order twice, leaving him short

5,000 shares. When he called to report the error to the broker, he claimed that he was kept on hold seven hours (the broker said it was only three hours) and he ultimately lost US$23,000 due to the error.

3.8 Bigger and Fewer

One very important effect that the shift to screens has had on the world of exchanges is that the incentive to be big is much greater for electronic exchanges. Economies of scale in the cyber world are much greater than they were in the floor world, and exchanges are racing each other to the bottom of the new electronic cost curve. In the floor-based world, adding new products or significantly increasing the volume of trade in existing products required more physical space on a trading floor and often more floor traders to handle the brokerage and market making. In the new screen-based world, new products simply require a little more space on a server. So new products and volume growth in existing products brings in more revenue without adding appreciably to costs, thus boosting profits. Moreover, profits have become very important, as most exchanges have shifted from a not-for-profit member-owned structure to a for-profit stockholder-owned structure. Given that volume growth pushes up revenues much more rapidly than costs, all exchanges want to be larger and they have been doing their best to become so.

The result is fewer and larger exchanges. Euronext, the pan-European stock exchange was built from the merger of four national stock exchanges between 2000 and 2002. Then Euronext went from pan-European to trans-Atlantic by merging in 2007 with the New York Stock Exchange (NYSE), which itself had merged with Archipelago, a former Chicago-based Electronic Communication Network (ECN) that had become an exchange by merging with the Pacific Stock Exchange.[33] NYSE subsequently bought the American Stock Exchange, a very old exchange that was the US innovator of exchange-traded funds (ETFs). A second trans-Atlantic exchange, NASDAQ OMX, was created in 2008 via NASDAQ's complicated merger with OMX, itself a Stockholm-based company that was born of the mergers of OM with stock exchanges in Stockholm, Copenhagen, Helsinki, Tallinn, Riga, Vilnius, and Iceland. A third trans-Atlantic marketplace was created by a European exchange buying an American one, namely Eurex's purchase of the International Securities Exchange (ISE), the world's first fully electronic derivatives exchange. This move, incidentally, restored Eurex's position as the largest derivatives exchange globally after losing it to CME Group for a brief period.

An extreme case of this trend can be seen in the United States. In 2004, CME accounted for 50 percent of all US futures volume. By 2008, CME's market share had almost doubled to 97 percent. The reason, of course, is that CME had acquired the second and third largest US futures exchanges, CBOT in 2007 and NYMEX in 2008, becoming CME Group. How did CME emerge on top, especially given the fact that it had been the number two derivatives exchange in the United States for most of the twentieth century, always lagging behind CBOT? CME was long known as being feistier, more innovative and more aggressive than its cross-town rival. Nevertheless, a large part of its emerging on top had to do with its consistent leadership and long-term vision regarding electronic trading. It was able to balance the inevitable tension between the fears of its members and the need to move boldly into this new screen-based world. While CBOT was experimenting with night session floor trading and jumping from one electronic trading platform to another, CME marched forward with a focus on a single electronic platform—GLOBEX. In addition, while CME was building volume on GLOBEX, NYMEX was so married to the idea of floor trading, as late as 2005, it was still trying to expand by setting up floor-based exchanges in Dublin, London, and Singapore. CME was also the first US derivatives exchange to become a for-profit, publicly traded company, which gave it more structural and financial flexibility than its member-owned brethren. Even though CME was slow to move into electronic trading compared with European and Asian exchanges, it did so much more effectively than its domestic rivals did.

4. Assessment—Are We Almost Done and Was It a Good Thing?

While it seems that we are in the very late stages of the transition from floors to screens—it has been going on for over three decades now—we may still have a while to wait for the time when all exchange trading is electronic. There are serious pockets of resistance. While tremendous strides have been made, there are still many transactions in equities, bonds and derivatives that still take place on the floor, over the telephone, or increasingly, via instant messaging systems. For example, very large equity transactions are likely to continue to be arranged away from the electronic exchange's matching engine. Such transactions are best done by brokers who know the players and can match orders with minimum market impact. Options have been a particular sticking point. With many options, trades consisting of more complicated combinations of contracts, many traders prefer to negotiate these on the floor of exchanges than on screens. Moreover, many option transactions that appear to be conducted on electronic platforms are actually prearranged in the "call-around market." In addition, while OTC trading has increasingly shifted to screens, the customized nature of OTC trading makes at least a certain portion of those trades likely to be negotiated over the phone for some time.

What's good about what has occurred? While individual traders may prefer to keep their own orders and trades hidden from view, they seem to want to know as much as possible about the orders and trades of others, so we would have to say that the transparency brought by electronic trading is a good thing. Likewise, the falling prices of both trades and market data have both delighted traders and brought in many more market participants, some of them doing huge volumes. No one will miss the "out trades," probably the most visible manifestation of the inherent inefficiency of the old system. Even the out-trade clerks who cleaned up the messes made by the brokers have surely found something more interesting to do.

What about the speed? Most of us love speed. Who would want to ever go back to dial-up Internet? Who doesn't thrill at watching new speed records set in Olympic events or on racetracks? And we all watch in slack-jawed amazement at the incredible increase in speeds at which trades can be done. Speed has become the new obsession in the trading industry. And as much as some of us might like to slow our lives down, when it comes to markets, we simply do not have that choice. Markets have always been about competition, and competition, to varying extents, has always been about speed. It is just that we have learned how to continually make these speeds blazingly fast.

What are the downsides to electronic trading? While the transition to screen-based trading has brought many benefits to the world, it is a clear example of Joseph Schumpeter's process of creative destruction. To create a new world, an old one had to be destroyed. Those who earned their livelihood on the old trading floors—the runners, the price reporters, and the traders themselves—saw their jobs disappear, sometimes overnight. The new jobs created in this transition required very different skill sets: runners could not easily become programmers, and floor traders could not easily become screen traders. The new proprietary trading shops generally preferred to hire bright, easily trainable new college graduates, rather than attempt to retrain middle-aged floor traders. They had acquired too many bad habits that were too difficult to unlearn.

The kids raised on video games had the speed, the motor skills, and the open minds to continually beat the older floor traders to the punch. A few of these floor traders were sufficiently visionary to set up prop shops and hire the new kids to staff them. There is no doubt that the transition has been painful. In early 2010, a documentary film called *Floored*[34] premiered in Chicago to sold-out audiences, made up largely of CME, CBOT, and CBOE floor traders. The film, which documents the disappearance of both floors and floor traders, poignantly captures the feelings of confusion and loss experienced by once successful traders who find their skills increasingly irrelevant. One trader rails against the trend as he angrily says "I hate email. I hate computers ... the computer is the worst and most evil thing of trading that I've ever seen. ... It's more devious ... trust me when I say these people are cheating on the computer. ... The people who are making money are the programmers."

The process of creative destruction has expanded beyond the exchanges to the institutions broking the trades. As mentioned earlier, small start-up firms are doing a tremendous portion of all trading both in equities and in derivatives. With direct access to the exchange, these firms have little need for the traditional broker/dealer or futures commission merchant. They only need these firms to clear and guarantee their trades, and do not need the traditional services like research and execution.

While the destruction of the old order naturally generates nostalgia and sadness amongst those who grew up in it, as well as concern over individuals caught in the process, it is an inevitable part of technological change and does not call for any regulatory intervention. As historian Will Durant wrote, "Death is life's greatest invention, perpetually replacing the worn with the new." The same holds true in technological change.

Regulators are happy about some things and worried about others. Electronic trading has solved one of the biggest regulatory headaches of previous decades, and that was the lack of a decent audit trail for trades. In floor trading, while outside orders were timed stamped when they came in, floor traders did not record the precise time they executed each of their trades. At one point the futures exchanges improved things by requiring all brokers and traders to record the 30-minute time bracket (and later the 15-minute time bracket) in which their trade took place. In addition, both the exchanges and the CFTC would use this information to attempt to reconstruct the trading day, so there would be a reasonable idea of when a trader made his own trade and entered a trade for a customer. However, without a precise time for each trade, neither the exchanges nor regulatory personnel were able to tell with certainty whether a broker had traded ahead of his customer, a major violation of both exchange rules and government regulations in most countries. This allowed front-running and a host of other possible abuses sometimes to go undetected. In the screen-based world, we know precisely when each transaction took place, making it much easier to detect violations.

At the moment, a few things seem to bother regulators, especially amidst the populist sentiment of the electorate following the recent financial crisis. High-frequency trading generally and flash trading in particular, along with colocation, strike some regulators as unfair, giving some traders an advantage over others and especially over the general public. Moreover, a number of regulators feel that market integrity and even financial system integrity could be compromised by a scenario of a well-financed but buggy algorithm gone wild when combined with direct market access. It is essential that these scenarios and risks are thoroughly explored and well understood by regulators contemplating various kinds of bans.

The technological changes taking place outside of the exchange servers will also continue to amaze, confuse, and startle us. Now that the technology genie has been let out of the lamp, he is not going back in, and markets will continue to evolve and develop. There will be abuses, false starts, unexpected twists and turns, and things that keep traders, exchange officials and regulators up at night. There will be so much that we simply cannot yet imagine, and there is no doubt that the journey will be an exciting one.

Notes

Thanks to Stuart School of Business graduate students Madhursh Rai and Rajeev Ranjan for research assistance in preparing this chapter.

1 William Batten, Chairman NYSE, "The ABC's of ABS," Draft, November 22, 1977, p. 2. Thanks to Larry Harris for pointing out that ABS apparently was first and supplying the foregoing reference and one other, available at: http://c0403731.cdn.cloudfiles.rackspacecloud.com/collection/papers/1970/1977_1122_ABSNYSE.pdf and http://c0403731.cdn.cloudfiles.rackspacecloud.com/collection/papers/1970/1976_0201_CentralProgress.pdf

2 Unless otherwise indicated, details in this section are taken from Patrick Catania, "Electronic Trading: A Brief History," in Patrick L. Young (editor), *An Intangible Commodity: Defining the Future of Derivatives*, Kent, England, derivatives.com Publishing, 2004, p. 51–55, and from discussions with Patrick Catania, who was an employee of INTEX during the period referenced.

3 It is difficult to imagine today when we can see all or much of the limit order book, but in the floor-based world, the most a customer off the floor would know was the price of the last transaction and possibly a recent bid and ask. By the time a market order reached the floor, it often would be executed at a worse price than indicated by the prices that had just been reported from the floor, and customers often felt they were being cheated. And because of the lack of an accurate trail, it was easier for brokers to front run customer orders. To make matters worse, when things got very busy, a fast market was declared and brokers were not held to all of the normal requirements of performance.

4 "Electronic Exchange for Futures, Intex, Opens in Slow Trading," *Wall Street Journal*, October 26, 1984, p. 1.

5 With options listed on only six Swedish stocks, the exchange made a pre-tax profit of US$24.4 million on revenue of US$121.8 million, *Wall Street Journal*, November 18, 1988.

6 This section draws upon Leo Melamed's recollections in Leo Melamed, *Escape to the Futures*, John Wiley and Sons, 1996, p. 336–39.

7 Roger D. Huang and Hans Stoll, "The Design of Trading Systems: Lessons from Abroad," *Financial Analysts Journal*, Vol. 48, No. 5 (September–October, 1992) pp. 49–54.

8 Lewis D. Solomon and Louise Corso, "The Impact of Technology on the Trading of Securities: The Emerging Global Market and the Implications for Regulation," *The John Marshall Law School Review*, Vol. 24 (1991), p. 299.

9 Michael Gorham and Nidhi Singh, *Electronic Exchanges: The Global Transformation from Pits to Bits*, Elsevier, 2009, p. 66.

10 The full 85 are listed in Gorham and Singh, though only the top 20 are displayed in the table here.

11 This discussion relies on discussions with David Colker, who served in many capacities at the Cincinnati Stock Exchange for two decades, retiring as CEO and president in 2006, and with Gary Lahey, former vice Chairman of CBOE and board member of the Cincinnati Stock Exchange.

12 In fact, brokerage firms may actually hold some of the limit order book that is not revealed to the exchange. For example, the hidden portion of an iceberg order may well be resident on the brokerage firm's server, not the exchange's.

13 Ivy Schmerken, "CME Expands Views of Order Book Data," *Advanced Trading*, March 26, 2009, http://www.advancedtrading.com/ exchanges/showArticle.jhtml?articleID=216400379

14 To put this in perspective, it takes about 6,000 ms to read this footnote.

15 Lisa Kassenaar, "Lime's Gorton Trades Fast, Seeks Car-Free Utopia," Bloomberg.com, March 23, 2008.http://www.bloomberg.com/ apps/news?pid=20601109&sid=aI7Vgoya5Bak&refer=exclusive

16 Larry Tabb presented the results in a video at http://advancedtrading.com/video-tabb/index.jhtml;jsessionid=MT122TWVOM 0G1QE1GHRSKH4ATMY32JVN

17 Jonathan Spicer and Herbert Lash, "Who's Afraid of High Frequency Trading?" Reuters, December 2, 2009 http://www.reuters.com/article/idUSN173583920091202?pageNumber=1&virtualBrandChannel=

18 Liz Moyer and Emily Lambert, "The New Masters of Wall Street," *Forbes Magazine*, September 2001, http://www.forbes.com/forbes/2009/0921/revolutionaries-stocks-getco-new-masters-of-wall-street.html

19 Cara Scatizzi, "On-Line Discount Brokers 2009," American Association of Individual Investors, *Computerized Investing*, January/February 2009. Survey of 18 American brokers found prices of US$5, US$7, US$8, and US$10, for typically up to 500 shares. The average price of a stock in the Dow Jones Industrial Average was US$47 at the time of the survey. Costs continue to fall. On March 10, 2010, Interactive Brokers charged US$0.005 per share, or US$1.50 for a 300 share trade. http://www.interactivebrokers.com/en/p.php?f=commission

20 Options traders paid a lower flat fee per contract.

21 Members got a 90 percent discount and paid only seven cents, but it was a member-owned exchange and it seemed fine for the customers to subsidize the members, especially since most members were providing brokering or market making services for the customers.

22 Larry Schneider, Zaner Group LLC.

23 Interactive Brokers offers both the traditional orders and algos, programs that allow customers to more actively manage their orders, especially useful when the trading has been automated on the customer's end.

24 When a firm allows a customer to send it orders directly to an exchange, this is known as sponsored access. If the customer is allowed to bypass the firm's risk management system, this is called unfiltered sponsored access. This unfiltered access is known in the equities world as naked access and in the futures world as direct market access. Carol L. Clark, "Controlling Risk in a Lightening-Speed Trading Environment," *Chicago Fed Letter*, Number 272, March 2010.

25 Carol L. Clark, "Controlling Risk in a Lightening-Speed Trading Environment," *Chicago Fed Letter*, Number 272, March 2010.

26 Two financial veterans believe the risks are great and have written that quality control in the financial industry is just not good enough and falls far short of standards in manufacturing. See Andrew Kumiega and Benjamin E. Van Vliet, "In Crisis, Give Credit to Quality," *Quality Progress*, December 2008, pp. 8–9.

27 Scott Patterson, "SEC Proposes Banning Naked Access," *Wall Street Journal*, January 14, 2010. http://online.wsj.com/article/SB10001424052748 704362004575000962550983250.html

28 They would try to confirm the details of these trades if there was sufficient time, either immediately, or later during quieter periods, but this was sometimes difficult to do when markets were very active.

29 David McNeill, "Fat Finger Trade Costs Tokyo Shares Boss His Job," *The Independent*, December 21, 2005.

30 "Not My Fault," Futures, December 1998, p. 12.

31 Note that exchanges have developed rules, with varying degrees of subjectivity, for breaking or busting trades when these trades were caused by glitches of various kinds. To simplify and standardize things, the SEC worked with all the US securities exchanges to come up with an industry rule that allows breaking a trade only if the price has moved by more than a specified percentage (10, 5, or 3 percent, based on the price level of the stock). This rule on "erroneous trades" became effective October 9, 2009. http://www.sec.gov/news/press/2009/2009-215.htm

32 Greg Ip, "Casualties in Online Trading Revolution Are Putting E*Trade on the Defensive," *Wall Street Journal*, June 13, 2000, pg. C.1.

33 The Pacific Stock Exchange itself was created by a 1957 merger of the San Francisco Stock and Bond Exchange and the Los Angeles Stock and Oil Exchange, but this was part of the earlier trend of merging regional exchanges, and not the current M&A frenzy driven by the tremendous economies of scale made available by electronic order matching. "Pacific Stock Exchange Equities Floor Passes into History," *Silicon Valley/San Jose Business Journal*, March 21, 2002.

34 Directed by James Allen Smith and produced by Trader Film LLC.

7

Demutualization and Self-listing

BENGT RYDÉN

▬▬▬ I. Overview

Securities exchanges around the world have undergone radical structural changes during the last decades. Demutualizations, self-listings, and mergers are important examples of such changes.[1] This chapter describes these phenomena and their role in the restructuring process of the world's stock exchanges.

I will discuss the main driving forces behind the process and some of its consequences. I will also try to evaluate their benefits and disadvantages and present some thoughts about possible future developments. My conclusion is that the changes mainly have had private as well as social benefits but that some problems related to potential conflicts of interest remain to be solved.

The description and discussion is to a large extent based on developments at the Stockholm Stock Exchange (SSE) where, as CEO, I took part in initiating and implementing most of the reforms described in this chapter. SSE was the first stock exchange to demutualize so we had to "invent the wheel." I also will try to give examples and conclusions from other exchanges. The main driving forces behind the discussed changes in the industry are much the same for all exchanges, but the form and character of the reforms vary from country to country and from exchange to exchange.

▨▨▨▨ 2. General Background to the Structural Reforms in the Securities Exchange Industry

The latest phase in the development of the organization and structure of the securities exchange industry should be seen against a historical background. Marketplaces for securities trading were set up during the seventeenth century in several European cities, among them Amsterdam, when trading moved from outdoors curb and coffeehouse activities to exchange buildings created for this purpose. The guild culture, which for centuries dominated economic and social life in Europe, greatly influenced these early securities marketplaces.

Against this background, stock exchanges naturally organized as member cooperatives where only members had the right to buy and sell securities among themselves and on behalf of their clients. To secure their businesses, the members agreed to self-regulate their markets.

In the late 1800s, public interest in equity share investments grew with the emerging industrialization and the creation of the joint stock company. With the increased involvement of public traders, governments started to intervene in stock trading to counteract swindling and other malpractices that had developed.

Sweden adopted its first stock exchange law in 1920. This law was in effect for 60 years until it was replaced by a new law that dramatically increased political intervention in the exchange business. The new law established a public utility framework for SSE, gave it a listing and trading monopoly, and provided that the government appoint a majority of the board of directors. The exchange had no owners—it was "self owned"—but in practice, the government dominated it. Government intervention in the stock exchange business was common in different forms around the world, as part of the strong regulation of capital markets of the time.

Such a governance structure obviously was not fit for the new environment that emerged in the last decades of the twentieth century, when a wave of deregulation and financial market reforms created a completely different environment for stock exchanges and securities trading. The exchanges, which for centuries lived in a culture of national monopolies and protectionism, for the first time faced competition. They slowly started to develop strategies of how to meet the new situation.

This was how issues of governance and organizational reform, and the business behavior of stock exchanges, came on their agendas.

3. A New World Order

Following the reforms of the Thatcher and Reagan governments, a wave of market liberalism swept over most parts of the world. The financial sector was deeply influenced by the new political sentiment. Nevertheless, market liberalism also changed the structure of several other industries with histories of public utility regulation and sheltered market positions, such as airlines, railways, energy, and telecom. These industries all went through radical structural changes in the wake of deregulation, new technologies, the entrance of new innovative companies, and the creation of global markets for many kinds of services. Traditional attitudes of protectionist nationalism gave way to more market-friendly attitudes, not least in Europe.

In the financial sector, the internationalization of investing and trading in financial products—made possible by the removal of foreign exchange controls—and the use of new information and communication technologies gradually increased competition among exchanges. Legislators often supported the efforts of the exchanges to adjust to the new situation by tearing down legal and other institutional obstacles to change. The ambition of the European Union to lay the foundation of a European market for financial services was an important part of this process.

The deregulation of financial markets created a completely new business climate in the industry. Equity financing and investing grew in importance as the number of public companies and of retail investors increased. New standardized financial products were developed, especially options, futures, and other derivatives. Investment funds became extremely popular. Pension savings in equity grew in importance. Many new firms were set up to profit from the business opportunities. After having been a slow growth industry for many decades, the financial sector gradually developed to become a high-growth industry.

4. Demutualization

During the course of the 1990s, many stock exchanges realized that the new environment presented both threats and opportunities, and many concluded that change was necessary. The core of their new strategies was to create a business culture to meet the competitive threats and to profit from the business opportunities. Many soon regarded demutualization—the transformation from a member or government, not-for-profit, entity to a for-profit corporation—as a logic step to take.

In many countries, this process was rather slow due to member resistance to giving up control of the exchange. This was clearly the case in the United States. However, when, in the second half of the 1990s, it became evident that several important exchanges were planning to demutualize and be run for profit, demutualization soon became the standard route to modernize the corporate structure of exchanges. Around the year 2000, many stock exchanges—among them all Nordic exchanges, Amsterdam, Borsa Italiana, Australia, Hong Kong, Singapore, Toronto, Frankfurt, London, Paris, NASDAQ, and New York—had demutualized, or stated they were planning to do so. As mentioned, SSE was the first exchange to demutualize, in 1993.[2]

I conclude from the many discussions I had with boards and managements of exchanges who were contemplating to demutualize that the financial solutions and new corporate structures that they choose varied substantially because of different traditions, governance, legislation, et cetera. For example, seat-based exchanges, which were the norm in the United States, encountered different issues than did exchanges where all members had access to trading. Moreover, exchanges that were strictly regulated by law had to enter into complicated discussions with politicians and civil servants to create understandings for the legal and regulatory reforms required to demutualize.

5. The SSE Case

Since SSE was first out and seemed to have set the tone for a number of followers, I will describe in some detail what we did and why.

As an outsider, it became clear to me soon after my arrival in 1985 that the organization, structure, and regulation of SSE was in need of reform to make it ready to meet the challenges of the emerging business environment of the financial industry. It was easy to see that this was not a specific company problem but rather an industry structure problem.

The first step, taken in 1987, was to initiate a reform of the trading system, from a traditional trading floor with an open outcry auction to electronic trading with a limit order book with automatic matching. The SSE introduced the new system in 1990 and fully implemented it in 1991 when the SSE closed the trading floor. For the members, this change was more controversial and dramatic than the coming demutualization.

The next step was to create the legal conditions to orient the exchange as a for-profit business that the management and the board thought necessary to make the exchange competitive. There were many obstacles to such an orientation in the law, for example the not-for-profit provision and the self-owned structure. Management and the board recognized that organizations without owners suffer from serious limitations to operating efficiently. In addition, SSE had a legal monopoly which, of course, is an obstacle to the creation of an efficient business culture. Another problem was the structure of the board, which had 22 members that included 14 government appointees with the remaining representing exchange members and issuers.

A new stock exchange law, passed in 1992, removed these and other legal obstacles to the reform of SSE that the board was planning. The reform aimed at providing the SSE with owners with an interest to operate the exchange efficiently for profit and with directors elected on competence by the owners and with responsibility to hire (and fire) the CEO.

The new company, Stockholm Stock Exchange AB, was set up as a daughter company to its mother SSE in 1992. It issued subscription rights for shares to its members and issuers on a 50/50 basis. The number of rights to each recipient was based on the value of fees paid to SSE during the previous five years. A total of 150 members and issuers subscribed to the share issue. The company took over the operations of the exchange on January 1, 1993, the same day as the new law became effective. The board had been reduced from 22 to 8 members who were elected by representatives of the owners. I was offered to stay on the board as CEO to continue the work of reforming the exchange.

The staff of about 50 was streamlined. After some time, the right to sell market information products was sold to an information vendor. A profit sharing scheme for all staff was introduced, based on distributing 20 percent of a defined "excess profit." This system served well as an important incentive for efficiency and hard work. Many of these events were parts of strategic work that had been going on for some time and which continued to engage the board, the management, and the staff for several years to come.

I had tried for some years to create a business culture at all levels in SSE. It was not until the demutualization/privatization that these efforts gradually proved successful. A substantial growth of trading, listing and income in combination with the profit sharing scheme contributed to this change of attitude.

However, my view that members, issuers and investors should all be regarded and treated as customers was a matter of some conflict. At this time, in the early 1990s, no stock exchange even talked about customers; the word did not exist in the stock exchange vocabulary. It took the members (and their board representatives) a long time to accept this view. The members argued that they should be treated as members only, not as any one customer. Moreover, the investors were their customers, not those of the exchange, they said. Although this conflict may seem absurd today, it shows how much business attitude has changed in the industry.

Contributing substantially to the business culture of SSE was the reform of the trading system. When the floor closed, the relationship between the traders/brokers and the exchange obviously changed character. In addition, with the introduction in 1992 of foreign, "remote," members who could trade online from wherever they were located, this relationship became totally different from the traditional one. This change also helped instil a business culture.[3]

In the years that followed the demutualization/privatization, several other important initiatives were taken to strengthen the exchange. The trading grew substantially by the addition of new members, many of whom were trading from their home offices in the Nordic countries, London, Zürich, Frankfurt, and Amsterdam. Direct access to the trading system was opened to institutional investors who started to trade online; this was the first step towards disintermediation of securities trading. The electronic order book was gradually opened to the general public so the retail investor also got access to the market and could trade in real time at minimal commissions. Negotiations were held to create a common Nordic exchange market. Quality assurance work was successfully completed when SSE was granted an ISO 2001 certification. The new business culture facilitated many of these changes.

The demutualization/privatization process in Sweden was relatively fast and smooth. The legislators were supportive and since the exchange had no owners and virtually no capital, there was no serious resistance or financial conflicts to handle with the members. It is my impression that many exchanges had to struggle hard to solve such problems.

▓▓▓ 6. Self-listing

As I have argued, demutualized for-profit exchanges can provide important benefits to their owners and users. In many cases, demutualization has been followed by the listing of the equity of the exchange on its own market—"self-listing." Early examples of such self-listings are OM/SSE, Australian Stock Exchange (ASX), Hong Kong Stock Exchange, and Singapore Stock Exchange. Soon Deutsche Börse, London Stock Exchange, Euronext, and NASDAQ followed suit.

The possible benefits of self-listing are much the same as for the listing of any type of business—access to the capital market; a liquid currency for growth through acquisition; educational effects of the market evaluation, and the risk of hostile takeovers; quality stamp through the due diligence process; and an exit facility for the owners.

The listing of SSE was not the result of a listing decision as such but rather of the merger of the already listed derivatives exchange OM and SSE in 1998 (see the following section). The possibility to list the SSE shares was briefly discussed at the time of the initial public offering (IPO) but considered to be premature and unrealistic; the equity of SSE was small as was the number of shareholders. In addition, the demutualization/privatization was undertaken during an economic crisis that seriously hurt the Swedish financial community and the equity market.

The listing of a stock exchange underlines the business orientation of the exchange even stronger than does a demutualization. As with any listed company, the exchange can be expected to be more financially driven and more motivated by short-term profit maximization. If the open ownership attracts outside investors, these will demand a return on their investment at par with their investment alternatives. This probably will not be the case if the owners are insiders (members, issuers) with other interests in the exchange than outsiders.

This conflict of interest can influence the allocation of resources to the self-regulatory functions of the exchange—setting rules, conducting surveillance, and enforcing the rules. In an increasingly competitive environment, exchanges may want to minimize resources to these regulatory functions.

However, such behavior may entail reputational risks which can be detrimental to the business of the exchange. For example, when SSE demutualized, it set up an independent disciplinary committee to handle cases involving possible breaches of exchange rules and to decide about enforcements against issuers and members. Before, these functions had been handled by the board. The stock exchange law was later amended to require that all authorized exchanges organize such committees.

In addition, several exchanges have separated the regulating and oversight functions from the for-profit business operations by establishing independent subsidiaries or departments, or by outsourcing these functions. This was done by ASX, NASDAQ, OM/SSE, and many others.

In many countries, conflicts of interest related to exchange regulatory activities have been handled through agreements between the exchanges and their government regulators. Nevertheless, the trend seems to be towards more of government regulation, whereby surveillance and other market regulatory functions are taken over by government supervisory authorities. The UK market is an interesting example of this trend, and Sweden is going in the same direction.

Another area of possible conflict involves trading in the exchange shares and the associated market surveillance. In many cases, among them Sweden, the conflict of interest problem has been solved by the government regulator taking sole regulatory responsibility over trades in the exchange shares while obligating the exchange to report any irregularities that it may observe.

In many countries, demutualized stock exchanges are regarded as public or semi-public utilities. Strong influence by "unfriendly" owners may be seen as contrary to the public interest. To counteract this risk, articles of association or laws regulating stock exchanges often restrict ownership interests to less than 5–15 percent. Surprisingly, no such restrictions were introduced in Sweden. Instead, the government increased its share holding in OM/SSE from the 7 percent it got at the time of the IPO to around 9 percent by purchasing OM shares on the market a couple of years after the OM/SSE merger. It later sold this holding when NASDAQ bid for OM.

7. Evaluation of the New Governance Structure

The corporate structure that emerged as a result of the vast changes in the exchange industry created a business culture that never before existed in the industry. It may be one of the fastest and most radical structural reforms that any industry has experienced. The new competitive landscape that emerged has forced exchanges to be more efficient, innovative and growth oriented than they were before. Output in terms of numbers of quotations, transactions, and listings per man-hour grew substantially for many years.

While the SSE output grew some 50–100 percent annually, the number of staff remained unchanged. Decisions were taken faster, new products and services were developed, and the overall quality of the SSE services improved. This benefited owners, issuers and brokers in several different ways. Trading and listing fees were reduced. The SSE share increased in value over 50 times during the five years from the IPO to the merger with OM.[4] And to judge from the growth in value of the shares of listed exchanges in general, the owners of these exchanges have benefited greatly from their investments.

However, demutualization also entails problems, some of which were discussed in the previous section. If the members continue to have a strong influence over strategic issues, such as pricing and investment policies, they may use their influence to their advantage and to the disadvantage of other interest groups, such as issuers or outside inves-tors. To avoid this, it may be necessary to allot shares and board seats so that members do not obtain voting majority positions among the shareholders or the board members.

Australia and Hong Kong have enacted provisions of this kind. As mentioned, in the SSE case, members and issuers each were offered to subscribe for 50 percent of the capital. Nevertheless, the interest of the issuers was weak, and those who became owners were passive. The power over SSE to a large extent continued to reside in the hands of the big Swedish banks, most of which stood together informally on strategic SSE issues.

This was most obvious in pricing matters, as has been the case at many other exchanges. Member interests often argue for reducing trading fees rather than promoting the growth of exchange profits. What trading members have seen as excessive profits have even induced them to jointly set up competing low-fee trading vehicles in an effort to drive down the fees of the exchanges. Such initiatives have been taken in the United States, Britain, Germany, and Sweden, among others. Moreover, they have been successful in forcing exchanges to cut their trading fees. The same phenomenon occurred in the clearing business. This demonstrates that member owners often continue to regard demutualized for-profit exchanges as public utilities and that they have difficulties in accepting their dual role as owners and customers.

8. The New Era of Mergers and Acquisitions

Stock exchanges were local actors until new communication tools, such as the telegraph and telephone, made the fast dissemination of market information possible. Many countries had a large number of exchanges, some of which continued to exist—often competing with each other—well into the mid-twentieth century. In European countries such as Spain, Portugal, Italy, and Switzerland, consolidation into one national exchange was implemented as late as in the 1990s. A similar process took place in countries such as United States, Canada, Brazil, and Australia. Nevertheless, Germany still defies this trend, probably because of strong local state political interests.

The new corporate structure created financial possibilities for the birth of transnational stock exchange groups. An important first case was the setting up of Euronext through a merger of the Paris, Amsterdam, and Brussels exchanges, which later took over the Lisbon Stock Exchange. Starting in the early 1990s, a Nordic consolidation came into effect that eventually combined Stockholm, Helsinki, Copenhagen, Iceland, and the three Baltic exchanges into one company. Later, London Stock Exchange (LSE) acquired Borsa Italiana. Even before these events, Deutsche Börse (Frankfurt Stock Exchange) made several unsuccessful efforts to grow internationally, mainly by merging with LSE in 2000. In addition, OM made an unsuccessful bid for LSE in 2000. A strong driving force was probably the fear of being left alone on the dancing floor.

The next step in this consolidation process occurred when the first truly global exchange groups were created. The New York Stock Exchange and Euronext agreed to merge, giving birth to the largest exchange in the world. NYSE may have been influenced by NASDAQ's gradual acquisition of LSE shares, but LSE turned down NASDAQ's proposals to merge. NASDAQ instead made an offer to buy OMX, and NASDAQ/OMX was created. In a matter of less than 20 years, the exchange industry structure changed from one characterized by many small member-driven, not-for-profit organizations to one dominated by a few global, listed corporate groups operating clusters of exchanges.

As often is the case with mergers and acquisitions, there is no single reason that explains this development. One obvious reason is economies of scale in the exchange industry. Consolidating transactions has become increasingly important as capital expenditure for technical development and infrastructure investment has grown. Economies of scope is another reason. A third one is the quest for growth that can be realized quicker through acquisitions.

Cash and derivative securities trading originally developed on completely separate marketplaces. The first financial derivatives exchanges were set up in Chicago in the 1970s. Some cash exchanges, such as NYSE and LSE, tried to complement their operations with derivatives products but with meager results. Instead, new derivatives exchanges were set up all over the world. In the 1990s, it became increasingly evident that combined cash and derivatives trading could offer both cost synergies and better services to clients. The result was a number of acquisitions and mergers between these two types of exchanges in their efforts to grow and become more efficient. Euronext's acquisition of London International Financial Futures Exchange (LIFFE) is an important example. Many national mergers of cash and derivatives exchanges took place in Europe, Asia and Latin America—but not in the United States where the demutualization of derivatives exchanges was slow.

In Sweden, the merger of OM and SSE was a very special case. Organized equity options contract trading started in 1985 through the auspices of a new securities firm, OM. Options trading grew substantially, and OM soon became very successful. Its shares were quoted on the small company market that SSE had set up.[5] In 1992, OM received subscription rights in the SSE and soon got an interest to acquire more rights and, later on, shares from issuers that had no interest in being owners of SSE. When OM, after a couple of years, had increased its holding to about 20 percent of SSE, discussions got under way to develop some type of cooperation between the two exchanges.

The parties could easily see that there were possible benefits from cooperation, especially in technical areas. In November 1997, SSE and OM agreed to merge, whereby OM, now listed on the SSE main list, offered new shares in exchange for SSE shares. Therefore, the merged exchanges were now listed on SSE as one exchange operating company. This is how SSE became self-listed. The listing of NYSE through a reverse takeover of Archipelago came about in a similar way.

During the period of structural reforms in the exchange industry, important changes occurred also in other parts of the value chain of securities trading. The production and distribution of pre- and post-trade information improved substantially. Many exchanges engaged in these activities which they regarded as adding value to the core business. The clearing and settling of transactions were modernized in many countries with the help of information technologies.

Central counterparty clearing organizations were created to guarantee correct and fast settlement of each trade. Simultaneously, similar modern and cost efficient solutions were developed for the registration of securities in central security depositaries, operated by organizations owned by the securities industry as cooperatives and/or by governments. Certificate dematerialization started in the Scandinavian countries in the 1980s, which significantly improved the efficiency of the post trade administration.

Some exchanges soon developed an interest in investing also in the post-trade business. They were nicknamed as "silos" because of their vertically integrated operations. Deutsche Börse was the first and probably best example of this new trend. The silos were criticized by some of the large international investment banks, and also by the European Commission, for obstructing the free access of market users to their preferred post-trade service providers.

9. The New Competitors

The latest, but certainly not the last, phase in the development of the securities trading industry was the emergence of trading platforms, so called "multilateral trading facilities" (MTFs), offering trading services to institutions at minimal fees. These platforms, among them Chi-X and Turquoise, have won substantial market shares in blue chip trading in Europe and United States. In January 2010, Chi-X was the second largest marketplace in Europe in equity turnover. LSE has been reported to have lost near 50 percent of its trading to such platforms in two years time, and it is not surprising that LSE has taken over a majority ownership of Turquoise. NYSE is also an obvious loser. These trading platforms do not have market surveillance or listing obligations but are free riding on the work done by the exchanges. In Europe, the legal basis for this dramatic change in the securities trading corporate structure was the Market in Financial Instruments Directive MiFID of the European Union, which became effective on November 1, 2007.

It is interesting that some of the new trading platforms (e.g., Turquoise and, in Sweden, Burgundy) have been set up by exchange members to drive down the trading fees of the exchanges. They seem to act more as user cooperatives than for profit companies and are so far experiencing substantial losses.

In addition, large investment banks have gradually ceased to bring trades to regulated markets for execution. Instead, they seek the benefits from internal matching.

It is not easy to see how the regulated exchanges can in the long run successfully compete in substantial parts of the market with these new low-fee trading vehicles. However successful in their transformation to business enterprises, they have a cost burden that their new competitors do not have. Although their legal obligations may have a positive bearing on the public trust in stock exchanges, it is possible that the oversight and listing functions must be fully taken over by government agencies to create a level playing field or to secure serious execution of these important functions.

▓ 10. The New Structure—Summary and Some Thoughts About the Future

As I have described in this chapter, the securities exchange industry has gone through dramatic changes during the last decades. Vast deregulation, new technologies, and the development of global markets for investment and trading have been the main drivers. The most important result is the emergence of a business culture created through new corporate structures and a behavior that has been fostered by the listing of exchanges. In just a few years, exchanges have developed new organizational forms that are completely different from traditional ones.

This development has improved the governance and the efficiency of exchanges to the benefit of investors, issuers, and intermediaries. Prices have been reduced and services have improved. Securities investing and trading has become a fast growing industry. On the other hand, the new structure has created new problems, most of which relate to conflicts of interest.

The most important of these, in my view, is the reluctance of members to accept their ownership role, but instead continue to act in their self-interest and against the interests of the other owners. This type of conflict ideally should be avoided when the shares of the demutualized exchange are first distributed or offered to the different interest groups.

There are also social benefits of the reforms of the securities exchange industry. National economies have been helped to grow faster when an increasing number of old and young companies have had better access to risk capital. The number of public companies has grown substantially in all parts of the world. Income, new jobs and new investment opportunities have been created. Possibilities for entrepreneurs to realize old dreams and new ideas have been facilitated. A climate of dynamism and market solutions has emerged to the benefit of economic growth. The importance of this development is perhaps of special relevance in former communist countries—and of course in China—all of which were eager to set up stock markets and exchanges in the early 1990s.

If these social benefits are true for nations, they are also true for the world. Securities investment and trading have become truly global activities.

However, the free market liberalism governing the stock exchange industry of today perhaps is not tenable in the long run for an industry that continues to have a character of public utility. If profit maximizing exchange operating companies cease handling listing and trading in small companies because it is a loss making business—what will "the public" then do? What will happen if serving retail investors becomes unprofitable? With increased pension savings in the equity market, politicians will have to take an interest in such possible problems, as they have already done in areas as energy, railways, postal services, and other sectors considered necessary as part of the social infrastructure in modern societies. Alternatively, will "the market" help solve the problem with small niche market operators picking up what the big ones have left? In any event, the line between public and private utilities will become even more difficult to draw.

Considering the social importance of financial markets and their infrastructure, it is surprising that the structural reforms described in this chapter, based on politically driven deregulation, were decided and implemented so fast and, in my view, often without the proper analysis—normally expected in cases of vast social and economic reforms. Politicians seem to have been taken by surprise and have not been able to resist the market liberalization wind that swept the world in the 1980s and 1990s. When problems caused by unfettered profit-seeking stock market operators come out in the daylight, we will probably have a new debate about the proper level of regulation of stock markets and exchanges and possibly a wave of reregulation. Conflicts of interest are so inherent in the present structure that such a reaction is bound to take place.

The world needs stock markets. However, they must be regulated to act as public and private utilities with a social purpose.

Notes

1 Demutualization is defined as the conversion of a securities exchange from a not-for-profit, member-owned entity to a for-profit corporation. Self-listing is defined as the listing of the share of an exchange operating company on its own market.

2 Privatization is a more accurate description of the SSE case since SSE, as already mentioned, was not member owned but rather government dominated with no owners.

3 SSE was the first cash equity exchange to close its floor and the first to have remote members trading electronically.

4 It should be mentioned that the initial issuance price was very low. Large dividends were also distributed.

5 OM was the first exchange in the world to list in 1987.

8

The Creation of Exchanges in Countries with Communist Histories

WIESLAW ROZLUCKI

1. Overview

This chapter considers the stock markets that have emerged during the transition from centrally planned to market economies. The transition occurred over the last 20 years and covered a wide geographical area spreading from Central and Eastern Europe (CEE) through Central Asia to China and Vietnam. A complete description of the different paths of transition in each individual country would be too voluminous for this chapter. Instead, this chapter concentrates on the common features and most important differences in the development of stock markets in the more than 30 countries that underwent transition.

The following analysis identifies the most important factors that contributed to the success or failure of individual stock markets that were re-established from a fresh start in the early 1990s.

2. Historical Background

During the pre-Communist period, practically all countries described in the following section had functioning commercial exchanges that dealt both in commodities and securities. Most exchanges were established as formal institutions in the nineteenth century (St.Petersburg 1816, Warsaw 1817, Moscow 1839, Budapest 1864, Prague 1872, Bucharest 1882). They provided facilities for trading government loans, corporate bonds and shares, promissory notes and other instruments. The proportion of traded instruments differed across markets. For example, in Warsaw, securities trading clearly dominated, but in Moscow, securities trading was small in comparison to commodity trading.

In 1912, 275 Russian companies were listed at the St Petersburg Exchange, with one-third of them cross-listed in Paris, London, or Brussels. At the Budapest Commodity and Stock Exchange at the time, 177 companies were listed, many of which also traded in Vienna. The Warsaw Exchange listed 130 companies and 82 bond issues in 1938, a number of which also listed on Western exchanges.

The operations of exchanges in the CEE were, in most cases, interrupted during the World Wars and finally terminated when the communist political system was installed (Russia 1917, Central Europe 1945).[1] In the following decades of central planning, the human experience in stock markets was largely lost. However, the recorded rules and practices of exchanges were not forgotten. When political conditions changed after 1989, memories of local stock exchanges influenced the transitions to market economies.

3. Privatization Strategies as Drivers of Capital Markets

Political events of the 1980s triggered the process of transition in Central and Eastern Europe. Among the more important movements and events were the Solidarity (*Solidarnosc*) movement in Poland, the Russian *perestroika*, the June 1989 elections in Poland and the tearing down of the Berlin Wall later that year. During the next few years, the governments and political systems changed dramatically in most of these countries.

Concerning the economic dimension, the transitions were based on liberalization, i.e., the removal of the commands and restrictions typical of centrally planned economies. Structural reforms included also privatization, which involved the sale or distribution of state-owned enterprises as well as the establishment of new private companies.

In many countries—particularly those in Central and Eastern Europe (CEE)—speed was an essential element of transition. Privatization, being always politically controversial, was carried out relatively quickly to reach a point of no return to the previous regime. In the early 1990s, the scope of privatization carried out in CEE was unprecedented in economic history. Privatization transformed thousands of state-owned enterprises (in Russia alone more than 30,000). The public debate during 1989–91 concentrated on how to privatize large numbers of companies as rapidly as possible, while taking into account shortages of available capital.

Examples of previous privatizations carried out in some Western countries in the late 1980s were available, but these privatizations (for example, British Telecom and British Steel in the United Kingdom and Paribas in France) were more similar to the initial public offerings (IPOs) of individual companies, rather than privatization of whole economies.

The challenge in CEE was much bigger: privatization of whole industries and economies. Case-by-case offerings would take dozens of years to carry out the privatization process. Hence, the idea of mass privatization was considered, through coupons or vouchers distributed among citizens. The concept of coupon privatization, discussed in Poland in the late 1980s, was effectively introduced in Czechoslovakia during the early 1990s. It was followed—with many modifications—in Russia, Ukraine, Romania, Bulgaria and other countries. Mass privatization was adopted, to a limited extent, in Poland and not at all in Hungary. Those countries sold most of their large state-owned enterprises either through public offerings or through direct sales to strategic—mainly foreign—investors.

The privatization strategies adopted (coupon privatization, employee ownership, IPOs and sale to strategic investors) were crucial factors in determining the future shape of securities markets in the transitioning economies. The framework of the securities markets that emerged in each country was to a large extent a by-product of the privatization method.

In the debate of the early 1990s, coupon privatization was considered to be most conducive to the development of domestic stock markets. Theoretically, before the process started, nobody could deny the best opportunities for the securities markets would arise when thousands of companies were readily available to millions of potential investors. The critical mass of liquidity would be easily achieved. In contrast, employee ownership was not considered as economically efficient and conducive to the development of public markets. Although politically popular, employee ownership was implemented mainly in the former Yugoslavia.

Privatization through IPOs was seen as very positive for the market, but too slow given the large volume of the planned privatizations. The direct sale of privatized assets to strategic, mostly foreign, investors seemed to be most effective from the productivity point of view. Future developments proved this point. However, it was the politically least popular method of privatization. Unfortunately, the positive externality effects on the local securities markets proved to be very limited. International strategic owners in most, but not all, cases are not interested in local public listings of their affiliated companies. This is particularly true if the local markets are in early stages of development, but already impose additional local reporting and compliance costs.[2]

4. Mass Privatization Markets

In those countries that opted for coupon privatization, securities markets were seen as mechanism for secondary trading of the coupons and/or shares in privatized companies. In Czechoslovakia, the nationwide network of RM-System (RMS)—used initially for coupon privatization—was subsequently transformed into a secondary trading platform. It started with periodic auctions and then moved later to continuous trading. More than 1,600 companies were registered for trading on RMS in 1993. Registration should not be understood as listing, as no disclosure and reporting requirements were imposed. In the early 1990s, thousands of newly privatized companies in CEE were not ready for disclosure standards similar to those used in mature markets. When speed and scale of transformation were essential, standards had to be compromised.

Regulation of the post-voucher-privatization markets was deliberately light. The slow process of regulation was not accidental. The idea behind light regulation and supervision of securities markets was to facilitate the concentration of ownership. Less informed investors were expected to sell their shares more readily and at lower prices to potential strategic investors. In Russia, this phase of development (until 1998) was nicknamed "the vacuum-cleaner market".

When millions of accidental, first-time investors became—free of charge—owners of securities, most of them wanted to sell out as soon as possible. Hence, all sorts of "investment funds" became popular. In Czechoslovakia, one such fund very quickly accumulated two-thirds of distributed vouchers. In nonregulated environments, pyramid schemes spread quickly (Russia, Romania, Albania), destroying investor confidence and hampering the development of regulated markets. The price paid for mass and quick privatization, with very low standards of disclosure and reporting, was high.[3]

Only a small fraction of people who received privatization vouchers became individual shareholders in the following years. Mass privatization—which initially looked very promising from an investor's perspective—has not produced a shareholder society. The markets originating from coupon privatization turned out to be transitional and have not transformed themselves into significant regulated markets. In Czech Republic, the RMS market accounts for only 2 percent of total equity trading in the country.

Equally transitional was the development of unregulated or loosely regulated "stock and commodity exchanges" in CEE. Liberalization and deregulation of economic activity in the early 1990s produced a legal environment where an enterprise called "commodity and stock exchange" could be easily established without any licensing process. This was in line with simplified liberal ideology of removing all "communist" restrictions of economic activity. The idea of free markets was initially understood in a literal sense. In Poland, before the first securities law was introduced in March 1991, more than 60 "commodity and stock exchanges" were established during 1989-90. The corresponding figure for Russia was more than 600 establishments. Most of those "exchanges" dealt with all sorts of wholesale goods and some early issues of securities, including shares in the exchanges themselves. The period of spontaneous, unlicensed activity in securities markets was short lived in Poland, ending effectively in 1991. In other countries, some loosely regulated exchanges operated throughout 1990s. Practically, all of them subsequently disappeared.

5. Regulated Securities Exchanges in the 1990s

In the early 1990s, many governments and other institutions in the CEE regarded the period of spontaneous activity as detrimental to market confidence. Governments (Poland), central banks (Czechoslovakia and Russia) and scientific institutes (Hungary) actively supported the initiatives to establish a modern infrastructure for the emerging securities markets. They assumed that securities markets played a much more important role than just as enablers of privatization. The markets were seen as a mechanism for mobilizing savings, allocating capital, providing price discovery and monitoring listed companies. This required the establishment of a modern infrastructure, consisting of a stock exchange, a central securities depository, licensed brokers and, last but not least, a regulator with adequate authority.

In each country, the extent to which the historical tradition of local stock markets could be used in rebuilding the necessary infrastructure was a fundamental decision. As indicated in the overview to this chapter, the history of national stock exchanges in CEE had been broken for too long during the communist period to be operationally continued in the 1990s. Despite some efforts (Budapest, Prague, Warsaw), local expertise was not available.

The necessary know-how to assist local initiatives came from abroad. It originated from individual stock exchanges (SBF Paris Bourse, Deutsche Börse, NYSE, Nasdaq), professional federations (FIBV - International Federation of Stock Exchanges/WFE - World Federation of Exchanges, FESE - Federation of European Stock Exchanges), regulators (US SEC, French COB - Commission des Operations de Bourse), securities depositories as well as institutions like US AID - Agency for International Development, British Know-how Fund, German FBF, Canadian government, the IFC - International Finance Corporation, World Bank and others.[4]

If a securities market is to operate in a professional manner, it has to be organized in every detail. The post-communist countries had a unique opportunity to organize their markets from scratch. There were no established institutions, practices, or vested interests. If a strong leadership and support of interested parties were provided, the market infrastructure could be established in a proper way from the beginning. In practice, however, many compromises had to be introduced.

The first three regulated stock exchanges in transition economies were those in Ljubljana in March 1990, followed by Budapest in June 1990 and Warsaw in April 1991. In Slovenia and Hungary, the financial community set up the exchanges, but in Poland, the government took the initiative. It took only six months for Poland to build the necessary infrastructure, including the Warsaw Stock Exchange, Central Securities Depository and Securities Commission. The Polish team was aided by the French experts of SBF Paris Bourse and Sicovam, as well as regulation experts from the US SEC. The simple market infrastructure was based on modern principles of electronic call auction trading, paperless central depository clearing and settlement, and high disclosure standards. Brokers had to be licensed by the Securities Commission, both as firms and as individuals. The first IPOs, which took place in Poland in December 1990, included prospectuses comparable with Western standards. The same can be said about the first Hungarian IPO (Ibusz travel agency) in early 1990. Poland, Hungary and Slovenia, the early developers of regulated stock markets in CEE, decided to build, right from the beginning, an institutional framework for their markets based on modern standards and practices. The established infrastructure was simple, but covered all the basic processes of a stock market.[5]

Creating properly regulated exchanges and other market institutions was more difficult in other countries. In Czech Republic, the Prague Stock Exchange (PSE), which started trading in 1993, was sometimes viewed as an unwanted child that the government did not support. Competing from the beginning with the RMS over-the-counter market (OTC), the PSE had to admit for trading more than 1,600 privatized companies, most of which were gradually delisted. The conflict between the PSE and RMS resulted in unnecessary fragmentation of the market and the failure to establish a single settlement and depository system in Czech Republic.

During the transformation, it soon became evident that establishing a stock exchange was not as difficult an aspect of building the market infrastructure as was initially thought. Central depository for securities, and particularly an independent and active regulatory body, often turned out to be missing infrastructural components.

Whereas in Poland, Hungary, Slovenia, Baltic countries, the entire market infrastructure was built relatively quickly, the process was much longer and controversial in other countries. In Russia, a Securities and Exchange Commission, having been established in 1992, only became active in 1996. In Czech Republic, it was established as late as in 1998. Loose regulation and supervision in many countries was motivated by vested interests, rather than lack of expertise. The economic interests of oligarchs, accumulating capital during privatization, were opposite to those of small shareholders, whose interests were best served by the principles of transparency and minority protection. Not all stakeholders equally appreciated tight regulation. Politicized enforcement and discretionary decisions brought disillusionment and loss of trust to public institutions and financial firms. In a number of countries, low confidence in stock market was strengthened by banking crises (Russia, Bulgaria, Romania) or general political instability (Ukraine).

The first decade of economic and political transition in CEE brought the establishment of basic stock market infrastructure in most countries of the region. The level of development was highly uneven. Whereas Hungary and Poland were most advanced, successfully initiating derivatives markets in the late 1990s, other countries like Ukraine and Bulgaria still struggled with early problems of assuring ownership rights and bringing securities trading to regulated markets. The processes of building national markets proceeded largely autonomously, almost unaffected by consolidation trends in Western Europe during the 1990s.

6. The long March Towards Maturity

After 2000, development patterns in the CEE markets, based on different principles, remained diverse. The most distinguishing factor was accession to the European Union (EU), which included ten countries: Estonia, Latvia, Lithuania, Poland, Czech Republic, Slovakia, Hungary, Slovenia, Romania and Bulgaria in 2004. A few years before the accession, the markets in those countries went through the process of harmonization of national regulations in accordance with EU rules and practices.

As a result, national regulations and structures of the ten new members became closer to each other and similar to Western Europe, but different from the rest of the CEE region. In each of the accession countries, market forces primarily, and regulation to a lesser extent, brought about a single, dominant stock exchange. The initial competition among trading venues practically disappeared.[6]

The post-accession period, which coincided with prosperity in the world economy, brought the CEE markets to much higher levels of capitalization, turnover and general development of local markets. The beneficial effects of EU accession were not spread evenly among stock markets of the region, however. In Poland, rising trading volumes and valuations triggered a wave of new listings, averaging more than 40 companies annually during 2004-2008, putting the Warsaw Stock Exchange among the top three European exchanges in this category. During the same period, the number of listed companies in Budapest and Prague remained rather stagnant, despite much higher valuations and trading volumes.

In Poland, an important change was observed in the behaviour of listed companies. Whereas in the 1990s, companies were content with public listing, during the next decade, they succeeded in raising new capital, usually through secondary public offerings. In terms of the value of public offerings, Russia has become the undisputed leader in CEE. Macroeconomic and political stability in the country in the early 2000s sharply increased the market capitalization of listed companies, particularly those owning natural resources. Moscow Interbank Currency Exchange (MICEX), originally a platform for interbank trading, became the dominant trading venue in Russia, with turnover close to that of the leading exchanges in Europe. At the same time, neighbouring Ukraine still faces the problems of inadequate regulation, decentralized infrastructure, resulting in dispersed, mainly OTC, trading in equities.

The first decade of economic transformation in 1990s created individual national stock markets in CEE. Their institutional development was not influenced by the worldwide trends of demutualization and consolidation. The post-2000 decade brought significant change. Many smaller markets started looking for partners that were able and willing to increase their level of activity. Two exchanges, Vienna and OMX Nordic, were particularly active in the consolidation process. OMX succeeded in taking over stock exchanges in Lithuania, Latvia and Estonia, while Vienna acquired dominant positions in the stock exchanges of Hungary, Slovenia and Czech Republic. Thus, during 2004-2008, six out of ten exchanges from the accession countries joined larger exchange networks.

The Warsaw Stock Exchange, the biggest in the region, did not participate in the consolidation process on either side. It planned its own IPO and listing in November 2010, striving successfully to attract more remote members and foreign listings.

During the last 20 years, many observers predicted that the biggest and most liquid companies of the CEE region would move their primary listings to bigger European or American financial centres. By and large, this migration has not happened. Companies from Central Europe trade mainly in their home markets. International investors find it easy to trade using either local or remote brokers who can access the main pool of liquidity. The situation is different with regard to Ukraine, Kazakhstan and, until very recently, Russia. Big companies from those countries, particularly those launching IPOs, chose to list in world financial centres, first of all in London, but also in New York and Frankfurt. A number of smaller issuers registered their secondary listings in Warsaw.

7. Centrally Managed Capital Markets in China and Vietnam

The rise of stock exchanges in the transition economies of China and Vietnam lies in sharp contrast to the CEE experience. In Europe, a stock market, its institutions and mechanisms, were seen to be in total opposition to central planning and the political system supporting it. There, a stock exchange had symbolic meaning as the ultimate expression of a free market, capitalist economy.[7] It was, therefore, almost unthinkable in the CEE that a genuine stock market, particularly in equities, could be tolerated in centrally planned economy.[8] Before the fall of the Berlin Wall in 1989, in the CEE region, a stock exchange was an academic and historical concept.

In contrast, in China, the stock exchanges in Shanghai[9] and Shenzhen were established at the end of 1990 with the toleration and support of the Communist Party. It was seen as yet another step in the ongoing liberalization of the Chinese economy, which had begun in the late 1970s. In contrast to CEE, the change of ownership of Chinese state-owned enterprises (SOEs) was meant to be limited and gradual. Instead of privatization, the concept of "corporatization" was introduced, later called "equitization" in Vietnam.

The development of these stock markets followed a top-down approach. The exchanges were not only established and supervised, but also indirectly managed by the government. According to a central plan, a stock market was supposed to raise new money for SOEs, monitor performance and improve capital allocation and efficiency of listed companies. To retain state control, only a minority of shares in Chinese companies, usually 35 percent, were tradable. The majority was to be maintained by the State and other SOEs. A separate class of shares was available to foreigners. The market was regulated and supervised by the Chinese Securities Regulatory Commission (CSRC), set up in 1992.

Raising new money required investor interest. Traditionally, very high savings ratios, coupled with willingness to take risks, provided good prospects on the demand side. Idle capital, kept in cash, was to be mobilized to develop listed companies. The initial response of Chinese investors was very encouraging. During 1991, 370,000 investment accounts were opened.[10] Interest was so intense that, in October 1992, a shortage of subscription certificates triggered investor riots in Shenzhen.

In 2009, after two decades of transition, the Chinese stock market looks very impressive in more ways than just absolute size. From the operational point of view, the market infrastructure proved robust and resilient during the high volatility in 2008-09. The listed companies, no longer exclusively majority state-owned, are able to raise seemingly unlimited capital in the domestic market. In raising capital, Chinese corporations have been far more successful that the CEE listed companies. With nearly 100 million investment accounts in China, it is not surprising that the stock exchanges in Hong Kong, Shanghai and Shenzen were the world's top three exchanges in terms of aggregate IPO value in 2009. The functioning of the market is still policy-based. The government has used a number of unorthodox policy measures related to IPOs, such as regional quotas, recommended price ranges or temporal bans (October 2008-June 2009).

In Vietnam, the role of the state in the development of the stock market was similar to that in China. The process of "equitization" proceeded "under the Party resolution and Government's action plan to restructure, reform, develop and raise efficiency of State Owned Enterprises [..]". Public trading in securities started ten years later than in China. A securities trading centre began to operate in Ho Chi Minh City in 2000, followed by Hanoi in 2005. Both centres were renamed as stock exchanges in 2007. The Vietnamese market, although actively trading over 200 securities, is still in the early phase of development. It still is developing its settlement, depository, regulatory and supervisory facilities. A complicating challenge in Vietnam relates to the government's double role as majority owner and regulator of listed companies.

Even a cursory review of the Chinese and Vietnamese markets shows that their emergence and pattern of development are far from the traditional, spontaneous origins of the European and American exchanges. On the other hand, their day-to-day operations, market practices and investor behaviour are not different from those observed in other world markets. It seems that stock exchanges throughout the world, while performing similar functions, will always have many local, distinctive features.

■■■■ 8. Twenty Years After: Results and Challenges

Starting from scratch in 1989, the emerging markets of formerly centrally planned economies developed rapidly, though unevenly, over the next 20 years. To assess their current position, comparable markets in emerging and mature economies should be analyzed. Both absolute and relative measures will be taken into account.

In terms of absolute size, the undisputed leader is China (Shanghai and Shenzen stock exchanges), followed by Russia (MICEX, RTS - Russian

Trading System). Despite their immature regulatory and market infrastructures, both markets rank high not only in absolute terms but also relative to their GDP. The sheer size and liquidity of many Chinese and Russian companies have attracted international investors who tolerate many regulatory issues in the domestic market environment.

Among medium-size markets, Warsaw, Budapest and Prague have achieved the highest positions in terms of stock market significance. If we compare market capitalization and turnover in equities to GDP, they are still below, but not far from, comparable mature European markets.

A major weakness of Prague and Budapest is the very high level of concentration of trading in the top five companies. Warsaw, on the other hand, is unique in attracting an impressive number of new listings, both in its main market and its "New Connect" alternative trading platform.

In some other CEE markets, statistical figures, particularly those relating to the number of listed companies, should be interpreted with caution. At many exchanges, the quoted companies have not passed the listing process and do not provide periodic and current disclosure. Such figures should always be compared with corresponding data on turnover and market capitalization.

The remaining markets of CEE, even those of Ukraine and Romania, are small, both in absolute and relative terms. When we compare stock market turnover with GDP of those countries, the corresponding figures are below 5 percent, i.e. 3-4 times lower than those of Budapest, Prague and Warsaw.

The stock markets that emerged from the centrally planned economies are very different. In terms of size, the capitalization of the Shanghai Stock Exchange is 1,000 times that of the Banja Luka in Montenegro. Even in the neighbouring countries of Poland, Slovakia and Belarus, the differences in size and maturity are enormous.

In qualitative terms, the contribution of domestic stock exchanges to the transition and economic development their economics is significant, but not crucial. Almost from the very beginning, stock exchanges provided a price-discovery mechanism—in stark contrast with previous bureaucratic procedures. The valuations obtained in the listing process were subsequently used as benchmarks for other listed and unlisted companies. Stock exchanges and market authorities have initiated public disclosure of audited financial statements, providing standards of transparency previously unknown in centrally planned economies. Even in China and Vietnam, where markets are more centrally managed than elsewhere, the rule of law has become more widely accepted.

The most important textbook contribution of stock markets is in providing an alternative source of capital to listed companies. In this respect, very few domestic markets have been successful, with China and Poland as notable examples. Raising capital has become more international, with the world financial centres taking the lead. The most recent developments have shown, however, that Shanghai and Moscow are becoming strong contenders in this field.

Are the many advantages of local domestic markets sufficient to allow them to survive? Integration and consolidation in the financial sector has been occurring in the more developed countries for almost two decades. As noted in the foregoing section, it has already involved the six national exchanges in CEE. Certain functions of a stock exchange, and particularly those of clearing and settlement, are subject to economies of scale, which favours consolidation. Some other services can be provided from abroad. Nevertheless, certain functions like searching for local companies suitable for listing, market surveillance, investor education and building an investor community are better managed locally, since they depend critically on knowledge of the local language, customs, local daily media coverage and local networking. These observations do not imply that domestic exchanges cannot be owned by foreign entities or should not be parts of bigger structures. There are many ways to create synergies and economies of scale.

In my opinion, domestic exchanges in these markets will survive, although not necessarily with all their present functions or as independent entities. The evolution of markets has never been unidirectional. This is clearly seen in the post-MiFID (Markets in Financial Instruments Directive) market structure in Europe, which is, contrary to initial expectations, more fragmented and less transparent than before. Keeping this in mind, and taking into account the growth potential in the region, one can optimistically look into the next 20 years. I am confident that, by the end of that period, the common denominator of "stock markets of formerly centrally planned economies" will disappear altogether.

9. Conclusions: Requirements for a Successful Securities Market

The economic transition to the market economy started in over 30 countries almost simultaneously at the beginning of the 1990s. Having reviewed their relative performance, some crucial success factors can be identified.

The most important of these factors seems to be a long-term strategy, based on high standards of organization and regulation of the markets. The strategy should be comprehensive, covering the total range of securities markets. A major deficiency in the area of regulation or post-trading activities can disrupt a smooth transition.

Investor confidence accompanied by an appetite for risk is the most valuable asset. The emphasis on speed and quantity, however politically justified, has not produced quality in the long run. The transformation of state-owned enterprises to become more compliant with listing standards and investor needs for governance structures has taken longer than initially expected. Moreover, initial conditions and, more specifically, historical traditions of stock exchanges have turned out to be positive but not decisive. Finally, the potential size of the market and the high rate of economic growth of a country have contributed positively to the overall development of the capital markets.

Relative stability and the rule of law are also important factors in creating securities markets. Extreme free-market liberalism or a laissez-faire approach produced unregulated securities markets, but did not prove to be the right recipe for success, either at the very early or later stages of market development. The lessons learned in the transition process have universal value: success in establishing new exchanges and the accompanying infrastructure is achievable but not guaranteed. Finally, let us hope that the exercise of rebuilding securities markets after a long period of nonexistence does not arise again.

Notes

1 Some failed attempts to re-establish exchanges were made in Soviet Russia in the 1920s, as well as in Budapest in 1946.

2 The concurrent debate on the basic model of financial market to be adopted was less political than that on privatization, but it was still controversial. One of the most frequent topics of discussion was whether to adopt a German bank-oriented model or an Anglo-Saxon market-driven financial sector model. This debate soon proved to be more academic than practical. The financial sector in CEE was underdeveloped in every respect: banking and insurance had to be transformed and expanded, and securities markets were nonexistent. Nobody denied the need for securities markets to be established, but opinions differed on priorities, urgency and their significance in national economies.

3 When speed and scale of privatization are politically accepted as priorities, the quality of market infrastructure has to be sacrificed. Unfortunately, quite often, low standards and bad practices, initially meant to be transitional, persist and become permanent.

4 Having been personally involved in establishing and running the Warsaw Stock Exchange for 15 years, I can say that no request for advice or assistance was ever denied to me. I remember this generosity with gratitude.

5 In those days, I compared those structures and practices to instant coffee that generally is not as good as slowly maturing coffee but which can be prepared very quickly.

6 Czech RMS was marginalized and Romanian RASDAQ (Romanian Association of Securities Dealers Automated Quotation) was taken over by Bucharest Stock Exchange in 2005.

7 In Poland in 1990, the Warsaw Stock Exchange was located in the former headquarters of the Communist Party. The decision was both practical (empty office space and excellent communications infrastructure) and—obviously—symbolic.

8 In Hungary, an exchange trading in bonds was set up in Budapest in 1988.

9 The first exchange in Shanghai was established as an association of brokers in 1891, renamed in 1904 as the Shanghai Stock Exchange

10 In the summer 2009, 700,000 new investment accounts were opened in China every week.

VISIONS OF THE FUTURE

9

The World's Exchanges as Social Agents

EDEMIR PINTO

I. Overview

This World Federation of Exchanges (WFE) anniversary book is a collection of essays. One of the characteristics of an essay, according to the French philosopher Julien Benda, is that it is devoid of a peremptory nature. Therefore, this text has no academic concerns, and makes no attempt to prove any economic, sociological, or statistical theories, and much less to establish any methodological commitments. The purpose of this text is merely to narrate, describe, and comment on the role of exchanges as social agents, which was the theme suggested to us.

We begin with a brief remark on what has been known as the "corporate social responsibility movement." This introduction is followed by a word on this historical moment in which the world's exchanges have been demutualizing and converting to electronic trading. These changes have brought the deepest transformations exchanges have seen in the last 500 years.

Next, we analyze the role exchanges play in helping to establish the best policies of corporate governance, together with the description of the rich experience of social transformation undertaken by BM&FBOVESPA in Brazil. The next section deals with the direct engagement of exchanges in the toughest challenge facing mankind today—sustainable development—along with some notes on practical examples.

This discussion ends with a few comments on other facets of social performance related to the exchanges, and finally with a tentative speculation on the future based on our only known parameter—the past.

2. Social Responsibility

The concept of Corporate Social Responsibility (CSR) is based on the ethical hypothesis that individuals and all public and private entities have certain commitments to the societies in which they live and operate, and in an even broader sense, to all mankind. This principle was recently introduced within the institutional framework of businesses and capital markets around the globe, and is derived from pressures of political activism, and not from the traditions of Western Judeo-Christian morality or legal systems.

Up until the 1980s, the concept of Social Responsibility was associated with voluntary deeds, donations, or bequests that the more affluent would bestow upon underprivileged communities or charitable organizations as retribution and compensation for their opulence. It was then an issue of individual conscience, while companies were simply entrusted with the task of generating wealth without much concern for the quality of life or welfare of their human and environmental surroundings. The induction of the CSR concept is gradually guiding the business sector to shoulder its social responsibilities.

Over the past few decades, the scope of Social Responsibility has broadened, especially as regards large corporations. Today, it is far more comprehensive than mere philanthropic contributions. An extensive network of political activism has emerged, involving multilateral institutions, governments, companies, civil society organizations, and individuals. Social Responsibility is no longer simply understood as a gesture of goodwill, but now constitutes a far-reaching attitude involving multiple initiatives related to business activities.

To put it briefly, the CSR movement is widely recognized to embody three elements: improvement of corporate governance; support to sustainable development models, namely, environment conservation; and promotion of social issues such as education, workplace relations, human rights, eradication of poverty, artistic and literary achievement, and a myriad of community-oriented issues.

Currently, critics with the economic and conservative political sectors have challenged the ideas and criteria involving Social Responsibility.

They argue that CSR objectives draw businesses away from their fundamental and primary economic roles. On the other side of the political spectrum, some question whether Social Responsibility acts as a deceptive façade to maintain the status quo.

However, reality seems to be radically different from either of these beliefs. In fact, it is clear that Social Responsibility has fully emerged and is now consolidating its place within the global corporate world. In all its shades and hues, Social Responsibility is a growing and irresistible trend from which there appears to be no possible—let alone desirable—return. Social Responsibility has become an integral part of the wealth generation process and is naturally accepted as such by investment communities around the world. It marches relentlessly towards progress and the enhancement of capitalist society, and towards the survival of the planet as we know it and hope to continue enjoying.

3. Historical Moment

Exchanges first emerged during the Renaissance from the darkness of the Middle Ages. They represented the logical evolution from markets in the public squares of large medieval cities where guilds were the financial institutions *par excellence* of that time. The major goal of these medieval guilds was to protect their members from external competition, thus ensuring their markets for products and services.

Early exchanges consisted of guilds of traders that were family-run, closed, and elitist in nature, just like all the other guilds of that time. It was only natural that they would be established this way, since the guild was the business standard of those times. The exchanges usually cited as forerunners are the Flemish exchanges of Bruges, Antwerp and Amsterdam; and Sir Thomas Gresham's Royal Exchange in Elizabethan London. Exchanges were also established in other major cities of that time. They used the same organizational model.

Guilds faded during the Industrial Revolution. Companies were more agile, efficient, and competitive organizations, and therefore replaced them as the dominant economic institutions. Exchanges then facilitated capital raising and growth for those companies throughout the following centuries. In a perfect symbiosis, the exchanges and their members grew in importance and economic power, thanks to the proliferation of joint-stock companies. Curiously, exchanges were not imbued with the progressive and competitive spirit of their traded companies.

Instead, they remained more like the guilds from which they originated. For 500 years, exchanges operated and existed as guilds, and so remained, like traces of the medieval economy, until the late twentieth century.

In the early 1990s, as some remaining mutual insurance companies were successfully converted into corporations, exchanges began a widespread movement towards their transformation into for-profit organizations by going through the so-called demutualization process. The first to undergo this change in 1993 was the Stockholm Exchange, followed by its Australian antipode in 1998. Now, according to data from the World Federation of Exchanges, almost 80 percent of the world's associated exchanges have crossed this authentic Rubicon.

Another revolutionary catalyst—technology—had been quietly lurking in the background since the 1970s. It also would arise to deconstruct ancient traditions. In the space of a few years, electronic trading platforms overshadowed the traditional floor trading systems and replaced them. The habit of traders meeting daily on the floor in face-to-face trading sessions disappeared nearly simultaneously with the fall of the traditional guild inspired organization model of the exchanges.

Five centuries of deeply entrenched habits changed in only two decades! Demutualization and electronic trading rocked the structure of exchanges around the globe, and changed forever their face and economic base, causing a true cultural shock for their communities, far bigger than the waves of deregulation that have been striking since the 1970s. Like a stroke of magic, financial intermediaries, who formerly owned the exchanges, suddenly became their customers. Corporate goals made a complete about-turn. The exchanges ceased to be exclusive service supporting entities and agencies promoting self-regulation. Instead, they began to seek financial results that would please their new masters—the shareholders.

Almost like an ironic paradox of fate, the new role of exchanges as social agents was forged in this troubled milieu where the demand for profit was running high. This apparent contradiction does not mean that there is any clash of goals, as the economic and social propositions might suggest. On the contrary, a wide range of complementary social activities now add to the broad world of Corporate Social Responsibility, and have become an irreversible trend for the future of humanity and the planet.

4. Corporate Governance—New Principles

In 1998, the Organization for Economic Cooperation and Development (OECD) began discussions on adopting a set of standards associated with action lines to define the recommended benchmark practices for corporate governance on an international level. Several multilateral organizations, governments, and private sectors worldwide were heard from, and, in 1999, the first Corporate Governance draft was published. A few years later, in 2004, after an extensive range of consultations and debates was held with participants and stakeholders, the OECD published a new, revised set of Corporate Governance Principles.[1]

By the end of the introductory page of this new set of principles, it immediately becomes clear that the text is presenting non-mandatory standards, and that these standards should be adapted to the various legal, economic, and cultural circumstances existing in each country, whether that country is an OECD member or not. As we will see later, these constitute extremely important details when analyzing what the implementation of a healthy corporate governance structure should look like, and in defining the role of exchanges in that process.

In the first paragraph of the preamble, the role of exchanges in conducting corporate governance initiatives is highlighted:

> "The Principles are intended to assist OECD and non-OECD
> governments in their efforts to evaluate and improve the legal,
> institutional and regulatory framework for corporate governance
> in their countries, and to provide guidance and suggestions for
> stock exchanges, investors, corporations, and other parties that
> have a role in the process of developing good corporate
> governance."

One can observe that other institutions associated with the issue, such as securities commissions and other regulatory agencies, are not mentioned directly, but underlie the scope of governments in the text. Even business associations, like those of banks, industries or commercial enterprises, are understood to be within the general scope of third parties. It is suggested that the exchanges—the only public entities cited in the text—play a central role in good corporate governance principles and practices, even though most exchanges had demutualized and been transformed into for-profit enterprises.

The guidelines laid out by the OECD are generic suggestions, just as noncoercive corporate governance principles should be. In reality, they make up a code of ethics containing macro-guidelines geared mainly to publicly traded companies, but that can also be applied to state-run or even non-public companies. The goal of the OECD's Corporate Governance Principles was to set a nonstatic benchmark—rather evolutionary in its own right—and, as such, it is adaptable to the varying circumstances within each country or region over time.

The content of the OECD document outlines its purposes. To avoid too many details here, we have broken it down into six chapters and their comments. The first chapter refers to the foundations upon which an effective corporate governance framework that ensures efficient and transparent markets should be built. The second and third chapters describe the rights and treatment of shareholders within these principles. The fourth chapter reflects a clear social concern, as it deals with the role of stakeholders interested in the life and inner workings of companies and the treatment the former deserve to receive from the latter. The last two chapters deal with transparency and the functions and accountability of senior management, that is, the board of directors and the executive officers.

It is clear that since publicly traded companies congregate at exchanges within their respective countries, one of the most relevant exchange roles is to ensure the promotion and practice of good corporate governance, as defined by the OECD. This is a vital task for the exchange community, when it comes to social responsibility. Instead of colliding with government regulations, the exchanges help by anticipating them and, in doing so, they foster more ethical and sound trading environments that will ultimately lead to greater assurance for investors and so enhance the efficiency of private sector initiatives.

5. A Brazilian Experience

In 2000, one year after OECD's first Corporate Governance Principles were published, the former São Paulo Stock Exchange (Bovespa), today part of BM&FBOVESPA, implemented a special trading segment that was named *Novo Mercado* (the New Market). Within this segment, companies were ranked according to how closely they adhered to the precepts of corporate governance. This was accomplished without hindering any of the other companies that were not adherents of these principles, since their shares were allowed to continue to trade on Bovespa's traditional main board.

The fact is that Bovespa's creation of *Novo Mercado* provided a podium on which companies adopting the highest standards of transparency and investor relations were able to stand out from the others. It soon became apparent that these *Novo Mercado* rankings helped improve the operating financial environment of the participating companies, resulting in more positive public reputations and easier access to domestic and international credit facilities.

Furthermore, besides creating the *Novo Mercado* segment to encourage the adaptation of companies to OECD's Corporate Governance Principles, Bovespa spearheaded a revolution in company customs, proving that Bovespa is a true agent of change that is fully aware of its social responsibilities. Bovespa went one step beyond OECD's recommendation by adapting corporate governance changes to local peculiarities and customs. These transformations focused on certain aspects of the democratization of Brazil's enterprises, business culture, and its society at large.

To understand the importance of those changes, it is necessary to make a quick immersion into the recent history of the Brazilian legal system.

The issuance of preferred shares without voting rights was long a deeply rooted tradition within Brazilian corporate law. During the 1930s, this custom was very common: The number of shareholders with no voting power accounted for 90 percent of the capital stock of some companies. Concerns about the concentration of control led to a review of corporate law in 1942, which limited the fraction of shares without the right to vote to 50 percent. However, a few decades later, during the 1970s, a new charter for joint stock companies raised the upper bound to two-thirds of a company's capital stock.

This change reflected the prevailing belief in the existence of enlightened entrepreneurs, corporate leaders capable of conducting business under the guise of their irresistible, wise leadership. It was the outcome of an authoritarian way of thinking stemming from the positivist philosophy that had created the Republic of Brazil and remained the dominant mindset in the country throughout most of the twentieth century. Shareholders were dismissed as mere suppliers of capital who should simply trust in the good conduct of the company, without voicing their opinions or asking any questions. In its final phase, capital markets law established that with only 16.7 percent of a company's capital stock, it was possible to run that company without any contestation.

The prevailing system of holding shares without voting rights, which was in effect in Brazil for many decades, caused several distortions at the corporate level and undermined the healthy development of Brazilian capitalism. To begin with, that model created a deceptive notion of democratization in business as the companies' capital stock was diluted into shares with no voting rights, while ownership was held by common stockholders. Two distinct shareholder castes were thus created: shareholders holding preferred shares and entrepreneurs who were owners of the voting common stock. As holders of different securities, a clear divide was created between them. This apartheid led to a complete dissociation between the entrepreneur holders of the common shares and the company's stock market which traded the nonvoting preferred stocks. The entrepreneurs had no interest in the shares traded at the exchanges, since they were not the assets that they held. When the controlling shareholder needed liquidity, they sold their stock in blocks, as though they were selling their company in its entirety. This system prevented the owners of the nonvoting preferred shares—the investors who actually held the majority of shares—from profiting from the appreciation of assets achieved by the sale of their businesses.

The legal shareholding system that existed in Brazil thus hindered the growth of companies set up as joint-stock companies. The so-called controlling shareholders failed to follow-up on the capital needs of their companies over time, while the market, as an impersonal and remote agent, would have been able to do so. In fact, companies operating under this regime became extensions of their owners and suffered from their financial limitations. These companies hardly ever developed institutional characters of their own. Concurrently, this system led to a consolidation of business ownership in Brazil. Heirs were effectively prevented from diluting their ownership interests by selling the common stocks, because there was no liquidity in the market for common stocks. This system was also characterized by the creation of holding companies and shareholder agreements, whose main purpose was to maintain the status quo, and thus preserve the artificial appreciation of ownership control.

Another negative effect of this corporate structure was found in the difficulties surrounding the implementation of professional management systems in joint stock companies. No matter how qualified and efficient the staff was, their loyalty was primarily to the controlling shareholder and not to the company itself or to its preferred shareholders, who were in fact the owners of the majority of the company's capital.

Novo Mercado's listing rules now require companies to adhere to the best corporate governance practices of transparency and fair and equal treatment of minority shareholders. These rules contain specific chapters with stringent standards. One of those refers to the composition of the boards of directors, whereby at least 20 percent of the board members should be independent. This means that they must not have any tie to the company or the controlling group. Another rule refers to the periodicity and quality of information to be provided, requiring that financial statements be established in accordance with international accounting standards (IFRS—International Financial Reporting Standards, or the US GAAP—Generally Accepted Accounting Principles). The listing rules mandate that these companies maintain 25 percent of their shares circulating in the market, a system known as free float.

Ownership transfers, securities trading by controlling shareholders, compulsory information disclosure, and the extent of rights and benefits of minority shareholders are all regulated in specific chapters of the *Novo Mercado* listing standards. Another *Novo Mercado* innovation was the implementation of an arbitration system within the Bovespa Stock Exchange for resolution of conflicts between companies, management, shareholders, et cetera, thus avoiding the sluggishness of the Brazilian legal system while improving the efficiency of the economy as a whole.

At the heart of the *Novo Mercado* rules is the requirement that companies wishing to ascend to this podium of excellence should only issue common shares with voting rights. This was actually the first effective move made towards the democratization of Brazilian capitalism in decades. It epitomizes the motto "one share, one vote," in a link with politics where each voter should be entitled to one vote.

Today, *Novo Mercado* is part of BM&FBOVESPA. Its rules led to the deconstruction of a perverse system of oligarchic control of companies through the proliferation of preferred shares without voting rights. In 2001, 19 companies had adhered to differentiated segments of corporate governance accounting for 4 percent of listed companies. By 2009, 159 companies had adhered, or 36 percent of the 434 companies listed on BM&FBOVESPA. Of these, 105 companies, or 24 percent, had only voting shares outstanding. As it can be seen, the journey has begun, but we still have a long and arduous way to go.

The most fascinating aspect is that this revolution was led by Bovespa within its own trading environment, operating limits and sphere of influence. There was no government intervention whatsoever at either the legislative, executive, or judiciary levels. No laws, decrees or court decisions were necessary. In fact, Bovespa was ahead of its time in replacing the policies of government agencies with its own socially responsible democratic policy.

Today, the *Novo Mercado* segment is globally acknowledged as a key initiator for improving not only corporate governance, but also the broadest spectrum of society. It is a shining example of how an exchange can become a social agent. The *Novo Mercado* segment significantly changed the shape of Brazilian capital markets by implementing a major renovation of its methods and procedures. Bovespa's role in creating *Novo Mercado* went beyond the mere self-regulatory activity and helped build an ethical and democratic framework that underpins the attitude of companies and spreading throughout society as a whole through the nation's business and financial markets.

▬▬ 6. Environmental Challenge and Sustainability

Besides Corporate Governance, another concern within the realm of CSR refers to the environment and sustainable development. The Exchanges have maintained a very active attitude towards these subjects, embodying them into several instruments of their actions. It is important to take a brief look on the historical background of this movement.

British scientist James Lovelock raised one of the first alarms about global warming in the 1970s. In his thesis, Lovelock addressed the Earth as Gaia, the goddess who personified our planet in Greek mythology. In his conception, the Earth is a living organism whose worst predator is mankind. Lovelock, who many consider to be the father of environmentalism, advanced the hypothesis that if Darwin had realized just how inextricably entwined life and the environment are, he might have discovered that evolution involves not only living beings, but also the entire surface of the planet. In consequence, we would all now see the Earth as the pulsing system it is with the awareness that we cannot continue to pollute the air or use the "skin of Earth"—its forests and marine ecosystems—as a mere source of products to feed ourselves and furnish our homes. Today, critics of his views exist, such as Washington University paleontologist Peter Ward, but nothing can diminish Lovelock's pioneering contribution.

During those early days of the fledgling environmental movement, a Norwegian physician, Ms. Gro Brundtland also stood out for her words and actions. She was appointed environment minister of her country in 1973 and, in 1981, she became Norway's first—and to this date only—female prime minister, an achievement which garnered her worldwide acclaim. In 1983, she was invited to chair a United Nations panel to study the environment and its relation to economic development. This panel became the Brundtland Commission, an organization that proved instrumental in establishing and disseminating the concept of sustainability throughout the world.

The final report issued by the Brundtland Commission popularized sustainable development, defining it as the act of meeting the needs of the present without compromising the ability of future generations to meet their needs. In other words, it recognized that the use of natural resources should be allocated in such manner as to preserve or replace those resources, so that our descendants may also enjoy them. In essence, sustainable development is the conscious and renewable use of the resources of what Lovelock defined as the "skin of Earth."

This report simultaneously outlined general recommendations such as granting funds for projects with sustainability criteria; fostering the protection of environmental macro-systems and supporting the creation of a United Nations sustainable development program. Certain guidelines were intended for countries addressing issues such as population growth, the need to assure the conservation and supply of water and energy, the preservation of biodiversity, the creation of clean and renewable technologies, urban planning, healthcare, education, housing, et cetera.

The Brundtland Report produced two basic milestones. It was, in one fell swoop, a cry of alarm about the depletion of the planet's natural resources and the risks of global warming, and the first supranational position ever endorsed regarding these issues. The conclusions and impact of the Report were translated into effective international measures such as the Eco-92 World Summit, and the Kyoto Protocol in 1997, and also fostered universal awareness about the urgency and need to make economic progress less detrimental to the environment.

7. The World's Exchanges and Sustainable Development

Although exchanges are still grappling with the consequences of the demutualization process, with innovations in information and communication technologies, and with new demands regarding corporate governance, they adhered to social responsibility standards. Many of the world's exchanges have endorsed sustainable development as foreseen in the Brundtland Report and all of its political ramifications.

The first initiative undertaken by the exchanges to respond to this global trend was the development of market tracking indices. Between 1999 and 2006, based on the performance of companies committed to sustainability, eight exchanges, all WFE members, voluntarily created 22 different indices to measure the stock performance of these companies in their respective markets without any external intervention.

In 2006, seven years after the first initiative by an exchange, that is, the NYSE Arca Cleantech Index, the United Nations published a booklet containing six principles that it considered relevant for "Responsible Investment." Similar to the document on OECD Corporate Governance, which in some ways was incorporated in the booklet, the recommendations developed by the United Nations are not mandatory, but rather a set of aspirations based on voluntary adherence. Although aimed specifically at institutional investors and asset managers, the UN program was launched in April 2006 by the then Secretary General Kofi Annan at an exchange where it could gain maximum impact and visibility, the NYSE. Even though the document is not directed at exchanges, this gesture explicitly recognized their importance as major agents in implementing the policies outlined in the program.

The *United Nations Principles for Responsible Investment* (UNPRI) are gathered under a single and comprehensive code of ethics called the ESG (Environmental, Social, and Governance) standards. The clear and highly focused objective of these principles is to raise awareness of institutional investors and asset managers to the importance of directing their formidable financial power to invest in companies engaged in good social and environmental practices. As a result, a vast supranational network of filters, pressures, demands, commitments, and moral suasion was created to stimulate the adoption of these principles.

The guidelines that have been set and subscribed to by investors and managers are divided into a few areas. The first guideline established that environmental, social and governance issues should be incorporated into the investment analysis and decision-making process of each institution. Next is the determination that all committed entities should maintain a high level of corporate activism, and add the aforementioned standards to their policies and practices as shareholders. The third point concerns the search for transparency regarding ESG matters by companies where financial resources are invested. The fourth guideline refers to the purpose of disseminating these principles throughout the investment industry. This is followed by the intention to act jointly with other signatories towards disseminating the proposed

ESG policies, and finally the shared commitment to promote their own activities in support of other subscribers to these principles, together with third party stakeholders.

With these basic rules in place, the fund managers who signed the UNPRI document began to require the companies of which they are shareholders, or to which they are lenders, to implement methods, procedures and processes that comply with the best available environmental, social and corporate governance standards. Those target companies, in turn, were instructed to require that their suppliers, distributors, dealers, and other members of their production chains follow identical behavior patterns.

The collective impacts of these measures on the reduction of greenhouse gases and on the other deleterious effects threatening the environment are as yet unknown. However, one can already see the unequivocal response from companies that have chosen to boycott products derived from the deforestation of the Amazon rainforest or from the exploitation of labor with practices akin to slavery.

Paradoxically, although not addressed to exchanges, the behavioral framework outlined by the United Nations PRI strengthened their responsibilities in the field of environmental and social issues and in corporate governance. Side by side with the voluntary work developed in the engineering of different indices for monitoring the actions of socially and environmentally responsible companies, exchanges began to see their own actions being subjected to greater scrutiny.

By 2006, most of the world's regulated exchanges had been demutualized, turning into for-profit entities owned by shareholders instead of members. Among their new partners were institutional investors who subscribed to the United Nation's ESG principles. Thus, the procedures adopted by exchanges in terms of social responsibilities pursued two distinct approaches: externally, by inducing companies under their umbrella—through the offering of public platforms and dedicated investment niches—or through their inclusion into differentiated indices; and internally, with companies seeking compliance to satisfy the demands of their own shareholders and their communities.

This twofold approach to ESG consolidated the authority of exchanges regarding social responsibility. While suggesting, indicating and ranking behaviors within the scope of listed companies, which is their field of exogenous influence, exchanges are at the same time compelled to conform to the highest standards of endogenous requirements in conducting their own businesses.

Following the publication of the United Nations Principles for Responsible Investments, exchanges continued with their policy of setting new indices to measure the performance of companies committed to ethics and sustainability. From 2006 to late 2009, 29 indicators were created, thereby more than doubling those that had been available since 1999. At the same time, the market saw a substantial growth in the specific niche of exchange-traded, closed-end funds designed to invest in companies that use clean technologies.

Some exchanges in East Asia have promoted even more explicit policies with regard to ESG-related issues, reinforcing their roles as social agents. In Malaysia, for instance, the publication of standardized annual social responsibility and sustainability reports by listed companies is on the way to become compulsory, and the Taiwan Stock Exchange is following Malaysia's footsteps. Shenzhen and Shanghai Stock Exchanges encourage listed companies to disclose their documents with similar purpose and frequency. They are concurrently engaged in an initiative supported by the Chinese government to accept only IPOs of companies that have passed a sustainability test. The Stock Exchange of Thailand set up an institute to encourage social responsibility and bestows annual awards on listed companies that excel in this area. In Australia, new principles of corporate governance were written for the Australian Securities Exchange, and all listed companies must state that they are following recommendations on ESG-related issues or explain why they are not.

Other tools established and then wielded by exchanges with regard to the environment are their markets for trading carbon credits, options, and related products. Institutions like the Montreal Exchange, NYSE Euronext, NASDAQ OMX, Deutsche Börse, Buenos Aires Stock Exchange, and BM&FBOVESPA are examples of institutions committed to the development of such market segments. The pricing established will be of fundamental use in commercial assessments of environmental degradation.

8. Social Initiatives

In addition to their roles as drivers of good governance and sustainability practices, the activism of exchanges as social agents also appears in other arenas. One such arena is the fight against extreme poverty. In this respect, two remarkable achievements of the Luxembourg Stock Exchange are noteworthy. The first is the creation of an agency that provides funding for investments in micro-finance, ensuring investors that their capital will be properly used. Micro-finance is today one of the most important drivers of small businesses in poor communities.

The second achievement is of paramount importance for public health in poverty-stricken regions: the establishment of an institution called the International Finance Facility for Immunisation (IFFIm), which focuses on raising funds for mass vaccination in areas of the world's 70 poorest countries that have the least developed healthcare infrastructures. IFFIm's ambitious goal is to raise US$4 billion to provide vaccinations and healthcare for 500 million children around the world by 2015.

Another area where regulated exchanges are socially active is the financial education of investors. Brazilian exchanges have much experience when it comes to educating and training investors and financial executives. In the 1970s, the former Rio de Janeiro Stock Exchange founded the Brazilian Institute of Capital Markets (IBMEC), which evolved into one of the country's most highly ranked private universities. Currently, BMF&BOVESPA is engaged with government agencies and private sector entities in the development of the National Strategy for Financial Education (ENEF), which is designed to introduce basic knowledge of finance into the programs of nonspecialized colleges and universities.

At the end of the 1990s, the former Bovespa began a broad public awareness program to disseminate basic savings and stock market concepts. Geared towards various sectors of society and focusing on individual investors, the program slogan is "the exchange goes where you are." The strategy was very successful, and excellent results have been reaped in recent years. In late 2009, BM&FBOVESPA boasted 500,000 active individual investors in its customer base compared with just a few thousand at the inception of the program.

BM&FBOVESPA also fosters social initiatives with a wide array of specific purposes. One such initiative is the Environmental and Social Investment Exchange, a pioneering program reproducing the same environment as that of a stock exchange through which selected social projects are publicized to help them raise support and receive donations from interested parties. Another example is the BM&FBOVESPA Athletics Club, which, in addition to the exchange, also receives support of third-party sponsors. The Athletics Club is comprised of nearly 100 of Brazil's best track-and-field athletes. All affiliated athletes receive a high level of training, technical coaching, medical assistance, and a stipend for living expenses. The Athletics Club is currently the eight-time consecutive champion of the Brazil Athletics Trophy (2002–2009).

BM&FBOVESPA based its decision to sponsor Olympic track-and-field athletes on two key considerations: the realization that there is an overall lack of support for athletics in Brazil, and the fact that athletics is a sport that allows for greater social inclusion of underprivileged youth. Another outreach initiative focused on training at-risk teenagers is the BM&FBOVESPA Job Training Association, which creates job opportunities and provides guidance for boys and girls between the ages of 15 and 20.

9. The Future

The world's exchanges represent the state-of-the-art of progressive social activism in the realm of economic freedom, in an economic system its detractors first called "capitalism." Unfortunately, the world has adopted and commonly continues to use this archaic and often derogatory label, which to some people denotes a system of values whereby material aspects prevail over human interests. Nothing could be further from the truth: the combination of these two facets—the pursuit of profit while meeting market demands in a climate of economic freedom that encourages competition and efficiency—is the source of a myriad of benefits that are today part and parcel of humanity's everyday life and comfort.

From energy sources such as steam, coal, oil, gas, and electricity for industrial, residential, or transport use to telecommunication facilities down to the simplest of electric household appliances, life's progress is truly evident. This myriad of innovations did not emerge under oppressive regimes with enormous state predominance and without regular markets, like the so-called economies of real socialism. Nor did trains, cars, trucks, the telegraph, the telephone, the fax, cell phones, computers, the Internet, X-rays, CT scans, sophisticated medications, radios, the cinema, televisions, DVDs, air conditioners, refrigerators, frozen meals, blenders, microwaves, et cetera come from the womb of government bureaucracies.

The revolution in agribusiness has reduced pockets of poverty and malnutrition around our world, though deplorably too many still remain due to the poor level of education available to local populations. All improvements and amenities that we enjoy today at increasingly lower costs are derived only from environments in which economic freedom—this supreme engine of progress—holds sway.

Behind the brands that compete to provide the wide range of products and services of which we are end users, there has been, there now is, and there always will be—directly or indirectly—a company with its stock or bonds listed on an exchange. It was at the exchanges that joint-stock companies took off as the enterprise model of the modern era, and ultimately they also became the place where funds have been raised to finance countless innovations since the Industrial Revolution. It was the ability of the exchanges to provide liquidity, streamline financial instruments, shape trading platforms, create products and service specialties, and set benchmarks that made the economic boom of recent centuries possible.

Nevertheless, though not originally planned or anticipated, excessive reliance on carbon-derived energy threatens the progress of modernity. Historically, this finding is fairly recent, but it has quickly become a serious concern for mankind. An urgent search is underway for new forms of clean, renewable, carbon-free energy to maintain the planet's environmental balance. This concern underscores the importance of genuine social responsibility, as does the maintenance of high ethical business standards, the so-called movement to affirm good corporate governance. Social Responsibility in all its aspects is a mission from which businesses, governments, civil society organizations, and populations cannot escape.

As primary agents and trailblazers in the process of economic adjustment to new social demands, exchanges are no exception. While setting indices, creating funds made up of firms with the best environmental performances, seeking IPOs of companies specializing in clean technologies, or enforcing ESG standards, one can clearly see a correction in the course of economic development. We march steadfast towards a world where carbon use must be reduced to preserve the quality of life and habitability of our planet, while maintaining the economic progress required by all societies.

Clearly, there is awareness and consensus among exchanges regarding the importance of their role in conducting socially and environmentally responsible policies. This trend is transmitted to companies that are awarded an important seal of quality on their quote screens. From simple awards or recognitions to inclusion in sustainability indices to recommendations or suggestions to rectify behaviors, we are gradually on our way to developing requirements that may or may not be followed, but must be justified. These are the first steps toward increasingly intense and demanding internal regulations, which will exert an impact on the improvement of business ethics and sustainable development, all of which is humanity's most pressing demand today.

As exchanges increasingly engage with the largest companies in every country to encourage or guide them to socially responsible practices, they are effectively contributing as agents of vital importance to improving their communities. At times in collaboration with governments, but in most cases independent of state assistance, exchanges are moving ahead of governments and achieving more tangible and objective results, such as in the case of BM&FBOVESPA's *Novo Mercado*. Within their scope and private jurisdiction, exchanges have spearheaded initiatives that have proven more effective than state laws. Lastly, ethics, corporate governance, sustainability, and social responsibility are demands of a global society, which will be better served by the markets represented by the exchanges and their listed companies because of the visibility the public listing process confers.

Exchanges will continue on their path to progress despite the risk of increasing government intervention that historically results from misinterpretations and distortions of naturally recurring, cyclic economic crises. Moreover, exchanges will continue to expand, being aware now of their new and growing social responsibilities, while adapting to the momentary circumstances in their home nations, just as they have always done throughout history. Nothing today heralds a different future, because markets will always survive as long as economic freedom is not wiped from the face of the earth, which is a highly unlikely scenario in today's world.

Notes

1 The OECD Corporate Governance Principals appear at http://www.oecd.org/dataoecd/32/18/31557724.pdf.

10

Regulated Exchanges and the Ethos of Public Capital Markets

ATSUSHI SAITO

▬▬▬ I. Overview

First, I would like to congratulate the World Federation of Exchanges (WFE) on its 50th anniversary. I am grateful for the opportunity the organization has given me to contribute my views relating to the future of regulated exchanges.

This essay is about the intellectual assumptions underlying today's capital markets. All great writers in classical economics explicitly included their moral philosophies in their arguments. Moral philosophy is the crucial element that moderates human behavior and provides for balance and cohesion in society, both as it grows more prosperous as well as during those times when it suffers wealth losses.

Over the past several decades, too many marketplaces and institutions failed to promote a classical balanced ethos for moral behavior in the markets. The financial system must regain this ethos. Rethinking and reaffirmation of our ethos must be one of the corrective measures that the world economy must address in the aftermath of the most significant financial crisis since the Second World War.

I begin by stating my agreement with the points made by Lord Adair Turner, Chairman of the UK Financial Services Authority, in his address to the International Organization of Securities Commissions (IOSCO) annual meeting in Tel Aviv in June 2009. The sense of his speech was that the recent financial crisis has been a shock to the intellectual assumptions of how markets work. In the future, we must devise regulations that will keep the benefits of the system while realizing that financial markets are not like other markets, and that they can be harmful to the real economy. In retrospect, many people were much too confident with the philosophical assumptions of the past several decades, and did not question them enough.

This essay reviews those intellectual assumptions, and the alternatives now proposed to them in some circles. It starts by postulating new work to be undertaken by exchanges and their corporate clients, and concludes by reaffirming the crucial and very particular role exchanges have in ameliorating the world's market economies. Until we reaffirm our intellectual assumptions and reestablish a balanced ethos of the markets, no appropriate corrective policies for the financial system can be found or implemented.

Let us remember that exchanges are central actors in market economies. The daily trading events of a regulated market reflect all economic achievements and difficulties as they occur. Among instruments measuring daily economic life in any country, none works more reliably or simply than the behavior of an exchange's marketplace. To appreciate how societies can make best use of what only an exchange can provide— the provision of multilateral transparent price discovery along with risk management products and services—readers would do well to step back from the headlines and reflect on the fundamental economic questions of our day. When the questions are answered and new policy directions are set, exchanges can be expected to perform their functions with even greater efficiency.

2. The Self-adjusting Free Market

The world now finds itself at an historical turning point. Its leaders must conduct a debate on whether to maintain the values and social ethics that have been in force since the Industrial Revolution or move towards a more protectionist economy based on government-set, schematically controlled distribution. Alternatively, without entirely abandoning all that has been good since the Industrial Revolution, creating a new form of financial capitalism through extensive revision of our economic system that further improves the effectiveness of the self-adjusting free market may be possible.

Whatever the outcome of the debate over our philosophical assumptions, all social systems require that exchanges play an important role. Prices fairly established by the public provide valuable signals for economic adjustment and financial risk management as asset values evolve.

Consider first the origins of the ideas underpinning today's social and economic system. Around 1730, Benjamin Franklin described the spirit of capitalism. In his thinking, he included the idea of self-interest as part of the philosophical basis of the social system taking form.

Adam Smith subsequently ignited the world in 1776 with his book, *The Wealth of Nations*. There, he developed the idea of the self-adjusting free market. This thought was bolstered by David Ricardo and others in the early 1800s. Much later, great economists such as Friedrich von Hayek and Milton Friedman developed and further spread the theory of the self-adjusting functions of the free market.

Halfway between the end of the Second World War and today, Margaret Thatcher and Ronald Reagan enthusiastically made these economic theories the basis for national strategies for their respective countries. In size and style, the New York and London financial markets have led the world for the decades since. The ideas of these two leaders are critical to understanding how the world's financial system got where it is now, and possibly, where it will go forward from 2010. Those theories, once praised, are now coming under scrutiny, and in many respects also harsh criticism.

As I write this essay, some thinkers and officials in the United States are exploring a shift from Wall Street-style capitalism to Washington-style state capitalism. In addition, in the run-up to Britain's parliamentary elections now just a few weeks away, the debate about state capitalism is central to the political campaigns. Both counties have strong histories of laissez-faire financial markets: The citizenry in both countries increasingly accept the idea of reforming market regulation.

In response to the acute financial crisis, many ideas for reform have been put forward. Among these are the imposition of a 50 percent tax on the bonuses of business managers, the registration of hedge funds, the adoption of the Tobin foreign exchange trading tax, the restriction of certain kinds of high-frequency trading, the banning of dark pools, the increase in equity capital requirements for banks in terms of quality and amount, and the regulation of bank leverage ratios. Among other countries, these discussions are occurring in the United States and

United Kingdom, two countries that only recently were among the most vocal champions of minimum regulation in the financial services sector.

The issue garnering the most attention in the United States today is whether to limit the European-style "universal banking system" by reinstating the Glass-Steagall Act or similar legislation, thus separating commercial banking from investment banking, or to separate those financial institutions permitted to trade for their proprietary accounts from those that are not.

France and Germany have from the outset supported heavier regulation of financial services. In these countries, the pendulum now swings even farther. While maintaining the universal banking system, these countries are considering ways to divide financial institutions into smaller sizes, and place them more clearly under government control.

Even in Tokyo, after the recent electoral victory of the Democratic Party of Japan, mistrust in the self-adjusting free market assumption has begun to manifest itself, although informed debate has yet to develop to the high levels seen elsewhere.

In many parts of the world, aspects of the classic economic model of the self-adjusting market simply have not been functioning. For instance, the lowering of interest rates in Japan in response to increasing current account surpluses was in line with traditional theories. However, what has been taught in classrooms cannot explain a rise in unemployment, a weakened currency, and a tumble into deflation. In much the same way, the United States has had a sustained trade deficit for the past 40 years—occasionally reaching 7 percent of GDP—but interest rates did not rise dramatically. Also, in the past 20 years (though not now), the dollar has been at its strongest with a trend of only mild inflation, coupled with no sharp increase of unemployment. How would Friedman and Hayek have explained the sudden rise in unemployment following the reduction in the deficit some years ago, and more recently the weakening of the dollar after the financial crisis?

The built-in stabilizers posited in the theory clearly are not working. No end appears in sight to the increase in social victims, rising prices, and the world's over-consumption of its natural resources. Adam Smith observed that competition arises from people seeking wealth in their own interest, in other words, that competition is the product of the pursuit of wealth based on the normal self-regard of human beings. To earn profits from one's products and services, as a matter of course their quality must be higher and their prices must be lower than those of competitors. However, this principle often is not working today.

In all of his writing, Adam Smith never mentions individual greed or the notion of monopoly of wealth. Possibly influenced by the Calvinist religious views of his day, he argued that if a man attains a certain amount of wealth and then seeks more of it, he will incur divine wrath. Also on the matter of human nature, Smith speculated that business managers and capitalists would increasingly feel subject to public scrutiny. Through this public exposure, he assumed that they must have within themselves, and must put forward publicly, a strong sense of social justice and ethics as an intrinsic element of their leadership. Smith adds that the commercial marketplace therefore must be naturally fair, just, and free of any fraud or unneeded intervention. To counterbalance the problem of competition as each person tries to advance at the expense of every other, he affirmed the importance of self-control and social regulation as requirements for the very existence of the free market.

Furthermore, Adam Smith did not necessarily approve of market economics as a system for pursuing self-interest. His theme focused on how social wealth could most effectively be created, and how such wealth could then be passed on to lower social classes. Thus, he arrived at a kind of "trickle down" theory of wealth, which poses the question of how within the highly stratified society of that day, the profits earned by upper-class estates and businesses could first be increased, and then how such wealth should be distributed to the other social classes.

Smith and other classical Western economists were as much sociologists as economists. Their analyses were balanced with a strong moral grounding. They would never have imagined serious economic thinking or commercial behavior without this essential, moderating ingredient.

Such questioning took place elsewhere in the world as the Industrial Revolution spread. The famous Japanese author, Soseki Natsume, who studied in the United Kingdom in 1900, wrote a book entitled *My Individualism*. In it, he spoke of the survival of the individual in society through work. He asserted that whatever profession one may take, the profit a person may obtain is dependent on his level of contribution to others, and that each man's job is the mandate of heaven. He explained that in a variety of professions, the amount of work done for oneself is equal to the amount done for others, and that the element which balances the differences across professions is money. This means that if measured quantitatively by money, regardless of profession, the amount one contributes to others and the amount received by others is the same in the end. According to Natsume, each individual pursues his/her specialty or individual interests with a self-centered mind. He then concluded that it is money which quantitatively balances the values of such individuals.

To elaborate on Natsume's thinking, because a profession is a means to increase one's wealth through monetary rewards given in appreciation of one's labor, as a matter of course scientists, monks, and artists are likely to be left worse off in monetary terms, because they pursue contentment based on values and views of life that are less highly remunerated by society. At the opposite end of the spectrum, if a man accumulates considerable monetary power through his labor, he must assume the social responsibility that such power entails. Within this purely monetary theory, Natsume ignores the moral purpose of each profession or form of work. In my view, this failure was likely due to the influence of the intense free market beliefs that prevailed in the United Kingdom during Natsume's stay more than a century ago.

Other influences came to affect the development of free-market thinking in the course of the eighteenth and nineteenth centuries. Free-market thinking originally developed with a keen respect for religious beliefs, ethics, and nature. Subsequently, it gave birth to the labor market theory through fierce competition between urban industrial managers and traditional farmers for control of labor as the full force of the Industrial Revolution in Britain was felt. The questions raised here remain constant social and economic issues, even if the immediate context looks less recognizable.

Perspectives from the natural sciences also filtered into the idea of the self-adjusting free market. Elements of Darwin's theories of survival of the fittest and natural selection came to be included as further justifications for why some workers did better than others. Later, the theory of labor supply contributed: in the crudest sense, only a fear of hunger will cause laborers to work. With these various strands of social philosophy, as society evolved over these two centuries, the theories of the self-adjusting free market developed by Adam Smith, David Ricardo, Thomas Malthus, and others came to be interpreted in new contexts.

3. Refuting the Free Market Theory and Its Effects

In recent years, important economists, including Joseph Stiglitz, view the recent financial crisis as a turning point. They affirm that the self-adjusting market in the perfect form posited by some cannot exist: Mankind and its institutions are not likely to be perfectible. They argue, therefore, that government intervention in the market is indispensable, and that only government intervention can correct recurring market imperfections, thereby restoring a more efficient distribution of resources and funds.

Some economists go so far as to denounce the theory of economic growth altogether, though not Stiglitz and many other likeminded thinkers. This denunciation is linked to the belief that economic growth breeds an unacceptable disparity in the balance between wealth and poverty. The main point of their argument is that they would not allow free-market theory to apply to the labor force, land, oil, natural resources, and the foreign exchange market which, in particular, can cause significant social instability. In their view, trading of labor and land, as if they were simple products, is neither morally nor socially permissible. They conclude that active adjustment by the government, and not self-adjustment by the market, is required to solve this basic social question.

These social thinkers recognize the importance of individual freedom. Their view is that the freedom of the poor and the downtrodden must be the same as that of the wealthy. They assert that the use of employed and unemployed workers and limited natural resources solely for the promotion of one's profit is actually in conflict with the true definition of freedom. The freedom that they champion is guaranteed by securing the right of insubordination against the government and against those business managers who have achieved social dominance under the banner of the free market theory. In the eyes of those who denounce the unhampered free market, government intervention will bring freedom to the lower social levels, where it could not be enjoyed before.

If closely examined, it becomes clear that philosophers who oppose pure laissez-faire principles believe that the government should also be a market player. This is the point at which those denouncing the unrestrained free market differ with the supporters of the self-adjusting market theory. The latter distinctly separate the role of market economies from the role of governments and criticize the application of state power in market functions.

Some of those who harshly denounce the free market also deplore the existence of capital that flows around the globe seeking the greatest opportunities for profit. This school of thought also regards globalization, which in many respects has come to replace the gold standard of monetary value, as an indirect cause of the recent financial crisis. However, many are genuinely concerned that if the idea of social harm perpetuated by the market economy is overstressed, an extreme reaction in the form of authoritarianism will take hold.

A look at world history shows protectionist solutions often arise in response to economic crises, such as the one being experienced now. The so-called socialist theory is one such example: It denied and attacked the laissez-faire principle, and, at the same time, acknowledged individual freedom and limited market functions. However, as the experiences of the twentieth century demonstrated, these did not function well either: Fascism and dictatorships of many kinds and forms, found in different cultures across the globe, suppressed personal freedoms, failed society as economic production systems, and led to massive losses of life through famines, internal oppressions, and wars.

This essay for the World Federation of Exchanges is being written at a critical juncture. Policy-makers must take care, and moderate voices must be heard. Parallels to worrisome times in the twentieth century exist: In 1939, after Peter Drucker fled fascism in Europe, he published a book entitled *The End of Economic Man*. Drucker viewed a world in which people were fascinated with the idea of National Socialism. In his book, he reflected on why and how this form of controlled socialist nation could come into existence.

Drucker identified two factors. First, fascism fed on the popular despair resulting from mass unemployment and large income disparities, which occurred when the prevailing philosophical premise for economics was extreme laissez-faire free capitalism. Profit-seeking as a singular commercial objective had become almost obsessive. Fascism also exploited the disappointment of those who had turned to Marxist economics earlier in the century. The roots of fascist movements in Europe and elsewhere can be found in the search for controlled market principles from the late 1920s to 1933, during which the self-adjusting free market theory collapsed.

Of all people, the operators of the world's financial exchanges must today ask themselves the same question people were posing 80 years ago: How does one reconcile freedom and equality with market economies? This essay attempts to address this issue.

In Western civilization, the legitimacy of authority is found in its purpose of improving the lives of the populace, spiritually, and in terms of living standards, even under absolute monarchs. Fascists came to denounce this form of authority. To avoid being fooled by dishonest government, clear and definitive rejection must be made as soon as a trend appears that might lead away from the legitimate exercise of government power, which is the material improvement of the people's lives and their spiritual enhancement. Drucker's recommendation for prudence and careful skepticism when looking into the heart of government workings reads like a textbook for today.

Following the recent crisis which began to unfold in 2007, movements toward protectionism have appeared in some countries. What is clear, however, is that we must not return to the terrible struggles of authoritarian states of right or left, all of which plagued the previous century.

4. Market Excesses

Events that led to the financial crisis of 2007–09 suggest that many financial business operators, especially those in the financial institutions of major markets, came to pursue what now clearly seems to be a greedy and almost fraudulent pursuit of profits. Their behavior appears inconsistent with the prevailing ethics and values held high as lynchpins of the industrial world.

Certainly, in retrospect, much evidence reveals a lack of common sense, moderation, and the exercise of individual responsibility. Unthinkable acts of deceit and ignorant arrogance have been too common in the competitive landscape of Wall Street and its counterparts throughout the world. Fischer Black and Merton Miller did not develop financial engineering tools in the 1970s and 1980s with the expectation that they would be misused two decades later in a flawed laissez-faire environment. Rather, the prevailing free market capitalist systems and their regulators allowed things to run out of control. They operated without sufficient care for rules or regulations, or even much reflection on the social purpose of finance, if any.

Free money policies in many countries exacerbated ethical problems. Too many governments accommodated policies in which leveraged financing spread to those with no money, and kept them poorly informed of the risks of leveraged consumption. In the United States, the Federal Reserve lowered interest rates from 6 percent to 1 percent from the period of 2000–2003. In so doing, the United States, which was in recession due to the bursting of the IT bubble, headed toward a new bubble. Given their responsibilities, one must question why authorities in central banks and finance ministries throughout the world did not ask more questions as evidence of problems mounted.

The laissez-faire, free-market type of capitalism, without the sufficient moderating influences of rules and regulations, failed to self-adjust. As it collapsed, this system then plunged the world headlong into the current global financial crisis and credit crunch, with its ever-increasing tally of victims and social offenses.

Economic history shows that governments in developed countries have intervened regularly to maintain free markets that function properly. As markets, laws, and technologies have evolved, authorities have adapted with appropriately complex arrays of new regulations, including antitrust laws, antimonopoly laws, and labor union laws.

Exchanges operate at the heart of regulated environments. The discipline associated with their regulations has enabled them to continue near normal operations during the current financial crisis. The hands-off approach to off-exchange trading seen in the United States over the past few decades and more recently in Europe stands in sharp contrast to the historical experiences of most other countries. Some of the solutions to current financial problems will come from careful analysis of why this was the case.

5. The Future of Market Development

Many observers today call for cautious reflection. Was the crisis actually a malfunction of the self-adjusting market, or a lack of morals and plain greed on the part of too many market participants?

I raise two sets of questions in this section of the essay. The first concerns the functioning of the financial market somewhat narrowly defined. The second involves broader social issues affected by market pricing, and the usefulness of market prices for decisions involving those broader social issues.

First, the efficiency of capital markets has been reaffirmed, and, at the same time, their limits also have been recognized. The public now generally believes that capital markets should be subject to some degree of external regulation for the sake of their efficient functioning. A serious issue now remains: Who should decide which regulations are necessary? Which regulations should be removed, and how? The cost clearly will be too high if these decisions are made among a narrow circle of policymakers relying only on the wisdom of hindsight.

Citizens in many countries have witnessed many attempts at pushing plans for total removal of government intervention that seek instead growth based solely on privatization and market liberalization. These efforts unfortunately too often have caused many socially disruptive phenomena such as unemployment, loss of housing, and tragic erosion of the social fabric.

In contrast, economic history demonstrates how regular, long-term capital formation has contributed to an increase in production efficiency. Capital formation has played a vital role in promoting wealth and the social welfare that depends upon it. Nations and societies have flourished when they have amassed large capital reserves that they could invest regularly in new projects. Adam Smith hoped that once capitalists gained a certain level of income, they would cease the pursuit of further wealth and seek a moral path that would reveal the value of wisdom in their lives. In parallel with this process, rapid investment of their "excess" capital would advance society in a virtuous circle. If capitalists did not hold themselves to highly ethical behavior, the government unavoidably would need to collect money through taxes to invest it in place of capitalists.

The critical issue implied here is that governments should maintain a high sense of morals, have genuine regard for the nation, and utilize capital efficiently on behalf of the governed. To put it in the terms of the free market theory under scrutiny, individuals would feel the pain of their overspending, and thus would be compelled to return to a more ethical, or certainly a simpler lifestyle. Governments, with comparatively less self-regard, are more inclined to wasteful spending and inefficient use of capital, and so should come under close and regular public examination. Systems for supervising the quality of government intervention in society must be devised. Countries must find a balance between the forces of the individual and his government, to construct sociopolitical systems that guarantee true democracy.

Turning closer to issues involving regulated exchanges, which have spread across the globe in the post-Second World War era, exchange markets represent the condensed essence of freedom and democracy, as my colleague Edemir Pinto of BM&FBOVESPA observes in the previous essay.

An idealized free market would be based on three democratic principles:

- Market information must not be concealed, disguised, or distorted. It must be made equally available to all participants.
- Trading must not be coerced by any parties.

- Buyers and sellers must not be controlled by any state or authority, and instead must be independent entities.

The establishment of effective capital markets will bring about efficient use of scarce savings by decreasing the costs of transactions. Trading costs arise from asymmetries in the information of market participants. If the asymmetries are too high, asset values may not be accurate. The poor valuation of assets is a key problem in controlled economies. The economic costs of poorly valued assets are another reason why a controlled economy and excessive intervention by the government should be rejected, even while accepting partial intervention and certain regulations.

Therefore, the issue is finding a meeting point between buyers and sellers, and so between supply and demand. This presents the question of how understandable and how transparent such rules can be made. To what extent can unnecessary trading costs be identified and eliminated? For exchange operators, the answer to this question must be ceaselessly pursued. The responsibility of the government and of market authorities is to seek a smoothly functioning balance of supply and demand, and then to decide how far conditions are from that point, and in what direction to move to assure the optimal outcome. At some point, though, a regulated market becomes costly to society. Beyond that point, no further reductions in the cost of operations can be obtained. Nevertheless, a regulated marketplace does provide returns to society, and transaction costs can easily be rationalized in comparison to the trillions of dollars destroyed in the recent crisis by unregulated markets in many countries.

The next set of issues has to do with the value of financial market prices for social matters, namely labor and limited natural resources. For example, if excessive government funds support unemployed workers in the private sector, and an unusual number of jobs are produced in public institutions, the hiring of workers by corporations at reasonable wages becomes impossible. Industrial competition would be damaged, ultimately resulting in the weakening of the nation as a whole, and leading to even more unemployment. Our prevailing economic system must be modified considerably to redress the pursuit of excessive profits and the distorted income distribution structure, while making the most of market freedom and the true nature of *homo economicus*, or economic man.

Equally, as this decade opens, another fundamental problem affecting the marketplace is approaching from a different direction: The idea of sustainability, already gathering strength and importance in recent years, is reaching the desks of all public policymakers. During the period from 1950 to the present, in which the world's population has grown from 2.5 billion to 6 billion, belief was placed in the self-adjusting functions of the market. However, this belief was not founded: Limited resources have been recklessly consumed in the pursuit of mass production, mass consumption, and material satisfaction. If this pace continues, the sustainability of life on earth will be threatened.

Many thinkers hope that some form of market adjustment will resolve the mass-production/mass-consumption business conundrum, though perhaps not market self-adjustment. They would pursue the creation of an equal society that balances the roles of the government and the market, and achieves steady growth and stability through ecological investment. To the extent possible, social forces themselves should encourage private enterprises to exercise self-discipline, instead of expecting the nation or government to define moral values or justice for all.

Today's debate on corporate social responsibility (CSR) is clearly advancing as an integral part of the philosophical rethinking of our economies, as posited at the outset of this essay. A public call is growing for discipline not only in corporations, but also in citizens, regions, and society as a whole. Under these circumstances, the pursuit of economic efficiency, environmental safety, education, health, and even more, social equality, should be recognized as additional responsibilities of corporations. The limited liability corporation is a remarkable social actor, one that has proven its adaptability over several centuries. It can rise to these challenges, too.

Financial exchanges have a role in this debate, through their work for enhancing transparent capital pricing and providing risk management tools, and through the example they set by their own operations as national economic leaders. By raising the sense of public morality in the market and utilizing a judicious mix of self-regulation and appropriate public regulation, more efficient asset prices will be discovered. Multiple social goods are at stake in this work: This moderate mix of the marketplace with some government guidance would be the more certain path to national affluence than a system of wealth distribution dictated by the nation or government.

Ideally, when business managers from around the world aim not only to fulfill their direct commercial duties but also to promote a stronger sense of ethics and social obligation, corporations will serve society well in many senses. Entrepreneurs will disclose information fully to the public, and conduct business under careful surveillance, forgoing the pursuit of excessive profits and seeking to contribute to social harmony and justice. I recognize that this idealized vision cannot be achieved easily. Sadly, such a situation cannot be achieved without proper oversight, regulation, and, in some cases, penalties. However, I do not doubt that corporations will be moving in this general direction.

The question arises of how to introduce effective monitoring of corporations from the outside. Though hard to implement, a much higher level of monitoring by third parties such as shareholders, independent directors, and consumers will be necessary. Such monitoring would nonetheless be more effective and flexible than the monitoring that would come from assuming that governments might find solutions in the form of constrictive new laws and regulations. However, this private monitoring would be inadequate if conducted only by shareholders. When a stock price rises, the shareholders too often cannot determine whether it was the product of logical and moral methods or accomplished through antisocial actions such as window-dressing accounting, or some other form of money-play, such as stock price manipulation. The cases of Enron and WorldCom made this perfectly clear. Little evidence suggests that shareholders questioned the quality of the management, financial figures, or the business model as they celebrated rising stock prices. I affirm that a broader collaboration of many social actors will be required to assure effective monitoring of corporate behavior, and to instill in it some sense of partnering, too.

As central institutions in market democracies, stock exchanges have consistently dedicated themselves to pursuing the best conditions to ensure capital market efficiency for the prosperity of citizens and the nation. Being an institutional fulcrum, the prices discovered on exchanges enable society to adjust to many changes in policy. For example, the debate on economic efficiency plays out well when reflected on an exchange: In one case, workers accept profits in the form of higher wages and then consume more in the market, while the government charges taxes which are then used as support for social services, including aid for the unemployed. In another case, corporations lower the cost of services and products, thus creating social demand. Whatever the social choice, asset values can adjust because of the exchange mechanism. The measure of effective exchange price discovery is not the accuracy of its foresight, but its ability to continuously grasp inaccurate predictions and expectations and reveal these to the public through higher or lower volumes, volatility, or bid-ask spreads.

The world is growing more complex. The absolute solutions of the past can no better solve the issues faced today than they can solve the issues of the future. A balance between embracing the free market and supporting it through regulation must be sought. The only question that should remain is how such a balance can be realized.

6. The Role of Regulated Exchanges

One fact stands out from the discussion of laissez-faire markets versus a moderate mix of government regulation guiding the market to assure fairness, transparency, and greater overall economic efficiency. Even during the chaos of 2008–09, regulated exchanges performed their functions of price discovery in a clear and efficient manner. The global crisis did not arise from the products traded on these venues, but from certain products traded outside of exchanges in less transparent over-the-counter (OTC) markets. Regulated exchanges, and the central clearing and settlement houses that operate in tandem with them, provide certainty of trade execution. This certainty was sorely lacking in the off-exchange markets.

Despite their singular success, another legacy of the liberal laissez-faire thinking of the past decades continues to harm regulated exchanges. Competition authorities thought it desirable—or came to be persuaded that it would be desirable—to experiment with competition between exchanges. In the United States and European Union in particular, they began to undermine the business model of regulated exchanges at the very time their success in transparent price discovery was needed most in this crisis by allowing—even encouraging—alternative trade execution platforms of various kinds and internalization of orders by intermediaries to proliferate.

These other venues do not have the obligations to pay for central market infrastructure that exchanges have. The trading conducted on these venues is not held to the same disclosure requirements as trading conducted on a regulated exchange. The result is a blurring of the price discovery process, and the creation of higher indirect costs. A market where neither the volume nor price of a transaction is required to be disclosed is in direct conflict with the first requirement of a true market: equal availability of market information to all participants. This activity not only impairs the transparency of the trading process, but also leads to deterioration in price discovery functions of the public markets that the regulated exchanges provide. Moreover, trading in these markets is significantly more difficult for regulators to monitor properly.

The opaqueness of trading processes found on these alternative trading venues negatively impacts investors, and raises the possibility of unnecessarily increasing the volatility of the market. Limiting information runs the risk of allowing only a specific group of participants to benefit from trading across many venues. Transactions may be occurring at prices which deviate greatly from their true value.

Competition between securities markets can be quite desirable for market participants, as it brings about benefits such as improved services. However, when such competition does not occur on a level playing field with all parties fairly sharing the costs of market infrastructure, as is now the case, that same false competition simply fragments the market. Presently, the alternative trading venues that are sapping business away from regulated exchanges owe their existence to the exchanges themselves. They are simple operations that are free-riding on the regulatory costs borne by exchanges and thus are able to compete for the same business without equal responsibility. Unfair competition will run the risk of degenerating into a "race to the bottom," which would ultimately result in a new form of economic chaos.

Exchanges cannot long continue to operate with one hand tied behind their backs, with their ability to fulfill their many obligations to society undermined. As stated at the start of this essay, extreme liberal views on economic life must be moderated, and the idea of competition authorities fragmenting the markets to somehow "improve" them must be refuted. To return to the opening of this essay, this tinkering— the experimentation with the structure of the regulated exchange environment with the intention of breaking it to pieces—was derived from the philosophy then prevailing, and which has proven so disastrous to the world economy. Exchange structure questions must be rebased on a commonly redefined, responsible public ethos necessary for a successful market economy.

Simply put, the role of the regulated exchange is that of providing capital for companies to grow, and investment destinations for individual savers, thus contributing to the creation of wealth for the general public. When exchange operators—and all other actors, public and private—remember these basics and work together, the social and investment outcome will be as optimal as any human institution can imagine and achieve.

A Free Option on the Future: Regulated Securities Exchanges Beyond 2010

STEPHAN MALHERBE, SIOBHAN CLEARY, AND NICKY NEWTON-KING

1. Setting the Scene

During the half-century celebrated by this book, the business of financial intermediation—bringing capital to new endeavors, securing a well-regulated set of investment choices for savers, and enabling risks to be laid off or assumed—has been one of the world's great growth industries. Regulated securities and futures exchanges have stood at the apex of the burgeoning business of financial intermediation.[1] Were we not so used to it, we would be startled that a single type of business could be so prominent that its street address would serve as shorthand for the entire economy and an index of its prices a key barometer of economic outlook. Wall Street, Threadneedle Street, Hang Sen, Sensex, CAC40: these and other such names have become accepted shorthand for economic wellbeing or otherwise.

There is no guarantee that this preeminence will last. During the 50 years, few other businesses have had that kind of sustained institutional prominence in the lives of nations, but there have been some. Metropolitan newspapers, national airlines, large broadcasters, major automobile companies, oil companies, and major high street and investment banks come to mind. When pondering the future of regulated exchanges, it is a sobering list. Major newspapers, and to a large extent traditional broadcasters, are being superseded by other forms of information delivery. Flag-carrier airlines have been undercut by wrenching competition following deregulation. Moreover, the recent global financial crisis has resulted in famed banks and automobile firms going under, being absorbed by competitors, or taken over by the state.

The crisp question is: will regulated exchanges turn out to be another artifact of the twentieth century, reduced to a peripheral status by nimble new competitors or emerging global giants? Alternatively, will regulated exchanges continue to evolve, successfully playing a critical role in financial intermediation and risk management around the world?

These questions assume that exchanges tend to have a similar structure and environment. A theme of this chapter is that this homogeneity, to the extent that it is still present, will disappear. The exchanges of tomorrow will face different competitive pressures, regulatory regimes, and degrees of protection from global rivals. To find a way through this increasingly complex picture, we first identify a handful of major trends that have transformed the operating realities for most exchanges.

2. Six Trends that have Transformed the World of Exchanges

Six large trends over the last quarter century have tested the adaptability of exchanges. In our view, however, the full impacts of these changes, momentous as they have been, still lie in the future.

2.1 The First Trend: from Club to Company—and its Corollary, Increased Regulatory Oversight

Initially, most of the national stock exchanges were for many decades owned by the brokers who were the direct users of their services. Those brokers did not consider themselves to be co-owners of a business, but rather members of a club operating a common asset. For reasons discussed elsewhere in this book, exchanges have in recent years moved away from this mutual structure. In retrospect, the demutualization of the Stockholm Stock Exchange in 1993 and the demutualization and listing of the Australian Stock Exchange on its own market in 1998 forged a path subsequently followed, fully or in part, by many other exchanges. According to the World Federation of Exchanges (WFE), as at the end of 2008, listed exchanges represented more than 40 percent of its membership, with an additional 18 percent having gone through the process of demutualization.[2] With ownership, exchange profit (as opposed to member profit) became the main driver. In the decade to 2008, the number of for-profit WFE members more than doubled to over 80 percent of the membership.[3]

In addition, with a clear profit motive, came increased oversight by regulatory authorities, and a strong policy preference for encouraging competition so as to discipline powerful, prominent businesses that were often thought of as a natural monopoly.

The other large change was in the relationship between the exchange and brokers, previously proprietors, now customers, and treated as such. This was never going to be an easy transition, and the scars may still bedevil exchange/customer interaction. Nevertheless, the tension between a business and its customers is a universal one: interests are sometimes aligned, and sometimes conflicting. How exchanges have struck a balance, and how they will do so in the future, will help determine the future shape of the industry, a point to which we shall return.

2.2 The Second Trend: Rapidly Intensifying Competition

Following the move from "club to company," regulators and customers alike began to view the exchange less as a public entity, and more as a service provider that ought to be exposed to the same competitive forces as other market participants.

Competition in trading services. The United States was the first to pass rules enabling privately owned alternative execution venues to compete with exchanges.[4] By 2008, the United States had more than 40 equity execution venues, comprised of a mix of registered stock exchanges, electronic communication networks (ECNs), alternative trading systems (ATSs), and new entrants.[5] The impact of the increase in competition has been swift: the New York Stock Exchange's (NYSE) trading market share in NYSE-listed stocks declined from over 70 percent in October 2005 to about 25 percent by March 2009.

On the other side of the Atlantic, European regulators followed the lead of their American counterparts with the introduction of the Markets in Financial Instruments Directive (MiFID) in 2007.[6] The objectives of MiFID are to ensure investor protection, to facilitate greater integration of the various markets within the European Community, and, importantly, to enhance competition amongst and between investment firms and market operators.

As in the United States, MiFID opened the door to a variety of institutions and businesses offering securities trading services. It did so through three significant moves. First, the directive expressly recognizes three categories of execution venue: the regulated market (the traditional exchange), the multilateral trading facility (MTF) and the systematic internalizer (SI). Secondly, MiFID abolished the "concentration rule" which was still operating in many European markets: this rule required investment firms to route orders to the national exchange. The concentration rule was replaced with a requirement that firms demonstrate that they had achieved best execution for their clients using whatever execution platform would achieve that. Thus did the privileged position of the traditional exchange come to an end in Europe.

The immediate consequence has been a proliferation of new equity execution venues across Europe. As at end December 2009, the Committee for European Securities Regulators (CESR) database showed that together systematic internalizers (13 registered) and MTFs (133 registered) outnumbered the 91 regulated markets.[7] Some of these new entrants are exchange customers who saw an opportunity to set up an exchange-independent execution venue and/or to self-provide (subject to the best-execution requirement). It is worth noting that customers have tended to be prodded into action when they felt that exchanges had been insufficiently responsive to their requirements. The establishment in the United Kingdom of the MTF Turquoise by a consortium of investment banks is a case in point. At the time that the project was announced, Alan Yarrow, the Chairman of the London Investment Banking Association said:

> "The exchanges have seen huge increases in their margins on a
> fixed price platform and haven't shared that proactively with their
> users. There is a huge degree of frustration out there. We have
> repeatedly put the point to them but they haven't listened so I
> commend this proposal."[8]

Other new providers are entities who already provide similar execution venues in the United States, inter-dealer brokers and in some cases, exchanges themselves.

This emergence of multiple alternative execution venues has resulted in fierce competition for the profitable aspects of the exchange business, predominantly trade execution, while leaving exchanges largely responsible for the nonprofit generating aspects such as market and company regulation. The new competitors tend to have much lower overheads than the traditional exchanges have, enabling entry with extremely competitive pricing.[9] Exchanges have had no choice but to respond with their own round of fee restructuring and tariff reductions. Often the alternative execution venues do not charge brokers to become members or charge a fee for real time market data. While doubts have been raised about the long-term sustainability of these low-cost models,[10] some of the new venues have made in-roads into trade volumes. By some estimates, Chi-X Europe, one of the more successful European MTFs launched in the wake of MiFID, accounts for some 25 percent of trading in London's FTSE 100 and 14 percent of German equities.[11]

With the changes, a further significant source of competition in trade execution appears to have emerged outside of the three types of platform envisaged by MiFID. This is trading on brokers' internal crossing networks—which networks are not currently registered under any of the existing MiFID classifications and are hence largely unregulated. The volumes are large: According to one estimate by the Federation of European Stock Exchanges, nearly 40 percent of all trade volume in Europe is now traded on broker's internal crossing networks.[12] FESE argues that these services constitute formalized execution service provision, and should hence be conducted in one of the defined MiFID categories and subject to the same regulation. MiFID is currently being reviewed, and it remains to be seen how these concerns are addressed.

Competition in data provision. It follows that, in many jurisdictions, the exchanges are no longer the only venue from which order information and trade data can and must be sourced. This creates problems for those exchanges for which the sale of data is a significant revenue component. The challenge is accentuated if MTFs continue to capture market share. After all, an exchange's ability to charge for data is linked to the extent to which those data represent the output of the main venue at which the prices of these securities are determined.

Competition in post-trade services. MiFID and other similar regulations focus predominantly on increasing competition in the trading space,[13] and hence most competition has been in trade execution. Competition in post-trade services has lagged, and an important question is whether the competitive dynamic we have seen in trade execution will play out there. This is true not least for exchanges that provide—or wish to provide—post-trade services such as clearing and settlement. However, competition in post-trade services also provides opportunities for exchanges—perhaps especially the opportunity to provide risk management services for over-the-counter (OTC) derivative trades, or lure these trades on to exchanges entirely.

The competition unleashed by regulatory change and market entry has not yet played itself out. Many jurisdictions have yet to see such an explicit opening of the exchange space to competition. For some, it may just be a matter of time: For example, in Australia, it was recently announced that market supervision would be taken from the Australian Securities Exchange (ASX) to be performed in future by the Australian Securities and Investments Commission (ASIC)—the apparent rationale being to open the field to competition in trade execution. Already two alternative execution venues—Liquidnet and Chi-X—have indicated an interest in obtaining licenses to operate in Australia.[14]

2.3 The Third Trend: Acquisitions as a Strategic Tool

Enabled by demutualization and encouraged by the globalization of their clients, some exchanges have joined in the more general merger and acquisition frenzy. These exchanges can be broadly grouped into "globalizers" wishing to diversify into new geographical markets, and "consolidators" expanding their business within a chosen geographic area.

The "globalizers" have attracted the most attention. Cross-continental exchanges that emerged in the mid-2000s include NASDAQ OMX and NYSE Euronext (with Euronext having acquired London-based Liffe not too long before that). The London Stock Exchange (LSE) found itself on the receiving end of a number of take-over attempts before it finally undertook its own acquisition of Borsa Italiana. A variant of the "globalizing" game has been the rush by exchanges and other market participants to stake their claim in fast-growing regions such as Asia and the Middle East, usually through minority stakes.[15]

Amongst the "consolidators," the most important recent transaction was the merger of the Chicago Mercantile Exchange and the Chicago Board of Trade, which resulted in the establishment of the largest publicly listed exchange by market capitalization. Consolidation has also occurred in a number of smaller markets. In Brazil, the Sao Paolo Stock Exchange and the Brazilian Mercantile and Futures Exchange merged to create BM&FBOVESPA, while in Australia the ASX acquired the Sydney Futures Exchange (SFE). The Johannesburg Stock Exchange acquired both the South African Futures Exchange and the Bond Exchange of South Africa.

How will these combinations fare in the future? One cannot generalize, but the advantages of scale, efficiency, and sheer heft seem at first blush to be more readily achievable by the "consolidators," not least because the difficulties of reconciling regulatory regimes and of managing cross-border teams are largely avoided. This may change if "globalizers" succeed in exploiting their scale to develop or purchase technologies more effectively. At this point, though, much-touted scenarios of a capital markets world dominated by a handful of global mega-exchanges with a global footprint now seem unlikely—at least in the short term. In fact, NYSE Euronext recently reported merger costs amounting to US$442 million and a resultant loss of US$182 million for the quarter ended June 2009. The interplay between globalization and the force of nation-states will be an important factor shaping the future, a point to which we return in the following section.

2.4 The Fourth Trend: Technology

Managing the exponential rate of technological change has become a critical challenge for exchanges. Technology facilitated the move from physical trading floors to electronic central order books, which then enabled and required ever greater transaction processing speeds, and expanded the reach and audience for exchange market data. Most importantly, technology cut costs per trade sharply, particularly for new entrants. Many exchanges have had to migrate from legacy systems and structures—a slow and often costly process—whereas more recent entrants into the market have escaped these migration costs by acquiring ultramodern, low-cost technology from the start.

The acceleration of technological change had some surprising effects. For all but a few exchanges, it meant that technology is now largely acquired rather than developed internally. Looking to the future, the rise of third-party technology providers has in some ways leveled the competitive playing field, allowing smaller exchanges to stay abreast of technological change. This means that the competitive battle will shift in good part to business models and market positioning, rather than technological differentiation.

One should not, though, dismiss the future role of technologically based differentiation altogether: in the section that follows, we posit that we may be entering a new era of product differentiation.

2.5 The Fifth Trend: "Emerging" Markets Move from the Periphery to the Centre

There is by now general recognition that the role of Asia in the global exchange business—as a customer, a destination and a marketplace—is on the cusp of even greater expansion. Already the shape and, to some extent, nature of the global flows of capital and savings have changed radically. Asia (excluding Japan) has become the principal source of new global savings. And those savings are in many instances intermediated by the state abroad through central bank reserves and other forms of sovereign wealth funds, and domestically (in both China and India) through state-owned banking sectors. Thirdly, enterprises and production facilities in the region are important recipients of capital. Other emerging economies, such as those found in Latin America, Eastern Europe, and Africa, are also starting to show some of the promise long-suggested by their mineral and agricultural wealth. While not showing the same levels or rates of growth as some of the Asian economies, they are attaining scales which make them too large to ignore.

New players on the investment, issuing and exchange sides of the triangle are now coming to the fore. More profoundly, the rules of the game, and hence the game itself, may change as a result. The first WFE half-century saw the emergence of an "Atlantic" consensus on exchange activities, in which the United States and the European Union assumed broadly similar views on regulating capital markets, including embracing a large degree of trading freedom, profit, free transfer of ownership, and competition. It is too early to say whether during the next half-century of WFE, exchanges will see a different "South South" consensus emerge, including the Indian Ocean giants and countries like Brazil and South Africa. It is already apparent that countries such as India and China are taking a nontraditional view on such key matters as exchange ownership and control.

2.6 The Sixth Trend: the Return of Risk—and a Declining Belief in Market Self-discipline

There is nothing like a financial crisis to remind one and all that risk is not a notional concept, and that optimal risk management is a critical objective. Following the American–European financial crisis of 2008, risk management has returned to center stage.

A silver lining for central counterparty systems. The bilateral risk management characteristic of over-the-counter (OTC) transactions has been particularly criticized. Market participants, policy-makers and the public have woken up to the fact that essentially unregulated OTC markets are sufficiently massive in size (for example, including the large majority of international derivatives markets) that defaults in these markets can endanger global institutions. In marked contrast, central counterparty (CCP) risk management structures, often operated by exchanges, have been lauded for the manner in which they handled various defaults stemming from the crisis, including that of Lehman Brothers.

US Treasury Secretary Timothy Geithner endorsed the CCP model in written testimony, saying:

> "Central clearing of standardized OTC derivatives will reduce
> risks to those on both sides of a derivative contract and make the
> market more stable. With careful supervision and regulation of the
> margin and other risk management practices of central
> counterparties, central clearing of a substantial proportion of OTC
> derivatives should help to reduce risks arising from the web of
> bilateral interconnections among our major financial institutions.
> This should help to constrain threats to financial stability."[16]

Hence, the emergence of a widely held view that OTC derivatives should at least be centrally cleared through a CCP-type structure, if not also standardized to the degree where they can be exchange-traded. As the memory of the crisis fades, bank and other users of OTC derivatives have pushed back against such regulations with increasing vigor. On balance, it is likely that CCPs—and possibly even exchanges with derivative offerings—will see a greater percentage of this activity. Some market participants, however, are apparently still not reconciled with the entities that they used to own, the exchanges, and they are arguing that if they are going to be required by regulation to utilize exchanges or clearing houses, then these should be run as utilities rather than as for-profit entities.[17]

Transparency. Another major factor blamed for the crisis was the lack of transparency that prevented regulators from identifying the systemic risk posed by certain institutions and their activities. Once again, OTC markets—opaque by nature—received their fair share of the blame, and greater transparency was held up as a means of preventing future crises of this nature. Exchanges, CCPs, and other central reporting venues were identified as mechanisms for enhancing market transparency. According to a recent report prepared for the Bank for International Settlements:

> "Introducing CCPs would improve transparency by allowing for
> easy collection of high-frequency market-wide information on
> market activity, transaction prices and counterparty exposures for

market participants who rely on them. The centralization of information in a CCP makes it possible to provide market participants, policymakers and researchers with the information to better gauge developments in various markets on the position of individual market participants."[18]

This demand for greater transparency has begun to extend into other market areas, with regulators on both sides of the Atlantic beginning to look more closely at, and to question the value of, so-called "dark pool" offerings provided by both exchanges and exchange-like competitors. We shall return to this point.

The 2008 crisis has largely been an Atlantic one. Nevertheless, in one respect, its consequences will be global: the renewed emphasis on risk and the reduced confidence in capital markets as self-regulating, self-policing entities will for many years cause a societal bias in favor of increased scrutiny and regulation.

3. Succeeding in the New Reality

3.1 The New Value Reality

When we consider the twentieth-century corporate titans mentioned at the start of this chapter, it becomes apparent that quite a few have come undone (national airlines, metropolitan newspapers, and broadcasters) or been strengthened (oil majors) by large changes in the core value of their products—that is, the prices people were prepared to pay for their products (airline tickets, media advertising slots, and crude oil) changed, and did so permanently. The causes are generally complex, involving profound technological changes, global shifts in markets, and entrants with brand new business models. Yet, the impact boils down to something quite simple: a large permanent change in price, usually a fall. It is similar, we believe, for the exchange business: The rich tapestry of exchange trends described in the preceding section boil down to three short, simple statements on *value*:

- **Trading services are being** *devalued*. As communication and processing costs will continue to fall, and competition intensifies, the long-term unit prices of standard trading services point inexorably downwards.
- **Risk management services are being** *revalued*. Following the financial crisis, the immense social value of the risk reduction offered by

exchanges and central counterparties is evident. If this currently widely shared realization changes the behavior of capital market actors, then the value of offering risk management services will increase—not necessarily in unit price increases, but in volume increases relative to the same fixed costs.

- **Regulatory services are being *unvalued*.** Traditional exchanges' regulatory and listings services are of great value to capital market participants and the economy as a whole. Yet, these services are not appropriately valued as a public good by market users or regulators. The result is that exchanges continue to struggle to monetize this value.

Not all exchanges will face the same combination of these value impacts, and not all will respond in the same way. In these shadings lies the difference between relative failure and success.

3.2 Strategic Responses to the Devaluation of Trading Services

Trading revenues remains the largest component of total exchange revenues, and in many cases, the reliance of exchanges on trading services revenues is growing. According to the WFE's survey of members, by 2008 trading contributed no less than 53 percent of overall revenues. This proportion has been rising steadily, up from 43 percent in 2003, and 39 percent in 1998. Hence, the gravity of a long-run secular fall in trading fees—the pricing pattern that seems most likely for markets where new trading competitors such as MTFs are active. The trend observed during the last ten years, during which falls in the unit prices of trading were compensated for by volume growth, may well not last. For example, it is worth contemplating the potential for entry by low-cost competitors who both force down prices and rapidly build market share.

Price falls need not be a cause for alarm. Trading is a digitized activity that works off a fixed-cost base. It is to be expected that prices will fall as processing and communicating digital information become ever cheaper. In such an industry, a business that *leads* the cost reduction curve will experience larger market share and higher profits while cutting prices. However, businesses that *lag* in cost reduction have a very difficult time, and in the worst case can find themselves in a "death spiral" of falling volumes and increasing losses.[19]

Broadly speaking, the exchanges in markets with these pricing pressures are responding with three strategies:

- *Leading the charge to win the low-cost game*—by exploiting scale and in certain cases by creating or buying MTFs.
- *Adding value to trading*—for example, by providing trading "privacy" in so-called dark pools, or by catering for the needs of high-frequency traders. An important variation on the value-adding theme is to assume the role of a liquidity aggregator offering smart order routing amongst the various trade execution venues.
- *Diversifying*—to new products and revenue streams. One increasingly prevalent example is achieving product diversity by providing access to securities traded on exchanges in other geographical areas.

3.2.1 Leading the Charge to Win the Low-Cost Game

The exchange business model remains a largely fixed cost, variable income model: In such a market, the company with the largest market share ought to prevail, occupying a "sweet spot" that combines sound margins and competitive pricing. In most markets, of course, traditional exchanges are still the market share leaders—yet they mostly seem quite far from the sweet spot. That is for two reasons. Firstly, exchanges may find it difficult to switch from the relatively relaxed mind-set of a sole franchise to the lean discipline required of a low-cost mass operator. An analogy from the airline business illustrates the point: It was easier for new airlines to adopt a budget model than for far larger scale flag carriers to reinvent themselves as low-cost contenders. The second point is that for an incumbent wishing to preempt low-cost rivals, it is often costly to reduce fees across its entire customer base. Internally and externally, there is a bias in favor of postponing the pain of such a price cut. This easily results in a price response that is too modest and too late, leaving an opening for an entrant to gain significant market share.

Therefore, for some exchanges, it may be difficult to succeed at the scale and low-cost game. Difficult, but not impossible. One way to overcome the inherent tensions between incumbency and insurgency is to create an MTF adjacent to the exchange's traditional trading activities. In its MiFID review, the CESR found that *nearly half* of the new equity MTFs operating in Europe since introduction of MiFID had been launched by exchanges.[20] Two high-profile examples: in late 2009, the LSE acquired 60 percent of Turquoise, a well-known MTF.[21] In addition,

Deutsche Börse has sought to expand its presence amongst retail traders through the acquisition of a 75 percent stake in Tradegate Exchange, a retail-focused MTF. As a result of the acquisitions, these exchange groups have a richer set of strategic responses from which to choose, if the low-trading-fee juggernaut rolls on.

3.2.2 Adding Value to Trading

Dark pools. When customers say unexpected things, good businesses listen with particular attentiveness. After more than a decade in which exchanges touted the advantages of a transparent central order book, large traders have made it clear that transparency can also have its costs. These traders have been attracted to so-called dark pools, a facility for completing large transactions privately and without the feedback effects of market responses, thus minimizing market impact cost. Some exchanges have responded to this need. SmartPool, a European dark pool for the execution of institutional order flow was created by NYSE Euronext in partnership with J.P. Morgan, HSBC and BNP Paribas. The LSE has stated that it will amalgamate Turquoise's dark pool component into the LSE's Baikal dark pool offering, while its "lit" platform will continue to offer pan-European equities trading.

Execution speed. As traders seek new ways to achieve above-average returns, new demands are placed on execution speeds and data dissemination.[22] For example, in cash equity markets, the rise of high-frequency trading has encouraged ever faster transaction speeds, with some venues now boasting sub-millisecond execution speeds. This is not a small part of the market: A recent report by the TABB Group[23] estimates that high-frequency trading now accounts for 70 percent of US equities trading volume. Like many other market developments enabled by technological advance (dark pools and flash orders come to mind), high-frequency trading is now being scrutinized by regulators in both the United States and the United Kingdom.[24]

Liquidity aggregation. In the current fragmented market environments of the United States and Europe, customers will value the ability to easily search through all the available execution venues for the best deal. Pro-active exchanges might provide this service, and help to solve the liquidity fragmentation problem. The provision of efficient and cost-effective data aggregation and smart order routing facilities enables an exchange to capture at least the order flow and a portion of the data revenue, if not the full transaction execution revenue.

3.2.3 Diversification

As trade in liquid securities becomes subject to more competition, exchanges look to new product and service areas for competitive advantage. For example, traditional cash equity exchanges *have broadened their trading activities into new securities.* Examples include adding derivatives and fixed-income instruments to equities trading to become a one-stop trading shop for investors. In some instances, this was done through an acquisition or merger of existing exchanges. Note the acquisitions mentioned earlier by the Johannesburg Stock Exchange of the South African Futures Exchange in 2001 and the Bond Exchange of South Africa in 2009; the merger of the ASx and the Sydney Futures Exchange (SFE) in 2006; and the merger of the Sao Paolo Stock Exchange and the Brazilian Mercantile and Futures Exchange in 2008. Other exchanges, such as the National Stock Exchange of India and Bursa Malaysia, have opted to expand their product ranges independently of acquisitions.

In addition, technology can be used to give exchange customers access to new products and geographies. Rather than seeking to cross-list products, exchanges can connect customers into other exchanges or platforms with different offerings. In effect, through joint initiatives with other exchanges, exchanges are seeking to establish themselves to their customer base as *portals for global trading.*

Another diversification play is to maximize revenues from *nontrading products* such as data analysis and dissemination, and clearing and settlement. In a few instances, the selling of information technology and/or infrastructure has gained prominence. Often, though, the diversification is more apparent than real; as the "new" revenue source is really derived from trading activity, it will lose steam if trading activity falls.

3.2.4 Will the Regulated Exchanges Win the Battle for Trading?

The simple answer is: time will tell. Exchanges with the will to change in the face of competition will likely prevail. Alternative trading systems may wax and wane as an investment priority for their backers. Moreover, many of these new businesses still have to find the equilibrium prices at which they will be viable.

What about exchanges that are operating in jurisdictions where they are the sole provider? In the short run, it may well be a feasible strategy for the incumbent to protect its domain against insurgents, for example by regulatory means. In this way, exchanges in developing markets might usefully buy time to build scale and adjust business models so as to fend off future competitors. Nevertheless, the protection strategy will not work forever: Investors and traders, both domestic and foreign, will seek more trading alternatives, and regulators are likely to become sympathetic. The protection strategy is best understood not as a means to eliminate future competition, but to prepare for it.

3.3 Strategic Responses to the Revaluation of Risk Management Services

The key post-crisis opportunity for exchanges is in post-trade risk management. As mentioned earlier, regulators now clearly believe central counterparty clearing to be more prudent than the naked reliance on the deal counterparty that one finds in OTC market. Hence, the global talk about the advantages of bringing OTC trades "on-market."

Exchanges have to act quickly to take advantage of the renewed appreciation of centralized risk management mechanisms. Work is needed on two fronts. The first is in the regulation and policy debate. In the midst of a financial crisis, multibillion dollar bail-outs of banks and insurers, and fiscal costs that may be paid by an entire generation made tangible the social costs of poor risk management, both unilateral and bilateral. When systemic risk becomes visible in this way, it is vital to undertake systemic reforms, for during normal times, when these costs are merely hypothetical, paying the smaller actual costs of forestalling these greater calamities is often resisted. Such is human nature. As the visceral memory of crisis recedes, the forces against any measure that adds to the bank-incurred cost of proprietary trading will strengthen. Therefore, this is a time for exchanges and other suppliers of centralized risk management to provide a strong voice for reform—and to do so for reasons that go beyond self-interest, that go to the long-term health, and hence political viability, of the sophisticated financial markets on which global economic activity depends.

The second front requiring action is customers, particularly the new and possibly reluctant ones migrating from the OTC environment. Exchanges will have to work hard to understand and be responsive to these customers and their particular requirements, a point to which we return in the following section. Moreover, all participants, not least customers, need to understand that competing on cost by lowering levels of risk management would not be responsible. Other forms of competition of course will be healthy and inevitable.

Some exchanges now provide clearing and risk management for OTC derivatives, with Intercontinental Exchange (ICE) gaining a first-mover lead in this realm.[25] Derivatives exchanges tend to own their central counterparty clearing infrastructure, though in Europe LCH.Clearnet is a notable independent clearing service provider in that context. In addition, in jurisdictions where there is a single national exchange operator, the exchange is often vertically integrated. The Singapore Exchange, Bursa Malaysia, Hong Kong Exchanges and Clearing (HKEx), and the Johannesburg Stock Exchange are just some examples of these types of vertically integrated exchanges.

Managed well, these and other risk management incumbents may have a lasting competitive advantage. There are several reasons for this. Financial risk management is an activity where trust and reputation matter greatly. Further, developing and deploying effective risk management models is not as straightforward as some might think—especially when it comes to historically nonstandardized OTC instruments: Risk management around the world may hew to the same set of principles, but it is far from being a commodity. Finally, perhaps even more than trading, risk management generates powerful returns to scale, with costs falling as volumes increase.

However, not all exchanges provide risk management. In the United Kingdom and United States, most equity exchanges have tended to focus until very recently on listing and trade execution services, with post-trade clearing and settlement performed by an independent third party (in the case of the United States, a quasi-utility). Exchanges that are not already providing CCP clearing services may seek to collaborate with or acquire existing clearing providers. NYSE Euronext recently received permission for its derivatives business, NYSE Liffe, to become a self-clearing recognized investment exchange. This means that in future it will be able to act as the CCP for its trades. Initially, NYSE Liffe will continue to outsource the performance of the clearing functions to LCH.Clearnet.[26]

Competition also will come from outside exchanges. The US-based Depositary Trust and Clearing Corporation (DTCC) has registered a wholly owned subsidiary, EuroCCP, in the United Kingdom to provide "low-cost" pan-European central counterparty clearing services, predominantly for equities. Similarly, Fortis Bank established the European Multilateral Clearing Facility (EMCF) in 2007.[27]

3.4 Strategic Responses to the Nonvaluation of Regulatory and Listing Services

The aftermath of the financial crisis of 2008–09 is not the first period where exchanges have been touted as the solution to a core weakness revealed by the crisis. The Asian crisis of 1997–98 led to a renewed focus on corporate disclosure and governance. Equities exchanges, wielding the power of listings requirements when they had the authority to set them, were widely seen as a key part of the solution. The post-history of the Asian crisis is still to be written, and perhaps it will emerge that exchanges have indeed played the heroic role in building corporate disclosure and sound governance that had been envisaged.

If they have, they have not been paid for it. According to the WFE's survey of its members, in 2008 listings fees accounted for only 6 percent of revenues—down from 18 percent ten years earlier, at the height of the crisis, and before the corporate governance movement had reached its apogee. Why is this? Do exchanges have a latent source of value waiting to be tapped, given that investors and governments alike continue to have deep concerns about the informational chasm between corporations and their shareholders?

There is little doubt of the immense social value of the listings function. Of course, exchanges are not alone: the listings function is part of an ecosystem that includes accountants, broking analysts, investors, and financial media. Nevertheless, it is in the realm of the listings rules that new approaches have been set, shareholder rights and managerial practicalities balanced, and entrenched interests overcome. Why, then, have exchanges not been able to monetize the extraordinary value they have created for shareholders and companies alike? The public nature of listings is an important part of the answer. A shareholder does not need to trade on an established exchange to have the benefit of the disciplines of its listings function. Thus, trading revenue has become disjoint from listings virtue.

Exchanges are learning that free-riding does not cease merely because one has complained about it. Given that the primary beneficiaries of "listings virtue" are the long-term holders of a firm's shares, it might be expected that companies, as the collective enterprise of those very shareholders, ought to be prepared to pay fully for the listings function and its benefits. That this has not happened is something of a mystery. However, value waits to be unlocked.

While it waits, risks abound. It should be of concern to all market users and stakeholders that exchanges may decide to give up their costly regulatory function if faced with competitors that free-ride on this public good. Moreover, who knows what innovations and improvements are left undone, because no one has the incentive to pursue them.

Further, it is by no means clear that national regulators ought to take over this function or would be able to perform it effectively.

Some exchanges in jurisdictions where national legislation lags international norms now require adherence to higher corporate governance standards. BOVESPA's Novo Mercado is a justly celebrated example of such initiative. In other jurisdictions, the exchange is potentially a more trusted and more sophisticated source and arbiter of these rules of corporate conduct.

This may also apply to other supervisory functions performed by exchanges. In many jurisdictions, the market regulators are reliant on exchanges to provide them with information they require in order to investigate and prosecute insider trading or other instances of market abuse. It is not clear how this is catered for in a more fragmented environment with potentially less regulation. The overall impression given is that regulators and users alike undervalue the public good nature of the regulatory services of exchanges.

3.5 How the Battle Between Exchange Models will be Decided

It is easy to be dogmatic about exchange models. Exchanges that are now for-profit, corporate entities (the "companies"), have every incentive to trumpet the success of their transformation, not least because of fears about potential entrants organized as customer-owned utilities. Indeed, since this corporate restructuring, markets have continued to grow, exchange service costs have fallen, and this sector continued to operate straight through a historic crisis. In contrast, customers and policy-makers of a certain persuasion can be nostalgic about the mutual exchange model (the "clubs"), omitting from their reveries the stresses and clashes of interests that led to the adoption of the non-mutual corporate model.

In fact, the battle between models will be decided not on the basis of opinions, but results. The decisive question will be: Which model, *in the circumstances*, is generally better at responding effectively to the challenging business environment described in the preceding section, and in particular to the three key elements: the devaluation of trading, the revaluation of risk management, and need to monetize the value inherent in listings and other regulatory functions?

In this respect, the utility model is not to be discarded. Utilities can display visionary leadership and respond flexibly and strategically to a changing environment. In some emerging economy settings, the utility model could fit more easily into a tapestry of policies that support domestic service provision and economies of scale.

We foresee a mix of models into the future, including hybrids that combine the profit incentive with some customer participation. Generally, though, we believe that the "company" offers a better chance of success than the "club." Exchanges organized as companies have a particularly strong incentive to adapt and prosper, as do their managers. The company form also allows for speedy responses to opportunities, including mergers and acquisitions. Perhaps most importantly, for-profit corporations can more readily access capital—capital that will be needed to fund the strategic responses to the new value reality.

There is some evidence that the "companies" do diversify more quickly. According to the WFE's 2008 member survey, for nonmutual exchanges, trading accounted for roughly 40–50 percent of all revenues with "services" contributing a further 25 percent plus. Listed exchanges were particularly well diversified, deriving nearly 40 percent of their revenue from other services. By contrast, the four responding exchanges that were associations of members derived over 80 percent of their revenue from trading. It is worth noting that exchanges that had pursued integration across asset classes relied less on trading revenue (57 percent) than did their single asset class peers (over 90 percent for derivative exchanges and 75 percent for cash only exchanges).

Finally, a word of warning to the "companies." The corporatized exchanges often still have work to do to win back the trust of their customers who might have found the transition from belonging to a club to being serviced by a company a jarring experience.

In every industry, the best for-profit companies succeed at winning over customers, and the same will be true of exchanges. More unusually, exchanges will have to deal with a blurring of the lines between customers, competitors, and partners, a phenomenon to which we now turn.

4. Co-opetition: Thinking Afresh about Customers and Competitors

The demutualization revolution meant that, for the first time, exchanges had to think about customers, and, with the coming of competition, competitors in a traditional, generic business way. Customers were customers, not members or owners. And competitors became a reality.

The demutualization revolution is now in a second, new phase, and again exchanges need to think about their customers and competitors afresh. This is because, in ways that are quite specific to the securities industry, the lines between customers, competitors, suppliers, and business partners are blurring. Customers are competing with exchanges, competing exchanges are cooperating, and both customers and competitors are becoming business partners of exchanges. In a fast-moving industry, this may become the most creative and dynamic area of strategy. At the same time, the lingering discomfort between exchanges and their customers needs to be addressed.

4.1 Customers Rediscovered

Demutualization gave exchanges the ability to respond to *market* demands as opposed to simply *member* demands. However, the pendulum may have swung too far, with exchanges being insufficiently attentive to direct user needs. The result has been some appetite for "remutualization," for example of execution services. Exchanges need to ensure that they understand the requirements of not just the end-users of their services, the issuers and the investors but also the intermediaries. These are, after all, their direct customers.

Exchange customers are more diverse than is generally imagined. For example, while most customers value low execution costs, their willingness to trade lower costs for lower market security or certainty of execution may vary. The high-frequency trader may demand high-speed execution, but the large institutional investor may be more interested in being able to execute his order without significant market impact. For some customers, being able to trade multiple asset classes in a single location may be important, whereas for others being able to seamlessly trade a given product class across geographies may matter more. Even within a category, interests may differ: some issuers of derivative instruments favor market liquidity and price transparency while others may wish to remain the main price-maker. In a competitive environment, a single exchange (or other provider) may not succeed in being all things to all people. Exchanges will have to make decisions around which customer needs will be fulfilled at the expense of others.

An important test for the customer skills of the exchanges will come in the form of efforts to attract current users of OTC instruments on-exchange, or into centralized risk management mechanisms. Absent regulatory fiat, customers will need to be persuaded that a move to centralized clearing is in their own interest as well as that of society. The key to success will be exchanges' ability to listen to OTC users' needs, and to respond effectively. In some cases, the exchange/customer divide is best crossed by including users in governance structures or advisory bodies to ensure that their voices are properly and effectively heard. Ultimately, customers will assess whether exchanges are responsive on the basis of service and cost, not by the presence of an advisory panel.

The most profound way of listening to customers is in fact to make them co-owners of your business—a trend apparent in various MTFs that have sought in this way to secure trading volume. These business models tempt some to say that the exchange world has come full circle, back to the world of mutual ownership. That is premature. It remains to be seen whether the trust benefits of such an arrangement outweigh the effect of different vantage points, particularly with respect to capital expenditure.

4.2 Competitors Redefined

An exchange and an MTF compete aggressively in one market but agree to co-operate in offering a new service. On the other hand, an MTF entering a new jurisdiction may decide to do so in partnership with the incumbent exchange. The common thread is combining competitors with complementary strengths to make a new business feasible. There is even is a word for it: "co-opetition," a combination of the two seemingly opposite notions of "co-operation" and "competition." Its proper definition is "the arrangement between competing firms to co-operate on specific projects or in certain areas of business for mutual benefit, even while remaining competitors in general"[28]—a venerable notion in technology, and a fairly novel, and potentially potent, one for exchanges.

In a recent example of co-opetition, the Singapore Exchange (SGX) has partnered with Chi-X global to create Chi-East, a pan-Asian, nondisplayed trading platform on which Australian, Hong Kong, and Japanese listed securities will be available for trading.[29] In response to customer demands, and perhaps making a preemptive strike against possible competition, both Bursa Malaysia and BM&FBOVESPA have entered into arrangements with CME Group under the terms of which members of the Brazilian and Malaysian markets are able to access CME (and vice versa) via CME's Globex network. In terms of the Bursa Malaysia/ CME agreement, the new Malaysian derivatives trading technology will be provided by CME and hosted in Chicago. BM&FBOVESPA is contemplating a similar network-type relationship for equities with NASDAQ OMX.[30]

5. Four Policy Paradoxes that will Shape the Future Playing Field

Exchanges, their customers and their competitors form three corners of a quadrangle. The fourth corner of the quadrangle is as important, that of the rule-makers, which in the world of exchanges comprises both regulators and financial policymakers. Crises empower and embolden policymakers, priming them for action and change. As it happens, policymakers face a particularly acute set of challenges right now. These challenges are best presented as four paradoxes. Why a paradox? It suggests that there is fork in the road where choices will have to be made. How these paradoxes are resolved, both by rule-makers and businesses, will shape the contours of the field of action for exchanges and their competitors.

5.1 The Regulatory Paradox

The regulatory paradox is hard to solve, but easy to state. Despite the post-crisis emphasis on enhanced regulatory supervision, the drive for increased competition has allowed for execution venues subject to different and lower regulatory standards to compete with the regulated exchanges. One important regulatory discrepancy is the ability of these competitors to free-ride on the listings function provided by the exchanges. This listings free-riding problem was noted by the Organization for Economic Cooperation and Development (OECD) in their report on "The Role of Stock Exchanges in Corporate Governance." [31]

In the foregoing section, we posed the question of whether the costs of providing regulation, particularly listings, could be fully and appropriately compensated for in the form of fees paid by listed entities such as companies. If that were not the case, exchanges facing trade-only competitors would increasingly be unable to perform this valuable regulatory function, or would systematically under-invest in it over time. This poses a severe long-term threat to capital markets if, as we believe, exchanges are uniquely well positioned to perform these critical functions.

5.2 The Liquidity Paradox

The second paradox goes to the heart of efficient capital markets. It is that while deep and liquid markets are valued as a good in and of themselves, the existence of multiple execution venues for the same instruments, serving the same customer base, may have the effect of fragmenting liquidity. Thus, while direct execution costs may decline as a consequence of competition between execution venues, overall transaction costs (or price discovery costs) may increase as a result of this liquidity fragmentation. The additional costs could arise from required investments in new liquidity-seeking technologies and data aggregation requirements, as well as from increased spreads in certain stocks. These points were raised with the Committee of European Securities Regulators as part of their MiFID review process, but it is not yet certain how this issue will be resolved.[32] The interplay between the market and regulator is important: above we raise the possibility of market-driven solutions; these may, or may not, remove the need for regulatory intervention.

5.3 The Transparency Paradox

The third paradox deals with the key issue of price discovery. It is diffi-cult to escape the irony that in this post acute crisis environment where transparency is so highly valued—at least by regulators—dark order execution venues continue to proliferate, driven by the needs of large trading customers. In Europe, the primary regulatory focus has been on the extent to which so-called pre-transparency waivers permitted in terms of MiFID have been applied consistently across member jurisdic-tions, ensuring the existence of level playing fields. In the United States, the focus has been on the issue of transparency itself. In calling for a response to new proposals to enhance the transparency of dark pools, Mary Schapiro, Chairman of the US Securities and Exchange Commission stated:

> "We should never underestimate or take for granted the wide spectrum of benefits that come from transparency, which plays a vital role in promoting public confidence in the honesty and integrity of financial markets."[33]

In October 2009, the US Securities and Exchange Commission released for public comment measures aimed at increasing the transpar-ency of dark pools to ensure that the trade and related activity occurring on these platforms form part of the broader price discovery process. The proposals are aimed at creating "the same level of post-trade transpar-ency for dark pools—and other ATSs—as for registered exchanges."[34] At the same time in Europe, the CESR is conducting research into the size and extent of dark pool trading to determine whether dark pool trading is harming market transparency and price formation, and thereby inform its recommendations in this regard to the European Commission. On the other hand, dark pools, as discussed earlier in this chapter, are a response to genuine needs of customers with large trades.

5.4 The Paradox of National Interests in a World of Global Capital

Mervyn King, Governor of the Bank of England, pointed out at the start of the financial crisis that "global banking institutions are global in life but national in death." There is some truth to this. These institutions may operate in a global arena, but when they run into problems, the national central bank must act as lender of last resort and it is often national governments that step in.[35] While this financial crisis has seen some focus on global regulation, national leaders naturally remain focused on what is necessary for the recovery and protection of their economy. This inward focus may result in the introduction of regulation that seeks to limit the free flow of capital, as well as the ability of local firms and exchanges to forge relationships with foreign enterprises. It is possible, though not yet certain, that the ability of foreigners to access local capital markets or to co-operate with local entities and vice versa may become more constrained in a post-crisis world.

One possible indicator of the emergence of such a trend is the proposed "Over-the-Counter Derivatives Markets Act of 2009" in the United States, which gives the US Commodity Futures Trading Commission the power to make rules and regulations "requiring registration with the Commission for a foreign board of trade that provides members of the foreign board of trade or other participants located in the United States direct access to the electronic trading and order matching system of the foreign board of trade . . ." The Act limits the ability of a foreign exchange or other market to enable US participants to trade contracts on it that are price-referenced to US securities contracts, unless the Commission is satisfied that the foreign market meets certain requirements.

Another example, from our discussion of global trends: the fast-growing Asian nations' divergence from the "Atlantic" consensus with respect to nationality ownership restrictions on exchanges.

One can expect these regulations to evolve, but it is not clear at this point in which direction that will be, and whether exchange services markets will become more national or global as a result.

6. A Free Option on the Future

In this chapter, we have made the case that the near-term future of exchanges depends on the ability of these organizations to navigate large shifts in the value of exchange services. To survive and prosper, exchanges will have to be better than their competitors in managing the long-run *de*valuation of trading services and the *re*valuation of risk management services—and also in turning to account the business and social value generated by their regulatory functions, particularly listings.

In the longer run, value too will be determining for the destiny of exchanges: In this case, we mean value in a broader sense than pricing trends—in the sense of creating new and lasting value for customers and society.

A high return to innovation. Taking a step back, it is worth recognizing that exchanges sit astride three key processes of modern economies:

- The allocation of resources through capital markets
- The custodianship and governance of long-term investments, particularly in companies
- The management of financial risks

These are important and complex areas in which new insights, service delivery models, and products that add value will yield enormous returns. There ought to be no limit to the ability of exchanges to devise new means of adding value to their customers.

At the same time, markets are on a strong growth trajectory. The financial crisis that forms the backdrop of the last few years ought not to obscure the momentous changes that are taking place in the world economy, and very much so in leading developing countries. By some reckonings, more than a billion additional workers have been brought into global trade during the last twenty years, resulting in astonishing increases in both productivity and incomes for the many individuals involved. This is an engine of growth that still has a long way to run, both in terms of the hundreds of millions of people still to be brought into the global economy, often from rural areas, and the additional productivity growth that many of the world's workers will experience in their lifetimes. As that process plays out over the next fifty years, the resulting massive long-run increase in global economic activity augurs well for exchanges.

Geared growth. In our view, the business of securities exchanges will grow even more quickly than the underlying economy. This is because within that economy, another momentous shift will be taking place. In fast-growing economies, virtually all the prodigious savings of China, India, and other countries have been channeled through savings banks and the reserve accounts of central banks. This is not a fixed or desirable state of affairs. In future, as macro-economic balances shift and long-term savings institutions throughout the developing world mature, a larger part of these massive savings flows should logically shift to investment in traded securities such as equities. Exchanges servicing the tens of thousands of companies that will be at the heart of this growth, and which may be headquartered all over the world, will prosper.

The business of exchanges is not simply trading, clearing, and settlement; it is to be a core part of the never-ending process of financial intermediation. Regulated exchanges all over the world have a free option to add extraordinary value to this process as the future unfolds.

Notes

1 Because of problems in ensuring information comparability, the "regulated exchanges" referred to in this chapter are the exchanges that are members of the World Federation of Exchanges (WFE).

2 Based on a review of 45 of the 51 member exchanges—"2008 Cost and Revenue Survey," Devai, R., *World Federation of Exchanges*, October 2008.

3 *Ibid*, p. 9.

4 The most recent US regulation, Regulation National Market Systems (also known as Reg NMS) was fully enacted in October 2007.

5 "Is market fragmentation harming market quality?" O'Hara, M. and Ye, M., March 10, 2009, Available at SSRN: http://ssrn.com/abstract=1356839.

6 MiFID was adopted in 2004, and finally implemented on November 1, 2007.

7 CESR MiFID database: http://mifiddatabase.cesr.eu/.

8 "LSE hit by bank plan to launch competing exchange," Moore, J., *The Independent*, November 16, 2006.

9 BATS Europe, for example, introduced a maker–taker pricing model that effectively results in it paying its customers to use its service. "Chi-X Europe wades into the fee war," Jeff, L., *Financial News*, August 28, 2009.

10 London Stock Exchange CEO Xavier Rolet was recently quoted as saying, "None of the MTFs can succeed in building their platforms with their current pricing levels." "They are too low and structurally unprofitable"; "Rolet wages war on LSE's newer rivals," Bates, V., *City AM*, November 26, 2009, http://www.cityam.com/news-and-analysis/6e2q16d85v.html.

11 "Chi-X gains ground on rival bourses," Grant, J., *Financial Times*, November 24, 2009.

12 FESE's estimate is based on an assessment of actual trade volumes between January 2008 and May 2009.

13 MiFID does, however, state in articles 35 and 46 that investment firms should be able to freely choose the most appropriate clearing and settlement provider, independent of its nationality. In addition, investment firms, in providing "best execution" for clients, are required to consider the total cost of trade including the cost of clearing and settlement.

14 Transcript of ABC News broadcast, August 30, 2009, http://www.abc.net.au/insidebusiness/content/2009/s2670943.htm.

15 Examples are NYSE/Euronext taking a 5 percent stake in the National Stock Exchange of India and concluding a strategic partnership with Qatar's Doha Stock Exchange, while Deutsche Borse acquired its own 5 percent stake in the Bombay Stock Exchange. NASDAQ OMX recently sold its 33 percent stake in NASDAQ Dubai to rival exchange Dubai Financial Markets (DFM) for a combination of cash and a 1 percent stake in DFM.

16 Tim Geithner, Written Testimony to the House Financial Services and Agriculture Committees, Joint Hearing on Regulation of OTC Derivatives, July 10, 2009.

17 In a joint response to the European Commission Working Group paper entitled "Ensuring efficient, safe and sound derivatives markets" published in July 2009, industry bodies International Swaps Derivative Association (ISDA), Securities Industry and Financial Markets Association (SIFMA), and London Investment Banking Association (LIBA) indicated that while they were not opposed to CCP clearing of suitable instruments, they believed that CCPs that are owned by for-profit clearing houses are "driven by revenue and commercial drivers, which are not obviously aligned with the core purpose of a CCP, namely risk reduction."

18 "Central counterparties for over the counter derivatives," Cecchetti, S., Gyntelberg, J., and Hollanders, M., *BIS Quarterly Review*, September 2009.

19 By analogy, note the momentous changes in the airline industry. It is better to be Ryanair than Aer Lingus.

20 CESR Report, pg 12. The remaining ones have been launched and backed by either investment firms or European equivalents of US-based alternative trading systems (ATS).

21 "LSE buys Turquoise share trading platform," Grant, J., *Financial Times*, December 20, 2009, http://www.ft.com/cms/s/0/3234208e-ed72-11de-ba12-00144feab49a.html. The remaining 40 percent is to be retained by existing shareholders. The LSE intends to make 9 percent of its shareholding available to new investors in the future.

22 This refers to a current trend where, to reduce execution times even further, trading houses physically locate their servers next to the servers of the execution venue.

23 "Survival of the Fastest," Stewart, N., *IR Magazine*, November 2009.

24 Letter from SEC Chairman, Mary Schapiro, to US Senator Ted Kaufman, December 3, 2009, http://kaufman.senate.gov/imo/media/doc/Schapiro%20letter%20to%20Kaufman1.pdf "FSA looks into high-frequency trading and dark pools," Finextra, August 4, 2009, http://www.finextra.com/news/fullstory.aspx?newsitemid=20337.

25 "Competition in OTC Clearing Comes with Its Own Risk—ICE CEO," Bunge, J., October 22, 2009, Dow Jones Newswire, http://www.nasdaq.com/aspx/stock-market-news-story.aspx?storyid=200910221302dowjonesdjonline000891&title=competition-in-otc-clearing-comes-with-its-own-risk---ice-ceo.

26 "UK FSA Gives NYSE Liffe Green Light to Launch European CCP in July," A-Team Group, 27 May 2009 http://www.a-teamgroup.com/article/uk-fsa-gives-nyse-liffe-green-light-to-launch-european-ccp-in-july/.

27 EuroCCP website, "About Us," http://www.euromcf.nl/?ID=25c.

28 Free Encyclopaedia of eCommerce, http://ecommerce.hostip.info/pages/266/Co-Opetition.html, accessed on November 29, 2009.

29 "LCH.Clearnet to clear for SGX-Chi-X dark pool," The Trade News, November 18, 2009, http://www.thetradenews.com/trading-venues/dark-pools/3897.

30 "NASDAQ OMX and BM&F Bovespa in partnership talks," Finextra, August 27, 2009.

31 OECD: Directorate for Financial and Enterprise Affairs, Steering Group on Corporate Governance, July 2009.

In the report, the OECD notes the important historical role played by exchanges in the regulation of listed companies and the promotion of corporate governance. While the report points out that concerns have been raised regarding the ability of exchanges as for-profit entities to continue to perform this function in a meaningful fashion, it also concludes that there is no concrete evidence that exchanges do not continue to play an important role in this regard.

32 "Impact of MiFID on Equity Secondary Markets Functioning," Committee of European Securities Regulators, June 10, 2009.

33 "SEC Issues Proposals to Shed Greater Light on Dark Pools," US SEC Press Release, October 21, 2009.

34 James Brigagliano, Co-Acting Director of the Division of Trading and Markets; "SEC Issues Proposals to Shed Greater Light on Dark Pools"; SEC website: http://www.sec.gov/news/press/2009/2009-223.htm.

35 The Turner Review: A Regulatory Response to the Global Banking Crisis, Turner, A., March 2009, p. 38.

Appendix: WFE Memorabilia

The founders in October 1961:

Amsterdam Stock Exchange
Association of German Stock Exchanges
Association of Swiss Stock Exchanges
Brussels Stock Exchange
London Stock Exchange

Luxembourg Stock Exchange
Madrid Stock Exchange
Milan Stock Exchange
Paris Stock Exchange
Vienna Stock Exchange

WFE members in January 2010:

Amman Stock Exchange
Athens Exchange
Australian Securities Exchange
Bermuda Stock Exchange
BM&FBOVESPA
BME Spanish Exchanges
Bolsa de Comercio de Buenos Aires
Bolsa de Comercio de Santiago
Bolsa de Valores de Colombia
Bolsa de Valores de Lima
Bolsa Mexicana de Valores
Bombay Stock Exchange
Bourse de Luxembourg
Bursa Malaysia
Chicago Board Options Exchange
CME Group
Colombo Stock Exchange
Cyprus Stock Exchange
Deutsche Börse
Hong Kong Exchanges and Clearing
Indonesia Stock Exchange
IntercontinentalExchange
International Securities Exchange
Irish Stock Exchange
Istanbul Stock Exchange
Johannesburg Stock Exchange

Korea Exchange
London Stock Exchange Group
Malta Stock Exchange
Moscow Interbank Currency Exchange
NASDAQ OMX Group
National Stock Exchange of India
New Zealand Exchange.
NYSE Euronext Group
Osaka Securities Exchange
Oslo Børs
Philippine Stock Exchange
Saudi Stock Exchange (Tadawul)
Shanghai Stock Exchange
Shenzhen Stock Exchange
Singapore Exchange
SIX Swiss Exchange
Stock Exchange of Mauritius
Stock Exchange of Tehran
Stock Exchange of Thailand
Taiwan Stock Exchange
Tel-Aviv Stock Exchange
The Egyptian Exchange
TMX Group
Tokyo Stock Exchange Group
Warsaw Stock Exchange
Wiener Börse

Past Chairmen

Mr. Pierre Sellier	Paris Bourse	1961–63
Baron C.J. Schimmelpenninck van der Oije	Amsterdam Exchange	1964–65
Mr. August Ribi	Swiss Exchange	1966–67
Mr. Paul Detroy	Brussels Bourse	1968–69
Mr. F. R. Althaus, C.B.E.	London Stock Exchange	1970–71
Dr. Jur. Fr. Priess	Deutsche Börse	1972–73
Mr. Pedro Rodriguez Ponga y Ruiz de Salazar	Bolsa de Madrid	1974–75
Dr. James J. Needham	New York Stock Exchange	1976
Mr. Remy Kremer	Bourse de Luxembourg	1976–78
On. Dott. Urbano Aletti	Borsa Italiana	1979–80
Mr. Yves Flornoy	Paris Bourse	1981–82
Mr. Pearce J. Bunting	Toronto Stock Exchange	1983–84
Sir Nicholas Goodison	London Stock Exchange	1985–86
Mr. Boudewijn F. van Ittersum	Amsterdam Exchange	1987–88
Dr. Gernot Ernst	Deutsche Börse	1989–90
Mr. John J. Phelan, Jr.	New York Stock Exchange	1991–92
Mr. Jean-François Théodore	Paris Bourse	1993–94
Dr. Bengt Ryden	Stockholmsbörsen	1995–96
Mr. Manuel Robleda G. de Castilla	Bolsa Mexicana de Valores	1997–98
Mr. HC Lee	Hong Kong Exchanges & Clearing	1999–2000
Mr. Antonio J. Zoido	Bolsa de Madrid	2001–02
Mr. Richard Grasso	New York Stock Exchange	2003
Mr. John A. Thain	New York Stock Exchange	2004
Mr. Takuo Tsurushima	Tokyo Stock Exchange	2005
Mr. Taizo Nishimuro	Tokyo Stock Exchange	2006
Mr. Massimo Capuano	Borsa Italiana	2007–08
Mr. William J. Brodsky	Chicago Board Options Exchange	2009–10

General Assembly Venues

1. London	1961	26. London	1986
2. Bruxelles	1962	27. New York	1987
3. Paris	1963	28. Amsterdam	1988
4. Amsterdam	1964	29. Tokyo	1989
5. Düsseldorf	1965	30. Frankfurt/Berlin	1990
6. Genève	1966	31. Hong Kong	1991
7. Rome	1967	32. Mexico	1992
8. Bruxelles	1968	33. Oslo	1993
9. Luxembourg	1969	34. Seoul	1994
10. London	1970	35. Santiago	1995
11. Vienna	1971	36. Hong Kong	1996
12. Hamburg	1972	37. New York	1997
13. New York	1973	38. Kuala Lumpur	1998
14. Madrid	1974	39. Bangkok	1999
15. Johannesburg	1975	40. Brisbane	2000
16. Tokyo	1976	41. Madrid	2001
17. Zürich	1977	42. Amsterdam	2002
18. Rio de Janeiro	1978	43. New York	2003
19. Luxembourg	1979	44. Tokyo	2004
20. Melbourne	1980	45. Mumbai	2005
21. Paris	1981	46. Sao Paulo	2006
22. Montreux	1982	47. Shanghai	2007
23. Toronto	1983	48. Milan	2008
24. Stockholm	1984	49. Vancouver	2009
25. Buenos Aires	1985	50. Paris	2010

CONFERENCE OF EUROPEAN STOCK EXCHANGES

12th - 13th October, 1961

Drapers' Hall

President of the Conference

Lord Ritchie of Dundee - Chairman of the Stock Exchange, London.

Present as Delegates were the following:

Amsterdam

Baron C.J. Schimmelpenninck van der Oije - Vice President, Amsterdam
                                          Stock Exchange.
Dhr. U.J.V. de Graaff - Director of the Amsterdam Stock Exchange.
Dhr. J.G.N. de Hoop Scheffer - Secretary of the Amsterdam Stock Exchange.

Brussels

M. Pierre Anciaux - President de la Commission de la Bourse de Bruxelles.
M. Alfred Delande - Vice President de la Commission de la Bourse de
                    Bruxelles.
M. Paul Cornette - Membre de la Commission de la Bourse de Bruxelles.
M. Gaston de Koninck - Membre de la Commission de la Bourse de Bruxelles.
M. Felix Bastiaens - Greffier de la Commission de la Bourse de Bruxelles.
M. Louis van Dessel - Secretaire du Comite de la Cote de la Bourse de
                      Bruxelles.

Luxembourg

M. Fernand Koster - Secretaire-General de la Bourse de Luxembourg.

Madrid

Sr. Don Pedro Rodriguez Ponga - Vice President, Madrid Stock Exchange.
Sr. Don Carlos de la Mora pajares - Member of the Committee, Madrid
                                    Stock Exchange.

Milan

Signor Giulio Rossi - Membro del Comitato Dirretivo del Borsa di Milano.
Dottore Giancarlo Boffa - Membro del Comitato Dirretivo del Borsa di Milan
Dottore Urbano Aletti - Membro del Comitato Dirretivo del Borsa di Milano.
Dottore Achille Boretti - Segretario del Comitato Dirretivo del Borsa di
                          Milano.

Paris

M. Pierre Sellier - Syndic de la Compagnie des Agents de Change de Paris.
M. Jean Boscher - Adjoint au Syndic de la Compagnie des Agents de Change
                  de Paris.
M. Georges Oudart - Adjoint au Syndic de la Compagnie des Agents de
                    Change de Paris.
M. Philippe Clement - Vice President de la Chambre des Courtiers en
                      Valeurs Mobilieres de Paris.
M. Daniel Petit - Secretaire-General de la Compagnie des Agents de
                  Change de Paris.

P.T.O.

Vienna

Dr. Eduard Karlik - Member of Committee, Wiener Börsekammer.
Dr. Robert Rintersbacher - Secretary General, Wiener Börsekammer.

Association of German Stock Exchanges

Eberhard Cl. Baron von Ostman - Vize Präsident der Rheinisch-Westfälischen
                                 Börse zu Düsseldorf.
Hr. Hans Weber - Präsident der Berliner Börse.
Hr. Otto Kuhn - Vize Präsident der Berliner Börse.
Hr. Joachim Schlieckmann - Hauptgeschäftsführer der Rheinisch-West-
                                 fälischen Börse zu Düsseldorf.

Association of Swiss Stock Exchanges

M. August Ribi - Vice President of the Zurich Stock Exchange.
Dr. Alfred Rossi - Secretary of the Zurich Stock Exchange.

London

Mr. F.R. Althaus - Deputy Chairman of the Stock Exchange.
Mr. J.A. Hunter - Member of the Council of the Stock Exchange.
Mr. R. Layton - Member of the Council of the Stock Exchange.
Mr. P.E.M. Shaw - Member of the Council of the Stock Exchange.
Mr. W.T. Henderson - Member of the Council of the Stock Exchange.
Mr. W.S. Wareham - Secretary of the Share & Loan Department, the
                                 Stock Exchange.

The following representatives of other Exchanges attended as observers:

Sr. Don Jaime Aguilar Otermin - Vice President, Barcelona Stock Exchange.
Hr. A. Eken - Chairman of the Board of the Copenhagen Stock Exchange.
Hr. S.A. Jensen - Member of the Board of the Copenhagen Stock Exchange.
Hr. G. Backhaus - Secretary of the Board of the Copenhagen Stock Exchange.
M. Rene Demoustier - Syndic de la Compagnie des Agents de Change de Lyon.
Hr. Hans Chr. Henriksen - President, Børskomiteen, Oslo.
Hr. Oscar Martens - Vice Chairman, Børskomiteen, Oslo.
Hr. Hans Arnessen - Secretary, Oslo Børs.
Dottore Giorgio Natali - Vice President del Comitato Dirretivo del
                                 Borsa di Roma.
Dottore Guido Colomba - Segretario del Borsa di Roma.
Hr. Kjell Hagglof - Chairman of the Swedish Stockbrokers' Association.
Hr. Elis Ponsbach - Secretary of the Swedish Stockbrokers' Association.
Hr. Stig Algott - Secretary General of the Stockholm Stock Exchange.

Sr. Don Luis Arandui Aguirre - Vice President of the Bilbao Stock
     Exchange was unable to attend owing to illness.

Minutes of October 1961 founding meeting

94ᵉ année. — N° 259.   Le Numéro : 0,50 NF   Vendredi 2 et Samedi 3 Novembre 1962.

JOURNAL OFFICIEL
DE LA RÉPUBLIQUE FRANÇAISE

LOIS ET DÉCRETS

ARRÊTÉS, CIRCULAIRES, AVIS, COMMUNICATIONS, INFORMATIONS ET ANNONCES

23 octobre 1962. Déclaration à la préfecture d'Ille-et-Vilaine. **Groupement professionnel régional de Bretagne.** But : contribuer à une meilleure organisation de la production et de la commercialisation des pommes de terre. Siège social : 34, place des Lices, Rennes.

24 octobre 1962. Déclaration à la préfecture de la Loire. **Conseil des parents d'élèves du lycée technique de filles et du collège d'enseignement technique annexé.** But : permettre aux parents des élèves de l'établissement de veiller à la défense des intérêts matériels et moraux de leurs enfants. Siège social : 29, rue Léon-Nautin, Saint-Etienne.

24 octobre 1962. Déclaration à la préfecture du Loiret. **Société de chasse Electricité-Gaz de France.** But : grouper les agents chasseurs Electricité-Gaz de France en vue du développement du gibier par la protection, le repeuplement, l'élevage, la destruction des nuisibles, la répression du braconnage et l'exploitation rationnelle de la chasse sur ce territoire. Siège social : 2, rue Emile-Zola, Orléans.

24 octobre 1962. Déclaration à la préfecture d'Arles. **Syndicat des ganaderos français.** But : défense des intérêts professionnels des éleveurs de taureaux de combat. Siège social : café de la Bourse, Arles (Bouches-du-Rhône).

25 octobre 1962. Déclaration à la sous-préfecture d'Aix-en-Provence. **Education populaire de l'école Saint-François-d'Assise.** But : organiser par tous moyens appropriés le fonctionnement matériel des écoles libres et notamment de l'école catholique Saint-François-d'Assise. Siège social : quartier Malouesse, Aix-en-Provence (Bouches-du-Rhône).

25 octobre 1962. Déclaration à la préfecture de la Charente-Maritime. **Association culturelle israélite de la Rochelle.** But : entretien et exercice du culte dans les départements de la Charente-Maritime, Charente, Vendée, Deux-Sèvres. Siège social : chez M. Kamoun, 58, rue Jean-Godefroy, la Rochelle.

25 octobre 1962. Déclaration à la préfecture de Loir-et-Cher. **Association d'action laïque du canton de Blois-Ouest.** But : veiller au respect de la laïcité. Siège social : 14, rue Saint-Honoré, Blois.

25 octobre 1962. Déclaration à la préfecture des Vosges. **Association amicale des anciens soldats d'A. F. N. d'Epinal et de sa région.** But : regrouper, dans un cadre d'amitié et de soutien, les anciens soldats de tous grades ayant servi en A. F. N. et perpétuer le souvenir de leurs camarades ayant trouvé la mort en A. F. N. Siège social : chez le président, M. Jean Monvoisin, 10, quai des Bons-Enfants, Epinal.

25 octobre 1962. Déclaration à la préfecture d'Ille-et-Vilaine. **Association des vieux travailleurs, des économiquement faibles et des retraités civils du canton de la Guerche-de-Bretagne.** But : aider moralement et matériellement les vieux travailleurs, les économiquement faibles et les retraités civils. Siège social : café Jannier, la Guerche-de-Bretagne.

26 octobre 1962. Déclaration à la sous-préfecture d'Aix-en-Provence. **Association des mères de famille des élèves de l'école maternelle de Beisson, Aix.** But : fournir aux enfants jouets, jeux éducatifs, matériel scolaire manquant et œuvre du vestiaire. Siège social : école maternelle Beisson, Aix-en-Provence (Bouches-du-Rhône).

26 octobre 1962. Déclaration à la préfecture de la Réunion. **Association philosophique et philanthropique L'Amitié.** But : étude des problèmes relatifs au perfectionnement intellectuel et moral de l'homme ainsi que la pratique de la solidarité. Siège social : rue Nicole-de-la-Serve, à Saint-Denis.

MODIFICATIONS

2 octobre 1962. Déclaration à la préfecture de police. **La Compagnie dramatique « La Guilde »** transfère son siège social du 16, rue des Amandiers, Paris, au 15-17, rue Malte-Brun, Paris.

2 octobre 1962. Déclaration à la préfecture de la Loire. **L'Association des parents d'élèves de l'enseignement libre du département de la Loire** transfère son siège social du 13, rue Elisée-Reclus, à Saint-Etienne, au 10, rue Mi-Carême, à Saint-Etienne.

3 octobre 1962. Déclaration à la préfecture de la Haute-Garonne. **L'Association amicale des arbitres du comité des Pyrénées de la fédération française de rugby** transfère son siège social du 11, place Sainte-Scarbes, à Toulouse, au café Capoul, 15, place Wilson, à Toulouse.

8 octobre 1962. Déclaration à la préfecture des Alpes-Maritimes. **Le Cercle Molière** transfère son siège social du 30, quai Saint-Jean-Baptiste, Nice, à la salle municipale, îlot Rey, rue des Serruriers, Nice.

9 octobre 1962. Déclaration à la sous-préfecture de Béziers. **L'Association sportive lycée de Béziers** modifie ses statuts conformément à l'annexe de l'arrêté du 4 septembre 1962. Siège social : lycée Henri-IV, Béziers (Hérault).

16 octobre 1962. Déclaration à la sous-préfecture de Montluçon. **L'Association sportive du collège de jeunes filles** change son titre, qui devient : **Association sportive du lycée d'Etat de jeunes filles de Montluçon.** Siège social : lycée de jeunes filles, Montluçon (Allier).

17 octobre 1962. Déclaration à la préfecture de police. **L'association Découverte du Monde** transfère son siège social du 3, rue Boudreau, à Paris, au 24, rue Royale, à Paris.

18 octobre 1962. Déclaration à la préfecture des Bouches-du-Rhône. **L'Association Soroptimiste internationale, Union nationale des Soroptimist-Clubs de France,** transfère son siège social du 1, rue Villaret-de-Joyeuse, à Paris, au 22, rue Francis-Davso, à Marseille.

18 octobre 1962. Déclaration à la préfecture de police. **L'Association générale des étudiants en droit et en sciences économiques de Paris** transfère son siège social du 51, boulevard Saint-Michel, Paris, au 6, rue Christine, Paris.

19 octobre 1962. Déclaration à la préfecture de la Gironde. **L'Association des étudiants laïques de l'université de Bordeaux Comité étudiant d'action laïque** change son titre, qui devient : **Comité laïque d'étudiants de Bordeaux.** Siège social : Fédération des œuvres laïques, place de la Ferme-de-Richemont, Bordeaux.

23 octobre 1962. Déclaration à la préfecture de police. **Le Groupement des parents d'élèves catholiques du lycée Molière** transfère son siège social du 4, avenue des Chalets, Paris, au 71 A, rue de l'Assomption, Paris.

24 octobre 1962. Déclaration à la sous-préfecture de Pontoise. **Cercle la que de Villiers-le-Bel.** Modification partielle des statuts. Siège social : mairie de Villiers-le-Bel (Seine-et-Oise).

24 octobre 1962. Déclaration à la préfecture de police. **L'Espoir d'Auvergne, Musiciens et danseurs du Massif Central,** transfère son siège social du 129, quai de la Gare, Paris, au 66, avenue Jean-Jaurès, Vitry-sur-Seine.

29 octobre 1962. Déclaration à la préfecture du Nord. **L'Association amicale des anciens élèves et amis des écoles des beaux-arts à Lille** transfère son siège social du 2, rue Alphonse-Colas, à Lille, au 18, rue du Capitaine-Verkindère, à Marcq-en-Barœul.

30 octobre 1962. Déclaration à la préfecture de police. **L'Association Les Petites Familles de France** (créée par les Amis de l'enfance délaissée) transfère son siège social du 66, boulevard de la Villette, à Paris, au 50, rue de Babylone, à Paris.

ASSOCIATIONS ETRANGERES

AUTORISATIONS
(Décret-loi du 12 avril 1939.)

20 octobre 1962. Arrêté du ministre de l'intérieur. (Autorisation enregistrée à la préfecture de police le 25 octobre 1962.) **Fédération internationale des bourses de valeurs.** But : promouvoir une collaboration entre ses membres dans le respect des relations traditionnelles que certains d'entre eux peuvent entretenir avec les bourses des pays tiers. Siège social : 129, rue Montmartre, Paris.

20 octobre 1962. Arrêté du ministre de l'intérieur. (Autorisation enregistrée à la préfecture de police le 25 octobre 1962.) **Comité international pour l'étude et le développement de la construction tubulaire.** But : recherches et expériences contribuant au progrès et au développement de l'emploi du tube d'acier dans ses diverses utilisations pour la construction tubulaire. Siège social : 30, boulevard Malesherbes, Paris.

Paris. — Imprimerie des Journaux officiels, 26, rue Desaix.

Journal Officiel - November 1962, registering FIBV

October 4, 1973

It is with great pleasure that I welcome
the distinguished members of the Federation
Internationale des Bourses de Valeurs as,
for the first time, you hold your General
Assembly in the United States.

Your decision to meet outside of Europe is
strongly indicative of the encouraging move
toward greater international cooperation.
With the present monetary and trade negotiations, the advent of large multinational
corporations and the massive inflows and
outflows of capital for investment purposes,
the reality of international economic inter-
dependence is more and more readily apparent
to all of us.

That groups such as the Federation can meet
to discuss common problems and seek solutions
across national boundaries augurs well for
the future. I wish you a highly successful
session, and I hope that by working together
in this way you will continue to spread the
international goodwill that is so basic to
world prosperity and peace.

Richard Nixon

President Richard Nixon welcome message to FIBV memebrs, October 1973

ADDRESS BY HIS IMPERIAL HIGHNESS THE CROWN PRINCE OF JAPAN

Address by His Imperial Highness
The Crown Prince of Japan
at the Gala Dinner of the World
Federation of Exchanges
44th General Assembly
13 October 2004 in Tokyo

Reprinted with the kind permission of the Tokyo Stock Exchange

His Imperial Highness the Crown Prince of Japan

Distinguished guests, ladies and gentlemen,

I am very pleased that the World Federation of Exchanges 44th General Assembly was brought to a successful conclusion with the participation of representatives from exchanges around the world.

Three centuries have passed since the first securities market was established in the 17th century. With the modernization of national economies, securities markets have now developed to the point that they are regarded as national assets which are indispensable to the social and economic activities of individual countries.

Exchanges have several important tasks as the centers of securities markets, which directly connect securities issuers with investors who offer funds. These tasks include encouraging the active and accurate disclosure of information by companies, as well as deepening the public's understanding of securities investment.
I myself have long had great interest in water transportation. Hubs of water transportation are centers of trade, and

it is there that commerce flourishes and securities markets, which support economic activities in the field of finance, exist there. In fact, adjacent to the place where the Tokyo Stock Exchange stands are commercial areas which have prospered through the ages, and canals still exist there. Nearby, there was also a landmark bridge called Kaiun-bashi, or "Marine Transportation Bridge." This is where the residence of the naval magistrate was located during the Edo Period. I find this link fascinating.

In our world of today, where the operations of securities markets cross borders and oceans and continue to broaden, I believe it is very meaningful that representatives of the leading exchanges in the world have convened to deepen mutual understanding. I hope that all gathered here today will make even further efforts toward developing securities markets from "national assets" into "global assets."

Thank you.

World Federation of Exchanges 44th
WFE General Assembly and Annual Meeting
October 11-15, 2004 Tokyo and Kyoto, Japan

WORLD FEDERATION OF EXCHANGES   3

Three former chairmen

Mr. Ponga adressing the FIBV delegates

FIBV General Assembly in NYSE Board Room, New York, 1973

Gala diner at Chateau de versailles - "Salon des Batailles" - September 1981

WFE Forum on Managing Exchanges in Emerging Economies, December 2002, Kuala Lumpur

FIBV Annual report 1991

Fédération Internationale des Bourses de Valeurs

monthly
news letter

1

january 1992

22. Boulevard de Courcelles, 75017 PARIS tel:(1)40.54.78.00 fax:(1)47.54.94.22

WORLD FEDERATION OF EXCHANGES

FOCUS

No 205 | March 2010
The monthly newsletter of regulated exchanges,
with key market figures

Cleared for take-off?

WJe50
50th Anniversary

| The role of central counterparties in financial crisis recovery by Marcus Zickwolff, CCP12 | Market safety and integrity for derivatives by Stefan Mai, Deutsche Boerse | Quest for transparency by Peter Clifford, WFE | Stock Exchanges since 1960 by Prof. Ranald Michie, Durham University |

WFE 49th Annual Meeting, October 2009

From left to right : Duncan Niederauer, Ravi Narain, Paul Chow, William J. Brodsky

Index

Note: Page numbers followed by "*f*" and "*t*" denote figures and tables, respectively.

United States Department of
    Agriculture (USDA), 201*n*32
universal banking system, 290
universal banks, Germany, 35
unregulated markets, 121
unvaluation, of regulatory services, 313
US Securities and Exchange
    Commission (SEC), 71, 325. *See*
    Securities and Exchange
    Commission (SEC)
US Treasury bills, 175
US Treasury bond futures, 175
utilitarian traders, 73–74, 77, 79,
    102, 105
utility model, 320

Value Line stock index futures, 180
value-motivated traders, 74–75, 82
Vienna Stock Exchange, 260
Vietnam, 252
    centrally managed capital markets
    in, 262
volatility, 72
    liquidity and, 92
Volcker, Paul, 198
Volcker Rule, 123
volume weighted average price
    (VWAP), 225

Wade, Jamie, 194
Wallenberg Group, 207
Wallison, Peter J., 115
Wall Street Crash, 9, 20
Wall Street investment banks, 39–41

Ward, Peter, 278
Warsaw, 253, 254, 257
Warsaw Stock Exchange, 253, 257,
    259, 260, 263, 266*n*7
Wealth of Nations, The, 289
Weitzman, Hal, 174
White, William R., 115
width, 91
Williams, Harold, 169
world's exchanges, as social
    agents, 269
    Brazil and, 274–78
    corporate governance, 273–74
    corporate social responsibility
    (CSR), 270–71, 299
    environmental challenge and
    sustainability, 278–79
    and historical movement, 271–72
    social initiatives and, 282–84
    and sustainable development,
    279–82
World Bank, 257
World Federation of Exchanges
    (WFE), 109, 133, 166, 167, 257,
    287, 304, 310
    anniversary book, 269
    survey of members, 319

Yarrow, Alan, 306
Ye, Mao, 135
Yeutter, Clayton, 192
Yugoslavia, 254

zero-sum game, 78–79, 105